CAREER OPPORTUNITIES IN THE FASHION INDUSTRY

Second Edition

PETER VOGT

Foreword by
ANGIE WOJAK
Director of Career Services,
Parsons The New School for Design

Career Opportunities in the Fashion Industry, Second Edition

Checkmark Books
An imprint of Infobase Publishing
132 West 31st Street
New York NY 10001

Library of Congress Cataloging-in-Publication Data

Vogt, Peter, 1967–
Career opportunities in the fashion industry / Peter Vogt.—2nd ed.
p. cm.
Includes bibliographical references and index.
ISBN-13: 978-0-8160-6841-8 (hc : alk. paper)
ISBN-13: 978-0-8160-6842-5 (pb : alk. paper) 1. Clothing trade—Vocational guidance. 2. Fashion—Vocational guidance.
I. Title.
TT507.V63 2007
746.9'2023—dc22 2006033396

Checkmark Books are available at special discounts when purchased in bulk quantities for businesses, associations, institutions, or sales promotions. Please call our Special Sales Department in New York at (212) 967-8800 or (800) 322-8755.

You can find Facts On File on the World Wide Web at http://www.factsonfile.com

Cover design by Takeshi Takahashi

Printed in the United States of America

VB Hermitage 10 9 8 7 6 5 4 3 2 1

This book is printed on acid-free paper.

CONTENTS

EDUCATION

OTHER FASHION CAREERS

APPENDIXES

FOREWORD

When the first edition of *Career Opportunities in the Fashion Industry* was published in 2002, technological advances had already begun revolutionizing the industry, and globalization of both consumer markets and apparel production and distribution activities was already well under way. An August 1997 article in the U.S. Department of Labor's *Monthly Labor Review* noted that while 2.4 million people had been employed in textiles and apparel in the United States in 1973, only 1.5 million held such jobs in 1996—a drop of about 38 percent. Now, the total number of U.S. jobs in textiles and apparel stands (as of 2004) at about 700,000, according to the U.S. Department of Labor's 2006–2007 *Career Guide to Industries.* Increasing imports, the use of offshore assembly, and greater productivity through new automation will contribute to additional job losses in lower-level positions and production.

Despite these job losses, the fashion industry is more robust than ever, with emerging designers and new labels appearing with increasing rapidity. Fashion retail continues to thrive; Americans spent more than $180 billion on fashion and apparel in 2005, according to The NPD Group, Inc. And the ongoing turnover of personnel throughout the industry—particularly in so-called white collar positions—means that while there may not be as many jobs available today, there will always be some jobs available as people come and go and the industry continues to evolve.

The fashion industry also continues to evolve in response to technology. Thus, for example, computer-aided design (CAD) has become as essential as great hand-sketching skills for designers. And content-rich, highly interactive fashion Web sites and Web logs (blogs) are revolutionizing how quickly trends and brand awareness are communicated to consumers.

Perhaps it is no wonder, then, that if you want to someday work in the fashion industry, you will need solid technical and technological skills, proven capacity to work well in diverse environments, an awareness (and acceptance) of the industry's ongoing transformation, and a resulting willingness and ability to continue your learning throughout your career. Hence, this new edition of *Career Opportunities in the Fashion Industry,* which completely updates the 65 occupational profiles from the first edition and features 10 brand new profiles covering jobs such as Web Content Producer, Technical Designer, Specification Technician, and Logistics Manager. Like the first edition, this updated and expanded edition of *Career Opportunities in the Fashion Industry* gives you vital information about career paths in the industry. The book offers a broad overview of career alternatives in the field, in addition to detailed information such as salary ranges and educational requirements for specific job titles, all of which make it an essential guide for anyone trying to navigate such a dynamic industry.

If you are considering a career in fashion, you should take the time to research the field thoroughly, because there are many different occupational options in addition to actual fashion design work (the career most people name when they think of jobs in the fashion industry). In fact, a significant number of students who graduate with four-year degrees in fashion design ultimately work in marketing and business rather than in a design capacity. So when you are mapping your career path, it is essential that you take a realistic and informed look at the occupation you are considering. There are numerous areas of expertise you may pursue, including textile design, merchandising, and production. You may find that your "passion for fashion" lies in an area you have yet to discover.

As director of career services at Parsons The New School for Design in New York City—one of the top art and design institutions in the world—I often find that students have misconceptions about the fashion industry. They assume, for instance, that one quickly becomes either a head designer or an independent designer. But it actually takes many years to attain success, and you must be a capable businessperson to thrive independently. Students often have unrealistic expectations about salaries as well. Young fashion designers frequently must be willing to start in low-paying positions and work long hours to establish themselves. In addition, the workplace is often very intense and volatile. You need to be aware of the atmosphere you might be working in and take that important factor into consideration as you develop your career goals and plans.

A young designer must display traits such as extroversion and independence. For example, assistant designers are often called upon to follow up with vendors. So they must be assertive and proactive to be effective. Also, an outgoing personality is helpful because networking is key to success in the fashion industry. Designers and others must be self-sufficient, yet also capable of working as part of a team. There is no better way to understand this dynamic than to take part in an *internship*—a short-term work experience in the field.

I cannot stress enough the importance of doing an internship before committing to a specific career path. Over the years, a number of students have come to me after completing their first internship in fashion design, only to have discovered that their personality, skills, or interests do not truly lie in the fashion world. Early experiential learning within the industry will help you direct your energies and career aspirations to paths that better fulfill your dreams and expectations. Rather than choosing design, for instance, you may discover that your personality and skills are better suited to retail, public relations, or perhaps an entirely different field, such as fine arts. Also, it is not unusual for recent alumni/ae to accept internships rather than full-time, salaried positions when they first graduate. This is because jobs in fashion are very competitive, and frequently designers must work in freelance or internship capacities during the early stages of their careers. This work, while often unpaid, is an essential part of networking, which leads to job opportunities in the industry.

Many recent fashion-design graduates report that they have found rewarding careers in fashion magazines, merchandising for major fashion retailers, and other related professional activities. While their academic experience in hands-on design is quite helpful and relevant, there are many other skills they must perfect in order to be marketable. For instance, a fashion designer must know CAD programs. But someone pursuing a career in marketing or production would need proficiency in Excel and PowerPoint too. It is very important that you develop computer skills that are relevant to your specific industry sector or specialization.

Flexibility is another key trait that you will need in order to flourish in the fashion industry. Often, recent graduates get a "foot in the door" at a major design house by initially accepting a position doing administrative work, which in turn can lead to a position within the design team. (That's why the Administrative Assistant occupational profile was added to this revised edition of the book.) You will want to work in retail sales before graduation too, because doing so increases your business savvy and your understanding of the all-important customer base.

Be sure you also stay on top of current industry trends and forecasts, particularly by reading industry publications in print and online. (You will find a helpful list of industry publications in Appendix III, "Fashion and Apparel Periodicals and Web Sites.") You simply must continuously build your knowledge base, and professional reading is among the best ways to do so. The fashion industry was already highly competitive when this book first came out in 2002. It has only gotten more competitive since.

Moreover, as the industry becomes more global, fluency in a language in addition to English—particularly Chinese or Spanish—will increasingly vault you to the top of a prospective employer's list of people to hire immediately. Your potential employer's company is more likely to be using a factory in China to manufacture its product rather than using a generations-old facility in the southern United States. So if—make that when—there is a production glitch at an apparel company's Chinese manufacturing facility, for example, a communication nightmare between the Chinese-speaking manager of the facility and the English-speaking point person at headquarters in the States is the last thing the company needs.

Fashion is an exciting—but ever-changing—industry. So consider *Career Opportunities in the Fashion Industry* to be an essential part of your professional research and growth. You will find that it is a valuable resource for anyone who is thinking about a job in the field. Fashion is a vital industry in which a creative, energetic person can thrive. If you want to explore or pursue a career somewhere in the world of fashion, I highly recommend that you read this book to gain greater insight into what you have to look forward to.

Angie Wojak
Director of Career Services
Parsons The New School for Design
New York City

INTRODUCTION
INDUSTRY OUTLOOK IN FASHION

Whether the economy is soaring, floundering, or somewhere in between, most Americans want and need good clothes, whether they're working or playing. That's why the fashion and apparel industry—the subject of this book—is expected to remain a dominant force in the American (and global) economy for many years to come.

But it won't be without considerable cost and constant transition, especially for the many blue-collar production workers in the industry. In fact, the changes are already well under way. As of June 2006, about 623,000 American workers were employed in the textile and apparel manufacturing industries, according to the U.S. Department of Labor. On the surface, that sounds like a lot of people—until you learn that just five years earlier, in June 2001, about 989,000 Americans worked in textile and apparel manufacturing. In other words, the industry lost about 37 percent of its jobs in the United States in just five years' time. And the Department of Labor predicts that employment in textile and apparel manufacturing will fall another 46 percent between now and 2014, due in great part to companies moving their manufacturing operations to low-wage countries overseas.

On the flip side, however, the white-collar segment of the fashion/apparel industry is remaining steady or even growing a bit in some cases. The retail sector of the industry, in particular, continues to thrive. In fact, Americans spent some $181 billion on fashion and apparel in 2005, according to the NPD Group, Inc., an international marketing information company that specializes in consumer purchasing and behavior. Add to that total the money Americans spent on shoes ($42 billion) and accessories ($30 billion), and the total is a shade over $250 billion. No wonder opportunities abound for people who are interested in apparel-related jobs like Store Manager, for example, or Merchandise Manager or Logistics Manager.

Then, of course, there's the Internet to take into account. Web site InternetRetailer.com reports that online sales of apparel and accessories in the United States reached $7.1 billion in 2005 (compared with $5.8 billion in 2000, according to NPD Group figures). That total represented about 2.8 percent of the industry's total sales in 2005, and it came on the heels of a recession that, according to many experts, began shortly before the terrorist attacks of September 11, 2001, and didn't officially end until sometime in 2003 (when the American economy was still soft in some ways). So career opportunities definitely exist for people who not only know the fashion and apparel industry but also have exceptional technological skills to boot—whether those skills are ultimately applied to e-commerce activities, Web site design and content production, or both.

The question that arises when all the dust clears: Is the fashion/apparel industry growing or declining? The answer: a little of both. It's much more accurate to say that, while the industry remains strong, it is changing substantially, as is the nature of work, both within the industry itself and in the many economic sectors somehow associated with fashion and apparel.

Where does this leave you, the job seeker interested in pursuing a career in the world of fashion and apparel? In need of accurate fashion/apparel career information that will help you explore established, emerging, and even declining occupations within the industry and then make informed decisions about the path you'll ultimately pursue in the field. *Career Opportunities in the Fashion Industry* will help you do just that, giving you both the knowledge and, especially, the essential strategies you'll need to land the job you want in a competitive yet exciting field that is, quite literally, evolving by the day.

ACKNOWLEDGMENTS

My thanks to the many professional organizations and experts in the fashion/apparel and textile sectors that provided information for this book. My thanks as well to the career centers at schools like the Fashion Institute of Technology and Parsons The New School for Design, both in New York City, whose staff members are "in the trenches" each day preparing students to enter the exciting world of fashion in whatever way they so choose.

Special thanks to Angie Wojak, director of career services at Parsons The New School for Design in New York City, who contributed to this book a foreword that is filled with sound advice for anyone considering a career in the fashion industry.

Thanks also to John Woods and Robert Magnan of CWL Publishing Enterprises in Madison, Wisconsin, without whom this book would never have been produced.

And finally, thanks to my most patient and loving wife, Lois, who helped research parts of this book and, perhaps more important, gave me the space, time, and moral support I needed to turn it from idea into reality.

HOW TO USE THIS BOOK

The job descriptions in this book provide an overview and discussion of 75 positions involving fashion and apparel. They are divided into seven categories. Each entry is organized as follows.

Career Profile

Duties: This describes the purpose of the position.

Alternative Title(s): This lists other titles for the position that may be found in employment ads. Some titles indicate closely related positions or more specialized positions.

Salary Range: This is an *approximate* indication of what an individual may expect to earn in this position as of late 2006. It reflects a range from entry-level to highly experienced. Highly experienced individuals or those with highly specialized skills may make considerably more than entry- or mid-level workers do. The salary range is best used as an *indication* of the relative value of the position compared to others, and should not be relied upon too much as an *exact* figure. Also, keep in mind that salaries vary considerably in different geographical areas, since the cost of living differs from place to place.

Employment Prospects: This is a rating ranging from "limited" to "excellent," with most falling in the "fair" or "good" category with respect to how easy or hard it is to get a position.

Advancement Prospects: This is a general indication of how easy or hard it is to move up the career ladder from the position.

Best Geographical Location(s): This section offers a general idea of the areas in the United States where job seekers will be most likely to find opportunities to pursue the position.

Prerequisites

Education or Training—This covers the level of education or training likely to be required by prospective employers, such as high school graduate, two-year college (associate degree), four-year college (B.A. or B.S. degree), or graduate degree (M.S. or Ph.D.).

Experience—This lists the type of work experience that employers prefer applicants to have for the position.

Special Skills and Personality Traits—This provides a brief indication of the work skills that are most essential to the position, and the personality traits most likely to lead to success.

Special Requirements—A few positions in the fashion industry require special certifications, unique physical attributes, and the like. This section highlights the job's special requirements.

Career Ladder

This section indicates the location of the position within a typical career path. Not all positions listed in the career ladder are discussed separately in this book. Smaller organizations may not have a formal career ladder, and may combine responsibilities from several positions. Large organizations, on the other hand, may have grades or steps within each level of the ladder.

Position Description

This describes in detail the tasks associated with the position, the typical workplace, and how the position relates to other positions. Bulleted lists are often used to summarize important tasks or considerations.

Salaries

This section discusses the factors that determine how much money a person will earn in the position. These factors include:

- the educational qualifications and experience of the individual at the time of hiring—higher education and more experience generally bring a higher starting salary
- whether the individual has particular skills that are in high demand
- the number of workers competing for openings (which can be influenced by educational trends and geographic location)
- economic growth and wage inflation.

You can refine this analysis by consulting the latest salary surveys you'll find in industry trade publications and/or on the Internet (see Appendixes II and III).

Employment Prospects

This section treats many of the above factors from the point of view of how they affect an applicant's chances of being hired. The discussion also includes trends that may influence future demand for the position, as well as tips on how applicants might improve their prospects for landing a position.

Advancement Prospects

This section discusses how likely it is to move up the career ladder from this position (assuming there is a career ladder), and the typical paths to advancement (such as specializing, pursuing freelance or self-employment opportunities, or going into middle or upper management).

Education and Training

The educational qualifications given in the Career Profile summary are expanded and include recommended courses or subject areas. Additional training or industry certification is included where appropriate.

Special Requirements

Any special requirements listed in the Career Profile summary are explained in more detail.

Experience, Skills, and Personality Traits

Experience and demonstrable skills are often as important as education. This section summarizes intellectual and social skills that are most important for being successful in the position. There is also some indication of the kind of personality most suited for the work, though it's important to remember that people and jobs are too complicated to "pigeonhole."

Unions and Associations

Some positions in this book are unionized. Most, however, are considered professional or specialist positions and have professional organizations devoted to them. This section characterizes the kinds of organizations that a person in this position may wish to join, and gives a few examples of those organizations. Appendix II lists the contact information for all of the organizations mentioned in the book's profiles (and many others).

Tips for Entry

This final section offers suggestions that can help you prepare for entering the position described. Some of the suggestions are geared toward high school or college students who are still deciding which courses, majors, internships, and other experiential learning activities to pursue. The other suggestions give pointers for gaining work experience and learning more about the position described.

Other Resources in This Book

The appendixes that end the book outline additional resources you can use to help you research careers and find jobs in fashion and apparel:

- Appendix I lists American colleges, universities, and other institutions offering educational programs related to fashion and apparel, textiles, and/or fiber sciences.
- Appendix II lists professional, industry, and trade associations and unions related to fashion and apparel.
- Appendix III lists some of the many consumer publications, trade publications, and Web sites devoted to fashion/apparel and textiles.
- A bibliography lists other sources of information you can use to learn more about careers in fashion and apparel.

TEXTILES

FABRIC LIBRARIAN

CAREER PROFILE

Duties: Develops and maintains a well-organized "library" of a company's fibers or fabrics, tracks which materials have been used in the past, and highlights new materials that apparel manufacturers can use in future products

Alternate Title(s): Textile Librarian

Salary Range: $30,000 to $60,000+

Employment Prospects: Limited

Advancement Prospects: Fair

Best Geographical Location(s): Major fashion centers such as New York City, Los Angeles, Paris, London, and other cities where fiber or fabric manufacturers' headquarters are located

Prerequisites:

Education or Training—A minimum of a bachelor's degree in a field such as textile development is generally required

Experience—For entry-level positions, college internship or co-op experience is preferred; for higher-level positions, extensive experience in textiles and/or apparel is essential

Special Skills and Personality Traits—Expertise in fabric and apparel trends and forecasts; strong sense of color; sound understanding of fibers and fabrics and their various uses; excellent research and organization skills; strong communication skills; outstanding computer skills, particularly with database and spreadsheet software; good interpersonal and customer service skills

CAREER LADDER

Fabric Library Director

Fabric Library Assistant Director/Coordinator

Fabric Librarian

Fabric Library Assistant/ Design Assistant

Position Description

Fabric Librarians can work in a variety of settings, but most often they work for fiber or fabric companies or textile- or apparel-related professional organizations. They maintain samples of material from previous seasons as well as samples of new materials that can be used by apparel manufacturers.

Fabric Librarians are resource people who help others, typically the staff of apparel manufacturers, make important decisions about the materials they should use in lines that will appear two, three, or even four years in the future. They have extensive knowledge of textile and apparel industry trends and forecasts, and they use that expertise, along with hundreds of actual material samples in their libraries, to help apparel manufacturing leaders determine which fabrics they should use in their products.

Sometimes, especially in smaller companies, Fabric Librarians hold other responsibilities in addition to their duties as librarian. In other cases, however, Fabric Librarians devote all of their time to their companies' fabric libraries, researching and compiling fabric resources lists; helping clients locate, identify, and select fabrics; reviewing previous fabric or apparel lines and choosing appropriate fabrics to be maintained in the library; and setting up computerized organizational systems so that the fabrics in the library can be easily found when needed.

Fabric Librarians must be highly organized, and, increasingly, they must have considerable computer skills. Most fabric libraries now have computerized databases. Just as today's public libraries store their book records on computers, most fabric libraries now maintain their fabric records on computers, often including scanned photos of the fabrics being archived. These libraries must still keep samples of the fabrics, or *swatches,* since the computer cannot completely duplicate a fabric's look or, especially, its feel and weight. But the fabric library that doesn't have its records computerized and, in many cases, available via the Internet is a step behind in today's textile and apparel industries.

Because Fabric Librarians have extensive knowledge of fabrics that manufacturers have successfully used in the past, as well as those that are predicted to be successful in the immediate future, they are often called upon to give presentations, either to individual clients or at industry events and shows. During these presentations, Fabric Librarians will often show samples of successful (or predicted to be successful) textiles and make suggestions about how the fabrics can be used. So, apparel manufacturers' fashion designers, merchandisers, product managers, and fabric researchers all look to Fabric Librarians whenever they need expert input on products they should be developing for their companies.

Salaries

Salaries for Fabric Librarians vary widely. Those who take on fabric library responsibilities as part of another job (e.g., fashion design assistants) might make only $30,000 a year or so to start. However, full-time Fabric Librarians, because of their expertise, can make $60,000 or more, especially at the managerial level in larger organizations.

Employment Prospects

The number of Fabric Librarian positions in the United States is quite small, so employment prospects in the field are limited. Positions are available, however, with fiber and textile companies and industry trade associations. Similar positions are also available in related fields (e.g., the furniture industry).

Advancement Prospects

Fabric Librarians, particularly those who do fabric library work as part of another job, can advance into higher-level fabric library positions, such as fabric library director or fabric library assistant director/coordinator. Sometimes Fabric Librarians can use their expertise at forecasting trends to move into other positions such as merchandiser, product manager, or upper management openings. Still, advancement prospects for Fabric Librarians are only fair.

Education and Training

Generally, Fabric Librarians need at least a bachelor's degree, preferably in textile development or a closely related field. Additional training may be acquired through internships or assuming some duties of the Fashion Librarian while holding lower-level positions. Courses in library science can be useful in developing organizational and archive skills.

Experience, Skills, and Personality Traits

Prospective Fabric Librarians can gain useful experience by participating in internships or co-ops during their college years, or by assuming some fabric library roles as parts of other jobs (e.g., fashion design assistant). Those who aspire to become fabric library directors need to accumulate at least five years of experience, along with extensive expertise in fabric and apparel trends and forecasts.

To be successful, Fabric Librarians must be highly organized. They also have to have a strong fashion sense and a well-developed sense of color; they have to know how to match fabrics with potential end uses, as well as which fibers and fabrics are likely to be successful in the marketplace a few years into the future.

Fabric Librarians also need strong research skills, good communication and interpersonal skills, and, increasingly, sound computer skills (especially in the area of database development and management).

Unions and Associations

Fabric Librarians keep up with industry trends and forecasts by participating in organizations like the American Apparel and Footwear Association (AAFA), the American Fiber Manufacturers Association (AFMA), the International Textile and Apparel Association (ITAA), and Fashion Group International (FGI).

Tips for Entry

1. Earn a bachelor's degree in textile development or a closely related field. While in college, participate in one or more internships or co-ops to gain practical experience under a Fabric Librarian or related professional.
2. Read industry publications and join industry organizations to start accumulating expertise on fabric and apparel trends and forecasts.
3. Pursue a part-time job at your campus library or another local library to gain experience as an organizer and resource professional.
4. Talk to one or more Fabric Librarians about what their jobs are like and how they got those jobs. Ask for their advice on how you too can pursue their career someday.

MARKET RESEARCHER, TEXTILES

CAREER PROFILE

Duties: Gathers and analyzes market data to help textile manufacturers determine which fabrics they should produce and in what quantities, not only for the present but also for the future

Alternate Title(s): Market Analyst, Market Research Analyst

Salary Range: $30,000 to $100,000+

Employment Prospects: Fair

Advancement Prospects: Fair

Best Geographical Location(s): Major urban areas, particularly where textile manufacturers' headquarters are located

Prerequisites:

Education or Training—A bachelor's degree is required, most often in market research, marketing, or statistics; often, a master's degree is required as well, in business administration, statistics, or a related field

Experience—Previous market research experience is essential; sales experience is very helpful

Special Skills and Personality Traits—Superior mathematical, statistical, research, and analytical skills; extensive knowledge of textile development, production, and applications; knowledge of textile and apparel industry trends and forecasts; strong written communication skills; ability to work well with other people; attentiveness to detail; ability to meet deadlines; accuracy and thoroughness

CAREER LADDER

Market Research Director/Manager

Market Researcher

Junior Market Researcher

Position Description

Market Researchers (sometimes called market analysts or market research analysts) in the textile industry use their data gathering and analysis skills to help textile manufacturers accurately determine which products they should develop, in what quantities, for what prices, and when.

Most Market Researchers work for larger textile producers, which are typically the only firms that can afford to have their own market research departments. (Smaller textile manufacturers will often *outsource* their market research efforts to specialized market research companies.) In general, Market Researchers gather two types of data: *quantitative* (i.e., numerical data such as sales figures and market share) and *qualitative* (less "tangible" but no less important data, e.g., verbal feedback from apparel production managers on how a certain fabric has fared in the manufacturing process). Their goal is to gather as much information as they can, from a variety of sources, so that they can make helpful product and production recommendations to their companies.

Market Researchers gather their data in a variety of ways. Often, they'll travel to talk with staff members of apparel manufacturing firms to get their insights on what fabrics are likely to be "hot" (and not so hot) in the coming months. They'll also attend fashion shows, both in the United States and abroad, to get a sense of the "pulse" of the fashion world and what types of fabrics are likely to be most in demand among apparel producers and, ultimately, consumers. Additionally, Market Researchers will sometimes conduct focus groups—events in which groups of consumers or apparel manufacturing personnel are asked to share their opinions on which fabrics and garments are currently doing well in the marketplace and which ones are likely to do well in the future.

Most Market Researchers turn to other sources, too, for useful information. Some Market Researchers in the textile industry will analyze government reports, for example, or data gathered by professional organizations in the textile or apparel industries. Others will collaborate with independent research firms to develop original surveys or analyze data from previously conducted studies.

Market Researchers are, essentially, professional prognosticators who base their predictions not on "gut feelings" or "instincts" (though both of those come into play at times), but on data and past experience. They forecast trends in fabric colors, looks, weights, textures, and makeups so that their companies know which products to develop, manufacture, market, and sell for maximum financial impact.

To do their jobs effectively, Market Researchers must be willing and able to work with many other professionals inside and outside their companies. They work closely with textile stylists, for example, to help determine an overall "direction" for their company. They gather input from textile sales representatives because they know how closely those professionals work with apparel manufacturers, and thus how much critical customer information they have. They even work with textile converters, helping them figure out which finished goods to produce and in what amounts.

Perhaps more important, Market Researchers need to monitor what their companies' competitors are doing—what fabrics those firms are developing, which companies they're marketing those fabrics to, and how much those fabrics cost. Market Researchers need to determine whether their own companies should be producing similar products, and figure out what markets would be willing to pay for those products.

Salaries

Salaries for Market Researchers in the textile industry can start as low as $30,000 at the entry level and rise to more than $100,000 at the managerial level. Salaries vary significantly according to one's level of experience, the size and location of the employer, and the specific job duties and responsibilities. The median salary in 2004 for market research analysts in all industries was $56,140, according to the U.S. Department of Labor. Salary information Web site Salary.com notes that median base salaries for market research analysts in all fields range from $43,843 at the entry level to $86,229 at the managerial level. Experienced Market Researchers in the textile industry who have a solid track record of making accurate (and thus profitable) predictions can command the highest salaries, especially if they move into high-level management positions within their organizations (as they often do).

Employment Prospects

Employment for Market Researchers in all industries is expected to grow faster than average between now and 2014, according to the U.S. Department of Labor. Moreover, a 2006 analysis by *Money* magazine and Salary.com ranked the market research analyst occupation as one of the "Top 10 Best Jobs" in the country in terms of predicted levels of growth, pay, and other factors. However, the number of Market Researcher jobs in the textile industry is quite limited, so employment prospects in the textile field itself can only be characterized as fair.

The best jobs will go to Market Researchers who have extensive experience in the field, a graduate degree, and a solid track record of success in the way of guiding their companies' product development and marketing decisions.

Advancement Prospects

The typical entry-level job in the textile field is the junior Market Researcher or junior market analyst position. With five or more years of experience, junior Market Researchers can advance to become Market Researchers or even senior Market Researchers.

Since, by necessity, Market Researchers develop an extensive knowledge of markets, products, product development, forecasting, and planning, they can sometimes advance to senior management and executive-level jobs in their textile companies.

Education and Training

To be a Market Researcher in the textile industry, you need a minimum of a bachelor's degree, in a field such as market research, marketing, statistics, mathematics, psychology, or management. Typically, a master's degree is required as well, particularly for high-level market research positions; the most common advanced degrees are in business administration, statistics, or mathematics.

Experience, Skills, and Personality Traits

The Market Researcher's job is not an entry-level position. Typically, Market Researchers in the textile industry start out as junior Market Researchers who work under more experienced colleagues and often carry out some of the more task-oriented activities of the job—setting up focus groups, compiling data, or conducting research in industry publications.

Market Researchers at all levels need to be very comfortable with numbers. They must be able to gather and analyze statistics and other types of data and make sound recommendations based on their findings. They must work well with people, both in their own work settings and in the "field," and have superior written communication skills to write detailed reports on their research.

Successful Market Researchers are detail-oriented, accurate, and patient; generally speaking, "answers" do not emerge from data quickly or easily. Market Researchers must be resourceful, especially when gathering data. Sometimes information is easy to find, but most often considerable effort is involved. Market Researchers must be willing to put forth that effort, and gather data from a variety of print, organizational, and people resources.

Unions and Associations

The Marketing Research Association (MRA) is an umbrella professional group for market researchers in all industries. Some market researchers (in textiles and elsewhere) are also members of the American Marketing Association (AMA).

Many Market Researchers in textiles keep up with industry trends by participating in field-specific organizations like the International Textile and Apparel Association (ITAA) and Fashion Group International (FGI).

Tips for Entry

1. Obtain at least a bachelor's degree in a field such as market research, marketing, statistics, or mathematics. Then work in the textile or apparel industry for a few years, to gain real-world experience, before pursuing a master's degree in business administration or statistics.
2. While in college, pursue at least one internship or co-op experience in market research in the textile industry, if possible. Even entry-level positions like junior market analyst require considerable textile industry experience and knowledge.
3. Take a part-time or summer job in fabric or apparel sales to get a better sense of consumer wants and needs and how textile and apparel manufacturers attempt to meet those wants and needs. Talk to customers as well as industry professionals (e.g., buyers, merchandisers) to better understand which fabrics are in highest demand now and which ones will likely be in highest demand in the future.
4. If possible, gain research experience by completing an academic research project (e.g., undergraduate thesis or master's thesis), working for a professor, or working for a local market research company (e.g., as a phone interviewer or mall patron surveyor). The better you understand how various data are gathered and why, the more likely you'll be able to gain entry-level employment in market research.
5. Talk to one or more Market Researchers in the textile industry. Ask for their advice and ideas on how you can best prepare to enter their career field someday.

PRODUCT MANAGER, TEXTILES

CAREER PROFILE

Duties: Oversees the conceptualization, design, manufacturing, selling, and distribution of a textile producer's fabrics in order to meet market demand and take advantage of new market opportunities

Alternate Title(s): Product Development Manager, Product Development Director, Product Development Engineer

Salary Range: $55,000 to $100,000+

Employment Prospects: Fair

Advancement Prospects: Fair

Best Geographical Location(s): Large urban areas where textile manufacturers' headquarters are located

Prerequisites:

Education or Training—A bachelor's degree is required in textile design, textile merchandising, textile development, or a related field; a graduate degree—usually a master of business administration (M.B.A.)—is often preferred

Experience—A minimum of five years of experience in textiles is generally required; usually, Product Managers have eight to 10 years of experience in the field

Special Skills and Personality Traits—Extensive knowledge of fabric design, production, sales, and distribution; extensive knowledge of trends and forecasts in the fabric and apparel industries; ability to take large projects from start to finish; sound knowledge of competitors' products; creativity; ability to collaborate with other high-level professionals; conceptualization skills; strong supervisory skills; research skills; marketing and sales skills

CAREER LADDER

Product Manager

Assistant/Associate Product Manager

Textile Stylist or Textile Designer

Product Development Assistant or Assistant Textile Stylist

Position Description

Product Managers identify new fabrics their companies will (or should) be producing. They're ultimately responsible for the conceptualization, design, manufacture, sales, and distribution of new fabric creations.

By necessity, Product Managers have to be "big picture" thinkers. They gather input from their various colleagues, then combine it with the findings of their own product research to determine which new products their firms should manufacture (and how they should develop and market existing products).

Product Managers must always be on top of trends and forecasts in both the textile and apparel industries, since those trends and forecasts will drive their product development decisions. As such, they spend considerable time traveling to fashion and textile shows, so that they can see new products and talk to other industry "insiders" about which fabrics are likely to be in the highest demand two, three, or even five years into the future.

In general, Product Managers have extensive textile experience and considerable knowledge of all aspects of the textile manufacturing process. As upper-level managers, they typically supervise many mid-level managers who in turn oversee the company's designers, stylists, colorists, market researchers, merchandisers, sales representatives, and other professionals. Since Product Managers assume so much responsibility for their companies' textile products—and, therefore, profits—they must work hard to collaborate effectively with the people they supervise, and to consistently come up with ideas that eventually turn into successful products.

Salaries

As upper-level managers with significant responsibilities over personnel, products, and company performance, Product Managers in textile firms are well paid. At a minimum, Product Managers can expect to make $50,000 a year, but much more often their salaries range from $75,000 to $100,000 a year or more. Many Product Managers in textile companies can earn additional income in the form of bonuses based on the sales performance of the products they create.

Employment Prospects

There aren't many Product Manager jobs in textile companies, in great part because those companies can only have one or at most a handful of people in such high-level positions. Therefore, employment prospects for Product Managers in textile companies are only fair.

Advancement Prospects

Product Managers are generally already in high-level management positions, so there often isn't much room for them to advance further. In some cases, however, Product Managers with a strong track record of performance move into even higher positions as executive managers, vice presidents, or even chief executive officers. Some can advance by moving to positions at larger or more prestigious companies.

Education and Training

Almost all Product Managers in the textile business have at least a bachelor's degree, in a field such as textile design, textile merchandising, or textile development. In many cases, they also have advanced degrees—most often an M.B.A.—that give them the financial, technical, and supervisory skills they need to be successful.

Experience, Skills, and Personality Traits

Product Managers in textile firms must have extensive knowledge of both the fabric and apparel industries. They have to be on top of the latest trends and forecasts, especially in the areas of colors and patterns of textile usage in the apparel industry.

To be successful, Product Managers also need to be "big picture" thinkers who can come up with creative ideas and make sure those ideas are effectively executed. They have to be able to work well with a host of other professionals, including the textile firm's designers, stylists, colorists, market researchers, merchandisers, and sales representatives, so that they fully understand how to conceptualize, design, manufacture, sell, and distribute new textile products for their companies.

Product Managers must be creative and full of ideas, and must oversee large projects successfully from start to finish. They must also have extensive experience in the textile industry or a closely related industry, perhaps as textile designers, textile stylists, or even production managers. The more Product Managers understand the different people and processes behind new and potential textile products, the more likely those products will ultimately succeed.

Product Managers today also need solid computer skills, particularly when it comes to databases and spreadsheets. Product Managers gather, analyze, and apply extensive amounts of data—everything from sales figures to production costs. These essential tasks—and the sheer amount of data they create—demand technological proficiency.

Unions and Associations

Product Managers generally participate in a variety of textile- and apparel-related professional organizations, most often to stay on top of trends and forecasts and consult with colleagues (and even competitors) in the textile industry.

Many Product Managers, for example, are involved with the Color Association of the United States (CAUS), which makes color predictions and recommends colors for the fabrics (and yarns) textile manufacturers are producing. Some Product Managers are also connected with the International Colour Authority (ICA), which makes color predictions for textile mills, textile converters, and other entities in the textile industry.

Product Managers can also join groups like the International Textile and Apparel Association (ITAA), the American Apparel and Footwear Association (AAFA), and Fashion Group International (FGI).

Tips for Entry

1. Earn a bachelor's degree in textile design, textile merchandising, textile development, or a related field. Consider pursuing an advanced degree (e.g., an M.B.A.), particularly after you've gained several years of experience in the textile or apparel industry.
2. Accumulate textile industry experience by working as a textile designer, a textile stylist, or a related professional. (Generally, Product Managers need at least five years of industry experience.)
3. Read industry publications and join industry organizations to begin accumulating knowledge of textile and apparel trends and forecasts.
4. Talk to one or more Product Managers in the textile industry to better understand their work and learn how you might advance to a similar position someday.

SALES REPRESENTATIVE, TEXTILES

CAREER PROFILE

Duties: Sells finished fabrics to apparel manufacturers and related businesses (e.g., fabric stores, furniture and drapery producers), sells fibers to yarn manufacturers, or sells yarn to fabric producers

Alternate Title(s): Account Executive (Textiles), Sales Manager (Textiles)

Salary Range: $30,000 to $100,000+

Employment Prospects: Good

Advancement Prospects: Good

Best Geographical Location(s): Positions are available throughout the United States, since Sales Representatives often oversee geographic "territories"

Prerequisites:

Education or Training—A bachelor's degree in business administration, marketing, fashion or textile merchandising, textile technology, or liberal arts is strongly recommended; many Sales Representatives also participate in company training programs lasting several months to two years

Experience—Previous sales experience, in any capacity, is helpful though not necessarily required; college or volunteer experience in making presentations is beneficial

Special Skills and Personality Traits—Excellent presentation skills; written and oral communication skills; sound knowledge of textile and apparel trends and forecasts; technical knowledge of textile development and production; ability to work well under pressure and deal with frequent rejection; excellent attention to detail; follow-through skills; competitiveness and aggressiveness; honesty; effective listening skills; friendliness; energy and enthusiasm; self-motivation

CAREER LADDER

Regional Sales Manager or National Sales Manager

District Sales Manager

Sales Representative

Sales Trainee

Position Description

Sales Representatives in the textile industry generally work in one of three distinct subgroups. Some Sales Representatives (or "Reps," for short) sell fibers to companies that manufacture yarns. Other Sales Reps sell those yarns to textile manufacturers, which use the yarns to create fabrics. And still other textile Sales Reps sell those finished fabrics to apparel manufacturers, which use the fabrics to produce clothes. (Note: In some cases, Sales Reps sell finished fabrics to other entities as well, e.g., fabric stores and companies that manufacture furniture, drapes, and other items requiring fabrics.)

Sales Reps can also be classified in terms of where they perform their day-to-day tasks. Inside Sales Reps work on the premises of their employer, calling prospective customers on the phone (in most cases) in an effort to sell their company's products. Outside Sales Reps, on the other hand, go to where their prospective customers are—they make their "sales calls" by traveling to the site of the prospective customer's company and making a sales presentation once there.

In many ways, Sales Reps are on the front lines of the textile and apparel businesses. Because they deal every day with the people who make decisions about which fibers, yarns, or fabrics to use in their products, Sales Reps are among the most accurate assessors of the current "pulse" of the textile and apparel markets. Their customers tell them which products are in demand and which products aren't. They can then take this information back to their own companies' decision makers so that those companies produce the fibers, yarns, or fabrics that are likely to sell well and be profitable.

Many Sales Reps travel frequently to call on various clients (usually within a predetermined geographic area, or "territory") and show those clients their companies' newest products. During these meetings, the Sales Rep might show samples of various fibers, yarns, or fabrics and answer customers' questions about the materials. As such, Sales Reps need to know their products well, both from a technical standpoint (i.e., what the materials are made of, how they're made, what their characteristics are) and a financial standpoint (i.e., what the materials cost to produce and what price they'll be sold for). Often, Sales Reps must know about their competitors' products as well, since customers will inevitably ask why they should buy and use one company's products over another company's products.

Sales Reps have to be excellent communicators. Each meeting with a prospective customer is another chance to either make a sale or be rejected. Often, the difference between a sale and a rejection is in the Sales Rep's presentation of his/her product(s). Sales Reps who can thoughtfully and enthusiastically talk about their products will be more successful than those who don't know their products very well and are indifferent (or worse) in their feelings toward those products.

When Sales Reps successfully make a sale, they have to be able to negotiate a purchase price that is fair to both the customer and their company. They must also take the customer's order accurately, give the customer a specific delivery date for the materials purchased, and ensure the customer receives the product by that deadline. If there are problems along the way—e.g., if a delivery is going to be delayed, or if the material the customer needs is on back order—it is the Sales Rep's responsibility to deal with them, along with any questions (or complaints) the customer may have as a result.

When Sales Reps aren't making presentations to prospective customers, they spend some of their time researching textile and apparel market trends and forecasts, so that they know what materials and fabrics are, or will be, "hot" and thus in high demand. They also visit with previous clients, to answer their questions and suggest new or innovative uses for the products they've purchased. Additionally, Sales Reps meet periodically with their companies' merchandisers, market analysts/researchers, designers and stylists, and other key decision makers to give them direct feedback on customers' product wants, needs, and expectations. And, of course, Sales Reps must set aside considerable time to prepare new presentations when they're about to "go on the road" and sell a new product or line of products.

Salaries

Entry-level Sales Reps, often called "trainees," typically earn about $30,000 a year to start, depending on their experience, their education and skills, their job duties and responsibilities, and their geographic location. In some cases they receive a typical salary that isn't impacted by their sales performance. Quite often, however, at least part of their salary is based on commission—a percentage of each successful sale. The more the Sales Rep sells, the more money he/she can make from commissions. Some companies pay their Sales Reps by having them "draw against" their commissions: The Sales Rep gets a set amount of money each pay period so that he/she knows what income to expect, but the money he/she receives is merely an advance payment of future commissions.

Sales Reps with three to five years of experience can easily make $40,000 to $50,000 a year or more, especially if they sell well and make significant money from their commissions.

With more experience, Sales Reps can advance to become district sales managers, regional sales managers, or even national sales managers. National sales managers can easily earn more than $100,000 a year.

Employment Prospects

Since textiles and apparel are among the most basic human needs, there is always a considerable need for both. Hence, employment prospects for Sales Reps in the textile industry are quite good. Every fiber, yarn, and fabric manufacturer has products to sell year after year, which means the need for Sales Reps is continuous.

Advancement Prospects

Sales Reps generally start out as sales trainees, working either in a company's on-site showroom or accompanying more experienced traveling Sales Reps as they make their rounds and sell their products. As sales trainees gain experience and industry knowledge, they're generally the first in line to take open Sales Rep positions.

Sales Reps with three to five years of experience and a strong track record of sales can advance to become district sales managers (who oversee the Sales Reps in a small geographic area—a state or part of a state, for example); regional sales managers (who oversee the district managers and Sales Reps in a wider geographic area—several states, for example); or even national sales managers (who oversee the regional managers, district managers, and Sales Reps throughout the entire country).

Sometimes, Sales Reps with years of experience also go on to higher-level positions in upper management, or even to become chief executive officer or president of the company.

Education and Training

Most companies expect entry-level Sales Reps to have a bachelor's degree in a field like business administration, marketing, fashion or textile merchandising, textile technology, or the liberal arts. Some professionals in the field say that the specific degree obtained isn't an issue; rather, they want entry-level candidates to have the breadth of knowledge and maturity that having a college degree requires.

Many Sales Reps learn the ropes of their jobs in company training programs, which can last anywhere from three months to two years. Through these programs, they learn about the company's specific products, processes, and procedures; develop their presentation skills; and learn under the tutelage of more experienced salespeople.

Sales Reps who wish to advance to higher-level positions often pursue advanced degrees—most often the master of business administration (M.B.A.) degree. Some Sales Reps also participate in training programs through local technical/community colleges so that they can better understand their companies' products, how they're made, and how they're best used.

Experience, Skills, and Personality Traits

Entry-level Sales Reps benefit from sales experience of any kind, preferably in the textile or apparel industry. Many have worked as sales associates in retail apparel or department stores. Others have held sales positions in different fields and industries, but find that their basic skill set transfers easily to the textile or apparel field.

Sales Reps need a host of widely varying skills in order to be successful. First and foremost, they must have excellent "people skills"—they must be friendly and outgoing, listen to people and understand what they're saying, and present themselves and their products well, either in person or on paper. They must also know their product(s) thoroughly so that they can answer customers' questions effectively and honestly.

Sales Reps also need to understand the broader textile and apparel industries, not to mention their competitors' products, so that they can effectively advise their customers on which fibers, yarns, or fabrics are likely to be successful in the current and future marketplaces.

To be successful, Sales Reps must be task-oriented. They're responsible for accurately documenting customers' product orders and ensuring that the products ordered arrive on time, in good condition, and at the agreed-upon price. If problems arise anywhere in that sometimes complex process, the Sales Rep must deal with those problems to the customer's satisfaction—if he/she wants to keep the customer!

Increasingly, Sales Reps must be technologically savvy as well, keeping track of customers and prospects in computerized databases; communicating frequently with customers and prospects via e-mail and even instant messaging in some cases; and using spreadsheet software to analyze current sales and project future ones. Moreover, since many textile companies today have customers of diverse backgrounds, Sales Reps are increasingly being called upon to be bilingual—in English and, most often, Spanish.

Sales Reps who do best in the textile industry are energetic, enthusiastic, aggressive, competitive, and persuasive. They're also able to deal with frequent rejection, part of the game for any salesperson. At the same time, however, they are honest and have a high degree of integrity. As all businesses in the fashion industry become more competitive, long-term relationships between textile or apparel producers and textile Sales Reps become essential. The Sales Rep who deals fairly with his/her customers will be one who earns their respect, their trust, and their dollars over a period of many years.

Unions and Associations

While there aren't any unions or professional associations specifically for Sales Reps in the textile industry, most Sales Reps keep up with industry trends and forecasts by participating in organizations like the American Apparel and Footwear Association (AAFA), the International Textile and Apparel Association (ITAA), and Fashion Group International (FGI).

Sales Reps in the textile industry and many other industries are often members of Sales and Marketing Executives International (SMEI) as well. The organization is a professional trade group for sales professionals in a wide variety of fields. Additionally, many Sales Reps (from all industries) are members of the American Marketing Association (AMA).

Tips for Entry

1. Earn a bachelor's degree in business administration, marketing, fashion or textile merchandising, textile technology, or the liberal arts.
2. While in school, pursue at least one internship, co-op, or related experiential learning activity to gain experience in the broad textile field or, preferably, in textile sales and marketing.

3. Take college courses in speech, communication, or similar areas to improve your oral and written communication skills. Consider joining a student organization, participating in a local Toastmasters group, or running for on-campus elected office so that you can work on sales-related activities.
4. Learn all you can about the textile and apparel industries by monitoring industry publications (in print and online) and getting involved in related professional organizations.
5. Contact current textile Sales Reps and ask to "shadow" them for a day to learn more about their work. Ask them how they got their jobs, and how you might get a similar job someday.
6. Get as much sales-related experience as you can, particularly in the textile or apparel industry. Work as a Sales Associate at a fabric store, or in an apparel or department store, so that you can learn more about the textile and apparel industries and, perhaps, meet working Sales Reps who visit to present their products.
7. Become technologically proficient by taking courses on how to use database software, spreadsheet programs, and contact management software. Consider taking courses in Internet and online research as well so that you can demonstrate to prospective employers your ability to find information on competitors and monitor industry trends and forecasts.

TEXTILE COLORIST

CAREER PROFILE

Duties: Chooses or helps choose the colors that will be used in textile designs, with the goal of creating color combinations that consumers (whether apparel manufacturers, retail buyers, or the eventual shopping public) will like and thus buy

Salary Range: $36,000 to $70,000+

Employment Prospects: Fair

Advancement Prospects: Fair

Best Geographical Location(s): New York City and other fashion centers, though positions exist in other parts of the country as well, particularly in New England and the Southeast, where the majority of textile manufacturers are located

Prerequisites:

Education or Training—A two-year college degree in textile design or fine arts is generally the minimum needed; many have a four-year college degree in textile design, fine arts, or a related field; coursework in color theory is essential; on-the-job training programs

Experience—None required; college internship/co-op or volunteer/apprenticeship experience is quite helpful

Special Skills and Personality Traits—Strong sense of color, along with specialized education in color theory; ability to realize how colors will look on different types of fabric and in different combinations; understanding of the nuances of textile construction and production; ability to research previously designed fabrics for color ideas; top-notch computer skills; ability to follow precise instructions to the letter; ability to roll with the inevitable changes that will occur during the process of determining colors and color combinations for a piece of fabric; ability to work well with other people; persistence and patience

CAREER LADDER

Textile Designer

Textile Artist

Textile Colorist

Textile Colorist Intern/ Trainee/Apprentice

Position Description

Textile Colorists are the professionals who decide—either on their own or, more often, in collaboration with textile artists, textile designers, and textile stylists—which colors and color combinations will look best in various textile designs. The goal is to come up with color offerings that will attract positive attention from customers, whether those customers are apparel manufacturers (that will use the fabric to produce their clothing items), retail fashion buyers (who will decide if the apparel that uses the fabric is worth stocking in their stores), or the general buying public (who will decide if they want to wear the fabric once it's been turned into garments).

Using their educational background in textile design or a similar field and an extensive knowledge of color theory, Textile Colorists work to determine which color combinations will work (or not work) in a given textile design. They may find, for example, that certain color combinations are unappealing while other combinations are attractive. Often, they must make these decisions with future color trends and forecasts in mind. The "hot" colors today aren't so much the concern as what will be hot one or two years down the road.

Typically, Textile Colorists work under textile designers or even a textile stylist who oversees the entire textile design operation. Usually, the Textile Colorist attempts to work out color combinations for designs already established by the textile designer. As such, the Textile Colorist must be willing to work within the parameters set by the textile designer, following directions carefully and yet having the persistence to suggest necessary changes.

Textile Colorists may work out various color combinations on paper or, much more often now, on computers with specially designed computer software programs. Work goes much faster and more efficiently when the Textile Colorist is a skilled computer user. The computer allows the Textile Colorist to experiment with various color combinations, and lets him/her easily save and, later, recall color combinations from previous textile designs.

To stay on top of color trends and forecasts, Textile Colorists often visit various fashion markets and attend industry events. Often, they belong to color forecasting organizations so that they can tap into well-researched predictions on which colors will be "hot" (and won't be "hot") in the next one or two years. Some Textile Colorists even do their own color forecasting for their companies—especially once they've accumulated several years of experience and, more important, a reputation for being accurate when it comes to their color trend predictions. To do this work, they typically must gather a variety of information from fiber producers, customers, and color research services, then carefully analyze that information, and perhaps supplement it with additional information before making their color predictions.

Usually, the Textile Colorist maintains a color library for his or her company, either alone or in collaboration with a color librarian. The color library allows the Textile Colorist and others in the company to quickly pull out samples of previous color combinations on various fabrics whenever there might be a question of how a certain color combination might look, in general or on a certain type of fabric. The more library samples a Textile Colorist has at his or her disposal, and the better organized those samples are, the easier the Textile Colorist's job becomes, especially when making critical final decisions about the colors and color combinations a textile manufacturer will produce in a given year.

Once all of the color decisions have been made for a line of fabrics, the Textile Colorist must develop precise color instructions for each piece of fabric that will be produced so that the color combinations look like they're supposed to. The Textile Colorist may even follow up with production personnel to ensure that each color and color combination turns out as expected.

Salaries

Salaries for Textile Colorists vary widely, usually starting at about $36,000 a year. Senior-level Textile Colorists with extensive experience can earn $70,000 a year or more.

Employment Prospects

Prospective Textile Colorists have a fair number of employment opportunities they can pursue, but competition for them can be tough. Most jobs are staff positions with textile manufacturers, located in fashion centers like New York City, or in the New England states and the Southeast, where many textile manufacturing operations are based.

The Textile Colorist job is often an entry-level position for people who have either a two- or four-year college degree and some basic experience they've gained through a college internship/co-op or a volunteer apprenticeship.

Advancement Prospects

With a few years of experience, a Textile Colorist often receives opportunities to do full-fledged textile design work. As a result, it's quite common for Textile Colorists to become textile artists and then textile designers after several years on the job. Later, they can move into positions as textile stylist or head textile stylist, overseeing the entire textile design process.

Education and Training

Most Textile Colorists have at least a two-year college degree in an area such as textile design or fine arts. Some Textile Colorists also have academic training in fashion merchandising, fashion marketing, or apparel production. A four-year college degree is a good idea for anyone who wants to move beyond the Textile Colorist position and into a textile designer or textile stylist position. Sometimes companies supplement academic preparation with their own targeted training programs for new Textile Colorists and similar professionals.

Whatever their postsecondary education, all Textile Colorists need to have extensive training in and understanding of color theory, fabric development and production, and textile construction.

Experience, Skills, and Personality Traits

Since Textile Colorists are often entry-level professionals, extensive experience isn't necessarily required to break into the field. However, college internship/co-op or volunteer/

apprenticeship experience is very helpful, as is a portfolio of textile coloring and even design samples highlighting your work.

All Textile Colorists need to have or develop expertise in color theory and color trends and forecasts. They must understand how different colors will look in different combinations and on different fabrics, so strong artistic abilities and visual sense are critical. Technical knowledge of fabric construction and textile production is also important. Computer hardware and software skills are also essential, since most textile companies now use computers in almost all of their product development and production processes.

Textile Colorists must be able to follow precise directions, yet have the wherewithal to suggest important color or color combination changes when necessary. Since they're always collaborating with other artistic and technical professionals, they must also be good team players who are able to communicate effectively with others, maintain their flexibility when the inevitable changes to their ideas arise, and be careful and accurate when carrying out color and color combination requests.

Above all, Textile Colorists need to be deadline-oriented can-doers. As one color development laboratory put it when it was looking to fill an open position for a Textile Colorist, "If you're a 'sure, I can do that' person, we would like to talk with you."

Unions and Associations

The American Association of Textile Chemists and Colorists (AATCC) is a professional trade organization for the textile chemistry field, with more than 5,000 individual and nearly 300 institutional members in 65 countries around the world. Members—among them Textile Colorists—focus their efforts on promoting research and the application of dyes and chemicals in the textile industry. Members can participate in a variety of workshops and subscribe to an assortment of industry-related publications.

Tips for Entry

1. Pursue a two- or four-year college degree in textile design or a related field like fine arts, textile manufacturing, or apparel manufacturing. During your time in school, talk to professors and campus career counselors to learn about Textile Colorist jobs and internships and similar opportunities.
2. Set up meetings with one or more Textile Colorists so that you can learn more about their day-to-day activities and how they got into their jobs and careers. (Note: If a face-to-face meeting is impossible, consider talking to people by phone or via email.)
3. Get involved with the American Association of Textile Chemists and Colorists (AATCC) and any other local, regional, national, or international organizations you can find that focus on textile coloring or textile design and manufacturing in general.
4. If you're a college student, seek an internship or co-op program that will allow you to get some practical experience working with a Textile Colorist and/or similar professionals. If an internship or co-op isn't an option, consider volunteering to be a gofer for a Textile Colorist or an entire textile design team.
5. Start building a portfolio of textile colors and color combinations you develop on paper or with computer software. Employers will expect to see your portfolio when they consider you for an entry-level job or an internship/co-op.
6. Keep up with general textile and fashion industry trends by reading industry trade publications and visiting industry-related Web sites. Pay particular attention to color trends and, especially, color forecasts for one or two years down the road. Try to understand how the color forecasters are making their predictions. Then monitor current color trends to determine the accuracy (or lack thereof) of forecasters' predictions from one or two years ago.

TEXTILE CONVERSION MANAGER

CAREER PROFILE

Duties: Oversees the various processes involved in turning uncolored, unfinished textiles into finished fabrics that can be purchased by apparel manufacturers, fabric retailers, and other companies that use textiles in their products

Alternate Title(s): Textile Conversion Supervisor

Salary Range: $35,000 to $75,000+

Employment Prospects: Limited

Advancement Prospects: Limited

Best Geographical Location(s): New York City area; New England and the Southeast, where textile manufacturing firms are located

Prerequisites:

Education or Training—A two- or four-year college degree in an area like textile technology, textile merchandising, or textile marketing is recommended; coursework in textile chemistry, fabric construction, dyeing, color analysis, and mathematics is also helpful

Experience—Extensive textile industry experience in general; textile manufacturing and finishing experience in particular

Special Skills and Personality Traits—Understanding of textile production procedures and the textile industry; expertise in textile dyeing, printing, and finishing processes; knowledge of yarns, weaving, and knitting construction; understanding of predicting textile needs in the marketplace; organizational skills; analytical skills; resourcefulness; detail orientation; problem-solving abilities; strong communication skills; excellent scheduling abilities; follow-up skills; extensive knowledge of textile trends and forecasts

CAREER LADDER

Textile Conversion Manager

Textile Converter

Assistant Textile Converter

Textile Converting Clerk

Position Description

Textile Conversion Managers are experts in textile finishing—dyeing, printing, and other processes that turn greige goods (uncolored, unfinished textiles) into finished fabrics that are typically used or purchased by apparel manufacturers, fabric retailers, and other companies featuring textiles in their products.

While working for a textile manufacturer—or, much more often these days, an independent textile converting company that serves textile producers and apparel manufacturers—the Textile Conversion Manager determines which dyes, prints, and/or other finishes textiles need based on how those textiles will be used. Working closely with the apparel manufacturers who will ultimately buy the finished fabric, the Textile Conversion Manager sees to it that the fabric that will eventually become children's play wear, for example, is more durable than, say, the material that will eventually become women's designer dresses. By developing standards of quality for each textile that goes through the finishing process, the Textile Conversion Manager works to ensure that the fabric that winds up in the hands of apparel manufacturers and, ultimately, consumers looks, feels, and works the way it's supposed to.

In situations where the Textile Conversion Manager works for a textile manufacturer (as opposed to an independent finishing firm), he or she often has responsibilities that go beyond finishing. Some Textile Conversion Managers who work for textile producers are heavily involved in determining which fabrics should be manufactured and in what quantities. They help calculate the amounts of fabric likely to be bought by the firm's customers (whether apparel manufacturers or other manufacturers) and then help set prices for those fabrics based on supply and production costs. Sometimes, Textile Conversion Managers are even involved in deciding what fibers the company will use in creating its textiles, and in what width and weight.

Textile Conversion Managers in independent textile conversion firms, meanwhile, are liaisons of sorts among textile production mills, independent dyeing and finishing plants (which often do dyeing and finishing work on a contract basis for the independent textile conversion company), and the buyers of finished fabric (e.g., apparel manufacturers). As such, they spend a healthy chunk of their time making sure that orders for finished fabrics are processed promptly and correctly. It's not unusual for them to be on the phone frequently with their counterparts in fiber mills, dyeing and finishing plants, and apparel manufacturing companies. They have to make sure that each player in the process of creating finished fabric is doing their part and doing it correctly.

Textile Conversion Managers must be well organized so that they can do the nitty gritty work of keeping accurate records of products, inventory, and production timetables; following up with various internal and external customers; and being involved in daily decisions regarding which fabrics will be produced and how they will be finished. At the same time, however, Textile Conversion Managers need to maintain a "big picture" focus. They have to understand the entire textile production process and the textile industry as a whole as well as the apparel industry if their companies are selling fabrics to apparel manufacturers. Keeping up with textile and apparel industry trends and forecasts is essential, as is constantly communicating with customers to determine their wants and needs where textiles are concerned.

Salaries

Entry-level assistant textile converters with the appropriate two- or four-year degree generally earn starting salaries of around $35,000 a year. Experienced Textile Conversion Managers, however, can earn $75,000 a year or more, depending on their experience and level of responsibility.

Employment Prospects

Since there are comparatively few textile manufacturers and independent textile conversion companies in the United States, job opportunities for Textile Conversion Managers are somewhat limited. Opportunities do become available with changes in personnel and retirements, but competition for openings can be tough.

Advancement Prospects

Applicants who have previous experience as converting clerks or assistant textile converters have the best opportunities for landing the higher-level textile converter and Textile Conversion Manager positions. Still, advancement prospects for Textile Conversion Managers and similar professionals are somewhat limited, mainly because the number of textile manufacturers and independent textile conversion companies in the United States is rather small.

Education and Training

Most Textile Conversion Managers have a two- or four-year college degree in a field such as textile technology, textile merchandising, or textile marketing. A few have academic backgrounds in apparel production as well.

All Textile Conversion Managers need coursework or training in textile science, fabric construction, color analysis, and mathematics as well. Some background in marketing is also quite helpful in most cases.

Experience, Skills, and Personality Traits

Textile Conversion Managers are not entry-level professionals. Indeed, most Textile Conversion Managers have extensive experience in textile production and/or the textile industry in general. They need that background in order to learn finishing processes, understand the various markets for different types of textiles, and build close working relationships with fiber producers and apparel manufacturers.

To do their jobs well, Textile Conversion Managers need to be highly organized and detail oriented. They must be able to carefully track textile production and finishing processes to make sure that the final fabrics purchased by apparel manufacturers and others meet expectations and quality standards. They also need to keep accurate records of textile orders and help ensure that those orders are filled quickly, efficiently, and correctly.

Textile Conversion Managers who work for textile production companies must have strong data-gathering and analytical skills, since they're often closely involved in determining which textiles will be produced, in what quantities, and at what price.

The most effective Textile Conversion Managers have superior communication skills, which they tap frequently in their dealings with counterparts in fiber production companies and apparel manufacturing firms. They must be able to understand the needs of their customers, whether apparel manufacturers or others, as well as the textile and apparel industries as a whole so that the fabrics their companies produce are ones that will be financially successful.

Unions and Associations

Some Textile Conversion Managers are members of the American Textile Manufacturers Institute (ATMI), a Washington, D.C.–based industry trade association whose members work in textile manufacturing or processing companies.

The New York City–based Textile Distributors Association (TDA) is a marketing association for textile manufacturers and converters that sell fabric and fiber for use in the apparel and home furnishings industries.

Tips for Entry

1. Pursue a two- or four-year college degree in textile technology or a related field like textile merchandising, textile marketing, or apparel production. While you're in school, participate in an internship or a co-op program that allows you to work in textile conversion or a closely related area.
2. Identify and talk to one or more people who currently work as Textile Conversion Managers or lower-level conversion professionals. Ask them how they got their jobs, what their day-to-day activities are like, and how you might break into the field.
3. Read textile and apparel industry publications (in print and online) to gain a thorough understanding of the textile market and its relationship to the apparel market and other markets that rely on fabrics.

TEXTILE DESIGNER

CAREER PROFILE

Duties: Uses a combination of artistic and technical skills to design new fabrics or modify previous fabric designs for use in the manufacture of apparel and related materials (e.g., household furniture, curtains)

Alternate Title(s): Fabric Designer

Salary Range: $30,000 to $100,000+

Employment Prospects: Fair

Advancement Prospects: Fair

Best Geographical Location(s): New York City and other fashion centers around the United States; New England and the southeastern United States, where most textiles are manufactured

Prerequisites:

Education or Training—A two- or four-year degree in textile design or a related field; on-the-job training through apprenticeships, internships, and volunteerships

Experience—Textile Designers begin as interns or apprentices to learn the artistic and technical skills they need to go on and become more involved with designing new fabrics

Special Skills and Personality Traits—Artistic and technical skills; excellent drawing and sketching skills; a well-developed sense of color and patterns; knowledge of textile and apparel production; understanding of fashion industry trends and forecasts; creativity and persuasion; good computer skills; good time management skills

CAREER LADDER

Freelance Textile Designer

Head/Senior Textile Designer

Textile Designer

Textile Design Assistant/Intern

Position Description

Textile Designers are part artists, part color experts, and part technical specialists who create new fabrics or modify the designs of previous fabrics so that they can be used in the manufacture of fashions. Many Textile Designers also work on related textile-based items, ranging from the everyday (e.g., curtains and furniture coverings) to the much more narrowly focused (e.g., cold-weather clothing and even space suits).

Textile Designers can specialize in a variety of ways. They may, for example, focus their efforts on print fabrics, for which designs are literally printed on pieces of fabric in large quantities. Print Textile Designers will generally develop their designs on paper, using their artistic skills and, to an increasing degree, their computer skills. The printed designs are then used to create samples and, eventually, large quantities of the fabric itself. Textile Designers who work with woven fabrics, on the other hand, use hand looms to weave new fabric designs. Once they come up with a design that has potential, they might use a computer program to see how the woven design would look in other colors or styles. Meanwhile, Textile Designers who work with knits use knitting machines to develop their new fabric ideas.

Since Textile Designers who work with wovens and knits are often tapping skills beyond the artistic, they typically need more advanced technical and computer skills than do designers of print fabrics. But all three types of Textile Designers must know how to effectively use computers and related software (e.g., Adobe Photoshop, Adobe Illustrator), because many of the tasks that used to be done by hand are now done mostly or entirely by computers.

Textile Designers can also specialize in the types of fabrics they work with (e.g., cottons, linens, wools, silks); the types of apparel markets they design for (e.g., men's, women's, children's); or the type of work they focus most of their attention on (e.g., designing new fabrics from scratch versus redesigning previously developed fabrics for new uses or "looks").

Because Textile Designers must be creative, they must devote considerable time to monitoring and observing the work of other designers and paying attention to the world around them. A new design idea could come from almost anywhere—a sample of fabric from another designer or from previously developed designs stored in a company's fabric library, an interesting wallpaper pattern or outdoor scene, or even a piece of art at a museum. Textile Designers are constantly observing the things they see around them, ensuring that new ideas will come to them.

The Textile Designer's work goes far beyond the artistic, however, especially with the recent explosive growth of computers and computer software, and the increasing complexity of textile manufacturing machinery. Textile Designers need to stay on top of new fabric developments, color and overall fashion trends, and emerging production processes in order to be successful. They also need to understand the entire textile production process in general, so that the designs they develop aren't cost-prohibitive to the companies they're working for. A creative, highly artistic design is one thing; but if the company can't profitably produce it, it will never see the light of day.

Textile Designers also need to understand and accept their roles in a process that is much bigger than themselves. Typically, the Textile Designer is a staff employee for a textile manufacturer. He or she will usually work under a textile stylist, who will either ask for fairly specific designs (i.e., a certain "look") or give the Textile Designer more creative freedom. In either case, the Textile Designer must be able to come up with ideas that will satisfy not only himself or herself, but many others in the company, and, of course, the final consumer, who makes the ultimate decision with his or her buying dollars about whether a certain fabric is "good" or not.

For the many Textile Designers who work for outside design houses or even, in some cases, as independent freelancers, meeting clients' wants and needs (versus one's own) is that much more important. The Textile Designer who can balance design freedom and creativity with meeting the desires of his or her customers is the one who will be most successful, especially over the long term.

Salaries

Salaries for Textile Designers vary significantly based on their level of experience, their education, and their reputation in the field. Entry-level textile design assistants usually earn around $30,000 a year to start. Senior-level Textile Designers with the appropriate credentials can earn $100,000 a year or more.

Employment Prospects

Competition in the textile design field is stiff. Opportunities do exist, but the best ones are reserved for Textile Designers who are willing to start small as trainees or interns and work their way up into full-fledged textile design positions by gaining experience under more seasoned Textile Designers.

Some Textile Designers find jobs in New York City, where many textile manufacturing firms base their design and styling departments. Other Textile Designer jobs exist in the New England states and in the Southeast, where many textile manufacturers' production operations are located. Still other opportunities exist with independent textile design firms.

Advancement Prospects

With a few years of hands-on experience, a person who starts out as an intern or a trainee in the textile design field can become an assistant Textile Designer or something similar, and then work as a full-fledged Textile Designer. Later, he or she might become a head Textile Designer, who oversees the work of other designers and has more managerial duties.

Some Textile Designers, once they've accumulated five or more years of professional experience in the field, decide to become independent freelancers who work for a variety of clients (either textile manufacturers or independent textile design firms) on a contract basis. Freelancers can make more money from their work, but they also give up some of the job security and other benefits they would probably have in a full-time staff position.

Education and Training

Most Textile Designers have a two- or four-year degree in textile design or a related field like fashion design or apparel production. Many also receive on-the-job training through apprenticeships, internships, and volunteerships.

Some Textile Designers pursue extra coursework or experience in graphic design and/or computer applications. Also, most develop and maintain portfolios of their previous designs, so that they can show them to prospective future employers or clients.

Experience, Skills, and Personality Traits

Hands-on experience is essential for breaking into the textile design field. Many who want to go into the industry gain such experience through college internships or co-op programs, or through apprenticeships or volunteerships they arrange on their own.

To be successful, Textile Designers need a combination of artistic and technical skills. They must draw and sketch well (especially if they intend to become print fabric designers), have an artistic flair and creativity, have a good sense of color and color combinations, and understand how an initial design can become a final product without being cost-prohibitive.

Technical skills are also critical to the Textile Designer's work. He or she needs to know about various fabrics and fabric constructions, finishes, and dyes, and keep current on emerging trends in all three areas. He or she must also be aware of trends and forecasts in the entire fashion industry—especially as they relate to colors, patterns, and fabrics that are expected to be "hot" perhaps one or even two years down the road. The various tools and machines that make up the textile production process need to be in every Textile Designer's field of knowledge as well. Also, the Textile Designer must not only be comfortable with computers but also skilled in using them to create new ideas. Computer-aided design (CAD) software and similar programs are no longer optional, but required for success in the field.

Textile Designers also need to be able to take their ideas from concept to reality, despite the many hurdles that might stand in the way, such as cost and production time constraints. Inevitably, the Textile Designer will have to work with other people, so effective written and oral communication skills are also essential. Time management skills are critical as well, since most Textile Designers, particularly those who work as independent freelancers, are working on several projects (perhaps for several clients, and with several deadlines) at once.

Unions and Associations

Some Textile Designers are members of the Surface Design Association (SDA), a California-based trade organization for professionals who work in surface design—the "coloring, patterning, designing, and transformation of fabrics, fibers, and other materials directed toward art and design," according to the definition on the SDA's Web site.

The Colorado-based International Textile and Apparel Association (ITAA) is an educational and scientific organization for members of the textile, apparel, and merchandising fields, while the Maryland-based Textile Association of America (TAA) serves more than 500 members worldwide, including museum curators, teachers, historians, artists, students, dealers, and collectors.

Tips for Entry

1. Offer to be a volunteer gofer for a Textile Designer in a textile manufacturing firm or an independent design firm. Practical experience is key to entering the textile design field.
2. Pursue a two- or four-year college degree in textile design or a related field like fashion design or apparel production. While you're there, be sure to participate in an internship or a co-op that will give you some hands-on experience in the industry.
3. Use the Internet and other sources to research various textile manufacturers and their specialties, as well as apparel manufacturers and the fabrics they tend to use most. Try to determine which companies use which fabrics from which designers, and why.
4. Keep up with trends and forecasts in the textile industry and the fashion industry by reading industry publications, getting involved with industry-related professional groups, and visiting industry-related Web sites.
5. Arrange to meet with one or more Textile Designers, perhaps one who works full-time for a textile manufacturer, another who works for an independent textile design firm, and a third who works as an independent freelancer. (Note: If an in-person meeting is impossible, arrange a phone call or email correspondence.) Ask the designers you meet with to advise you on how to break into the field, and on the education, experiences, and skills you'll need to succeed. Also ask about internship or volunteer opportunities you could pursue with their organizations.
6. Start a portfolio of your textile design ideas and creations so that you'll have something tangible to show prospective employers and others in the field.

TEXTILE RESEARCH SCIENTIST

CAREER PROFILE

Duties: Studies the technical aspects of fibers and fabrics in order to improve existing fibers and fabrics and develop better ones

Alternate Title(s): Research and Development Scientist, Textile Technologist, Textile Technician, Textile Tester

Salary Range: $30,000 to $90,000+

Employment Prospects: Good

Advancement Prospects: Fair

Best Geographical Location(s): Cities where textile mills are located, most often in the American Southeast, South, and Northeast

Prerequisites:

Education or Training—A bachelor's degree in chemistry, chemical engineering, textile science, or physics is generally the minimum educational requirement; often, a master's degree or Ph.D. in one of these same fields is required as well

Experience—Extensive textile research and development experience is required for high-level positions; experience in textile manufacturing is also quite helpful

Special Skills and Personality Traits—Solid understanding of how fibers, yarns, and fabrics are developed and produced; strong research skills; analytical and problem-solving abilities; interest in scientific principles and the scientific method; patience and persistence; accuracy; flexibility and creativity; well-developed sense of curiosity

CAREER LADDER

Textile Development Executive

Textile Research Scientist

Textile Technologist

Textile Lab Technician

Position Description

Textile Research Scientists are the people textile and apparel manufacturers turn to when they want to improve existing fibers, yarns, and fabrics and develop new ones that will make products more durable, more visually appealing, easier to take care of, and more cost-effective to make and sell.

Textile Research Scientists are experts in the technical aspects of fiber, yarn, and/or fabric construction. Working for fiber manufacturers, textile mills, or private testing and development laboratories, they study the ways their companies can blend existing fibers to create new fabrics. They also develop new synthetic fibers that textile and apparel manufacturers can use in their products to create more consumer interest in them and thus increase their sales and profits.

Much of the Textile Research Scientist's work involves studying what others in the field are doing in the way of fiber and fabric research. They devote part of their time, for example, to reading academic and technical journals describing various research findings. They also attend professional conferences, where they might present their own findings or attend educational sessions where they learn about the discoveries of others in the field.

Textile Research Scientists are critical to their companies because they exert considerable influence over what products will be made, how, and in what quantities. If, for example, a team of Textile Research Scientists comes up with a way to strengthen an existing fiber, their company will then be able to sell that fiber to other firms for a higher price, and therefore, greater profit. Or, if a Textile Research Scientist figures out a simple way to construct a certain piece of fabric, his/her company can eventually expect to save hundreds of thousands or even millions of dollars in manufacturing costs.

Thus, the Textile Research Scientist's ideas and discoveries often have a direct impact on a company's performance—not to mention the fibers and fabrics that go into the materials and clothes used every day by average consumers.

Salaries

Salaries for Textile Research Scientists can easily be over $70,000 a year, especially if they have advanced degrees. However, reaching this level of income generally requires at least five years of experience. Those who start out as textile laboratory technicians or textile testers can reasonably expect to earn salaries in the $30,000 to $35,000 range.

Generally speaking, the higher one's level of education, the higher the salary he/she earns. Scientists with a master's degree or Ph.D., for example, earn considerably more than new graduates with bachelor's degrees.

Employment Prospects

Employment Prospects for Textile Research Scientists are good, in great part because fiber, yarn, and fabric manufacturers are constantly looking for ways to improve existing materials and develop new ones. Research and development (R&D) budgets in many organizations are quite high because companies realize that their current and future success lies in creating and improving products.

Advancement Prospects

Since Textile Research Scientists are fairly high-level employees, they have already advanced considerably within their organizations. Some of them, however, do go on to management positions in R&D (they become textile development executives/managers, for example). In a few cases, they move up to even higher positions in a textile or apparel manufacturing operation, because of their technical knowledge and their understanding of product development.

Education and Training

Practically all Textile Research Scientists (even in lower-level positions like textile lab technician or textile tester) have at least a bachelor's degree, in a field like chemistry, chemical engineering, textile science, or physics. Most, however, also have graduate degrees, either at the master's level or, often, the doctoral level.

Experience, Skills, and Personality Traits

Textile Research Scientists have extensive experience that they've gained through their academic pursuits and practical work in the textile industry. College students who want to become Textile Research Scientists would do well to participate in at least one internship or co-op program that allows them to, for example, work with or as a textile lab technician, a textile tester, or a textile technologist.

All Textile Research Scientists must have a strong interest in scientific principles and methods, as well as a thorough understanding of how fibers, yarns, and fabrics are developed, constructed, and manufactured. Analytical and problem-solving skills are essential, as are strong written and oral communication skills, which are especially useful in helping Textile Research Scientists clearly communicate their findings and recommendations to company decision makers.

Because their work can take months or even years in some cases, Textile Research Scientists must be patient and persistent and able to see the big picture while also focusing on important, and sometimes minute, details. Accuracy and organization are critical as well.

Perhaps most important of all, Textile Research Scientists must be curious by nature, and willing to work toward answering their own questions and the questions of others.

Unions and Associations

Many Textile Research Scientists and related professionals are involved with the American Association of Textile Chemists and Colorists and generalist organizations like the International Textile and Apparel Association.

Depending on their specific area of interest, Textile Research Scientists might be members of other organizations as well. Those with a background in chemistry, for example, might be involved in the American Chemical Society or the American Institute of Chemical Engineers.

Tips for Entry

1. In college, participate in school- or academic department–sponsored research opportunities so that you can gain experience using the scientific method to study existing products/ideas or to develop new ones. Additionally, participate in at least one internship or co-op experience, preferably in the research and development (R&D) department of a textile manufacturer.

2. Work or volunteer in a textile manufacturer's R&D department, perhaps as the assistant to a textile lab technician or a textile tester. Such experience will introduce you to people who can give you other opportunities.
3. Talk to one or more Textile Research Scientists to learn more about their work, discover how they got their jobs, and ask for their advice on how you can pursue their career someday.

TEXTILE STYLIST

CAREER PROFILE

Duties: Oversees the conceptualization, development, and production of part or all of a textile producer's annual fabric line; coordinates the efforts of design and production staff to ensure that each line's "look" is correct

Alternate Title(s): Creative Director, Textiles

Salary Range: $55,000 to $100,000+

Employment Prospects: Limited

Advancement Prospects: Fair

Best Geographical Location(s): New York City and other fashion centers around the United States

Prerequisites:

Education or Training—A bachelor's degree in textile science, textile design, textile merchandising, textile technology, or textile marketing is generally required; coursework in art, advertising, marketing, apparel design, and/or fashion merchandising is also quite helpful

Experience—Extensive experience in the textile industry; several years' experience as a textile artist, textile colorist, and/or textile designer

Special Skills and Personality Traits—Extensive textile and apparel industry experience and knowledge; ability to work easily with both textile designers and the people in the manufacturing mill; excellent research skills; ability to maintain close contact with merchandising, marketing, and forecasting staff and services; ability to consistently oversee the development of fabric lines that will be appealing to customers (apparel manufacturers and the general consuming public) one or even two years down the road; "big picture" skills; resourcefulness and problem-solving abilities; creativity; strong sense of color; analytical and research skills; sound background in both the textile design and textile manufacturing processes; a willingness to travel frequently and visit national and international markets, as well as geographically dispersed production mills

CAREER LADDER

Creative Director (large companies)

Textile Stylist

Assistant Textile Stylist

Textile Designer

Position Description

Textile Stylists are supervisory professionals who use their extensive industry knowledge and experience to oversee the conceptualization, development, and production of each new annual line of fabric produced by their companies.

Typically working at least one year before the fabrics from a particular line will start showing up in clothes available for purchase in stores, Textile Stylists have the ultimate responsibility for developing a fabric line's overall "look" and then making that look a reality. To do their jobs successfully they have to communicate and coordinate with a number of other professionals and divisions within their companies.

For example, Textile Stylists work closely with textile designers, who actually create new textile concepts. Generally, the Textile Stylist guides the textile designers (and, often, the textile colorists and textile artists as well) by telling them which particular colors, textures, and weights they should use in their upcoming designs. The Textile Stylist gathers this critical information through considerable research. He or she typically travels to national and international markets to stay on top of current fabric and fashion trends and forecasts. He or she might also get line-planning insights from in-house or outside forecasting services, editors of trade publications, and industry associations. All the while, the Textile Stylist also draws from his or her past experience and industry knowledge to determine which direction the textile designers should take in their work.

Textile Stylists work closely with staff at the textile production mill, to ensure that all of the fabrics in a particular line are manufactured correctly. Additionally, most Textile Stylists maintain close contact with apparel manufacturers—their companies' customers—to learn what fabrics they want produced and to make suggestions about how manufacturers might use certain textile products in their garments. Meanwhile, Textile Stylists must also collaborate with their companies' merchandising and marketing staffs to plan future fabric lines, and, often, with other Textile Stylists under their supervision. Some companies assign different Textile Stylists to oversee fabric development for each of the men's, women's, and children's segments of the marketplace.

The Textile Stylist's job is an extremely diverse one carrying a great deal of responsibility. Consistent success (i.e., developing, year after year, fabrics that are in demand from apparel manufacturers and the consuming public alike) will mean high profits for their companies. Consistent mediocrity or failure, however, will generally mean low profits or even losses for their companies. So no one assumes a position as a Textile Stylist without extensive industry experience, education, knowledge, and a large number of industry contacts and resources.

Salaries

Salaries for Textile Stylists are among the highest in the industry, and for good reason. The decisions they make and the goals they achieve will have a tremendous impact on the textile producer's profitability and, by extension, its reputation within the textile and apparel manufacturing sectors as a whole.

Textile Stylists usually earn at least $55,000 a year, and often that number can reach $100,000 or more. Compensation may also include bonuses based on success.

Employment Prospects

Given the amount of education, experience, knowledge, and industry contacts the Textile Stylist needs to be successful, breaking into this position is quite difficult, and opportunities are limited.

Generally, prospective Textile Stylists need to work for several years in other positions before breaking in as an assistant Textile Stylist and moving on to full-fledged Textile Stylist. Many work for several years as textile artists or textile colorists first, and may then work for several more years as textile designers. Once they've accumulated considerable experience, they may then assume an assistant Textile Stylist role, in which they will generally help the Textile Stylist with tasks like scheduling appointments with customers, checking in with production staff to monitor problems and progress, maintaining swatch books of fabric samples, and handling assorted clerical details and correspondence.

Advancement Prospects

Perhaps surprisingly, advancement prospects for Textile Stylists are somewhat better than initial entry prospects. While the possibilities are somewhat limited, Textile Stylists have the opportunity to become head Textile Stylists or even creative directors for an entire textile company division, or possibly the entire company.

On the other hand, Textile Stylists sometimes move into other related positions, either within their own companies or, on occasion, in new companies that they start on their own. Some, for instance, opt to pursue careers in merchandising or marketing, while others become consultants or forecasters.

Education and Training

Generally speaking, Textile Stylists must have at minimum a bachelor's degree in a field such as textile science, textile design, textile merchandising, textile technology, or textile marketing. Coursework in art, advertising, marketing, apparel design, and/or fashion merchandising is also quite helpful.

Experience, Skills, and Personality Traits

Textile Stylists need extensive and diverse experience in the textile and/or apparel manufacturing industries because their job performance depends on it. The Textile Stylist who doesn't have considerable industry knowledge and contacts will find it hard to gain employment and probably won't last very long.

Since their jobs encompass such diverse activities, Textile Stylists must know the textile and apparel industries thoroughly. Specifically, they need to understand the textile design process and how textile designers do their jobs. They must constantly stay on top of fabric and apparel industry trends and forecasts through research, whether that means traveling to industry events and shows, consulting with in-house and outside colleagues, reading industry publications, or staying closely involved with industry associations. All the while, Textile Stylists must have the ability to communicate effectively with manufacturing staff at the fabric production mill to ensure that each fabric line is made as directed. Also, they need to build strong working relationships with merchandising and marketing professionals who can help them monitor changes in the fiber, yarn, textile, and apparel markets, as well as apparel manufacturers that can help them monitor what clothing producers want. Based on this information, they can make suggestions to help the clothing producers use fabrics in innovative, cost-effective ways.

The skills and personality traits the Textile Stylist needs are as diverse as the job itself. Textile Stylists must be excellent researchers and analysts who can gather important data (from a variety of sources), make sense of them, and use them to make sound decisions about the fabrics their companies should produce. They also need to fully understand practically every part of the textile and apparel production industries so that they know how decisions and actions in one area will affect other areas.

Additionally, Textile Stylists must be creative and resourceful problem solvers who have good taste, a strong sense of color and texture, and the ability to see and understand both the big picture and the hundreds of small details that make up the fabric production process. Also important, Textile Stylists must be skilled communicators who can present their ideas to a host of diverse colleagues and absorb other colleagues' ideas.

Unions and Associations

Since their day-to-day work encompasses such diverse areas of responsibility, Textile Stylists can get involved with a wide range of professional associations in the textile and/or apparel fields. Among them: the Color Association of the United States (CAUS), the International Textile and Apparel Association (ITAA), the Surface Design Association (SDA), and the Textile Society of America (TSA).

Tips for Entry

1. Pursue a part-time or summer job in a retail fabric or apparel store. Retail experience will help you understand why and how consumers make their fabric and/or apparel buying decisions, which is essential to the success of the Textile Stylist.
2. Build upon your education by pursuing a textile-oriented internship or co-op program, and, later, by taking a position as a textile artist, textile colorist, or textile designer.
3. Identify and talk to one or more Textile Stylists to see how they got their jobs and to get their advice on how you can pursue a similar path. Gain an understanding of what it takes to become an assistant Textile Stylist, who is generally a textile-stylist-in-training, and then make plans to pursue education and experiences that will lead you toward that goal.
4. Research as much as you can about the textile and apparel industries, especially in the way of trends and forecasts. Monitor industry and consumer publications and Web sites, get involved with one or more professional organizations in the textile and/or apparel fields, and, if possible, attend trade shows and similar events.
5. Try to gain broad knowledge and experiences versus overly specific ones. Textile Stylists work with diverse people doing diverse things in diverse settings. So the more you know about the broad range of activities going on in the fabric and apparel development, production, merchandising, and retail sectors, the better prepared you'll be to step into the Textile Stylist's role if and when you get the chance.

PRODUCTION/ MANUFACTURING

ACCESSORY DESIGNER

CAREER PROFILE

Duties: Designs accessories such as jewelry, handbags, hats, gloves, ties, belts, shoes, and hosiery that go with various apparel items

Alternate Title(s): Jewelry Designer, Handbag Designer, Hat Designer, Glove Designer, Tie Designer, Belt Designer, Shoe Designer, Hosiery Designer

Salary Range: $100 to $100,000+

Employment Prospects: Fair

Advancement Prospects: Fair

Best Geographical Location(s): Major cities where apparel accessories are produced

Prerequisites:

Education or Training—A bachelor's degree in art, fashion design, or a related field is quite helpful, but not required

Experience—A portfolio of previously created products is critical, as is experience marketing and selling previously created products

Special Skills and Personality Traits—Creativity; networking and marketing savvy; technical skills in a specialized area (e.g., hats, shoes, hosiery); ability to react to marketplace trends and forecasts; self-motivation and the ability to work independently; sketching and drawing skills; problem-solving skills; initiative; knowledge of fabrics and other materials (e.g., leathers, metals); accounting and budgeting skills; ability to set and meet deadlines

CAREER LADDER

Director, Accessory Design Firm

Accessory Designer, Staff

Accessory Designer, Freelance

Position Description

Accessory Designers conceptualize, create, and sell the accessories people wear with their clothes—for example, jewelry, handbags, hats, gloves, ties, belts, shoes, and hosiery (pantyhose or socks).

In almost all cases, Accessory Designers specialize in a certain type of accessory. Shoe designers, for example, use their knowledge of the foot's anatomy as well as their expertise in shoe and apparel market trends and forecasts to come up with shoes that will be both comfortable and fashionable. Similarly, jewelry designers draw upon their knowledge of various metals and marketplace demands to create necklaces, rings, earrings, and watches that people will want to purchase.

Most Accessory Designers also specialize in terms of whom they design for, such as women (the top users of accessories), men, or children.

Many Accessory Designers start out self-employed and market their products to both manufacturers and the general public. To determine what the marketplace wants and will pay for, Accessory Designers must pay close attention to trends and forecasts in both their own specialty area and in the apparel and fabric industries in general. So they often will attend industry trade shows to see what's hot, to show their products to potential buyers/users, and to make important personal connections with other people in the industry that may someday lead to profitable business relationships.

Sometimes, Accessory Designers work for manufacturers or even retailers, in much the same way fashion designers will work for apparel manufacturers or retailers. Instead of creating accessory designs for themselves or their own independent companies, they instead develop designs for the company they work for, which then produces those designs or markets them to other firms.

Self-employed Accessory Designers must devote considerable time and energy to sales and marketing activities. It's one thing to have a potentially popular design for, say, a hat or a belt. But if the marketplace or manufacturers and retailers don't know about that design, it will never be produced. So self-employed Accessory Designers need to be willing and able to "hustle" to meet with manufacturers and retailers so they can present their designs, attend industry events to get ideas and meet influential people, and persist when they hear the inevitable "no's" from potential buyers until they hear a "yes."

Salaries

Salaries for Accessory Designers vary enormously. Some self-employed Accessory Designers just starting out may make only a few hundred or a few thousand dollars a year, depending on sales of their designs and products. A select few who hit it big, however, can easily make hundreds of thousands of dollars a year if one of their creations becomes popular or is picked up by a major manufacturer.

Most Accessory Designers earn wages somewhere in between these two extremes. The median salary for fashion designers in general was $55,840 in 2004, according to the U.S. Department of Labor.

Employment Prospects

Employment prospects for Accessory Designers are fair, although a great deal of success in the field depends on self-motivation, drive, and persistence. Many opportunities do exist both for employment and self-employment, but only those with perseverance and marketing and networking savvy will successfully find those opportunities. Self-employed designers will find the hardest part of getting started is making a name for themselves and establishing effective industry contacts. Once this is accomplished, they should have an edge when pursuing staff jobs, for which competition can be stiff.

Advancement Prospects

Some self-employed Accessory Designers go on to be highly successful, both financially and critically, though many more earn a more modest living with their designs. Accessory Designers who work for manufacturing or retail companies can move into many other types of positions, particularly in fashion design if they choose to pursue a formal degree in that area. Designers who remain self-employed may become directors of their own firm designing and producing accessories. This is also an option for staff designers with a reputation for creating "hot" items.

Education and Training

A bachelor's degree in a field like art or fashion design is quite helpful to the aspiring Accessory Designer. Such a course of study provides valuable technical knowledge. Most schools with programs in this area also offer opportunities for students to make useful industry contacts through their instructors or special events. However, there is no generally required educational or training path for Accessory Designers.

Experience, Skills, and Personality Traits

To be successful, Accessory Designers must be able to show people their work, using a portfolio, actual samples of the product, or both. Any self-employment or work experience that will allow you to gain hands-on experience in accessory design will therefore be enormously helpful.

Accessory Designers, particularly those who are self-employed, must have as many business-related skills as design skills. They need to thoroughly understand trends and forecasts in their specialty area (e.g., jewelry, handbags, hats, shoes) as well as trends and forecasts in the broader apparel and fabric industries. Accessory Designers must also be able to market and sell their ideas to manufacturers, retailers, or the general public.

Technical skills and creativity are essential to Accessory Designers as well. Accessory Designers must be able to sketch and draw their initial ideas and then turn those ideas into reality.

Accessory Designers need to be self-disciplined and self-motivated, able to work independently, and adaptable to the marketplace in order to make a healthy living. They also have to be able to identify and solve problems as well as set and meet deadlines.

Perhaps most important of all, Accessory Designers must have above-average people skills since they will be required to network with people in their specialty areas and in the broader apparel and fabric industries. Much of an Accessory Designer's success depends on his or her ability to promote his/her ideas to the right people, at the right time, and with the right words and actions.

Unions and Associations

Any organization that will help an Accessory Designer stay on top of trends and forecasts and meet key players in the apparel industry is a useful investment.

The Council of Fashion Designers of America (CFDA), based in New York City, is one of the fashion design industry's top professional associations in the United States. Other key organizations include Fashion Group International (FGI), the International Association of Clothing Designers and Executives (IACDE), and the National Association of Fashion and Accessory Designers (NAFAD).

Accessory Designers can also get involved with organizations geared toward their specialties. Jewelry designers, for example, might join Jewelers of America, while shoe designers can participate in activities of the American Apparel and Footwear Association.

Tips for Entry

1. Strongly consider pursuing a college minor, or even a double major, in business administration or marketing so that you gain sound skills in promotion and sales.
2. Talk to some local boutique owners and retailers about your accessory design ideas. Tap their expertise to see if the creations you have in mind would sell in the marketplace, and ask them how you could make that happen.
3. Create some actual accessories and show them to industry insiders for their feedback. Keep these samples so that you can continue showing them to people in the industry.
4. If possible, attend accessory, apparel, and fabric shows in your area, both to understand industry trends and to meet people working in the accessory, apparel, and/or fabric industry.
5. Try to find a mentor—someone who has become a successful Accessory Designer and who would be willing to teach you how to do the same thing, either on your own or as an employee of a bigger company.

COSTING ENGINEER

CAREER PROFILE

Duties: Determines the total cost of manufacturing each individual apparel item, accounting for the costs of labor, raw materials, salaries, and overhead (e.g., facility lighting and heating costs, equipment costs)

Alternate Title(s): Cost Engineer, Cost/Costing Analyst, Cost/Costing Estimator, Cost/Costing Coordinator

Salary Range: $30,000 to $80,000+

Employment Prospects: Fair

Advancement Prospects: Fair

Best Geographical Location(s): Cities and regions where apparel manufacturing factories are located, particularly the New England states, the Southeast, and California

Prerequisites:

Education or Training—A minimum of a bachelor's degree is generally required; educational background in industrial engineering, production management, or textile engineering is helpful

Experience—Internship or co-op experience is helpful for entry-level positions; higher-level jobs call for several years of experience in the field

Special Skills and Personality Traits—Excellent research and analysis skills; strong mathematical abilities; detail orientation and organization; accuracy; precision; decisiveness; exceptional communication skills; willingness and ability to work effectively with other people and meet strict deadlines; patience and determination

Special Requirements—Certification through professional organizations like the Association for the Advancement of Cost Engineering International (AACEI) is helpful but not required

CAREER LADDER

Costing Supervisor/Director

Costing Engineer

Costing Clerk

Costing Trainee/Intern

Position Description

Costing Engineers use scientific principles and skills to determine how much it will cost to produce each individual item developed by an apparel manufacturer. Their conclusions play a key role in setting the retail price of an item when the consumer sees it on the store shelf or rack.

To produce their cost estimates, Costing Engineers look at a host of variables. First, they must factor in the cost of raw materials, such as the fabric used to make the garment, and any accessories (e.g., buttons, zippers, snaps) that are part of the garment. Next, the Costing Engineer examines the cost(s) of labor, in particular employees' salaries and benefits. Finally, the Costing Engineer must include overhead costs as well, such as the costs associated with lighting and heating/cooling the manufacturing plant. As the Costing Engineer examines each potential production cost, he or she documents his or her findings on a cost sheet so that a final production cost tally emerges at the end of the process. This allows the Costing Engineer to easily pinpoint whether certain production costs are unduly inflating the overall production cost of a particular item.

The data Costing Engineers gather for each prospective apparel item are used in several ways. Initially, the data become part of an overall profit/loss estimate, which the design and manufacturing decision makers use to determine whether the item can be profitably produced. If the manufacturer decides to go ahead and produce the item, the Costing Engineer's data are then used to pinpoint a final retail price for the item in stores. That price has to be high enough to achieve a predetermined profit goal for the manufacturer.

To do their work well, Costing Engineers must be skilled researchers and analysts who can gather accurate data in a variety of ways. Sometimes, for example, they will examine employee payroll and time sheets to figure out how many combined work hours went into producing a certain quantity of a certain garment. In other cases, they might visit the company's different production plants to observe operations and consult with production managers in hopes of finding ways to reduce overall production costs. In other cases, Costing Engineers might work with Industrial Engineers in time-motion studies to determine whether there are any unnecessary or overly complex steps in the production process that can be changed or eliminated, thus saving production time and money.

Costing Engineers work closely with other apparel manufacturing professionals, particularly fashion designers, piece goods (fabric) buyers, and quality control engineers. If, for example, a fashion designer wants to use a fabric that will drive overall production costs too high, it's up to the Costing Engineer to point the problem out and perhaps offer alternatives. Similarly, if a piece goods buyer insists on purchasing a certain overly expensive fabric, the Costing Engineer will likely have to be the person to caution against it. In these and other cases, tact and diplomacy are essential to the Costing Engineer, as is the ability to clearly explain the logical financial reasons behind his or her conclusions.

Salaries

A new college graduate with the appropriate academic preparation will typically earn an annual starting salary in the mid to high $30,000s at the entry level, often in the position of costing clerk or costing trainee. With experience, however, Costing Engineers can earn much more. The median annual earnings for Costing Engineers in all fields was $49,940 in 2004, according to the U.S. Department of Labor. Highly experienced Costing Engineers with extensive fashion or textile industry background can easily earn $60,000 a year, and in some cases can merit $80,000 a year or more.

Employment Prospects

Apparel manufacturers will always need to know how much it costs to produce the items they create, so job opportunities for prospective Costing Engineers are fairly consistent. The U.S. Department of Labor reports that Costing Engineers (in all fields) held 198,000 jobs in 2004. Seventeen percent of those jobs were in manufacturing sectors, including apparel production.

Between now and 2014, the Department of Labor predicts, job opportunities in cost engineering will grow faster than average.

Advancement Prospects

Costing clerks or trainees who gain several years of experience can move into costing analyst or Costing Engineer positions that pay more but also encompass more complex job tasks. In very large manufacturing firms, a Costing Engineer might advance further to a costing supervisor or costing director position, overseeing the entire costing process for the manufacturer.

Costing Engineers sometimes go on to pursue related opportunities in production management, plant management, industrial engineering, or similar areas.

Education and Training

Most Costing Engineers have at least a bachelor's degree in Industrial Engineering, Production Management, Textile Engineering, or a related field. Many have also gained on-the-job training by participating in college internships or co-op programs.

Special Requirements

As their careers progress, many Costing Engineers supplement their education and training by participating in certification programs offered by industry organizations like AACE International: The Association for the Advancement of Cost Engineering International. Such certification is not required, but it may give one an advantage over uncertified Costing Engineers.

Experience, Skills, and Personality Traits

Costing Engineers usually begin as entry-level costing clerks or trainees to gain costing experience under the supervision of an experienced Costing Engineer or costing supervisor/director. Many prospective Costing Engineers gain additional experience while they're in college by completing internships or co-op assignments in cost engineering or a closely related area.

To be successful, Costing Engineers must be highly analytical first and foremost. They need to use their mathematical, research, and problem-solving skills to collect useful production cost data, make sense of those data, and then make sound recommendations (to fashion designers, fashion buyers, quality controllers, and others) that will ensure the manufacturer's ability to produce a particular garment cost-effectively.

Costing Engineers need to be well organized, detail oriented, accurate, and precise to avoid mistakes that have the potential to be quite expensive for the manufacturer, not only in terms of dollars but also in terms of its reputation in the industry.

Additionally, Costing Engineers must have strong computer skills, exceptional knowledge of the entire apparel production process, the ability to deal with pressure and stress, and the ability to meet often ironclad deadlines. Costing Engineers need good people skills and excellent oral and written communication abilities so they can work effectively as members of a larger team of professionals. Efficient coordination is essential to ensure that a manufacturer's garments are produced in a way that maximizes the company's chances for tidy profits.

Unions and Associations

Many Costing Engineers in the apparel industry and elsewhere are members of AACE International: The Association for the Advancement of Cost Engineering International (AACEI), a Morgantown, West Virginia–based professional trade organization. Others are involved in the Society of Cost Estimating and Analysis, a nonprofit organization "dedicated to improving cost estimating and analysis in government and industry."

To keep up with developments in the textile and apparel fields, Costing Engineers can also participate in the activities of the American Apparel and Footwear Association (AAFA) and/or the International Textile and Apparel Association (ITAA).

Tips for Entry

1. While you're in school, be sure to participate in internships or co-op programs so that you can begin accumulating experience in cost engineering or a closely related area.
2. Identify one or more Costing Engineers and ask to speak with them (in person or via phone or email) about what they do and how they got their jobs. Ask them to advise you on ways you can best prepare for a cost engineering career or a similar career.
3. If possible, visit a textile or apparel manufacturing company's factory so that you can physically see all of the costs associated with producing a particular garment.
4. Start thinking about the products you buy from a production cost perspective. What do you suppose went into that shirt you bought the other day, in terms of raw materials, labor, and overhead? Does the retail price you paid justify itself from a production cost perspective?
5. Get involved with AACE International: The Association for the Advancement of Cost Engineering International or a similar professional organization so that you can start reading about the cost engineering field, attending industry events, and meeting people in the industry. The knowledge and contacts you gain can help you land an entry-level position in the future.

CUTTER

CAREER PROFILE

Duties: Cuts out various pieces of fabric during the apparel production process, most often using electric cutting machines or computerized cutting systems

Alternate Title(s): None

Salary Range: $17,000 to $40,000

Employment Prospects: Fair

Advancement Prospects: Fair

Best Geographical Location(s): Eastern, southeastern, and southern states, as well as California, where apparel production facilities are located

Prerequisites:

Education or Training—High school diploma required; increasingly, a technical school certificate or degree is preferred

Experience—On-the-job training is common

Special Skills and Personality Traits—High degree of accuracy and attention to detail; knowledge of apparel construction and mass production principles; computer skills; good hand-eye coordination; ability to perform repetitive tasks for long periods of time; physical strength and excellent eyesight

CAREER LADDER

Production Supervisor

Marker Maker or Grader

Cutter

Cutter Apprentice

Position Description

Cutters cut out the various pieces of fabric during the apparel production process, so that those pieces can later be sewn together by sewing machine operators and, eventually, shipped out to customers.

Cutters work closely with spreaders, who spread out long pieces of fabric and stack them in layers that can be several inches thick. The Cutters then cut out the various pieces of fabric, which have been laid out by the marker maker (the person who determines how to best arrange the various pieces to minimize waste during cutting).

Cutters rarely cut fabric by hand (though it does happen, particularly in specialized couture fashion houses). Instead, they typically use automated tools. They might, for example, use an electric saw that resembles a jig saw, and whose blade moves rapidly up and down through many layers of fabric. Or, they might employ a computer-guided cutting system, which automatically cuts through the layers of fabric with a computer-guided blade. In some cases, Cutters may even use water-jet cutters or laser cutters, which are extremely precise.

Part of the Cutter's responsibility is determining the best cutting tool for the specific job at hand. Cutters have to figure out the proper cutting speed and blade for each type of fabric so that all of the finished pieces of material retain their quality.

Accuracy and precision are critical in the cutting process. Cutting mistakes can almost never be fixed; so the Cutter that does make a mistake typically costs his/her company many yards of wasted fabric and, thus, wasted time and lost money. So even though the work itself is highly repetitive, Cutters must be sure to maintain their concentration at all times.

Most Cutters work "in-house" for apparel production companies. Some, however, work for independent cutting companies that perform cutting work for apparel manufacturers on a contract basis.

Salaries

Salaries for Cutters range between $17,000 and $40,000 a year, depending on one's skills and level of responsibility. Experienced Cutters—particularly those with command of another language besides English (e.g., Spanish, Chinese)—can earn $35,000 to $40,000 a year in supervisory positions.

In 2004, the median annual salary for textile cutting machine setters, operators, and tenders was just under $20,000, according to the U.S. Department of Labor.

Employment Prospects

There were only about 28,000 textile cutting machine setters, operators, and tenders in 2004, according to the U.S. Department of Labor, with the number expected to decline between now and 2014. However, the Department of Labor adds in its 2006–07 *Occupational Outlook Handbook,* "improvements in productivity will allow many of the presewing functions of design, patternmaking, marking, and cutting to be done domestically, and employment of workers who perform these functions will not be as adversely affected."

Thus, employment opportunities for prospective Cutters are fair—especially since some jobs do become available over time due to retirements and job changes.

Advancement Prospects

Cutters can move laterally to assume similar production positions in the grading, marker making, or spreading areas. Occasionally, they may also rise into supervisory positions, either in the cutting area, a similar area, or a larger company division.

Education and Training

Cutters need at least a high school diploma in most cases. But they'll increase their employability by having a certificate or degree from a two-year college and demonstrating sound computer skills. Cutters who have solid command of a language besides English (e.g., Spanish, Chinese) and strong supervisory skills will be in the best position to take higher-level jobs that offer better pay.

Experience, Skills, and Personality Traits

In most cases, cutter apprentices learn their trade on the job under the tutelage of more experienced Cutters.

To be successful, Cutters must be highly accurate and detail oriented in order to minimize or eliminate costly cutting mistakes. They also need to understand apparel construction and mass production principles.

Increasingly, Cutters need to have sound computer skills. In many cases they have to use computer-guided cutting systems, which they must be able to both operate and troubleshoot if necessary.

Cutters also need good hand-eye coordination, physical strength, excellent eyesight, and the ability to perform repetitive tasks for long periods of time.

Unions and Associations

The primary union for Cutters and similar workers is UNITE HERE!, which formed in 2004 with the merger of UNITE (Union of Needletrades, Industrial, and Textile Employees) and HERE (Hotel Employees and Restaurant Employees International Union). The union represents nearly half a million workers in the United States, Canada, and Puerto Rico.

Cutters and other garment workers can keep up with the broader apparel manufacturing industry by tapping into the American Apparel and Footwear Association (AAFA), a national trade association for the apparel industry and its suppliers.

Tips for Entry

1. Pursue a certificate or two-year degree at a local technical or community college, especially to gain sound computer skills.
2. Get a summer or part-time job in an apparel production facility so that you can begin to learn about the entire clothing manufacturing process and, in particular, the cutting process and related activities such as production pattern making, grading, and marker making.
3. Talk to one or more Cutters to learn more about their specific jobs and how they got those jobs. Try to understand the ever-increasing role of computers in the typical Cutter's everyday work activities.
4. Consider taking some courses to learn a language besides English—particularly Spanish or Chinese. Increasingly, apparel industry manufacturing jobs are being done by people whose first language isn't English.

FASHION DESIGNER

CAREER PROFILE

Duties: Conceptualizes, produces, and promotes new clothing and accessory (e.g., shoes, belts, ties) designs, for apparel manufacturers, specialty and retail stores, or individual clients

Alternate Title(s): Clothing Designer, Apparel Designer

Salary Range: $18,000 to $200,000+

Employment Prospects: Fair/Limited

Advancement Prospects: Fair

Best Geographical Location(s): Large cities, particularly fashion centers such as New York City, Paris, Milan, and London

Prerequisites:

Education or Training—Although no formal education or training is required, a two- or especially four-year college degree in fashion design or a closely related field is often strongly preferred by employers

Experience—Several years of experience as an intern/trainee, design assistant, and junior designer

Special Skills and Personality Traits—Drawing and sketching skills; creativity and artistic ability; sewing skills; computer skills, particularly in the area of computer-aided design (CAD) and in specific software programs like Adobe Photoshop, Adobe Illustrator, and Macromedia Freehand; persistence; ability to deal with ambiguity and the lack of a "normal" daily routine; current knowledge of fashion trends and forecasts; knowledge of manufacturing processes; ability to deal with pressure, stress, and deadlines; willingness to consider profitability issues in concert with proposed designs; outgoing personality and the ability to network with others in the industry; ability to work effectively alone and in teams

CAREER LADDER

Fashion Designer

Associate Designer or Junior Designer

Assistant Designer

Designer's Assistant

Position Description

Fashion Designers conceptualize, produce, and market new clothing and accessory designs for apparel manufacturers, specialty and retail stores, and, occasionally, individual clients such as movie stars and other celebrities.

Fashion Designers are involved in the development and production of a line of clothing practically from start to finish. Their duties go far beyond dreaming up and sketching new ideas, and so they often work long hours, especially when beginning their careers. They must keep up with fashion trends by reading industry publications, attending fashion shows, and talking to colleagues inside and outside their own companies; become aware of forecasted trends so that they know what particular designs are likely to sell best months or perhaps even years in the future; understand various fabrics and how those fabrics will impact a garment's production and its eventual cost to the consumer; create patterns and samples of garments in order to make any adjustments necessary for each garment's appearance, or look; and constantly market their designs and promote themselves in order to create future business opportunities.

As their job title implies, however, Fashion Designers spend a considerable amount of their time developing new apparel ideas or, more often, adapting or borrowing from the ideas of others. Rarely is a "new" design actually new; instead, it's typically an amalgamation of ideas from various sources of inspiration such as fashion shows; industry and consumer-oriented newspapers, magazines, and, increasingly, Web sites; and actual visits to retail stores to check out the competition.

Designers usually begin the design process by sketching their ideas so that they can better visualize the garment's colors, patterns, fabric, trimmings and accessories, and overall look. The sketches are used to develop patterns for the garment, which in turn are used to create samples. The samples can then be hung on stands or worn by live models so that the Designer can judge each garment's appearance, make any necessary adjustments, and start planning for the garment's manufacture.

To ensure that garments can be produced efficiently and cost-effectively, Fashion Designers need to understand the manufacturing side of the apparel business, something that may not seem obvious at first glance. While a garment's final price may be of no concern within what's called the couture market—made up of very wealthy customers—most typical consumers are influenced significantly by an item's retail price. Fashion Designers, then, must create garments whose design, fabric makeup, and manufacture aren't so costly as to drive the final retail prices too high for consumers.

While a great deal of the work of Fashion Designers is creative in nature, much of it is also marketing- and publicity-oriented. The savviest designers know how to create a buzz around their products and, often, themselves through fashion shows and positive media coverage. A designer's smartly cultivated reputation can make a significant difference in sales, and spark financial backing should she or he decide to start an independent fashion house.

Fashion Designers can specialize in a variety of ways. Some designers focus their efforts on children's apparel, while others create women's wear or men's wear. Designers can also specialize in the types of fabric or other materials they use, or in the types of apparel they create (e.g., evening gowns, swimsuits, outdoor clothing, uniforms).

Most Fashion Designers remain relatively anonymous, working for clothing and apparel manufacturers and adapting men's, women's, and children's clothing so that it can be sold on a mass-market basis to ordinary, everyday consumers. Some Fashion Designers, however, do become well-known in the field and among members of the general public by creating garments for specialty stores or high fashion department stores. The most famous designers can end up working for famous individual clients, particularly for events like the Academy Awards; but the number of designers who reach this level is quite small (the Princeton Review Online Web site estimates the odds of becoming an "internationally famous designer" as being about 160,000 to 1).

Salaries

Salaries for Fashion Designers vary widely depending on a host of factors, including the designer's talent, educational background, experience, professional reputation, and employer or work setting. A beginning designer's assistant or trainee/intern working for an apparel manufacturer can expect to earn a starting salary of around $20,000, give or take a few thousand dollars. After picking up three to five years of experience, an assistant designer or associate designer might make $40,000 a year or more. Senior-level designers can command salaries of $100,000 a year or more. The most famous designers—while relatively few in number—can easily earn $1 million a year. The median annual salary for Fashion Designers was $55,840 in 2004, according to the U.S. Department of Labor. For the growing number of Fashion Designers who are either freelancing for a variety of established clients or attempting to start and grow their own apparel companies, income can be close to nonexistent, in the six-figure range, or, most typically, somewhere in between.

Employment Prospects

The fashion design world is highly competitive, so it's somewhat difficult, though certainly not impossible, to break into the field. In general, there are more aspiring Fashion Designers than there are available jobs in the field, though demand in the industry can change with both the state of the economy (the better the economy, the more opportunities available) and consumers' fashion tastes and preferences. Most designers work for established companies, although increasingly some designers—especially younger ones with creativity, an entrepreneurial bent, and marketing savvy—are seeking self-employment as either freelance designers (for a variety of established clients) or as independent (or "indie") designers. In all, about 17,000 people worked as Fashion Designers in the United States in 2004, according to figures from the U.S. Department of Labor.

Advancement Prospects

Advancement tends to come slowly for Fashion Designers. It's not uncommon to break into the field as an intern/trainee or a designer's assistant who must handle many of the less-than-glamorous tasks associated with the design process. Slowly, though, the intern/trainee or designer's assistant can begin designing a few simple pieces and perhaps, over a period of several years, start establishing a line or at least a partial line of apparel. Eventually, it's possible to move into a senior design role, which may involve overseeing a company's entire design process and managing the people who are a part of it. Highly successful designers may take on management responsibilities, either as the head of their own company or for their employer.

Education and Training

While some Fashion Designers have been wildly successful without having attended college, most experts in the industry agree that a two- or four-year college degree in fashion design or a similar field is quite helpful, both for breaking into the field and advancing within it. Many American colleges and universities offer academic preparation programs in fashion design. Among the more well known: the Fashion Institute of Technology and Parsons The New School for Design in New York City, and the Rhode Island School of Design in Providence.

It's critical to also gain some practical experience in fashion design through an internship or co-op program, both for the skills it can teach and the personal and professional connections it can create. Many schools have career centers staffed by counselors who can help arrange these experiential activities.

Experience, Skills, and Personality Traits

Practical, hands-on experience is critical in the fashion design field. As such, many beginning designers start at the bottom as interns/trainees or designer's assistants so that they can begin gaining experience in the field. The people who advance most rapidly in the industry are those who have made the most of their entry-level jobs, in terms of both gaining new skills and connecting with key people.

Fashion Designers must be creative and imaginative first and foremost, and they must have the ability to effectively communicate their visions and ideas to others, be they colleagues or consumers. Drawing, sketching, and sewing skills are important, as is the ability to use computer-aided design (CAD) programs and software packages such as Adobe Photoshop, Adobe Illustrator, and Macromedia Freehand. Knowledge of fashion trends and forecasts is essential, as is the willingness to keep up with those trends and forecasts by reading professional publications, attending fashion shows and similar events, and networking with colleagues in the field. Fashion Designers must also understand the entire apparel manufacturing process, not just their part within it, so that they can develop designs that are cost-effective to produce without being overly expensive in the eyes of consumers.

Fashion Designers must also possess an array of "soft" skills that are key to success in the field. Among them are passion and self-motivation, persistence, the ability to deal with ambiguity, and the lack of a predictable daily routine. They must also have the ability to deal with stress, pressure, deadlines, and unforeseen events. They should be comfortable working alone as well as part of a team. Perhaps most important of all, they need a willingness to get to know others in the field and build a professional network that leads to new opportunities.

Unions and Associations

The Council of Fashion Designers of America (CFDA), based in New York City, is one of the fashion design industry's top professional associations in the United States. Other key organizations include Fashion Group International (FGI), the International Association of Clothing Designers and Executives (IACDE), and the National Association of Fashion and Accessory Designers (NAFAD).

Tips for Entry

1. Start developing a portfolio of sketches and drawings illustrating your fashion design ideas. Try to come up with a diverse collection of possibilities.
2. Begin reading industry publications like *Women's Wear Daily* and consumer publications like *Cosmopolitan* and *Vogue* to learn about current fashion trends and forecasted trends. Knowledge of what's hot and what's going to be is critical.
3. If you decide to earn a college degree in fashion design, be sure to gain some practical experience while you're in school through an internship, a co-op program, or even volunteering. Be willing to start at the bottom and work your way up to the job you want, as many of today's Fashion Designers had to do themselves.
4. Do whatever you can to get to know people in the fashion design industry. If possible, talk to some Fashion Designers to learn more about what they do and to build a networking relationship with them. The more connections you build in the field of fashion design, the more opportunities you'll uncover or create for yourself.
5. Look for ways to gain fashion design experience informally, for example, by offering to help design and produce the costumes for a school play.
6. Visit apparel company Web sites, fashion-oriented Web sites like FashionCareerCenter.com, and the career center Web sites of colleges and universities offering fashion design degrees. Look through various design-related job listings to get a sense of the specific education, experience, and skills employers are looking for in entry-level and higher-level Fashion Designers.
7. Learn how to use software packages such as Adobe Photoshop, Adobe Illustrator, and Macromedia Freehand, all of which have become essential tools in the world of fashion design.

FASHION FORECASTER

CAREER PROFILE

Duties: Uses research findings, extensive fashion industry experience, and, to some degree, intuition to predict which fashions will be hot one or two years in the future

Alternate Title(s): Fashion Trend Forecaster, Fashion Color Forecaster

Salary Range: $50,000 to $100,000+

Employment Prospects: Limited

Advancement Prospects: Limited

Best Geographical Location(s): New York City and other fashion centers

Prerequisites:

Education or Training—A bachelor's degree in fashion design, fashion merchandising, textile design, textile merchandising, or apparel production is preferred; training in research and statistical methods is important

Experience—Several years of experience in the fashion industry, often in product development, marketing, merchandising, or retail

Special Skills and Personality Traits—Extensive fashion industry knowledge and experience; research and analytical skills; ability to gather information from a variety of sources and make accurate predictions about colors, fabrics, patterns, shapes, and forms that will be popular one or two years in the future; strong quantitative (math) skills; top-notch writing and speaking skills; ability to present complex information in a way other people can readily understand

CAREER LADDER

Fashion Forecaster

Fashion Merchandiser/Marketer/ Product Developer

Retail Sales Associate/Manager

Position Description

Fashion Forecasters use their research and observation skills, their extensive fashion industry experience and education, and even their intuition to predict, one to two years ahead of time, which fashion looks, colors, fabrics, silhouettes (i.e., garment shapes or forms), and design details will be hot in the future. Textile and apparel manufacturers, apparel and textile design firms, fashion retailers, and corporate fashion buyers use this information, combined with their own research, to make decisions about the products they'll produce or buy 18 months or two years from now.

Fashion Forecasters look at previous fashion trends, as well as current trends, in an attempt to identify patterns and consistencies that will help them determine which fashions or fabrics will appeal to consumers during the fashion season that is one or even two years away. They gather information from a wide variety of sources: industry trade shows all over the world, professional trade associations (some of which offer their own fashion forecasts), company sales records from a wide geographic area, trade publications and Web sites, consumer publications and Web sites, and consultants, just to name a few. They must also be keen observers of the world around them, for significant cultural events can also influence fashion trends, both in the present and in the future.

Some apparel and textile manufacturers have their own forecasters or rely on professionals in other roles who assume forecasting as part of their overall job descriptions, but most Fashion Forecasters work for outside consulting firms, many of them located in New York City and other fashion centers. These firms are often referred to as fashion information services or fashion forecasting services, and they typically have subscribers, such as apparel and textile manufacturers, who pay annual fees in exchange for the services the forecasters provide.

The Fashion Forecaster's job can be broken down into three basic parts. First, the Fashion Forecaster gathers information from wide-ranging sources. Next, he or she sorts through and analyzes that information and determines what fashion trends he or she will be predicting. Finally, the Fashion Forecaster must take the information and present it in an understandable way. That might mean writing and designing a specialized report for subscribers, developing color or fabric swatch cards highlighting the colors and/or fabrics that are expected to be hot in the next year or two, putting together an audio/visual presentation, or even making fabric and color samples for distribution to subscribers. The idea is for the Fashion Forecaster to display the information gathered and the predictions made in a way that makes sense to the reader or viewer.

All Fashion Forecasters are quick to point out that their predictions are just that—predictions—and not absolute truths. No Fashion Forecaster is 100 percent accurate, and none expects to be. Instead, the goal is to be as accurate as possible as often as possible, so that, over time, the Fashion Forecaster builds up a reputation of being accurate much more often than not.

Salaries

Their extensive expertise generally allows Fashion Forecasters to command high salaries or charge substantial fees if they work for independent fashion forecasting firms, as many do. Most Fashion Forecasters earn at least $50,000 a year, and many earn $100,000 a year or more.

Increasingly, fashion forecasting firms are offering their reports online, charging several hundred or even a few thousand dollars for each of them. For the occasional large project, a forecasting firm can bill $150,000 or more.

Employment Prospects

Since breaking into the Fashion Forecasting field requires extensive industry experience and education, employment prospects are quite limited, particularly at the entry level. Some forecasting firms and associations do offer internships and related opportunities in which college students or entry-level professionals who are interested in Fashion Forecasting can get some hands-on experience in the field. Still, most professional jobs in the field are reserved for those who have at least five to 10 years of fashion world experience. Most Fashion Forecasters enter the industry in positions that allow them to begin building their knowledge and experience.

Advancement Prospects

While advancement opportunities in the fashion forecasting field are somewhat limited, they can be excellent for the Fashion Forecaster who builds a reputation of making accurate trend predictions. Companies invest enormous sums of money in developing their products. As such, they want and need accurate information about what types of products are likely to sell well in the future. The Fashion Forecaster who can consistently provide that information will always be a hot commodity, whether he or she works for an independent consulting firm or, as is sometimes the case, decides to start a consulting firm of his or her own. Successful Fashion Forecasters may demand higher compensation or take on more prestigious projects.

Education and Training

Fashion Forecasters need a strong educational background in fashion. Many in the field have at least a bachelor's degree in a field like fashion design, fashion merchandising, textile design, textile merchandising, or apparel production. Most are also heavily involved in industry professional associations, which often offer educational seminars and other ongoing training opportunities for their members.

Fashion Forecasters who work for independent consulting firms, many of which have only a few employees, can also benefit by having business-oriented education or training in a field like marketing.

Experience, Skills, and Personality Traits

Extensive fashion industry experience is perhaps the most important asset a Fashion Forecaster can have. It's best if that experience is diverse and includes retailing, merchandising, design, product development, or some combination thereof. Perhaps more than anyone else in the industry, Fashion Forecasters must have wide-ranging knowledge of the fashion and textile industries, as well as the ability to continuously learn about those industries in a variety of ways.

Since so much of their work involves research, Fashion Forecasters need to be skilled data gatherers who are able to get information from a wide array of sources. They must then be able to organize that information, carefully analyze it, pinpoint consistencies (and, often, inconsistencies as well), and draw logical conclusions that will lead directly to the predictions they make. All along the way, they need to use their mathematical and statistical skills, their gift for synthesizing large amounts of data, and their ability to remember past information and trends (for comparing and contrasting purposes).

Once they've completed the research and analysis phases of their work, Fashion Forecasters must be decisive and confident in the final recommendations they make. They must also call upon their excellent written and oral communication skills, and, increasingly, their computer and Internet skills, to quickly and clearly present their findings to their clients—the apparel and textile company decision makers who will use the predictions to make product development choices.

Unions and Associations

The New York City–based Color Association of the United States (CAUS) is the oldest color forecasting organization in the country. It's unique in that it makes its trend forecasts by tapping the expertise of a 12-member panel of professionals working in a variety of creative industries.

Similar organizations include Intercolor, made up of industry professionals around the world who meet twice a year in Paris to discuss color trends and forecasts; and the International Colour Authority (ICA), which also meets twice a year (in London) to provide color trend predictions for the apparel industry and related industries.

Tips for Entry

1. Pursue a college degree in fashion merchandising, fashion design, textile design, or a related field to begin learning about the broad fashion and textile industries.
2. Look for internship or volunteer opportunities with Fashion Forecasting firms so that you can gain some initial experience in the field.
3. Arrange to talk to one or more Fashion Forecasters so that you can learn more about how they got into the field and get their advice on how you might prepare for their particular career.
4. Follow as many fashion industry trade publications and Web sites as you can, and monitor fashion- and general-interest consumer publications and Web sites as well. Broad industry knowledge is key to the success of any Fashion Forecaster.
5. Take a retail fashion job so that you can gain insights into the buying habits of average, everyday consumers. As many Fashion Forecasters will tell you, consumers are the ultimate decision makers when it comes to what fashions will be hot and what fashions will languish on the store's racks.

FIT MODEL

CAREER PROFILE

Duties: Models garments for fashion designers, so that designers can judge each garment's fit, or for retail buyers visiting an apparel manufacturer's showrooms to review merchandise

Alternate Title(s): Fitting Model, Fitter's Model, Showroom Model

Salary Range: $0 to $30,000+

Employment Prospects: Limited

Advancement Prospects: Limited

Best Geographical Location(s): Major cities, especially those where apparel manufacturers' headquarters and/or showrooms are located, such as New York, Los Angeles, Dallas, or Chicago

Prerequisites:

Education or Training—No specific education is required, though modeling school training is highly recommended; coursework in fashion design or a related field is helpful

Experience—No specific experience required, though previous fit modeling experience is helpful

Special Skills or Personality Traits—Specific body proportions required in most cases; awareness of fashion and style; attractiveness; self-confidence; outgoing demeanor; knowledge of garment construction, fabrics, and the technical aspects of fit; ability to stand for long periods of time; willingness and ability to do clerical and other support work in some cases

CAREER LADDER

Model or Various Fashion Jobs

Fit Model

Position Description

Fit Models are living mannequins who perform one of two basic functions. Some Fit Models work closely with fashion designers and their colleagues, modeling samples of various garments so that the designer can check on each garment's precise fit and feel before it goes on to be produced in mass quantities. Other Fit Models work in apparel manufacturers' showrooms, modeling various garments for retail buyers so that the buyers can see how each garment looks on a live person.

Many Fit Models work only sporadically or part time. A Fit Model who works with a certain fashion designer, for example, may be asked to come in to work only a few days a week, for a few hours at a time. Similarly, Fit Models who work in apparel manufacturers' showrooms may work many hours during the busy buying seasons and not as many hours during the rest of the year.

Some Fit Models do work full time, but in many cases, they don't do fit modeling 40 hours a week. Rather, they do fit modeling part-time and then perform administrative duties, such as answering phones, filing, or making travel arrangements.

Fit Models who work with fashion designers are often on their feet for extended periods of time, modeling many garments each day. They might be asked to use their education and experience to make suggestions about adjustments and alterations that should be made to a particular garment. They also have to be able to clearly explain how well or poorly a particular garment fits and why, so that the fashion designer and his/her colleagues know precisely what they need to do to make the garment fit properly. Only when the fit of the garment is exactly correct can it go into mass production.

Fit Models who work in apparel manufacturers' showrooms also need to be on their feet for long periods of time. They also have to know how to stand properly, pose, and move so that the garments they're wearing look good to the retail buyers who are assessing them.

While some Fit Models have full-time positions as employees of apparel manufacturers, many work for outside agencies and are paid on a per-hour or per-day basis, with part of their earnings going to the agency. Work can be somewhat unpredictable for this latter group of Fit Models, though those who have the right connections and the right body proportions can model often enough to make a good living. Some even begin as young children, earning money for their future education and meeting people who could someday help them break into other parts of the fashion industry.

Salaries

Salaries for Fit Models vary considerably. Some Fit Models work for little or nothing, doing their fit modeling in addition to a more well-defined, traditional job within a company. Many other Fit Models work only sporadically, on a contract basis, and are then only paid by the hour or the day, with no benefits such as health care or retirement contributions.

Fit Models who have the precise measurements and body proportions a company needs, however, can earn $30,000 to $35,000 a year—and occasionally much more (it's not unusual for some Fit Models in New York City to earn $200 an hour)—especially if the company has difficulty finding someone else with the same measurements and proportions. Fit Models who take on other tasks within the company, such as clerical work and answering phones, can sometimes use the wide-ranging experience they accumulate to move into other, more lucrative positions.

Employment Prospects

Employment is often somewhat sporadic for many Fit Models, particularly if they work as part-timers or contractors for a modeling agency versus full-time for an apparel manufacturer. So generally speaking, employment prospects for Fit Models are limited.

Opportunities are available, however, particularly for prospective Fit Models who are willing and able to handle other tasks beyond modeling, for example, clerical work. Fit Models who have and can maintain the body proportions a company needs can work with that same company for years.

Advancement Prospects

Fit Models who gain experience and connections in the field can advance to other types of modeling. Some Fit Models move into other positions in the fashion industry by virtue of the experience they gain through both modeling and clerical work. It's not uncommon, for example, for a Fit Model who helps out with promotional activities to move into a full-time position in fashion promotion. Fit Models may also go on to other modeling jobs.

Education and Training

Fit Models aren't required to have any specific educational background, but they can gain an edge by attending modeling school so that they learn how to stand, pose, and move properly. Modeling school also teaches prospective Fit Models about speaking, makeup, and hair techniques that can be valuable to their repertoire of skills and knowledge.

Fit Models who work with fashion designers in particular also benefit by having some coursework or a two- or four-year degree in fashion design or a related field, so that they have a sound understanding of fit and form.

Experience, Skills, and Personality Traits

In most cases, perhaps the most unusual requirement for Fit Models is being a specific size. A job ad for a female Fit Model, for example, will often specify the height, waist size, hip measurements, bust size, and thigh measurements of the person needed for the position. Typically, female Fit Models need to be a size 8 or 10, while male Fit Models need to be a size 40 or 41 regular or long. However, as the apparel industry changes and more garments are developed for people of all shapes and sizes, so, too, grows the need for Fit Models of varying proportions.

Fit Models who work for fashion designers must be able to stand for long periods of time. They also need some knowledge of garment construction, fabrics, and the technical aspects of fit so that they can advise the designers.

Fit Models who work in apparel manufacturers' showrooms need to be fashion-conscious, attractive, stylish, and poised, with a friendly, outgoing personality.

Many Fit Models must also be willing and able to take on other duties in addition to their modeling duties—for example, answering phones, filing, and making travel arrangements—since actual fit modeling rarely takes up a full 40-hour workweek.

Unions and Associations

The primary union in the modeling field is The Model's Guild, based in New York City. The Guild represents both models and modeling-related professionals.

Tips for Entry

1. Think about attending modeling school to learn modeling basics. Consider pursuing coursework or a two- or four-year degree in fashion design or a related field.
2. Volunteer to do some modeling for a local fashion show or a nearby retail store. Get some photos from each of your modeling experiences so that you can develop a portfolio of your work.
3. Meet with some representatives of modeling agencies to see what sort of fit modeling opportunities they can offer you.
4. Watch industry publications and career-related Web sites for fit modeling jobs that call for a person with your specific physical measurements.
5. Talk to one or more people who work as Fit Models, and ask them how you can break into the field.
6. Read books and magazines on modeling and visit modeling-oriented Web sites to educate yourself about the industry.

INDUSTRIAL ENGINEER

CAREER PROFILE

Duties: Helps a textile producer or an apparel manufacturer make its products most efficiently and cost-effectively through the management and organization of workers, production methods, and technology

Alternate Title(s): Manufacturing Engineer

Salary Range: $50,000 to $70,000+

Employment Prospects: Good

Advancement Prospects: Good

Best Geographical Location(s): Eastern and southern United States

Prerequisites:

Education or Training—A college degree is generally required, preferably in industrial engineering, textile engineering, production management, or textile or apparel manufacturing; some textile and apparel manufacturers also offer their own specialized training programs for new Industrial Engineers

Experience—Practical, hands-on experience through internships or co-op programs is critical

Special Skills and Personality Traits—Analytical and research skills; strong mathematical and computer skills; organizational abilities; detail orientation, resourcefulness; decisiveness; excellent communication, teamwork, leadership, and persuasion skills

CAREER LADDER

Industrial Engineer

Junior Industrial Engineer or Trainee

Industrial Engineering Intern or Co-op Student

Position Description

Whether they work for textile producers or apparel manufacturers, Industrial Engineers have one overriding concern in their work: ensuring that their firms produce their products as efficiently and cost-effectively as possible.They do that by managing and organizing the firm's workers, production methods, and technology.

Combining principles of engineering with their knowledge of textile or apparel equipment and processes, Industrial Engineers are efficiency experts who work to develop production methods that cost the least (in terms of money, time, and energy) yet maintain quality in the final product. They regularly study production processes by conducting time-and-motion research, analyzing equipment and technological tools, examining worker productivity and methods, and studying a plant's overall layout and design. Their goals: to spot potential production problems; collaborate with their colleagues and, sometimes, production workers and supervisors to develop solutions to those problems; and implement the solutions and evaluate the results.

Much of the Industrial Engineer's time and energy is spent gathering data and analyzing it. The data may examine variables like the amount of raw material a manufacturing plant is using, the time it takes for an item to make its way through the entire production cycle, the total actual or estimated costs of various production strategies, or the financial savings that may result from the purchase, installation, and use of new technologies on the production line.

However, an Industrial Engineer's work isn't entirely technical or object-oriented. Since Industrial Engineers are problem identifiers and solvers by their very job descriptions, they spend a good portion of their time collaborating and communicating with others, sometimes in person, sometimes in writing. To pinpoint the causes of a certain production bottleneck, for example, the Industrial Engineer might not only look at figures, but also meet with production workers who do the tasks associated with the bottleneck. In this way, the Industrial Engineer can gather data firsthand, especially qualitative data (i.e., data that can't be measured in numerical terms) that probably wouldn't show up in other studies or research approaches.

Junior Industrial Engineers might be involved in day-to-day research and problem identification. At higher levels, however, Industrial Engineers are more often called upon to supervise the work of lower-level Industrial Engineers. They also collaborate more often with other middle- and upper-level managers in their companies, focusing more on big-picture tasks like planning, and perhaps even production forecasting, instead of problem solving.

Industrial Engineers might also find themselves doing a wider variety of tasks if they work in smaller textile or apparel production firms. In these cases, the Industrial Engineer might also take on overall plant management duties in addition to his or her regular tasks.

Some Industrial Engineers travel frequently to visit and work with production plants in other geographic locations. Others may have a certain amount of responsibility for ensuring worker safety, especially when those workers are dealing with complex and sometimes dangerous machines.

Whatever their specific duties, Industrial Engineers will always be concerned with improving production processes so that their employers, whether textile or apparel manufacturers, create the best possible products in the least possible time and at the lowest possible cost.

Salaries

Entry-level Industrial Engineers across all industries earned an average starting salary of just under $52,000 in spring 2006, according to the National Association of Colleges and Employers, a trade organization made up of college career services professionals and employers of new college graduates. The U.S. Department of Labor, meanwhile, notes that the median annual salary for Industrial Engineers in all disciplines was just over $65,000 in 2004.

Employment Prospects

According to the U.S. Department of Labor, employment opportunities for Industrial Engineers across all industries will rise about as fast as average through 2014, thanks in great part to companies' ongoing efforts to reduce costs and increase productivity.

Advancement Prospects

Advancement opportunities for Industrial Engineers in general, and those working in the textile or apparel production industries in particular, are good. Entry-level professionals who start their careers as junior Industrial Engineers or trainees can move into full-fledged Industrial Engineer positions after gaining a few years of experience and, perhaps, pursuing an advanced degree. Later, they can find even better opportunities at the directorial or managerial levels, and sometimes they can become consultants for companies that specialize in helping production firms become more efficient, cost-effective, and productive.

Education and Training

Most Industrial Engineers have at least a bachelor's degree in a discipline like industrial engineering, textile engineering, production management, or textile or apparel manufacturing. Some also benefit from their companies' own specialized training programs for new Industrial Engineers.

Industrial Engineers who hope to advance to managerial or directorial roles often pursue an advanced degree—for example, a master of business administration (M.B.A.) degree—to gain more engineering and/or management skills.

Experience, Skills, and Personality Traits

Most Industrial Engineers gain experience in the field by pursuing internships or co-op assignments with textile or apparel manufacturers while they're still in college. When they join firms as junior Industrial Engineers or trainees, they typically get involved in day-to-day research, analysis, and planning activities that give them the skills and experiences they'll need to advance within the company or the field.

Industrial Engineers, no matter which setting they work in, must be analytical, research-oriented, resourceful, and thorough to be successful. They use their strong mathematical skills and, increasingly, their computer skills practically every working day, along with their planning skills, their problem identification and solution skills, their resourcefulness, and their organizational and follow-through abilities.

Since much of their work involves other people, Industrial Engineers also need strong communication skills (both written and oral), leadership, teamwork, and decision-making skills. They must be able to handle stress and deadlines, unexpected problems, and even personnel with maturity and poise, so that everyone and everything in the company is effectively working toward the goal of efficient and cost-effective, yet high-quality, production.

Unions and Associations

Many Industrial Engineers from across disciplines are members of the Institute of Industrial Engineers (IIE), a professional trade organization for the field. The organization produces industry publications, offers career information for the field, and holds local, state, and national conferences for its members.

Tips for Entry

1. Research industrial engineering and similar academic programs at colleges and universities that interest you. A college degree in industrial engineering or a related field is all but required for breaking into industrial engineering in textile or apparel manufacturing companies.
2. Contact the Institute of Industrial Engineers and ask the organization to send you information about career opportunities in the broad industrial engineering field.
3. Arrange to meet with one or more practicing Industrial Engineers who work in the textile or apparel production industry (or a closely related industry). Find out what their daily work involves, ask them how they got their jobs, and see what types of job and internship opportunities are available within their companies and others.
4. If you're a college student pursuing a degree in industrial engineering or a similar field, be sure to do at least one internship or co-op before you graduate. Even for entry-level positions, employers seek applicants who have some practical, hands-on experience in the field.
5. Use Internet Web sites to search for industrial engineering jobs in the textile and apparel industries, and in other industries. Take notes on the key education and skills being sought by most companies, the typical job duties of Industrial Engineers, the typical skills Industrial Engineers must have, and the typical salaries Industrial Engineers are making. Use the information you gather to plan for appropriate educational and work experiences.

LOGISTICS MANAGER

CAREER PROFILE

Duties: Ensures that finished apparel items are received from various manufacturing facilities (in and out of the United States) and then transported—at the right time, in the right quantities, and in the right condition—to the retail and wholesale facilities that ultimately make them available to the buying public

Alternate Title(s): Logistics Director, Director of Logistics

Salary Range: $50,000 to $100,000+

Employment Prospects: Fair

Advancement Prospects: Fair

Best Geographical Location(s): Large cities where apparel manufacturers' distribution headquarters are located

Prerequisites:

Education or Training—A bachelor's degree in logistics, supply chain management, business administration/management, or a closely related field is generally required; some higher-level positions may require an advanced degree such as the master of business administration (M.B.A.)

Experience—Generally, a minimum of three years of experience is required in an area such as warehouse management, distribution center management, or shipping and receiving management; often, five to eight years of experience are preferred

Special Skills and Personality Traits—Solid organizational and multitasking skills; knowledge of importing/exporting laws, regulations, and procedures; exceptional ability to understand the big picture while also attending to numerous details, deadlines, and the daily pressure that accompanies them; outstanding written and verbal communication skills; fluency in a second language besides English (especially Chinese and/or Spanish); strong collaboration and teamwork abilities; proficiency with basic computer software; comfort with numbers and quantitative tasks; sound negotiating and contract development skills; proven analytical and problem-solving abilities; ability to roll with changes when plans go awry

CAREER LADDER

Vice President of Logistics

Logistics Manager

Traffic Coordinator or Distribution Center Manager

Warehouse Manager or Warehouse Specialist

Position Description

If you want to understand the field of logistics, there is perhaps no better source than the Council of Supply Chain Management Professionals (CSCMP). Logistics Managers, the CSCMP notes, ensure that "the right product, in the right quantity, in the right condition, is delivered to the right customer at the right place, at the right time, at the right cost."

Indeed, an apparel manufacturer may come up with, for example, the hottest pair of jeans on the planet. But if those jeans don't physically make their way from the manufacturer's production and distribution facilities to a store where you and other consumers can buy them, then there's no point in their being created in the first place. Somehow, those jeans—"in the right quantity, in the right condition"—have to get into consumers' hands. The Logistics Manager is one of the key people in the apparel industry who help make that happen.

Logistics Managers use their outstanding organizational, planning, and follow-through skills to work with both their own employees and various outside vendors who make sure a great shirt gets from Point A to Point B. It's a complicated task that isn't nearly as easy as it might sound. For starters, Logistics Managers have to understand various shipping laws and regulations, especially those regarding imports, as in the case where an American apparel firm has its products produced in another country and then has those products shipped to the United States. Ultimately, Logistics Managers are responsible for transporting products in the most efficient (and therefore cost-effective) manner. The less an apparel manufacturer spends on logistics, the more profit it can count on from the products it makes and sells.

To do their jobs well, Logistics Managers must be solid team players who have the comparatively rare ability to see the big picture and attend to many essential details at the same time. One moment, the Logistics Manager might be planning the transportation process and schedule for an entire line of new apparel; the next, he or she might be on the phone with a shipping company, using his or her communication and negotiation skills to hammer out a contract dispute or shipping snafu.

Logistics Managers must also be able to hire, train, and effectively supervise lower-level (but no less important) employees who specialize in certain parts of the overall logistics process (e.g., planning, shipping, analysis, scheduling, packing). All the while, Logistics Managers must constantly evaluate the performance of these employees as well as all the third-party vendors with whom they work. If any part of this complicated chain doesn't perform satisfactorily, it is up to the Logistics Manager to make necessary changes—which involves tact in some cases and firm resolve in others.

Salaries

Logistics Managers in the apparel industry usually make at least $50,000 a year, but often they earn considerably more—perhaps $75,000 to $100,000 and up—depending on their experience, education, and level of responsibility. Theirs is a high-pressure job that, for better or worse, has a significant impact on an apparel manufacturer's bottom line. So Logistics Managers tend to be compensated accordingly, often receiving bonuses based on individual and/or team performance.

Logistics Managers across all industries (including apparel manufacturing) earned an average annual salary of $81,000 in 2005, according to a survey conducted by *Logistics Management* magazine. However, Logistics Managers in the textiles and apparel sector, the survey found, earned an average salary of only $60,500 in 2005.

Employment Prospects

Since Logistics Managers in the apparel industry are already in upper-midlevel jobs, their employment prospects can only be characterized as fair. Considering, however, that American businesses (across all industries) spend nearly $800 billion a year on logistics (according to the Council of Supply Chain Management Professionals), it's safe to say that there will always be some opportunities for Logistics Managers who want to work in the apparel industry.

The U.S. Department of Labor reports that as of 2004, about 53,000 Americans worked as logisticians, and that employment in the field is projected to grow about as fast as average between now and 2014.

Advancement Prospects

Logistics Managers who build the necessary skills, knowledge, and—especially—track record of solid performance can go on to take executive-level positions in logistics (e.g., vice president of logistics), where they can easily earn more than $100,000 a year (and often significantly more, especially when potential bonuses are taken into account). Some Logistics Managers also go on to other high-level positions that are outside the logistics arena (e.g., chief operations officer).

Education and Training

Most Logistics Managers have at least a bachelor's degree in a discipline such as logistics, supply chain management, business administration/management, or a closely related field. Some Logistics Managers also go on to pursue graduate degrees—particularly the master of business administration (M.B.A.)—which can be an essential part of advancing to even higher-level positions in or out of the logistics arena.

Experience, Skills, and Personality Traits

Logistics Managers typically begin their careers in lower-level (often *much* lower-level) jobs that are somewhere within the logistics realm—e.g., warehouse specialist, distribution center specialist, planner, or analyst. Along the way, they must refine essential skills in organization, follow-up, scheduling, negotiating, planning, analyzing, and communicating (with both internal and external customers).

To be successful, Logistics Managers in the apparel industry need to know—and make sure their company follows—myriad laws, regulations, and procedures, especially when it comes to activities like importing and shipping. They must also have the ability to see the big picture while attending to numerous details, deadlines, and the daily pressure that accompanies them. It's one thing to understand how logistical processes are supposed to work; it's another thing to be able to execute those processes successfully, solving the inevitable problems that arise along the way.

Solid communication skills (written and verbal) are also critical to the Logistics Manager's success, and these days fluency in a second language besides English (particularly Chinese or Spanish) is essential in the many companies that work with overseas manufacturers, shippers, and distributors. Logistics Managers need to have outstanding quantitative and analytical skills as well, along with proficiency in basic computer software (such as Microsoft Office applications), sound negotiating and contract development skills, and strong collaboration and teamwork abilities.

Unions and Associations

Many Logistics Managers across all fields are members of the Council of Supply Chain Management Professionals (CSCMP), a professional association with more than 9,000 members in 63 countries. Some are also members of the American Society of Transportation and Logistics, which offers various certifications to logistics professionals across all industries.

Tips for Entry

1. Complete at least a bachelor's degree in a discipline such as logistics, supply chain management, or business administration/management. Consider pursuing an advanced degree (e.g., a master of business administration [M.B.A.]) as well, especially if you want to eventually land an executive-level job.
2. During college, gain some practical experience in logistics or a closely related discipline through an internship or a co-op assignment within an apparel manufacturer's logistics division.
3. Do whatever you can to get to know some working Logistics Managers in the apparel industry. If possible, talk to some Logistics Managers (i.e., informational interviewing) to learn more about what they do and how they got to where they are now. (Consider joining a professional association, such as the Council of Supply Chain Management Professionals, so that you can attend its events and participate in its Internet listservs as well.) The more connections you can make with Logistics Managers who are already in the field, the more potential opportunities you'll uncover for yourself.
4. Visit apparel company and job search Web sites to look for Logistics Manager job listings. What key skills and abilities, experiences, education, and traits do companies seem to be looking for in the Logistics Managers they want to hire?

MARKER MAKER

CAREER PROFILE

Duties: Determines how best to arrange various pattern pieces on fabric to minimize waste during the cutting process

Alternate Title(s): Marker

Salary Range: $19,000 to $30,000+

Employment Prospects: Limited

Advancement Prospects: Fair

Best Geographical Location(s): Eastern, southeastern, and southern states, as well as California, where apparel production facilities are located

Prerequisites:

Education or Training—A high school diploma is required; increasingly, a technical school certificate or degree is preferred

Experience—On-the-job training is common, although some two-year colleges with Marker Maker certificate programs offer apprenticeship/internship opportunities

Special Skills or Personality Traits—High degree of accuracy; detail orientation; expertise in apparel construction and mass production principles; knowledge of body proportions and garment fitting; sound computer skills; mathematical abilities; persistence; ability to work both independently and with team members; proficiency in a language besides English (e.g., Spanish, Chinese)

CAREER LADDER

Production Supervisor

Grader or Production Pattern Maker

Marker Maker

Marker Maker Apprentice/Trainee

Position Description

Marker Makers use their problem-solving skills, mathematical abilities, persistence, and computer skills to figure out how to minimize wasted fabric in the apparel production process. Specifically, they position production patterns on fabric (or paper the same size as the fabric) in a way that uses the most fabric and wastes the least. Their goal is to create a tight marker, or a marker that uses the highest percentage of fabric possible.

As part of their job, Marker Makers also determine the total amount of material that will be needed to cut the fabric for each item of clothing being produced. Additionally, their markers serve as layouts for cutters to follow in the cutting process.

When computers were a minimal or nonexistent part of the apparel production process, Marker Makers relied on their experienced judgment to figure out the most efficient pattern piece layouts. Today, however, computers are a major part of the marker-making process in all but the smallest of companies. Tasks that used to take Marker Makers many hours or even days to complete can now be completed in just a few hours or less. For many Marker Makers from the "old school," however, the introduction of computers has meant retraining or even reassignment or job loss. The results for apparel production companies, however, are considerable time and material savings, which translate into dollars saved as well.

While many apparel manufacturers do their marker making "in house," some outsource the task to private companies that handle marker-making activities (and similar activities like grading and pattern making). As such, it's almost as likely that today's Marker Maker will work for an outside specialty firm as an apparel production company.

Salaries

Salaries for Marker Makers range from $19,000 to $30,000, depending on location, the employee's qualifications and experience, and the specific duties of the job. Marker Makers who also handle related tasks (such as grading) tend to have the highest salaries.

Employment Prospects

Employment prospects for Marker Makers are generally poor because most marker making is now done with computers, and the apparel industry is losing many jobs to foreign workers at offshore assembly and outsourcing companies. Limited job openings do exist, however, thanks to retirements and job changes by other workers.

Advancement Prospects

Marker Markers can advance to positions as supervisors, either of the marker-making process or of other production divisions. In some cases, they can also become graders or production pattern makers.

Education and Training

Marker Makers need at least a high school diploma. But increasingly, they're expected to have a certificate or degree from a two-year college that offers training in computer-assisted marker making. Employers also value college degrees because college graduates tend to have more experience working with diverse individuals in team settings.

Marker Makers who have sound command of a second language besides English, such as Spanish or Chinese, have an edge over those who don't, since many apparel producers are hiring employees whose first language isn't English, or working with production firms in other countries.

Experience, Skills, and Personality Traits

In many cases, marker maker trainees/apprentices learn their trade on the job under the tutelage of more experienced Marker Makers. In some cases, though, they have already gained hands-on experience through internship/apprentice programs sponsored by their colleges.

To be successful, Marker Makers must be extremely accurate and precise. Mistakes in the marker-making process can cost thousands of dollars in wasted material and time. Marker Makers must also be detail-oriented and persistent so that they eventually figure out the best way to lay out pattern pieces for minimum waste.

Today's Marker Makers must also have sound computer skills, since they almost always use computers in the modern production environment. Additionally, Marker Makers need to have expertise in apparel construction, knowledge of body proportions and garment fitting, and an understanding of mass production principles, especially as they relate to the unique aspects of the apparel industry.

Often Marker Makers work alone or in very small groups. However, more and more Marker Makers must be good team members who can communicate effectively with others, whether in English, Spanish, Chinese, or another language.

Unions and Associations

The primary union for Marker Makers and similar workers is UNITE HERE!, which formed in 2004 with the merger of UNITE (Union of Needletrades, Industrial, and Textile Employees) and HERE (Hotel Employees and Restaurant Employees International Union). The union represents nearly half a million workers in the United States, Canada, and Puerto Rico.

Marker Makers and other garment workers can keep up with the broader apparel manufacturing industry by tapping into the American Apparel and Footwear Association, a national trade association for the apparel industry and its suppliers.

Tips for Entry

1. Pursue a certificate or two-year degree in marker making at a local technical or community college. While in the program, participate in any internship/apprenticeship programs that are offered, to gain hands-on experience under a veteran Marker Maker.
2. Get a summer or part-time job in an apparel production facility so that you can begin to learn about the entire clothing manufacturing process and, in particular, the marker-making process.
3. Talk to one or more Marker Makers to learn more about their specific jobs and how they got those jobs. Try to understand the ever-increasing role of computers in the typical Marker Maker's everyday work activities.

MERCHANDISER

CAREER PROFILE

Duties: Determines the product "direction" an apparel manufacturer will take each fashion season by closely studying apparel market trends and forecasts, previous sales results, production costs, and other production considerations

Alternate Title(s): Product Developer, Merchandise Planner

Salary Range: $50,000 to $200,000+

Employment Prospects: Fair

Advancement Prospects: Fair

Best Geographical Location(s): New York City and other fashion centers such as Chicago, Los Angeles, and Dallas

Prerequisites:

Education or Training—A minimum of a bachelor's degree is required, in an area such as fashion merchandising, apparel production, fashion design, or marketing; a master of business administration (M.B.A.) is helpful; participation in a company's retail or executive training programs is also a plus

Experience—At least five years of apparel-industry experience (usually closer to 10); some sales or retail experience

Special Skills and Personality Traits—Strong analytical skills; ability to gather data and translate research into profitable decisions about production "direction"; a well-developed sense of fashion and extensive knowledge of apparel industry trends and forecasts; ability to collaborate effectively with other professionals; organizational skills and detail orientation; decisiveness; ability to be calm under pressure; good problem-solving skills; strong mathematical skills; ability to maintain focus on the bottom line (i.e., profits/losses)

CAREER LADDER

Merchandising Director

Merchandiser

Merchandising Assistant

Fashion Buyer

Position Description

The American Marketing Association defines *merchandising* as "the planning involved in marketing the right merchandise at the right place at the right quantities at the right price." It's no wonder, then, that the Merchandiser's job involves such a variety of activities.

Merchandisers are high-level executives in apparel manufacturing organizations who use both their creativity and their business acumen to determine the product "direction" the manufacturer will take each fashion season. They're the professionals who are ultimately responsible for researching, planning, and deciding upon the particular fashions and/or accessories the manufacturer will produce, and whether those fashions and/or accessories will be profitable or not.

Much of the Merchandiser's job involves market research. For starters, Merchandisers thoroughly monitor industry publications (in print and online) so that they're aware of current and forecasted fashion trends. Additionally, Merchandisers study previous sales figures to determine which items sold well and why, and which sold poorly and why. They frequently travel to fashion showroom demonstrations, fashion shows, fashion trade shows, and other events in the United States and other parts of the world to talk to other professionals about industry trends and get ideas for new products. Some Merchandisers, in fact, spend up to 25 percent of their time "on the road."

Merchandisers collaborate with a host of colleagues to gather key information from them and deliver important information to them. In working with members of the sales staff, for example, Merchandisers can get a good sense of what buyers want for their stores and, ultimately, their customers (i.e., consumers). By working with fashion designers, Merchandisers can get feedback from the designers themselves, as well as the fashion stylist(s) who supervises them, about colors, styles, and silhouettes (i.e., garment outlines) that are or will be "hot." In turn, Merchandisers can inform the designers and the stylist about market and trend information they have gathered. Together, the Merchandiser, the designers, and the stylist can develop an initial plan for the items an upcoming fashion or accessory line might feature.

Since Merchandisers are responsible for the overall profits of a line of apparel, they also work closely with their production staffs. Specifically, they have to know enough about the production process and collaborate closely enough to determine whether each planned item can be produced cost-effectively or not. If it costs the company too much money to make a particular item, it must be dropped from the overall line, no matter how creative or innovative it might be.

In small apparel manufacturing companies, there may be just one Merchandiser. But in most larger companies with several divisions, there's at least one Merchandiser for each division. Each Merchandiser has "bottom line" responsibility: the decisions he or she makes will greatly affect the company's financial success. In many cases, the Merchandiser's knowledge, plans, and actions are literally linked to tens or even hundreds of millions of dollars' worth of potential sales each year. The Merchandiser's mistakes can have critical consequences, while his or her successes can lead to great financial rewards for the company as well as the Merchandiser.

Salaries

Since Merchandisers have extensive apparel industry experience as well as considerable bottom-line responsibility, salaries in the field are usually high. While some people in the field make only $50,000 to $60,000 a year, it's more common for Merchandisers to make $80,000 to $100,000; a few Merchandisers make $200,000 a year or more, particularly if they have a solid record of past performance and a reputation for financial success.

Employment Prospects

All apparel manufacturers need Merchandisers, and the largest companies employ more than one, so employment opportunities for prospective Merchandisers are relatively good, even though the total number of Merchandiser jobs is relatively small.

The best employment opportunities will go to those who have at least a bachelor's degree and, perhaps more importantly, significant experience in the apparel industry, particularly in sales positions (e.g., showroom sales rep, retail sales manager).

Advancement Prospects

Merchandisers who oversee strong profitability for their divisions or companies can move up to become merchandising directors, who oversee the work of other Merchandisers. From there, they can advance to assume a high-level management position, like vice president for merchandising. Both promotions lead to even higher salaries and greater bottomline responsibilities, not to mention additional personnel management duties.

Education and Training

All Merchandisers need at least a bachelor's degree, in an area like fashion merchandising, apparel production, fashion design, or marketing. Courses or other types of training in advertising and promotion are also helpful.

Many Merchandisers have advanced degrees, for example, a master of business administration (M.B.A.). Some have also participated in a company's retail or executive training programs, in which they've gained either retail or wholesale sales experience that they can use to better understand their customers, fashion buyers, or general consumers, who are the final purchasers of a company's products.

Experience, Skills, and Personality Traits

At a minimum, Merchandisers need five years of apparel industry experience, preferably including experience in retail or wholesale sales. Most Merchandisers, though, have even more experience—seven years or, in many cases, 10 years or more.

Merchandisers are highly skilled researchers. They must gather data from a variety of sources, such as industry publications and associations, industry colleagues, fashion shows and trade events, and fashion and color forecasters, and then analyze those data to determine what they mean in terms of the products the apparel manufacturer should develop and sell. The Merchandiser needs extensive industry knowledge (especially about color and style trends and forecasts), a strong fashion sense, and a solid understanding of his or her many customers. Merchandisers must know what products have sold well and why, and what products will sell well in the future and why.

To do their jobs well and ensure solid financial performance for their companies, Merchandisers need to be exceptional collaborators with their colleagues inside and outside the firm. Within the company, Merchandisers must be able to work closely with diverse groups of people, including sales staff, production staff, designers and stylists, piece goods (raw materials) buyers, and their fellow senior executives. Outside the company, meanwhile, Merchandisers must develop strong relationships with fashion buyers, apparel industry experts (e.g., editors of trade publications, color forecasters, members of professional organizations in the field), and even textile producers (who closely monitor fabric trends, particularly in the areas of "hot" colors and designs). No Merchandiser can work well or perform well alone.

Merchandising isn't a career for hesitant types. Merchandisers must be able to not only make sound decisions, but also carry them out. Good judgment is essential, but it isn't enough; Merchandisers also need to be organized to ensure that their product development plans are carried out. They must be able to keep track of the many details that make up the much larger apparel production process and use their follow-up skills to make sure every detail is taken care of.

The successful Merchandiser is a team-oriented problem solver who has exceptional communication skills, product development and marketing expertise, creativity, and the ability to work well under pressure while juggling a variety of different tasks and responsibilities. The highest-performing Merchandisers are also collaborative team players who go far beyond their own expertise to tap the knowledge of others in order to ensure solid profits for their companies.

Unions and Associations

Since Merchandisers are involved in such a variety of activities, they tend to tap the resources of a variety of organizations as well. While they don't have their own professional association or union, Merchandisers participate in organizations that cover the broad apparel and textile manufacturing industries—for example, the American Apparel and Footwear Association (AAFA), the International Textile and Apparel Association (ITAA), Fashion Group International (FGI), or more narrowly focused groups like the Color Association of the United States (CAUS).

Tips for Entry

1. While you're in school, gain experience in fashion merchandising by participating in internships, co-op programs, or similar activities.
2. Get a retail sales job in the fashion industry or a similar field so that you can better understand how and why consumers make their apparel buying decisions. (If possible, talk to the fashion buyer[s] in your store, to learn more about what they look for in the clothes they purchase for the store.)
3. Identify one or more people who work as Merchandisers and ask them to tell you how they got their jobs. Get their advice on how you can best prepare to become a Merchandiser someday.
4. Closely monitor (in print and online) industry publications, in both the apparel and textile sectors, so that you begin to develop knowledge about the fashion industry and the key players within it. Merchandisers need to have extensive industry knowledge in order to successfully plan, develop, and sell apparel and accessories that will be profitable for their companies.
5. If you're a college student, find a way to gain experience working with a variety of people, such as leading a student organization, or volunteering in your community. Merchandisers tap the expertise of a diverse group of people whose jobs and backgrounds vary widely.

PATTERN GRADER

CAREER PROFILE

Duties: Reduces or enlarges patterns created by a pattern maker for producing clothing across a range of sizes

Alternate Title(s): Grader

Salary Range: $19,000 to $25,000

Employment Prospects: Limited

Advancement Prospects: Limited

Best Geographical Location(s): New England, the Southeast, and California

Prerequisites:

Education or Training—A two-year college degree in an area like pattern making technology from a technical college or fashion school is preferred; on-the-job training

Experience—Experience as a pattern grading assistant/trainee is helpful, as are basic computer skills and experience with pattern making and pattern grading computer software and hardware

Special Skills and Personality Traits—Understanding of garment construction and pattern making; solid computer skills; drafting and mathematical abilities; manual dexterity; ability to be precise and accurate; deadline orientation; willingness to continuously analyze and solve problems

CAREER LADDER

Pattern Grader

Pattern Grading Assistant

Pattern Grading Trainee

Position Description

Pattern Graders are the people who ensure that the clothing items produced in apparel manufacturing firms all over the world ultimately come in different sizes. If not for their efforts, "one size fits all" might be the only size any garment comes in.

Pattern Graders work closely with pattern makers, who develop clothing patterns based on designers' sketches or samples. Once the pattern maker has come up with a final production pattern for a particular garment, it's up to the Pattern Grader to take that pattern and reduce and enlarge it into different sizes. This provides the manufacturer with graded patterns it can use to produce the item in a range of sizes (e.g., small, medium, large, extra large).

By necessity, the Pattern Grader's work requires precision and accuracy. A mistake could cost the manufacturer dearly in terms of lost money, since both fabric and manhours would go to waste as a result. To minimize the chance for errors, most manufacturing firms now use computer hardware and software in their pattern grading and related activities. Thus, today's Pattern Grader spends considerable time operating the hardware and software instead of making calculations and creating various patterns by hand.

Pattern grading, generally speaking, is much more science than art. The Pattern Grader doesn't really have much of an opportunity to customize patterns or alter them in any other way. Instead, he or she must use analytical and mathematical skills to determine the "right answer"—the proper sizing and proportion of various pattern pieces, whether they're larger or smaller than the original pattern.

Most Pattern Graders work for large apparel manufacturers in the New England states, the Southeast, California, and other areas. Some, however, work for outside companies that perform grading services and often, other services like patternmaking and marking, for a number of manufacturers that outsource the work to these companies. Whatever the setting, Pattern Graders are usually under some sort of deadline pressure. Most of the time, they must work on several projects at once, yet complete them all in the timeframe allowed by the rest of the production process.

Salaries

The median annual salary for fabric and apparel pattern makers (which includes Pattern Graders) was about $29,000 in 2004, according to the U.S. Department of Labor. However, since Pattern Graders often work under pattern makers and other apparel manufacturing staff, their salaries are usually lower—between $19,000 and $25,000 in most cases. Some Pattern Graders with extensive experience and technical skills earn slightly more.

Employment Prospects

Pattern grading is a fairly small occupation that is likely to become even smaller thanks to technological developments and the combining of pattern grading with similar jobs like pattern making. Still, limited opportunities do exist as a result of employee turnover and the ever-increasing need for people who have technical education, skills, and experience.

Many people who enter the field begin as pattern grader assistants or trainees, who may handle initial pattern preparations for computer processes and perhaps be involved in double-checking final grading results for accuracy.

Advancement Prospects

Advancement opportunities for Pattern Graders are generally limited, though those who have a college degree and extensive experience can move into other manufacturing positions such as pattern making or production management. Advancement depends on skill level and the availability of open positions.

Education and Training

Prospective Pattern Graders who have a two-year degree from a technical college or fashion school will generally have an advantage over those who don't, particularly if they've earned a degree in pattern-making technology or a related field and learned how to use pattern grading hardware and software.

Some Pattern Graders might also break into the field through on-the-job training, but this is becoming less common as computers handle the bulk of the grading work in many manufacturing firms.

Experience, Skills, and Personality Traits

All Pattern Graders must have considerable knowledge about garment construction and pattern making. Computer skills, particularly experience with computer-aided design (CAD) programs, are essential, since most apparel manufacturers now rely on computers for most of the pattern grading and related functions.

Since Pattern Graders work in a fast-paced environment, they must also be able to deal with stress and deadlines, and juggle several different projects at once. All the while, however, they need to be extremely accurate and precise because mistakes could cost their companies dearly in terms of wasted fabric, lost man-hours, and money.

Analytical and mathematical skills, manual dexterity, problem-solving abilities, and organizational skills are also keys to the Pattern Grader's success. The Pattern Grader needs strong written and oral communication skills as well, particularly since an increasing number of work environments call for skills in a language other than English (e.g., Spanish, Chinese).

Unions and Associations

The primary union for Pattern Graders and similar workers is UNITE HERE!, which formed in 2004 with the merger of UNITE (Union of Needletrades, Industrial, and Textile Employees) and HERE (Hotel Employees and Restaurant Employees International Union). The union represents nearly half a million workers in the United States, Canada, and Puerto Rico.

Pattern Graders and other garment workers can keep up with the broader apparel manufacturing industry by tapping into the American Apparel and Footwear Association, a national trade association for the apparel industry and its suppliers.

Tips for Entry

1. Identify and talk to one or more people who currently work as Pattern Graders. Ask them about how they got into the field and what advice they have to help you break into the field.
2. Learn as much as you can about apparel design, construction, and manufacturing by visiting industry Web sites, contacting professional organizations in the field, and reading industry-related books and periodicals.
3. Spend a day or longer shadowing a Pattern Grader at work—that is, actually following him or her in his or her job. Pay attention to the technical skills the Pattern Grader uses as well as the "soft" skills (e.g., communication with others) he or she must employ to work effectively.
4. Try to land a summer job in an apparel manufacturing firm so that you can learn more about pattern grading and related activities firsthand.

PATTERN MAKER

CAREER PROFILE

Duties: Translates a fashion designer's garment idea into pattern pieces used first to make initial product samples, and later, in more precise form, to produce the garment in mass quantities at the factory

Alternate Title(s): Assistant Designer

Salary Range: $19,000 to $85,000+

Employment Prospects: Fair

Advancement Prospects: Fair

Best Geographical Location(s): New York City, as well as regions of the United States where apparel is manufactured, such as New England, the Southeast, and California

Prerequisites:

Education or Training—A minimum of a two-year college degree in a field such as pattern-making technology, although increasingly employers are demanding that Pattern Makers have a bachelor's degree in pattern making, pattern engineering, fashion design, or a related field

Experience—Apprenticeship or college internship; retail sales experience and textile or apparel design experience are helpful

Special Skills and Personality Traits—Excellent technical skills as well as expertise in body proportions; accuracy and precision; patience and persistence; detail orientation; strong organizational skills; ability to work well with one's hands and with numbers; ability to handle multiple projects at once; strong computer skills; background in a language besides English (e.g., Spanish, Chinese)

CAREER LADDER

Production Manager

Pattern Maker

Assistant Pattern Maker

Pattern Grader

Position Description

Pattern Makers, sometimes called assistant designers, are responsible for taking a fashion designer's garment idea and creating the patterns needed for actually producing the garment, whether it's for a single sample or a huge quantity of garments that will be sold to retailers and, ultimately, consumers.

Working closely with the fashion designer or the entire design department, the Pattern Maker will initially create a first pattern for a particular garment idea. The first pattern is used to create an initial sample of the garment. Later in the process, the Pattern Maker will develop a final pattern or production pattern, a much more technically accurate pattern (sometimes called a "perfect" pattern) that will be used to manufacture the garment in mass quantities for the consuming public.

Either by hand or—much more often today—with the help of computer software, the Pattern Maker creates a pattern piece for each part of the garment. Once all of the pattern pieces are finished, the Pattern Maker develops construction specifications so that the final garment will be manufactured exactly as planned. The Pattern Maker must be extremely precise and accurate in this work, since mistakes can cost the manufacturer significant money in wasted material and production time.

Sometimes, particularly in smaller apparel manufacturing firms, the Pattern Maker is responsible for similar tasks as well. He or she may, for example, oversee the work of sample makers, the people who create sample garments from the first patterns. Or, the Pattern Makers might assist with marking (laying out the pattern pieces on fabric in a way that maximizes use of the fabric and minimizes waste) or grading (creating pattern pieces in different sizes for smaller and larger versions of the garment). On occasion, the Pattern Maker can do some design-related work as well, such as assisting with draping work or even contributing apparel design ideas.

While flat pattern making—drawing pattern pieces by hand on a flat table—used to be the rule in apparel manufacturing firms, it's the exception today; most manufacturers now use computerized pattern-making techniques and systems. Typically, the Pattern Maker has to know how to use a computer-aided design (CAD) program and/or specialized pattern-making software to do his/her job effectively in today's apparel manufacturing environment. As the technology continues to evolve, Pattern Makers will be expected to have even more technical skills and education. Indeed, salaries are already increasing significantly among the many Pattern Makers who have both extensive experience and well-developed technical skills.

Technical skills alone, however, won't make a Pattern Maker effective. Since Pattern Makers are in many ways go-betweens between the design side and the manufacturing side of an apparel manufacturing operation, they spend considerable time interacting with people who may be quite different from each other. The Pattern Maker, then, must be able to communicate just as easily and effectively with idea-oriented designers as with task-oriented manufacturing employees, who are ultimately responsible for turning all of a company's ideas into tangible reality.

Salaries

Salaries among Pattern Makers vary widely but are on the rise in many cases. Wages for entry-level Pattern Makers who have little or no experience and work for small companies can be as low as about $19,000 a year. The median 2004 wage for Pattern Makers, however, was just under $29,000, according to the U.S. Department of Labor.

With extensive experience and solid technical skills, Pattern Makers can earn substantially higher salaries. It's quite common to see Pattern Maker job advertisements listing salaries of $40,000 to $60,000, with a few listing salaries of more than $85,000.

Employment Prospects

Pattern making is a relatively small occupation, with about 9,200 people working in the field as of 2004, according to the U.S. Department of Labor. Most Pattern Makers work in New York City or in other areas of the country (e.g., New England, the Southeast, California) where apparel manufacturing is a common economic activity.

Prospects for finding a job in the field are fair, particularly for people who have the appropriate education, experience, and technical skills.

Most people who enter the field begin as assistant Pattern Makers, responsible for creating less complex patterns or perhaps performing some marking, grading, and cutting duties. Others enter the field after apprenticeships or internships under experienced Pattern Makers.

Advancement Prospects

Because they have a combination of technical and people skills, Pattern Makers can advance within their organizations in a variety of ways. They may simply take on higher-level pattern-making work, increasing their responsibilities and their salaries in the process. They might also advance to become fashion designers, or production managers who oversee the entire production process within an apparel manufacturing company.

Education and Training

In the "old days," most Pattern Makers began their careers as apprentices to more experienced Pattern Makers; they learned most or all of what they needed to know on the job. Today, however, it's becoming increasingly important for prospective Pattern Makers to have at least a two-year college degree in a field such as pattern-making technology, if not a bachelor's degree in pattern making, pattern engineering, or fashion design. In these educational programs, prospective Pattern Makers learn about computer software and basic pattern-making techniques, along with the fundamentals of the apparel design and manufacturing process.

Experience, Skills, and Personality Traits

To be successful in today's technologically sophisticated workplace, Pattern Makers need to have strong technical and computer skills. Software packages such as Gerber PDS (Pattern Design System) and Adobe Illustrator are now commonplace in the pattern-making environment. Pattern Makers must also be willing to continuously learn about new equipment and pattern-making processes. Manufacturers are always on the lookout for ways to save time, materials, manpower, and money, so Pattern Makers must be willing to adapt to some degree of constant change.

Pattern Makers also need strong analytical, mathematical, and problem-solving skills; extensive knowledge of body proportions and apparel design and fitting strategies; excellent hand-eye coordination and manual dexterity; and the ability to handle many projects at once, often under myriad deadlines.

To accompany their technical skills, Pattern Makers also need a host of "soft skills." Among them: patience and persistence, accuracy and precision, orderliness and organization, and the ability to attend to many details as well as problems that inevitably emerge in the pattern-making process. Also important, Pattern Makers must have strong people skills. They may be dealing with an idea-oriented designer one minute, and a "how-are-we-going-to-do-this" factory line employee the next. The Pattern Maker must be able to communicate effectively with both, whether in person or in writing.

Increasingly, Pattern Makers must have command of a language besides English—Spanish, for example, or Chinese—since they often deal with colleagues and customers whose first language isn't English.

Unions and Associations

Some Pattern Makers are members of UNITE HERE!, which formed in 2004 with the merger of UNITE (Union of Needletrades, Industrial, and Textile Employees) and HERE (Hotel Employees and Restaurant Employees International Union). The union represents nearly half a million workers in the United States, Canada, and Puerto Rico.

Pattern Makers can keep up with the broader apparel manufacturing industry by tapping into the American Apparel and Footwear Association, a national trade association for the apparel industry and its suppliers, as well as design-oriented organizations such as the Council of Fashion Designers of America and Fashion Group International.

Tips for Entry

1. Take advantage of any pattern-making internships or co-op programs offered by your school.
2. Identify and talk to one or more people who currently work as Pattern Makers. Ask them about how they got into the field and what advice they have to help you break into the field.
3. Learn as much as you can about apparel design, construction, and manufacturing by visiting industry Web sites, contacting professional organizations in the field, and reading industry-related books and periodicals.
4. Practice developing patterns from clothes you already own. Try to figure out how patterns are created from a designer's initial drawings.
5. Spend a day or longer shadowing a Pattern Maker at work—that is, actually following him or her in his or her job. Pay attention to both the technical skills the Pattern Maker uses as well as the "soft" skills (e.g., communication with others) he or she must employ to work effectively.
6. Try to land a summer job in an apparel manufacturing firm so that you can learn more about pattern making and related activities firsthand.
7. Learn at least the basics of a language besides English (e.g., Spanish, Chinese) by taking courses or participating in a self-study program.

PIECE GOODS BUYER

CAREER PROFILE

Duties: Works with an apparel manufacturer's fashion designers and merchandisers to determine which fabrics, or "piece goods," and trims to buy for the company's new fashion collections, then orders and receives those raw materials

Alternate Title(s): Piece Goods and Trim Buyer, Fabric and Trim Buyer, Fabric Coordinator/Specialist, Fabric Sourcing Coordinator/Specialist

Salary Range: $30,000 to $80,000+

Employment Prospects: Fair

Advancement Prospects: Fair

Best Geographical Location(s): Fashion centers like New York City, New England, and the Southeast

Prerequisites:

Education or Training—A college degree in textile technology, fashion merchandising, fashion design, or a related field is generally required, as is on-the-job training in assistant or internship positions

Experience—Several years as an assistant Piece Goods Buyer, working closely with the head Piece Goods Buyer on buying decisions and building strong relationships with textile companies

Special Skills and Personality Traits—Extensive knowledge of the textile and fashion industries; knowledge of fabric and fashion industry trends and forecasts, as well as new textiles and trims; ability to build effective working relationships with fashion designer and merchandiser colleagues as well as fabric and trim vendors; excellent organizational and follow-through skills; strong mathematical, analytical, and problem-solving skills; sound negotiation abilities; persistence and assertiveness; patience; strong communication skills; ability to work well as part of a team; knowledge of a language besides English (e.g., Spanish, Chinese)

CAREER LADDER

Piece Goods Buyer

Assistant Piece Goods Buyer

Position Description

Working closely with fashion designers and merchandisers, Piece Goods Buyers decide which fabrics, or "piece goods," and trims (zippers, buttons, snaps) an apparel manufacturer should buy to produce its latest fashion collections. The Piece Goods Buyer then visits various textile production firms to look at fabrics and trims and place orders for them. Finally, once an order has been placed, the Piece Goods Buyer makes sure that the fabric and trim orders arrive at the apparel company's manufacturing facility, on time and in good condition.

Piece Goods Buyers have to know the textile market thoroughly, so they devote considerable time to research and staying on top of fabric and fashion trends and forecasts. They accomplish this by reading industry publications, talking to textile production personnel, visiting textile manufacturers in other cities, and attending textile industry trade shows. Piece Goods Buyers continually pass on the information they gather to their fashion designer and merchandiser colleagues. Together, they determine which fabric and trim purchases to make. The Piece Goods Buyer and his or her staff must then go ahead and place orders for the agreed upon raw materials.

Ordering materials might sound easier than it really is. The Piece Goods Buyer must first ensure that each order is for the appropriate quantity of the correct fabric, a step that usually involves many phone calls and emails to the textile manufacturer. Once the order is in process, the Piece Goods Buyer has to follow up to make sure the order will arrive at the apparel company's production facility on time. And after the order actually shows up at the production facility, the Piece Goods Buyer must once again follow up to make sure the correct fabric has arrived, in the proper amount.

The Piece Goods Buyer usually negotiates a mutually reasonable price for the fabric and trim as well. The goal is to buy the best fabrics and trims possible for the least possible money, thus increasing the chance that the cost of producing the apparel company's line won't exceed the amount of money budgeted for the process.

As you might guess, Piece Goods Buyers, especially those who work for large apparel manufacturers, can easily be responsible for hundreds of thousands of dollars' worth of purchasing decisions each year. They have to know what they're doing, not only in terms of the materials they order but also in terms of the way they manage their operations. Poor decisions or mistakes on the part of the Piece Goods Buyer can cost an apparel manufacturer thousands or even millions of dollars. So the Piece Goods Buyer who establishes a pattern of being misinformed and disorganized won't last very long.

Salaries

Beginning assistant Piece Goods Buyers generally earn salaries in the $30,000 to $35,000 range. Once they're promoted into full-fledged Piece Goods Buyer positions, however, they could make $80,000 a year or more—especially if they have extensive experience and the increasingly critical ability to speak and understand a language besides English (e.g., Spanish, Chinese).

Employment Prospects

Since apparel manufacturers will always have to buy raw materials for their products, opportunities for prospective Piece Goods Buyers are somewhat plentiful. The best opportunities will go to those who have a related college degree; solid experience, beginning with internships and/or co-ops during college and continuing on through entry-level positions; and command of a language besides English (e.g., Spanish, Chinese).

Advancement Prospects

Those who start out at the assistant Piece Goods Buyer level can move into a full-fledged Piece Goods Buyer position after accumulating several years of experience working under someone in that position. Sometimes, Piece Goods Buyers can go on to related positions as well—for example, in merchandising or fashion buying.

Education and Training

Most Piece Goods Buyers have at least a bachelor's degree in a field like textile technology, fashion merchandising, or fashion design. Many have also received on-the-job training through college internships or co-ops.

Experience, Skills, and Personality Traits

Experience as an assistant Piece Goods Buyer is perhaps the best preparation for a full-fledged Piece Goods Buyer position. But experience alone won't make the Piece Goods Buyer successful. He or she must have top-notch textile and fashion industry knowledge as well, including a solid understanding of textile and fabric trends and forecasts. Like his or her fashion design and merchandising counterparts, the Piece Goods Buyer typically has to know what will be "hot" at least a year or perhaps even two years in advance.

Piece Goods Buyers must also be skilled negotiators who can get the best price on the fabrics and trims they buy for their companies. In today's global marketplace, that often means calling on one's fluency in (or at least working knowledge of) a language besides English—usually Spanish or Chinese. They also need exceptional organizational and follow-through skills to ensure that the raw materials they order actually reach their destination at the apparel manufacturer's production factory, by deadline and in good shape. Rarely does the ordering and procurement process go smoothly, so the Piece Goods Buyer must also have good problem-solving abilities, not to mention a willingness to be assertive if necessary.

An indecisive Piece Goods Buyer won't be on the job for very long. Indeed, every Piece Goods Buyer must have the ability to make up his or her mind, and to do so based on a combination of sound textile and fashion market research, past experience, and, to a degree, gut instincts.

Increasingly, Piece Goods Buyers need well-developed computer skills, along with above-average analytical and mathematical abilities, sound oral and written communication skills, and the ability to work well with members of a diverse team. They must do whatever it takes to stay on top of the textile and fashion industries, whether that means something as simple as reading industry publications or as time-consuming as traveling to different cities to meet with textile producers.

Unions and Associations

The International Textile and Apparel Association (ITAA) and the American Textile Manufacturers Institute (ATMI) both serve Piece Goods Buyers and related professionals. Some Piece Goods Buyers also participate in similar professional organizations like the International Textile Manufacturers Federation (ITMF) and the American Apparel and Footwear Association (AAFA).

Tips for Entry

1. While you're in college, participate in an internship or co-op program so that you can gain experience in Piece Goods Buying or a similar sector of the apparel or textile industry.
2. Monitor both textile and fashion industry publications, in print and online, to learn about and stay on top of trends and forecasts in fabrics and apparel. Piece Goods Buyers are in a unique position of needing some degree of expertise in both textile development and fashion design and merchandising.
3. Identify one or more Piece Goods Buyers and ask to talk to them (in person or by phone or email) about their jobs and how they got them. What advice do they have to help you break into the field?
4. Pay close attention to the component parts of the fashions you own or see in stores. What fabric was used to create a particular garment, and why was that fabric chosen? What trim pieces (e.g., buttons, zippers, snaps) had to be accounted for in the design of the garment, and how were they likely selected by the Piece Goods Buyer?
5. Pursue educational or training programs that allow you to develop your analytical, research, and problem-solving skills—three of the most important skill areas for Piece Goods Buyers.
6. Learn at least the basics of a language besides English (e.g., Spanish, Chinese) by taking courses or participating in a self-study program.

PRODUCT MANAGER, APPAREL

CAREER PROFILE

Duties: Oversees the conceptualization, design, manufacturing, selling, and distribution of an apparel producer's garments

Alternate Title(s): Product Development Manager, Director of Product Development, Category Manager

Salary Range: $60,000 to $120,000+

Employment Prospects: Fair

Advancement Prospects: Fair

Best Geographical Location(s): Major urban areas where apparel manufacturers' headquarters are located

Prerequisites:

Education or Training—A minimum of a bachelor's degree is required, in a field such as business administration, marketing, or apparel production; Product Managers often have advanced degrees as well, such as a master of business administration (M.B.A.)

Experience—At least five years of experience are required, preferably relating to apparel development or product management; Product Managers often have eight to 10 years of experience in the field

Special Skills or Personality Traits—Extensive knowledge of trends and forecasts in apparel and fabrics; sound understanding of garment construction and its associated costs; understanding of competitors and their products; analytical and problem-solving skills; "big picture" orientation combined with attention to detail; strong communication skills; ability to work well with other people of diverse backgrounds; practicality; supervisory skills; research skills; marketing and sales skills; ability to lead large projects from start to finish

CAREER LADDER

Vice President for Product Development

Product Manager

Associate Product Manager

Merchandiser

Position Description

Product Managers in apparel manufacturing companies have a unique combination of business, technical, and creative responsibilities. Their basic task is to oversee the conceptualization, design, manufacturing, selling, and distribution of either one particular segment of a company's garments or its entire line of garments.

Product Managers collaborate with a host of other high-level professionals, including fashion designers, fashion directors, merchandisers, market researchers, sales representatives, and production managers, to determine which products an apparel manufacturer should be creating, in what quantities, at what time, and at what price. To make accurate decisions, Product Managers also need to be experts in apparel and fabric trends and forecasts. They devote considerable time to reading industry publications, traveling to attend industry events and fashion or textile shows, participating in industry-related professional organizations, and conducting other research.

In some cases, Product Managers also oversee the modification of existing garments the company produces. For example, if a garment that has sold well in the past suddenly starts to lose steam in the marketplace, the Product Manager and his/her colleagues have to figure out why and whether the product should be revamped or dropped from the company's line altogether. "Can we manufacture the product more cost-effectively?" "Can we sell the product through channels we haven't used before?" "Should we change the product's colors or fabrics?" These questions and many others are the ones typically asked by the Product Manager.

Product Managers also work hard to stay on top of what their competitors are doing. In some cases, the Product Manager has to figure out how his/her company's products will coordinate with the products being made by other companies. In other cases, the Product Manager has to determine how his/her company's products can simply outperform competitors' products in the marketplace.

In many ways, Product Managers' "big picture" skills must coexist with their ability to focus on important details. For example, a Product Manager may have a superb idea for a new product. But if he/she determines it can't be produced at a cost the will allow it to be priced correctly for consumers, he/she must be able to move on to other possibilities. So the typical Product Manager must be equal parts "dreamer" and "realist" in order to be successful.

Salaries

Most Product Managers working for apparel manufacturers make at least $60,000 a year, and many of them make more than $120,000 a year. They can command such excellent salaries because of the considerable responsibility they have for making their companies financially successful.

Employment Prospects

Competition for Product Manager positions is considerable, and there aren't many of these high-level positions to go around. So employment prospects for Product Managers are only fair. The best opportunities will go to candidates who have extensive product development or related experience that they've gained in other positions or companies.

Advancement Prospects

Product Managers, because of their extensive experience and high-level responsibilities, sometimes advance to become part of apparel manufacturers' executive leadership teams. Others, who might oversee only one part of their company's line, are often promoted to oversee the firm's entire line of products.

Education and Training

At a minimum, prospective Product Managers need a bachelor's degree, most often in a field like business administration, marketing, or apparel production. Many Product Managers go on to complete advanced degrees as well, such as a master of business administration (M.B.A).

Experience, Skills, and Personality Traits

The Product Manager's job is not an entry-level position. In almost all cases, Product Managers have at least five years of experience in apparel manufacturing, often in the area of product development or merchandising. Frequently, prospective Product Managers have even more experience, perhaps eight years or more, before they're able to assume such a key position in the company.

Product Managers won't go far if they don't have extensive knowledge of apparel and fabric industry trends and forecasts. They simply must know which products are selling well and, as importantly, which ones are likely to sell well two, three, or even five years down the road. So they have to be able to find and understand industry-related information, whether it comes from industry publications or organizations, colleagues (in their own companies and others), or fashion shows, textile shows, and similar events.

To be successful, Product Managers must also be "big picture" thinkers who are able to conceptualize new ideas. At the same time, however, they have to be "realists" who can closely examine important details like production costs, timing, competitors' products and plans, and trends and forecasts, so that they make sound decisions about the products their companies will produce and sell.

Product Managers need good analytical and problem-solving skills, fashion savvy, organizational skills, and sound research skills. They also have to be practical yet creative, and be able to work with a host of other people with diverse backgrounds and perspectives. Perhaps most important of all, they must be strong leaders who understand how to make people work well together and develop and execute ideas that will make their companies successful.

Unions and Associations

Product Managers generally participate in a variety of apparel- and textile-related professional organizations, most often to stay on top of trends and forecasts and consult with colleagues (and even competitors) in the apparel and textile arenas.

Product Managers often participate in groups like the International Textile and Apparel Association (ITAA), the American Apparel and Footwear Association (AAFA), and

Fashion Group International (FGI). Some are also involved with their textile counterparts in organizations like the Color Association of the United States (CAUS), which makes color predictions and recommends colors for the fabrics (and yarns) textile manufacturers are producing.

Tips for Entry

1. Accumulate product development, product management, and merchandising expertise by working as a sales representative or account executive, merchandiser, or product developer in an apparel company setting.
2. Read industry publications and join industry organizations to begin accumulating knowledge of apparel and fabric trends and forecasts.
3. Talk to one or more Product Managers in the apparel industry to better understand their work and learn how you might advance to a similar position someday.

PRODUCTION MANAGER

CAREER PROFILE

Duties: Oversees the complex process of turning an apparel company's approved fashion designs into tangible, factory-produced products

Alternate Title(s): Production Supervisor, Production Coordinator

Salary Range: $35,000 to $100,000+

Employment Prospects: Fair/Good

Advancement Prospects: Fair/Good

Best Geographical Location(s): New York City and other major cities where fashion manufacturers' headquarters are located

Prerequisites:

Education or Training—At least a two-year college degree, although a four-year degree in a discipline such as apparel production management or industrial engineering is often preferred; on-the-job training as an industrial engineer or as a supervisor of factory subsections

Experience—A minimum of five to 10 years of production-related experience, typically in industrial engineering, supervisory, or production assistant positions

Special Skills and Personality Traits—Planning and people skills; apparel production and construction knowledge; ability to use problem-solving skills to ensure that garment production is as efficient—and therefore cost-effective—as possible; communication skills; foreign language skills; analytical skills; ability to focus on both the big picture and the small details

CAREER LADDER

Senior Production Manager

Production Manager

Production Supervisor/Coordinator or Assistant Production Manager

Production Assistant

Position Description

If apparel production in the factory were a football game, the Production Manager would be the quarterback, leading the rest of the factory's team toward the common goal of producing quality apparel and accessories efficiently and cost-effectively. He or she would have to ensure that every member of the squad was doing his or her job well, lest the entire team suffer the consequences.

The Production Manager has total responsibility for an apparel production factory's operations, processes, personnel, and performance. When all is said and done, a factory that produces apparel and accessories on time and at the lowest possible cost will be a credit to the Production Manager and his or her planning and execution efforts. Conversely, however, the factory that takes too long to produce items and spends too much money in doing so will be evidence of the Production Manager's inability to successfully develop the operations, personnel, and processes to do the job right. The Production Manager's job is a critical one.

Production Managers oversee a wide range of activities. First and foremost, they're ultimately responsible for the factory's employees—specifically, hiring, training, motivating, scheduling, and even protecting them. While most hiring of line employees is done by lower-level managers, the Production Manager must ensure that each employee is well trained and supervised. Moreover, the Production Manager is responsible for making sure that the factory under his or her management is in compliance with local, state, and federal laws related to worker health and safety. That means understanding often complex regulations from government bodies like the Occupational Safety and Health Administration (OSHA), for example, and, more importantly, making sure the factory is in compliance with such regulations.

Production Managers must also work to ensure that the entire factory is as efficient as possible. As such, the Production Manager typically oversees a group of supervisors, each of whom is responsible for a particular function within the firm—for example, patternmaking, cutting, sewing, pressing, shipping, and warehousing. If just one cog in the machine isn't functioning properly, the entire production operation will suffer. The Production Manager makes sure—either directly or through his or her managers—that every cog in the operation is working smoothly.

More and more these days, especially after passage of laws like the North American Free Trade Agreement (NAFTA), Production Managers have to travel to foreign locations where apparel manufacturers' factories are located because the cost of labor in these locations is far less than it is in the United States. In some cases, up to 50 percent of a Production Manager's time must be devoted to travel to places like Mexico, Central America, the Caribbean, and even Asia. Frequently, the Production Manager must be fluent in a language besides English—often Spanish or Chinese—to communicate with the personnel in these factories and see to it that they and their operations are functioning properly.

Production Managers can spend even more time on the road by going to industry trade shows and similar events, where they learn about new technologies and new processes aimed at improving production efficiency in apparel factories.

In large companies, Production Managers oversee multimillion-dollar budgets, hundreds or even thousands of employees, and a variety of distinct operations (e.g., cutting, sewing, warehousing), all under the pressure of production deadlines, cost restrictions, personnel concerns (e.g., labor union disputes with management), and an assortment of other stresses. All the while, they have to ensure that complex equipment keeps running properly, retailers' orders are produced and shipped on time, manufacturing inefficiencies are consistently identified and then eliminated, and workers from bottom to top in the organization are safely doing the work.

Salaries

Production Managers often begin their careers as production assistants, who make $30,000 to $35,000 a year. From there they can become production coordinators/supervisors or assistant Production Managers, who make $50,000 to $60,000 a year or more.

Once production supervisors/coordinators or assistant Production Managers advance to the Production Manager level, they typically make at least $70,000 a year—though that amount is often higher, particularly if the Production Manager earns a bonus for excellent performance of his/her facility.

In some cases, a Production Manager can advance to become senior Production Manager or even vice president of production, which almost always means a salary of at least $100,000 a year—and often considerably more.

Employment Prospects

Prospective Production Managers who are willing and able to travel or even relocate will have the best opportunities for jobs, since production factories can be spread all over the United States and, very often, other parts of the world. There are more than 20,000 apparel and textile manufacturing firms in the United States, so jobs for Production Managers and related professionals are reasonably plentiful.

Advancement Prospects

Production Managers typically have extensive industry experience, as theirs is a high-level position. But some of them go on to assume even higher-level positions—for example, as the vice president of production overseeing all of an apparel manufacturer's factory operations instead of only one or a handful.

Education and Training

Most Production Managers have a two- or four-year college degree in apparel production management or industrial engineering. Advancement is difficult without a college degree, though it is possible. Many have also accumulated on-the-job training by working in lower-level positions like industrial engineer, production supervisor, or assistant Production Manager.

The most effective Production Managers have thorough knowledge of and training in the factory's various operations, including pattern making, cutting, sewing, pressing, warehousing, and shipping.

Experience, Skills, and Personality Traits

Production Managers usually move into their jobs after they've accumulated at least five years of industry experience. More often, they have closer to 10 years of experience, and in some cases even more. It's essential that Production Managers understand various plant operations and motivate the workers within each of those functional areas.

Since their jobs depend, ultimately, on other people, Production Managers need to have excellent communication skills as well as the ability to hire, train, and motivate employees effectively. Often, they also have to be fluent in a language besides English—such as Spanish or Chinese—so that they can communicate with employees of diverse cultural backgrounds and countries and understand their ideas and concerns.

Production Managers must be master analyzers and planners who can spot production problems and fix them so that the manufacturing operation makes items as quickly and cost-effectively as possible. They regularly call upon their mathematical, data-gathering, and troubleshooting skills as well as their ability to see both the "big picture" and the small but important details of the production operation.

To do their jobs well, Production Managers need to be sound decision makers who can work well with diverse groups of people. They must have top-notch planning skills as well as the ability to follow through on their plans to make sure those plans are being carried out by the plant's middle managers and line employees. All the while, Production Managers must thoroughly understand the many laws and regulations the factory needs to comply with in order to keep all of its workers healthy and safe from on-the-job injuries. The Production Manager who can juggle the huge array of planning skills, people skills, apparel production, construction knowledge, and technical know-how is the one who will oversee a factory that produces quality goods, on time and for manageable cost.

Unions and Associations

While there is no specific union or professional association specifically for Production Managers, many monitor the apparel industry by participating in the American Apparel and Footwear Association (AAFA) and/or the International Textile and Apparel Association.

Some Production Managers who have training and experience in industrial engineering also belong to the Institute of Industrial Engineers (IIE) and similar professional groups.

Tips for Entry

1. Pursue at least a bachelor's degree in apparel production management, industrial engineering, or a similar field. While you're in college, participate in internships or co-op programs that allow you to gain hands-on experience in apparel production and related operations.
2. Identify and talk to one or more Production Managers who work for apparel manufacturing firms. Find out how they got where they are, and what advice they have to help you prepare to become a Production Manager someday.
3. Know the apparel industry and apparel production operations and processes. If possible, take a part-time or summer job in an apparel production factory so that you can learn one or more operations like pattern making, cutting, or sewing.
4. Find ways to gain experience working with a team. Production Managers rely on every part of the production team to do its job. As such, part of their responsibility is to motivate employees and make sure they're functioning well together. If you can gain similar experience by, for example, leading a college student organization or a community volunteer group, you'll learn how to work closely with others toward a common goal.

QUALITY CONTROL SPECIALIST

CAREER PROFILE

Duties: Ensures that garments, or fabrics/textiles used to make garments, are produced at required quality levels; identifies and resolves problems in production processes so that all products meet the required quality levels and specifications

Alternate Title(s): Quality Assurance Engineer, Quality Control Inspector, Quality Assurance Inspector, Quality Assurance Specialist

Salary Range: $30,000 to $100,000+

Employment Prospects: Good

Advancement Prospects: Good

Best Geographical Location(s): Major cities across the United States, particularly those where apparel manufacturers' headquarters and/or manufacturing facilities are located

Prerequisites:

Education or Training—A bachelor's degree in an area like industrial engineering, product management, textile technology, or apparel production is generally required; a graduate degree such as a master of business administration (M.B.A.) is helpful

Experience—Extensive work experience and technical training

Special Skills and Personality Traits—Good problem-solving skills; analytical skills; thoroughness; ability to see both the "big picture" and the individual parts of the production process; sound understanding of textile or garment production processes; ability to recognize high-quality and low-quality products; decisiveness, accuracy, and follow-through skills; computer and communication skills; diplomacy and tact; fluency in a language besides English (e.g., Spanish, Chinese)

Special Requirements—Various certifications possible from organizations such as the American Society for Quality

CAREER LADDER

Director of Quality Control/Assurance

Quality Control/Assurance Manager

Quality Control/Assurance Inspector

Quality Control/Assurance Technician or Assistant

Position Description

Quality Control Specialists (often called "QC" Specialists) can work for either apparel production facilities (and sometimes apparel importers) or textile production companies.

QC Specialists who work for apparel production firms are responsible for ensuring that garments are produced at required quality levels. They develop standards of production and make sure they're met by identifying problems in production and rectifying them through changes in equipment, personnel, processes, or a combination of the three. They also ensure that the finished product meets predetermined specifications in terms of size, color, construction, and fabric so that it will be saleable to the final customer, be it a consumer or a retail store.

QC Specialists who work for textile production companies examine fibers, yarns, and fabrics to ensure they meet often precise standards and specifications. As they might in an apparel production facility, QC Specialists in textile production companies must be able to identify production problems and solve them.

QC Specialists may be called upon to ensure the quality of both raw materials and finished products and everything in between. As such, they often spend a healthy share of their time traveling to various production facilities, sometimes in other states or even in other countries. In some cases, QC Specialists spend more than half of their work time on the road, evaluating foreign production facilities and processes, perhaps checking on the quality of finished garments a company is going to import and then sell. Sometimes they even establish new relationships with offshore production facilities, something that is becoming increasingly common following passage of the North American Free Trade Agreement and similar free trade pacts.

At the managerial or directorial level, QC Specialists are typically responsible for quality control for the entire production process. As such, they supervise lower-level QC personnel, hire and train those personnel, and work with other members of the larger production management team to ensure that garments are assembled quickly, correctly, and cost-effectively.

To do their jobs well, QC Specialists need extensive knowledge of textile technology and garment construction, which means knowing how to use complex machinery and computers. But they must also have sound "people skills," since they must often confront people who are doing low-quality work or who must learn to collaborate more effectively with their co-workers.

Salaries

At the entry level, QC Specialists in the apparel and textile industries typically earn $30,000 to $35,000 a year, depending on their education, experience, and geographical location. With additional experience and an advanced college education, QC Specialists can take on middle- and upper-management jobs that pay much more, often in the $60,000 to $75,000 range. QC Specialists who rise to the highest levels due to their education, experience, and certifications can make $100,000 a year or more.

Employment Prospects

As apparel manufacturers and textile developers continue to see that high-quality products mean more money for their companies (in terms of both cost savings in production and revenues from product sales), they'll continue to employ an abundance of Quality Control Specialists and related professionals. The U.S. Bureau of Labor Statistics reports that as apparel manufacturers and textile producers increasingly depend on quality to gain market share, they'll invest more and more in hiring and keeping competent Quality Control Specialists.

Advancement Prospects

At the entry-level, a Quality Control Specialist might perform product testing and inspection duties, often under the guidance of a more experienced professional. As they gain more experience, both technical and people-oriented, Quality Control Specialists have many opportunities to advance to middle- and upper-management positions. These involve more oversight of the entire quality control process; more personnel hiring, training, and supervision responsibilities; and more opportunities to identify and solve complex quality control problems involving entire divisions or companies.

Education and Training

In most cases, Quality Control Specialists have a college degree in industrial engineering, production management, textile technology, apparel production, or a related field. Those who move into higher-level positions often pursue graduate degrees—for example, a master of business administration (M.B.A.)—as well as industry certifications from organizations such as the American Society for Quality (ASQ).

Many Quality Control Specialists also seek out education or training in various computer applications. Additionally, with the spread of production to foreign countries and the increasing number of immigrants who work for apparel and textile production companies in the United States, Quality Control Specialists are pursuing coursework or training in foreign languages (often Spanish or Chinese) as well as foreign cultures.

Experience, Skills, and Personality Traits

Quality Control Specialists often begin gaining experience as assistants, working under more experienced professionals in the field. Mid- or upper-level management positions are reserved for professionals with extensive experience and education.

To be successful in their work, Quality Control Specialists need to have extensive knowledge of the entire textile or apparel production process. They must understand how the process is supposed to work and identify and fix problems when they arise. Analytical skills are essential to the job, as are decisiveness and assertiveness, organization and follow-through skills, the ability to handle stress and deadlines, and a willingness to travel, often on short notice, in response to a problem that has emerged.

Quality Control Specialists must also have good people skills, especially at the middle- and upper-management levels. As managers, they're typically responsible for hiring and training other quality control professionals, clearly communicating (orally or in writing) problems that have been identified and ways they must be solved, and confronting people who may be wholly or partially responsible for those problems. When they're called upon to work with or for production facilities in foreign countries, Quality Control Specialists must also be able to communicate well with people from diverse backgrounds, often using a second language (e.g., Spanish, Chinese) to do so. A Quality Control Specialist may be able to identify problems and perhaps even develop solutions; but if he or she can't effectively communicate ideas to the people who need to understand them, his or her efforts will likely be in vain.

Unions and Associations

Many QC Specialists and related professionals are members of the American Society for Quality, a Milwaukee-based trade association promoting "learning, quality improvement, and knowledge exchange to improve business results, and to create better workplaces and communities worldwide." Some QC Specialists are also involved with the American Apparel and Footwear Association (AAFA), a trade organization whose membership includes apparel manufacturers and related suppliers.

Tips for Entry

1. If possible, arrange to talk to one or more Quality Control Specialists who work for apparel manufacturers or textile producers. Better yet, ask to "shadow" one of them for a few hours or a whole day, so that you can see what their work is really like.
2. Seek a college degree in an area such as industrial engineering, production management, textile technology, or apparel production/manufacturing so that you can start to understand the entire textile/apparel manufacturing process and how it is impacted by the people and technology associated with it.
3. Gain experience in the quality control field by pursuing an internship or co-op program through your college.
4. Learn at least the basics of a language besides English (e.g., Spanish, Chinese) by taking courses or participating in a self-study program.
5. Start studying the garments you see in stores. How are they constructed? Are they well made? How many people and processes were probably involved in their production?

SALES REPRESENTATIVE, APPAREL

CAREER PROFILE

Duties: Travels to stores in a predetermined geographic area or territory to present a manufacturer's newest apparel lines to fashion buyers, who order such merchandise for sale in their stores

Alternate Title(s): Field Sales Representative, Manufacturer's Representative, Manufacturer's Agent, Wholesale Representative, Account Executive

Salary Range: $28,000 to $150,000+

Employment Prospects: Good

Advancement Prospects: Good

Best Geographical Location(s): All over the United States

Prerequisites:

Education or Training—A bachelor's degree is preferred, either in a specific field (e.g., fashion merchandising, business, marketing) or a broad liberal arts field; on-the-job training under the supervision of a more experienced Sales Representative or sales supervisor is also common

Experience—Previous sales experience is a plus

Special Skills and Personality Traits—Excellent communication and listening skills; outstanding presentation abilities; outgoing personality; ability to be persistent without being overly pushy; honesty; self-motivation; organizational and follow-through skills; knowledge of products manufactured by one's own company as well as the competition; awareness of apparel industry trends and forecasts; solid computer skills—especially contact management and spreadsheet software

CAREER LADDER

Sales Manager

Sales Supervisor

Sales Representative

Showroom Sales Representative or Assistant

Position Description

Sales Representatives, or Reps, are a key first link in the chain of events that results in fashion and accessories appearing in stores throughout the United States.

Sales Representatives who work for apparel manufacturing companies (usually just one but sometimes more than one) travel to various stores in a predetermined geographic area (or "territory") to present a manufacturer's newest apparel lines to fashion buyers. Their goal is to convince each fashion buyer to place an order for merchandise, which will then be sold to consumers in that fashion buyer's stores.

Today, most fashion buying takes place in manufacturers' showrooms in New York City and other fashion centers, usually during one of several market weeks that occur periodically throughout the year. As a result, the demand for traveling Sales Reps has declined somewhat in recent years. Still, the need exists for Sales Representatives who can meet with fashion buyers in the buyers' own cities, especially since market weeks are rather infrequent events and fashion buyers must continuously stay abreast of new apparel and accessory items.

Sales Representatives spend a great deal of their time on the phone, and even more so in recent years with the explosion of cell phones and pagers. They're constantly in touch with fashion buyers they've previously sold to, making sure the buyers have received the merchandise they've ordered and scheduling follow-up appointments in the hope of selling them more merchandise. Sales Representatives also make cold phone calls to fashion buyers they haven't worked with before, with the goal of gaining their business.

The Sales Rep's work can be thankless at times. A Representative might set up an appointment with a fashion buyer in a store that's three hours' drive, only to have the buyer not show up for the meeting because of a last-minute complication. Rejection and disappointment are simply part of the Sales Representative's job. Experienced Sales Reps know that every "no" they hear brings them one step closer to the "yes" they want. So they must remain persistent, yet patient in their dealing with buyers.

Often, Sales Reps will meet with fashion buyers one on one. Sometimes, however, Sales Reps will do presentations at hotels or in similar venues so that they can meet with several fashion buyers at a time. Whether interacting with one buyer or a group of buyers, the Sales Rep's job is essentially the same: he or she must use product samples, sketches, photographs, fabric samples or "swatches," press clips, and any other potentially helpful materials to convince the fashion buyers to purchase merchandise. In order to succeed, the Sales Rep must listen closely to what fashion buyers want and need, answer buyers' questions thoroughly and honestly, and, in some cases, even help buyers sell merchandise in their stores. This may include assisting them in the planning and execution of "trunk shows," in-store fashion shows that often feature live models showing off the apparel company's latest lines.

Since Sales Representatives have such close working relationships with fashion buyers and, by extension, consumers, they also frequently contribute to important planning and production decisions that their apparel manufacturing companies must make. High-level Sales Reps with extensive experience, for instance, frequently help merchandisers, fashion designers, and senior executives choose the company's final line of clothing and accessories. They also pass along to merchandisers and designers the opinions they regularly receive from fashion buyers, so that the merchandisers and designers can plan and create upcoming lines with the buyers' feedback in mind.

Most of the time, Sales Reps are frequent travelers, either within the boundaries of one state or, more often, covering a group of states. It's not unusual for a Sales Rep to be on the road four or even five days a week, which can make it difficult to have a family or be involved in outside-of-work activities. Still, for people who enjoy traveling and have a persuasive flair, working as a Sales Representative is often an excellent job that can lead to a variety of higher-level positions, either in sales or in other areas within the fashion industry.

Salaries

Beginning sales assistants typically earn $28,000 to $35,000 a year, though salaries can be a bit lower or higher depending on the job and the company. With experience, Sales Reps can earn $50,000 to $75,000 a year in many cases. Highly experienced Sales Reps, particularly those who advance into sales supervisor or regional/national sales manager positions, can easily earn $100,000 a year—and sometimes considerably more.

Most Sales Reps receive a "base salary" (money they get regardless of their sales) plus "commissions" (a percentage of the amount of merchandise they sell). Sales Reps are also frequently eligible for bonuses based on their performance, whether those bonuses come in the form of money or other rewards like trips or merchandise.

In many cases, Sales Reps who use their own cars to travel receive financial reimbursement to cover the costs of gas and automobile maintenance. They almost always receive additional money for meals, particularly when they use a lunch or dinner to "wine and dine" an existing or potential client.

Employment Prospects

While the number of traveling Sales Representatives has decreased somewhat in recent years, there are still plenty of opportunities, particularly with medium-sized apparel companies serving small and/or remote markets. However, competition can be stiff for Sales Rep jobs. The best opportunities go to those who have a bachelor's degree and some sort of sales experience, whether in retail or showroom sales.

Advancement Prospects

Many of today's top fashion executives got their start in sales, either at the retail level or as in-house or outside Sales Representatives. The ability to sell is one of the most cherished skills in the entire fashion business, and those who have it can go far.

Sales Representatives who perform well can become Sales Supervisors who oversee the work of other Sales Reps. Eventually, they can advance further to become assistant sales managers and then sales managers overseeing an even larger sales force. A few sales managers continue to move up to become regional sales managers (responsible for sales efforts in a large geographic region) and then national sales managers (responsible for nationwide sales).

Geographic flexibility is key to the Sales Rep's prospects for employment and advancement. Often, the apparel company's need for a salesperson exists in another nearby (or not-so-nearby) state. The Sales Representative who is open to relocating will have more potential job opportunities to pursue than the Sales Rep who is unwilling or unable to move.

Education and Training

While it's possible to become a Sales Representative without a college degree, most Sales Reps today have at least a bachelor's degree in an area like fashion merchandising, marketing, or business. Some Sales Representatives have degrees in the liberal arts, an advantage, according to one sales manager, when it comes to carrying on intelligent conversations with current and prospective clients.

Most Sales Representatives receive additional training as soon as they begin their jobs, under the direction of a more experienced Sales Rep or sales supervisor.

Experience, Skills, and Personality Traits

Sales Representatives who have previous sales experience, either at the retail level or as showroom sales assistants, have a definite advantage over those who don't. The best Sales Representatives also have thorough knowledge of the fashion industry, as well as their own companies' products and the products of their competitors.

It's important for Sales Representatives to have a thick skin and to be able to take rejection in stride. At the same time, Sales Representatives must be patient and persistent; they know that every "no" they hear brings them a step closer to "yes," but only if they refuse to give up on their selling and relationship-building efforts.

Sales Representatives need outstanding communication skills, especially in the way of making oral presentations to prospective clients and listening to their wants and needs. The successful Sales Rep is friendly and personable, enthusiastic and outgoing, and genuinely interested in working with people. He or she is also persuasive without being pushy. Perhaps above all, the successful Sales Representative is honest in his or her dealings with fashion buyers.

However, no Sales Rep will succeed without self-motivation. In most cases, the Sales Representative doesn't have a watchful boss who oversees his or her day-to-day activities. Indeed, most Sales Reps make their own decisions about who to see and when. They can rely only on themselves to do the work they need to do, and they have to set and meet their own schedules and deadlines. If a Sales Representative lacks self-discipline and organizational skills, he or she won't remain a Sales Representative for very long.

Unions and Associations

While there aren't any unions or professional associations specifically for Sales Representatives in the fashion industry, most Sales Reps keep up with industry trends by participating in organizations like the American Apparel and Footwear Association (AAFA), the International Textile and Apparel Association (ITAA), and Fashion Group International (FGI).

Sales Representatives in the fashion industry and many other industries are often members of Sales and Marketing Executives International (SMEI) as well. The organization is a professional trade group for sales professionals in a wide variety of fields.

Tips for Entry

1. While you're in college, participate in internships and co-op programs that allow you to gain sales and marketing experience in the fashion industry or a related industry (e.g., textiles).
2. Take a part- or full-time job as a retail sales associate so that you can begin accumulating sales experience in the apparel industry. Often, prospective Sales Representatives who have some previous sales experience have a competitive advantage over those who don't.
3. Seek work as a showroom sales assistant for an apparel manufacturer so that you can gain experience serving fashion buyers, the people you'll be working with closely as a Sales Representative.
4. Arrange to talk to one or more Sales Reps about the work they do and how they got to where they are. Ask for their advice on how you might someday become a Sales Representative.
5. Arrange to talk to one or more fashion buyers. Ask them to give you a brief overview of their work and responsibilities so that you fully understand what they do and why. The better you know fashion buyers, the more effective you'll be as a Sales Representative (whose clients are fashion buyers).
6. Monitor industry and consumer fashion and textile publications (in print and online) so that you start building up knowledge of fashion and textile trends and forecasts. Pay special attention to what various apparel manufacturers are developing, promoting, and selling. You may be working for one of those manufacturers as a Sales Representative someday, or perhaps competing with one of them as a Sales Representative for another manufacturer.

SAMPLE MAKER

CAREER PROFILE

Duties: Creates sample garments based on the ideas of fashion designers, using a sewing machine, hand-sewing techniques, or both

Alternate Title(s): Sample Hand, Sample Sewer

Salary Range: $18,000 to $35,000

Employment Prospects: Limited

Advancement Prospects: Limited

Best Geographical Location(s): New York City and other fashion centers

Prerequisites:

Education or Training—A high school diploma or a general educational development (GED) certificate is generally required; a one- or two-year college degree with course work in garment construction techniques is helpful

Experience—Must have experience sewing different types of garments (e.g., shirts, pants, coats) using different types of fabrics

Special Skills and Personality Traits—Knowledge of hand and machine sewing techniques; expertise in garment construction; sound hand-eye coordination and manual dexterity; ability to follow the fashion designer's directions precisely and accurately; ability to perform repetitive movements with hands and feet; enough focus to complete work quickly and well

CAREER LADDER

Sample Maker Supervisor

Sample Maker

Sewing Machine Operator

Position Description

Sample Makers are the professionals who take fashion designers' ideas for garments and turn them into tangible reality, at least initially.

Using their hand and machine sewing skills and their sound knowledge of garment construction, Sample Makers closely follow the fashion designer's sketch, initial pattern, and written directions to create a first sample, or prototype, of what the proposed garment will look and feel like. Often, the Sample Maker then helps the fashion designer fit the sample on either a mannequin or a live model. In almost every case, the designer, in consultation with the Sample Maker and perhaps others, decides to make changes to the garment. The Sample Maker makes those revisions as well, until the sample matches what the designer originally had in mind. The final sample then accompanies a technically specific final pattern and detailed specifications to the company's production facility, where the garment is manufactured in mass quantities.

The Sample Maker's work can be exacting and somewhat tedious at times. However, some Sample Makers take on other responsibilities in addition to their sewing duties. They may, for example, advise fashion designers on whether their designs work from an aesthetic perspective or a materials and construction point of view. In other cases, Sample Makers may help out with draping and other activities that are part of the overall design process. Experienced Sample Makers may move into positions where they're not only sewing garments, but also supervising the efforts of other Sample Makers or, in some cases, training them on sewing techniques.

Sample Makers can become so skilled at what they do that some fashion designers have been known to fight over them! Many become highly trusted right hands to the designers they work with, often increasing their salaries and responsibilities in the process.

Salaries

The salaries Sample Makers earn are quite low in many cases, especially if they work only part-time or sporadically. Sample Makers usually make just slightly more than factory sewing machine operators do, which was a median of just under $18,000 in 2004, according to the U.S. Department of Labor. That fact is reflected in the 2004 median salary for hand sewers, which was just under $19,000, according to Department of Labor figures.

In some instances, though, Sample Makers can earn considerably more for their efforts. Experienced Sample Makers who also have supervisory duties and/or an advisory role in the design process can make up to $35,000. And the many Sample Makers who work as self-employed independent contractors have the potential to make even more, depending on how much work they land and how much it pays.

Employment Prospects

Though some in the industry have called sample making a dying craft, there are still some jobs available to prospective Sample Makers. Opportunities also exist for self-employed independent contractors who prefer to pursue jobs with a variety of companies. The best opportunities will go to those who have extensive sewing skills and industry experience, a solid reputation in the industry (especially among fashion designers), and the willingness to further their education by taking college courses or participating in company or outside training programs.

Advancement Prospects

While a few Sample Makers move up to supervisory positions or even assistant designer roles, many have trouble advancing in the field without pursuing a two- or four-year college degree. Sample Makers who are fought over by fashion designers, however, can at least earn a salary increase in most cases, and perhaps the opportunity to take on additional responsibilities involving the design process.

Education and Training

Sample Makers need at least a high school diploma or a general educational development (GED) certificate. They must also have extensive training and experience in hand and machine sewing techniques and garment construction. Some Sample Makers pursue one- or two-year college degrees to get additional education in garment construction and perhaps take courses in fashion design.

Experience, Skills, and Personality Traits

Sample Makers need to be skilled sewers, whether using a sewing machine or sewing by hand, and know how to work with a variety of fabrics to create a variety of garments (e.g., shirts, pants, dresses, coats). Their work requires patience and precision as well as the ability to follow detailed instructions, whether those instructions are in the form of written specifications, sketches, patterns, or some combination thereof.

Sample Makers must also be able to visualize what a fashion designer's idea is supposed to look like in tangible form. To do so, they need to be able to communicate effectively with the designer and understand how colors, fabric, and form work together to create a garment that is pleasing to the eye.

In order to be successful, Sample Makers must have excellent hand-eye coordination and manual dexterity, solid knowledge of garment construction, the willingness and ability to do somewhat repetitive work involving both their hands and their feet, and the ability to work quickly and yet still come up with a quality product.

Unions and Associations

Some Sample Makers are members of UNITE HERE!, which formed in 2004 with the merger of UNITE (Union of Needletrades, Industrial, and Textile Employees) and HERE (Hotel Employees and Restaurant Employees International Union). The union represents nearly half a million workers in the United States, Canada, and Puerto Rico.

Sample Makers can keep up with the broader apparel manufacturing industry by tapping into the American Apparel and Footwear Association (AAFA), a national trade association for the apparel industry and its suppliers, as well as design-oriented organizations such as the Council of Fashion Designers of America (CFDA) and Fashion Group International (FGI).

Tips for Entry

1. Identify one or more Sample Makers and ask if you can talk to them (in person or by phone or e-mail) to learn more about what they do and how they got their jobs. What advice do they have to help you become a Sample Maker or a similar professional?
2. Practice sewing, either by hand or on a sewing machine. Make your own clothes, either from store-bought patterns or your own designs. Later, you can show these "samples" of your work to prospective employers.

SEWING MACHINE OPERATOR

CAREER PROFILE

Duties: Uses single- or multiple-needle sewing machines to assemble cut pieces of fabric into a completed garment, usually as part of an assembly line or team

Alternate Title(s): Garment Sewer

Salary Range: $12,000 to $21,000

Employment Prospects: Fair to Limited

Advancement Prospects: Limited

Best Geographical Location(s): Most jobs are found in eight U.S. states: Alabama, California, Georgia, New York, North Carolina, Pennsylvania, Tennessee, and Texas

Prerequisites:

Education or Training—A high school diploma plus on-the-job training is helpful; a two-year college degree is helpful for some supervisory positions

Experience—Sewing experience is helpful, as is on-the-job training and mentoring

Special Skills and Personality Traits—Physical stamina; good hand-eye and foot coordination; conscientiousness; ability to follow directions; ability to work well with other people; basic computer skills

CAREER LADDER

Line Supervisor or Team (Module) Leader

Sewing Machine Operator

Position Description

Sewing Machine Operators use single- or multiple-needle sewing machines to sew fabrics or other materials, such as leather or fur, into finished articles of clothing, which are then marketed and sold to consumers.

Sewing Machine Operators typically work in large or small factories, hand-feeding materials under a sewing machine's needle(s) and starting and stopping the machine with a foot pedal or knee lever. Generally, Sewing Machine Operators specialize on one machine so that they gain expertise performing a particular operation, such as making sleeves or stitching hems.

Traditionally, the Sewing Machine Operator has worked as one part of a bigger, assembly-line process. In recent years, however, many garment manufacturing firms have begun moving to a modular manufacturing system, in which Sewing Machine Operators work together in "modules," or teams. Each operator in the module still specializes in one operation, but most operators are also trained to take on any of the other operations performed by their team. That way, they can fill in for other workers when necessary. Manufacturers believe that the modular manufacturing system ultimately increases garment quality and reduces production time, while giving Sewing Machine Operators and other team members greater responsibilities and more opportunities to communicate with each other.

Most Sewing Machine Operators work a standard five-day, 35- to 40-hour week, although some work during second shifts and on weekends since manufacturers don't like leaving expensive machinery idle. Occasionally, Sewing Machine Operators must also work overtime, especially during peak production periods.

Work as a Sewing Machine Operator can be demanding from a physical standpoint. Sewing Machine Operators often sit or stand for long periods of time, perhaps leaning over tables and their operating machinery. Due to the nature of the work itself, the Sewing Machine Operator's work environment can often be noisy as well, not to mention hot. Modern factories have alleviated these conditions to some degree through better design and computer automation, but older factories still tend to be somewhat congested, badly lit, and poorly ventilated.

While garment manufacturers continue to invest in better equipment and computerized systems, it is quite difficult for them to make their garment sewing processes more efficient and fully automated. Consequently, the nature of the work of many Sewing Machine Operators and other garment assemblers has remained relatively unchanged over the years.

Salaries

Sewing Machine Operators earn anywhere from $12,000 to $21,000 a year. The median salary for Sewing Machine Operators in 2004 was just under $18,000, according to the U.S. Department of Labor.

Some Sewing Machine Operators also receive modest fringe benefits. A few large employers, for example, offer on-site childcare for their employees. Other manufacturers that operate their own retail stores allow employees to buy apparel products at considerable discounts.

Employment Prospects

The U.S. Department of Labor reports that employment of Sewing Machine Operators is expected to decline between now and 2014, since many of these jobs are being lost to lower-wage workers in countries outside the United States. As of 2004, about 256,000 people were employed as Sewing Machine Operators in the United States, down from about 287,000 in 1998. That downward trend is expected to continue.

Several factors are behind the expected changes. One is imports, which now account for about half of domestic apparel consumption in the United States. That figure is expected to go up even more as the American market is opened further by such initiatives as the North American Free Trade Agreement (NAFTA) and the Agreement on Textiles and Clothing (ATC) of the World Trade Organization.

Another factor focuses on production costs in the United States versus other countries. In most cases, American clothing manufacturers can get more for less by taking their sewing and other manufacturing operations to countries where wages are typically much lower for Sewing Machine Operators and other workers.

Finally, advances in technology will also play a role in the projected job losses. While it's difficult if not impossible to fully automate the sewing processes in garment manufacturing firms, some of the processes can be streamlined by new technology, thus eliminating some Sewing Machine Operator jobs and similar jobs.

Despite the gloomy employment projections for Sewing Machine Operators, the U.S. Department of Labor points out that job openings will continue to arise each year from the need to replace workers who move to other occupations or retire.

Advancement Prospects

Generally speaking, advancement opportunities for Sewing Machine Operators are limited. Workers can move up to supervisory positions, especially if they have a high school diploma and, even better, some college education, along with previous work experience. Increasingly, thanks to modular production systems, workers are also becoming more responsible for their own self- and team-management concerns.

Education and Training

A high school diploma is helpful but not required for entry into the Sewing Machine Operator occupation. Workers who have some college education and previous experience are most likely to advance to supervisory or management positions.

Increasingly, Sewing Machine Operators must also have some basic computer skills, along with training in teamwork, management, and interpersonal communication.

Experience, Skills, and Personality Traits

Sewing knowledge and experience are essential to the success of a Sewing Machine Operator. Since the work is so physically demanding, stamina, patience, good hand-eye and foot coordination, and excellent concentration skills are also necessary.

Sewing Machine Operators must also be able to learn by doing, since they are generally trained for their work by more experienced operators. Additionally, as a result of the move to modular production systems, Sewing Machine Operators must be able to work and communicate well with other people, learn how to perform multiple operations on multiple machines, and adjust to production changes brought on by automation technologies and computers.

Unions and Associations

The primary union for Sewing Machine Operators is UNITE HERE!, which formed in 2004 with the merger of UNITE (Union of Needletrades, Industrial, and Textile Employees) and HERE (Hotel Employees and Restaurant Employees International Union). The union represents nearly half a million workers in the United States, Canada, and Puerto Rico.

Sewing Machine Operators can keep up with the broader apparel manufacturing industry by tapping into the American Apparel and Footwear Association, a national trade association for the apparel industry and its suppliers.

Tips for Entry

1. Identify and talk to some people who currently work as Sewing Machine Operators to get their insights on and suggestions about the field.
2. Contact UNITE HERE! to get more information on working as a Sewing Machine Operator or similar manufacturing employee.
3. Learn how to sew well, by hand and with a machine, and try to gain as much knowledge as you can (through reading, Internet research, etc.) on sewing, fabrics/textiles, and fashion design.
4. If you're interested in taking on supervisory or team leader responsibilities, consider pursuing postsecondary education, perhaps at a two-year community college.
5. To prepare yourself to work well with other people, participate in group volunteer activities in your community, or take local community education courses dealing with team performance, management, and interpersonal communication.

SHOWROOM SALES REPRESENTATIVE

CAREER PROFILE

Duties: Shows fashion buyers a manufacturer's or designer's new lines of apparel and accessories; attempts to convince each buyer to place orders for merchandise; ensures that the merchandise ordered reaches the buyers' stores on time and in saleable condition

Alternate Title(s): Showroom Salesperson, Showroom Representative (Rep), Account Executive

Salary Range: $28,000 to $100,000+

Employment Prospects: Good

Advancement Prospects: Good

Best Geographical Location(s): New York City, Philadelphia, Dallas, Atlanta, Miami, Chicago, Los Angeles, and wherever else showrooms are located

Prerequisites:

Education or Training—A bachelor's degree in fashion merchandising, marketing, business, or a related field is preferred; on-the-job training programs are helpful

Experience—Previous sales experience, particularly fashion-related, in a part-time or summer job is very helpful; participation in college internships or co-op programs is also helpful

Special Skills and Personality Traits—Outgoing, friendly personality; considerable knowledge of both the manufacturing and retail sectors of the apparel industry; excellent presentation skills; ability to listen well and address questions/concerns effectively; outstanding organizational and computer skills; ability to handle pressure; fluency in a language besides English (e.g., Spanish, French, Italian) is a big plus

CAREER LADDER

Showroom Sales Manager

Showroom Sales Representative (Rep)

Showroom Sales Clerk/ Trainee/Assistant

Position Description

Showroom Sales Representatives, or "Reps," typically work in the New York City showrooms of various apparel manufacturers and designers. Their job is essentially threefold: to show fashion buyers a manufacturer's or designer's new line(s) of apparel and accessories; to convince each buyer to place orders for merchandise; and to ensure that the merchandise ordered reaches the buyers' stores on time and in saleable condition.

Showroom Sales Representatives usually begin at the entry level as showroom sales clerks or trainees. In this position, they typically handle clerical and "gofer" work. They may be responsible for writing up buyers' merchandise orders, for example, either by hand or by entering the information into a computerized database or a similar order management system. Sometimes, clerks or trainees might also deal with buyers on the phone or via e-mail to schedule appointments or to troubleshoot any problems. On occasion, clerks or trainees even serve as apparel models, wearing clothing for buyers so that they can see what it looks like on an actual person.

With experience, showroom sales clerks or trainees can become full-fledged Showroom Sales Representatives, whose duties and responsibilities are more complex. Showroom Sales Representatives are the people who work most closely with visiting buyers. They attempt to present the manufacturer's or designer's latest collection in a way that grabs the buyers' attention and interest. Their goal is to convince each buyer to place a merchandise order for his or her retail store(s).

If that happens, the Showroom Sales Representative must take the order. It's the Showroom Sales Representative's responsibility to ensure that each buyer's order is accurately taken and then processed. A mistake—for example, writing down the wrong quantity of jeans or the wrong date of delivery for those jeans—can and will cost time and money to both the buyer and the rep's employer.

Once an order has been placed, the Showroom Sales Representative must then make sure that the merchandise ordered reaches the buyer's store on time and in saleable condition. Here again mistakes can be and are costly, to both the buyer and the representative's employer.

Showroom Sales Representatives, given their interaction with both fashion buyers and their firms' fashion designers and fashion merchandisers, also serve as messengers between buyers and the designer(s)/manufacturer. Since Showroom Sales Representatives deal directly with fashion buyers, they quickly get an accurate sense of what the buyers want and need for their stores, and, ultimately, what their consumers want. The best Showroom Sales Representatives pass this important market pulse information on to the fashion designers in their companies, so that the designers continually have a good idea of what buyers want and don't want, and can develop apparel and accessory items accordingly.

Showroom Sales Representatives can eventually move up into the showroom sales manager's position. Showroom sales managers oversee the entire showroom sales operation—personnel, merchandise, buyer relations, and budgeting and finances. They supervise and train the other showroom sales staff, and ensure that garment samples are always available for buyers to see. They develop relationships with new buyers, who could potentially bring in millions of dollars' worth of sales, and deal with the most difficult problems buyers are having, especially if losing one or more of those buyers would mean losing millions of dollars' worth of their business. Sometimes, showroom sales managers get involved in planning their companies' merchandising concepts as well, and on occasion they even participate in selecting a designer's or manufacturer's final line of clothing for each season.

Showroom sales staff are also often called upon to help out during fashion shows and industry trade events. Almost every showroom sales professional can expect to work additional long hours during the four to six market weeks or fashion weeks each year, when fashion buyers from all over the world descend on New York City to look at manufacturers' new lines and place orders for their stores.

Salaries

Entry-level showroom sales trainees/clerks/assistants can expect to earn starting salaries of about $30,000 a year, give or take a few thousand dollars. Salaries for more experienced Showroom Sales Reps can go up substantially. Most receive commissions on the sales they make, and some receive performance bonuses as well. Thus, Showroom Sales Reps with several years of experience and solid selling skills frequently make $70,000 a year or more. Showroom sales managers, because of their considerable responsibilities, can earn even more—typically $100,000 a year or more.

Employment Prospects

While showroom sales is a competitive part of the industry, opportunities for landing an entry-level showroom sales job are reasonably good. Indeed, many people who now work in fashion sales or related careers began their working lives as trainees in a manufacturer's or designer's showroom.

Prospective showroom sales trainees who have a college degree, good communication and presentation skills, and some sales experience have the best opportunity to land this type of job.

Advancement Prospects

With experience and additional education (for example, a master of business administration [M.B.A.] degree), showroom sales trainees can advance to become Showroom Sales Reps and, eventually, showroom sales managers. They can often move into similar roles within their companies, in the merchandising or marketing divisions, for example, or even at the officer or directorial level.

Some highly experienced Showroom Sales Reps and managers opt to start their own companies by becoming manufacturers' agents, independent sales professionals who represent several noncompeting manufacturers and who draw on their extensive industry experience and contacts to work effectively with many buyers from many different companies.

Education and Training

A college degree isn't required to break into the showroom sales field, but most industry insiders say that a college degree in fashion merchandising, marketing, business, or a similar field gives an applicant an advantage over other applicants who don't have a college degree. A degree may become necessary for applicants who eventually want to move up into higher-level positions in the showroom sales sector or the fashion industry. The best educational programs, industry experts say, give students a combination of fashion/apparel knowledge, people skills, and presentation skills.

Experience, Skills, and Personality Traits

Retail sales experience is helpful to anyone who wants to become a Showroom Sales Representative. College internship or co-op experience is also an asset, as is participation in an apparel manufacturer's on-the-job training program.

Interpersonal skills are probably the most important trait a Showroom Sales Representative can have. Sales reps need to be highly skilled communicators who are able to present merchandise in an attention-grabbing way. Increasingly, Showroom Sales Reps also benefit from fluency in a second language besides English—for example, Spanish, French, or Italian—given the diversity of people with whom they deal. Showroom Sales Reps also need to be friendly and personable, yet also poised, confident, and assertive enough to go beyond simply making a good presentation so that they can actually succeed in making sales to buyers.

Showroom Sales Representatives also need to be good "schmoozers," who can, for example, take new prospective buyers out to dinner, get to know them better, and, hopefully, convince them to order merchandise. Social skills are critical to the success of every Showroom Sales Representative, as is the ability to dress and groom well for credibility's sake.

People skills alone, however, won't make a Showroom Sales Rep successful. Organizational and follow-through skills are essential. It's one thing to be able to convince a buyer to order some merchandise, but if the Showroom Sales Rep bungles the buyer's order—or, worse, forgets about it entirely—both the buyer and the rep's firm get hurt financially. The buyer may well decide to take his or her business elsewhere next time, to the potential tune of millions of lost dollars for the Showroom Sales Rep's company.

Increasingly, computer skills are playing a greater role in the Showroom Sales Representative's work. Computerized databases and other order processing systems handle the bulk of buyers' orders these days. The Internet, meanwhile, has given buyers another way to communicate with Showroom Sales Representatives.

Finally, Showroom Sales Reps must have considerable knowledge of both the retail and manufacturing sectors of the fashion business. In many ways, they work in between these two sectors, dealing with buyers who make merchandise purchases for the retail stores and designers who create the clothes. In order to work effectively with both, Showroom Sales Representatives need to know how the entire fashion industry works, and be able to serve as a liaison of sorts between buyers and designers.

Unions and Associations

Some Showroom Sales Reps are members of Sales and Marketing Executives International (SMEI), a national trade organization for sales and marketing professionals. Others monitor industry trends and develop relationships with colleagues by participating in professional associations like the American Apparel and Footwear Association (AAFA) and Fashion Group International (FGI).

Tips for Entry

1. Gain retail sales experience by pursuing a part-time or summer job, preferably one that's fashion-related. The more sales experience you can accumulate, the better your chances will be to break into the field.
2. Pursue a college degree in fashion merchandising, marketing, business, or a related field. While you're doing so, be sure to participate in one or more internships or co-op programs so that you can gain some practical, hands-on experience in the industry.
3. If possible, visit New York City or another city where fashion designers and manufacturers have showrooms. Go into as many showrooms as you can to see what they're like. If it's not terribly busy during your visit, you might even talk to one or more of the Sales Reps to learn how they got their jobs and what advice they have to help you break into the field.
4. Contact one or more Showroom Sales Representatives and see if they'll speak with you (in person or via phone or e-mail) about what they do. The best way to learn about a particular career field is to talk to people who are actually working in that field.
5. Study the fashion industry thoroughly by monitoring industry publications and taking college courses in fashion merchandising, fashion design, and fashion marketing. Showroom Sales Representatives need extensive knowledge of industry trends, forecasts, and procedures to be successful.
6. Visit manufacturers' and designers' Web sites to see if they offer any training programs that would allow you to take on an entry-level showroom sales job and

"learn the ropes" of the field. Even if you already have a college degree, some companies prefer to enroll you in their own training programs in order to groom you for a sales-related position.

7. Practice your public speaking skills. If you're a college student, for example, take speech/communication courses that force you to work on your presentation abilities. Successful Showroom Sales Representatives must know not only their product, but also how to effectively present it to fashion buyers.
8. Learn at least the basics of a language like Spanish, French, or Italian.

SKETCHER

CAREER PROFILE

Duties: Creates technically precise sketches of a fashion designer's ideas, either for pattern making, presentation, and/or manufacturing purposes or for the designer's record; assumes some clerical, organizational, and "gofer" responsibilities

Alternate Title(s): Assistant to the Designer, Designer's Assistant, Graphics Assistant

Salary Range: $30,000 to $40,000+

Employment Prospects: Fair

Advancement Prospects: Fair

Best Geographical Location(s): New York City and other fashion centers, particularly where expensive or couture design houses are located

Prerequisites:

Education or Training—A bachelor's degree in fashion design or fashion illustration is almost always required; formal training in art, design, textile, and garment construction concepts; proficiency with computer applications (e.g., computer-aided design [CAD] software, Adobe Photoshop, Adobe Illustrator) is essential

Experience—Previous experience as a college intern or co-op student is quite helpful; applicants must also have a portfolio highlighting their talents

Special Skills and Personality Traits—Excellent drawing skills; precision and accuracy; ability to work quickly while maintaining quality; understanding of art, design, and color principles; familiarity with pattern-making and draping techniques; a strong sense of fashion styles and trends; solid attention to detail; organizational skills; knowledge of garment construction and manufacturing; flexibility; resourcefulness; ability to work well under pressure and meet deadlines; patience and persistence

CAREER LADDER

Fashion Designer

Assistant Fashion Designer

Sketcher or Assistant to the Designer

Sketching Assistant

Position Description

Sketchers, and their lower-level counterparts, sketching assistants, create freehand or computer-based sketches of fashion designers' design ideas, for two basic purposes. First, the Sketcher's sketches are used for pattern making, presentation, or manufacturing purposes. They are used during the apparel design and production process itself. Second, Sketchers often do drawings after a line of clothing has already been produced, in order to update the *designer's record,* an archive of the designer's designs from previous collections. Computer applications are more common in handling this second sketching function.

Sketchers take idea-oriented sketches that the designer or assistant designer has produced and make them much more technically precise for manufacturing or recordkeeping purposes. Originality isn't a trait the Sketcher uses in his or her work. Rather, the important thing is to ensure that others' design ideas are accurately represented, and to do so quickly, often under the pressure of time constraints and deadlines. In the case of sketching for recordkeeping purposes, it often means including with each sketch a fabric swatch or sample, accessory samples, and a specification sheet outlining the construction details of the garment.

In most cases, the amount of sketching a Sketcher actually does isn't enough to justify a full-time position. Thus, Sketchers typically take on a variety of additional responsibilities, many of them clerical. They may, for example, serve as a designer's fitting model on occasion, or even contribute their own design ideas from time to time (especially once they've gained some experience with the company and/or a particular fashion designer). More often than not, however, Sketchers take care of the sometimes unexciting but always important detail or "gofer" work, such as answering the phone or e-mail messages; setting up and perhaps attending appointments with fashion buyers and salespeople; conducting market research; or running errands.

The work hours for Sketchers can be long and irregular, depending on the fashion designer they're working with and the time of year. Things can be especially hectic for Sketchers when they have to assist with fashion shows or other promotional activities. Still, the work is diverse, if not always creative, and it can often lead to better job opportunities later. It usually allows the Sketcher to make important industry contacts, some of whom may become employers or colleagues in the future.

Salaries

Sketchers who work mostly or exclusively on sketching activities can expect to earn around $30,000 a year to start. Those who advance to take on other tasks—particularly related to designing—can earn $40,000 a year or more, depending on their specific backgrounds, job duties, skills, and responsibilities.

Employment Prospects

There aren't many sketching-exclusive jobs anymore; in many companies, sketching duties are handled by people (e.g., designer's assistants) who also have a variety of other responsibilities. Today, sketching-exclusive jobs are generally confined to the expensive couture design houses. Sometimes Sketchers can work on staff or on an independent freelance/contract basis for apparel manufacturers or even pattern companies catering to the home sewing market.

Advancement Prospects

Once someone has broken into the industry as a Sketcher, he or she can advance in a variety of ways. The on-the-job education and experience the Sketcher receives can serve as a stepping stone to higher-level opportunities, particularly in the fashion design area. Some Sketchers, for example, go on to become assistant designers or even designers. A few of today's top designers, in fact, got their start as Sketchers, albeit 20 or more years ago in many cases.

Education and Training

To become a Sketcher, you generally need a bachelor's degree in fashion design, fashion illustration, or a closely related field. Course work in art, design principles, textiles, and apparel construction is essential. Computer skills are critical, especially when it comes to computer-aided design (CAD) applications and widely used software like Adobe Photoshop and Adobe Illustrator. It's also quite helpful for prospective Sketchers to have a solid understanding of pattern-making and draping techniques, color theory, and fitting strategies.

Prospective Sketchers must have a portfolio with various samples highlighting their talents in drawing, color usage, form, and style.

Experience, Skills, and Personality Traits

Though the Sketcher's job is usually an entry-level position, college internship or co-op experience is helpful for breaking into the field. If an internship or a co-op is impossible, volunteering to work with a staff or freelance Sketcher is another potential way to gain experience and make important contacts in the field.

Sketchers must have exceptional drawing abilities, a strong sense of color and two- and three-dimensional design principles, and solid knowledge of apparel construction. Creativity is critical as well, though the Sketcher must often be able to temper that creativity in order to accurately produce sketches of others' ideas.

Sketchers also need to be detail-oriented and precise, able to work quickly without sacrificing quality, and well organized so that they can meet deadlines and complete projects without forgetting anything or making mistakes.

Since they work with a range of different professionals, Sketchers must also be strong communicators who are flexible and patient. At the same time, however, Sketchers need to be self-motivated, ambitious, and persistent if they hope to accumulate the experience and contacts they'll need to move into more prestigious jobs in their own companies or in others.

Unions and Associations

Sketchers have no formal professional association or union of their own, but many of them participate in the same sorts of organizations fashion designers participate in—for example, the Council of Fashion Designers of America (CFDA), Fashion Group International (FGI), the International Association of Clothing Designers and Executives (IACDE), and the National Association of Fashion and Accessory Designers (NAFAD).

Tips for Entry

1. Be sure your academic preparation includes coursework in the principles of art, design (two- and three-dimensional), color theory, textile design and development, and garment construction. While you're in school, participate in one or more internships or co-op programs so that you can gain experience in sketching- and/or design-related activities and, as important, cultivate personal contacts in the fashion industry.
2. Arrange to talk to one or more Sketchers (either in person or via phone or email) to learn more about their work and to get their advice on breaking into the field. If possible, ask if you can "shadow" one or more of your interviewees for a morning or an entire day to see their day-to-day activities.
3. Start building a portfolio of drawings and similar works that you can show to prospective employers or internship/co-op supervisors. No employer will consider you for a job—or even an internship—unless you have at least the beginnings of a portfolio of your work.
4. Practice drawing apparel and accessory items. For example, take some of your own clothes and see if you can reproduce them in great technical detail. The best of your practice drawings can go into your portfolio, at least initially until you can replace them with other, more professional samples.
5. Find some books or visit some Web sites that have sketches of different pieces of apparel. Try to get a sense of the different drawing styles and tools used to produce these renderings. You might even want to contact the artists themselves to ask them questions about their pieces.
6. Become proficient with computer-aided design (CAD) programs or software packages like Adobe Photoshop or Adobe Illustrator by taking courses or participating in a self-study program.

SPECIFICATION TECHNICIAN

CAREER PROFILE

Duties: Assists the technical designer(s) with the key clerical, organizational, evaluation, and communication tasks that must be completed to ensure an apparel manufacturer's garments are produced with technical accuracy and the right fit for the consumers who ultimately buy them

Alternate Title(s): Assistant Technical Designer, Technical Design Assistant, Specification (Spec) Writer, Assistant Fit Technician

Salary Range: $30,000 to $55,000+

Employment Prospects: Fair

Advancement Prospects: Good

Best Geographical Location(s): Large cities, particularly fashion centers such as New York City and Los Angeles

Prerequisites:

Education or Training—A minimum of a two-year degree in pattern making or a closely related area is required; a four-year degree in apparel design, apparel technical design, or a closely related discipline is often preferred

Experience—One to four years of experience (which can include internship and/or co-op experience) in technical design or a closely related area

Special Skills and Personality Traits—Knowledge of pattern making, grading, and garment design and construction; ability to write detailed comments at fittings and then help communicate those comments clearly to manufacturing personnel; knowledge of measuring techniques and sewing construction terminology; sketching skills; strong computer skills, particularly in applications such as Microsoft Excel, Microsoft Access, Microsoft Outlook, Adobe Illustrator, Adobe Photoshop, and product data management (PDM) software from companies like Gerber Technology and Lectra; superior written and verbal communication skills; strong detail orientation and organizational skills; ability to multitask and be flexible; exceptional teamwork skills; quantitative skills; ability to handle pressure and meet often strict deadlines; prioritizing and decision-making skills

CAREER LADDER

Senior Technical Designer/ Technical Design Manager

Technical Designer

Associate Technical Designer

Specification Technician (Spec Tech)

Position Description

Specification Technicians—more commonly called Spec Techs—help a manufacturer's technical designer(s) in the quest to turn the new garment ideas of fashion designers into the new garment products that consumers ultimately buy.

The technical design process is, ultimately, about ensuring that each finished garment fits the consumer the way it's supposed to. So technical designers—with the help of Spec Techs—work closely with fashion designers to figure out the exact measurements for each new garment design; determine how that garment should fit and how it should ultimately be constructed; and create detailed plans—or specifications ("specs")—to be used by manufacturing personnel to create the actual garment in large quantities.

The Spec Tech plays a key role in this entire process, particularly when it comes to carrying out nitty-gritty clerical and organizational tasks assigned by the technical designer. As the spec tech and the technical designer oversee the fitting of a garment sample, for example—either on a mannequin or, much more often, on a live fit model—it is the Spec Tech who is often charged with writing detailed notes (called comments) on his/her and the technical designer's observations about how well (or not) the garment fits and what changes, if any, need to be made to the garment before it goes to the production stage. Later in the process, the Spec Tech is often responsible for using special software to create a detailed specification package (or "spec pack") that will be used by the manufacturing facility and its staff to create the garment itself in mass quantities.

Depending on the company, the Spec Tech may also be responsible for communicating with manufacturing personnel—which increasingly means being fluent in a language such as Chinese or Spanish—to answer any questions or concerns they may have about producing a particular garment.

In some companies, the Spec Tech and technical designer jobs are combined into one position. But in larger organizations, the jobs are separate, with the Spec Tech typically answering to the technical designer or an intermediary (such as an associate technical designer).

Salaries

Spec Techs are entry- to mid-level professionals who can earn anywhere from $30,000 to $55,000 a year or more depending on their education, experience, skills, and responsibilities. Those who have the combined job title of Spec Tech/technical designer tend to earn higher salaries, while those who are solely Spec Techs usually earn slightly less.

Eventually, Spec Techs can advance to become technical designers making $45,000 to $65,000 a year—or even senior technical designers or technical design managers who command salaries of $100,000 a year or more.

Employment Prospects

Spec Techs have only fair employment prospects because their numbers are relatively small. College graduates who have a year or two of experience in technical design (or a closely related discipline) and solid connections in the world of fashion design have the best chance of landing a job as a Spec Tech.

It's difficult to quantify just how many Spec Techs are working in the United States today. For the purposes of comparison, however, about 17,000 people worked as fashion designers in 2004, according to the U.S. Department of Labor.

Advancement Prospects

Once Spec Techs have accumulated a few years of experience, they can often advance to an associate technical designer or technical designer position in their own company or elsewhere. Later they can advance to higher-level senior technical designer or technical design manager positions.

Some Spec Techs who become technical designers eventually move into the more creative role of fashion designer, where they can come up with their own garment designs instead of executing the garment designs of others.

It's difficult to quantify growth prospects for Spec Techs. But for the purposes of comparison, employment of fashion designers is expected to grow more slowly than average between now and 2014, according to the U.S. Department of Labor.

Education and Training

At a minimum, Spec Techs generally need a two-year degree in pattern making or a closely related discipline. More often in today's global marketplace, however, Spec Techs need both the technical training and the soft skills (e.g., communication, teamwork) that come from a four-year degree, typically in fashion/apparel design, fashion/apparel technical design, or a closely related area.

Experience, Skills, and Personality Traits

Spec Techs need to understand the basics of key design-related tasks such as pattern making, grading, measuring and calculating (i.e., quantitative/numerical skills), and fitting. Like their technical designer counterparts, they must also have thorough knowledge of garment design and construction techniques.

Since they're often charged with carrying out the many clerical details involved in the technical design process, Spec Techs must also have exceptional computer skills. At a minimum, they should have solid command of programs such as Microsoft Excel (spreadsheet) and Microsoft

Access (database) as well as illustration software such as Adobe Illustrator and Adobe Photoshop. Moreover, Spec Techs need to know how to use often complex product data management (PDM) software produced by companies like Gerber Technology and Lectra, which allows them to put together the detailed specification packages ("spec packs") manufacturers need to produce garments correctly.

The most successful Spec Techs have a wide assortment of essential soft skills and key personality traits to complement their sound technical knowledge. Among the most important soft skills and personality traits: written and verbal communication (so Spec Techs can interact well with both on-site colleagues and, especially, off-site manufacturing personnel); solid organizational skills, attention to detail, thoroughness, and follow-through capabilities; flexibility, adaptability, and multitasking skills; the ability to prioritize tasks and handle the inevitable pressures involved with juggling many projects at once; and outstanding teamwork skills.

Frequently, Spec Techs must be fluent in a language besides English (e.g., Chinese, Spanish) as well.

Unions and Associations

While there are no specific unions or associations for the discipline, many Spec Techs keep current in the overall fashion industry by participating in organizations such as Fashion Group International (FGI) and the International Association of Clothing Designers and Executives (IACDE).

Tips for Entry

1. During college, gain some practical experience in technical design or a closely related discipline through an internship, a co-op program, or even volunteering.
2. Begin reading industry publications like *Women's Wear Daily* and *DNR (Daily News Record),* along with consumer publications like *Cosmopolitan* and *Vogue,* to learn about fashion trends and forecasts.
3. Do whatever you can to get to know some working Spec Techs (and technical designers) in the industry. If possible, talk to some Spec Techs (i.e., informational interviewing) to learn more about what they do and how they got to where they are now. The more connections you can make with Spec Techs (and technical designers) who are already in the field, the more potential opportunities you'll uncover for yourself.
4. Visit apparel company and job search Web sites to look for Spec Tech job listings. What key skills and abilities, experiences, education, and traits do companies seem to be looking for in the Spec Techs they want to hire?

SPREADER

CAREER PROFILE

Duties: Spreads out fabric on long tables during the apparel production process, so that it can be cut into pieces that will be sewn into finished garments

Alternate Title(s): None

Salary Range: $12,000 to $25,000

Employment Prospects: Limited

Advancement Prospects: Fair

Best Geographical Location(s): Eastern, southeastern, and southern states, as well as California, where apparel production facilities are located

Prerequisites:

Education or Training—A high school diploma is often required; a technical school certificate or degree is sometimes preferred

Experience—On-the-job training is common

Special Skills and Personality Traits—High degree of accuracy and detail orientation; knowledge of apparel construction and mass production principles; computer skills; ability to do repetitive tasks for long periods of time; physical strength; excellent eyesight and the ability to detect subtle differences among bolts of fabric

CAREER LADDER

Production Supervisor

Cutter, Marker Maker, or Grader

Spreader

Spreader Apprentice

Position Description

Spreaders take lengthy bolts, or rolls, of fabric and spread them out on long tables so that they can be marked with various pattern pieces. Workers called cutters then cut the fabric into the pieces that will eventually be sewn into finished garments.

In most of today's factories, Spreaders use computerized spreading machines to do their work. The machines help the Spreaders lay out the fabric in dozens or even hundreds of layers, which will all be cut at the same time during the cutting process.

Spreaders have to make sure that the fabric they lay out is completely smooth and straight before cutting begins. If it isn't, the pattern pieces will be cut improperly, costing the company money in terms of wasted effort and materials.

Accuracy and precision are critical in a Spreader's everyday work. Aside from spreading fabric, Spreaders are also responsible for closely examining each bolt of fabric as it is laid out. They have to be sure, for example, that the shading matches between different bolts of the same fabric, since inconsistencies will lead to the possibility that garments will be composed of slightly mismatched pieces of fabric. Additionally, in the many cases in which a garment will feature patterned fabric, Spreaders are responsible for ensuring that each long piece of the fabric is precisely lined up on top of the one directly underneath as well as the other layers below and above.

In smaller companies, Spreaders also do the actual cutting of the fabric, and sometimes participate in related activities such as marking or grading.

Salaries

Salaries for Spreaders range between $12,000 and $25,000 a year, depending on their specific duties and skills, their training, and their responsibilities. In 2004, the median annual salary for all textile cutting machine setters, operators, and tenders was just over $20,000, according to the U.S. Department of Labor.

Employment Prospects

There were only 28,000 textile cutting machine setters, operators, and tenders (which includes Spreaders) in 2004, according to the U.S. Department of Labor. That number will likely fall in the coming years as more of these types of jobs are lost to lower-wage workers in countries outside the United States.

Advancement Prospects

Spreaders can move laterally to assume similar production positions in the grading, marker making, or cutting areas. Occasionally, they may rise into supervisory positions, either in the spreading area, a similar area, or a larger company division.

Education and Training

Spreaders need at least a high school diploma in most cases. But they'll increase their employability by having a certificate or degree from a two-year college and demonstrating sound computer skills.

Experience, Skills, and Personality Traits

In most cases, spreader apprentices learn their trade on the job under the direction of more experienced Spreaders.

In order to be successful, Spreaders must be highly accurate and detail oriented to minimize or eliminate costly cutting mistakes that might result from fabric being wrinkled or misaligned during the spreading process. Spreaders also need to understand apparel construction and mass production principles.

Increasingly, Spreaders need to have sound computer skills as well, since the spreading machines they use are typically computerized.

Spreaders must also have physical strength and the ability to perform repetitive tasks for long periods of time. Additionally, they need excellent eyesight so that they can examine the consistency of fabric among different fabric bolts and, in the case of patterned fabrics that need to match up at the garment's seams, ensure that the layers of the fabric line up precisely so that they're cut properly.

Unions and Associations

The primary union for Spreaders is UNITE HERE!, which formed in 2004 with the merger of UNITE (Union of Needletrades, Industrial, and Textile Employees) and HERE (Hotel Employees and Restaurant Employees International Union). The union represents nearly half a million workers in the United States, Canada, and Puerto Rico.

Spreaders can keep up with the broader apparel manufacturing industry by tapping into the American Apparel and Footwear Association (AAFA), a national trade association for the apparel industry and its suppliers.

Tips for Entry

1. Get a summer or part-time job in an apparel production facility so that you can begin to learn about the entire clothing manufacturing process and, in particular, the spreading process and related procedures like production pattern making, grading, marker making, and cutting.
2. Talk to one or more Spreaders to learn more about their jobs and how they got those jobs. Try to understand the ever-increasing role of computers in the typical Spreader's everyday work activities.

TECHNICAL DESIGNER

CAREER PROFILE

Duties: Works closely with fashion designers (or fashion design teams) and manufacturing staff to make sure garments are produced with technical accuracy and have the right fit for the consumers who ultimately buy them

Alternate Title(s): Technical Design Coordinator, Technical Coordinator, Technical Manager, Technical Specialist

Salary Range: $45,000 to $100,000+

Employment Prospects: Fair

Advancement Prospects: Good

Best Geographical Location(s): Large cities, particularly fashion centers such as New York City and Los Angeles

Prerequisites:

Education or Training—A minimum of a two-year degree in pattern making or a closely related area is required; a four-year degree in apparel design, apparel technical design, or a closely related discipline is often preferred

Experience—Three to five years of experience in technical design, with higher-level positions generally requiring five to 10 years of experience

Special Skills and Personality Traits—Solid skills in pattern making, grading, and garment design and construction; sketching ability; knowledge of various fabrics; ability to judge a garment's fit on either a mannequin or, more often, a live fit model; ability to write detailed comments at fittings and then communicate those comments clearly to manufacturing personnel; strong computer skills, particularly in applications such as Microsoft Excel, Microsoft Access, Adobe Illustrator, and Adobe Photoshop; superior written and verbal communication skills; strong detail orientation and organizational skills; ability to multitask and be flexible; exceptional teamwork skills; quantitative skills

CAREER LADDER

Senior Technical Designer/ Technical Design Manager

Technical Designer

Assistant/Associate Technical Designer or Specification Technician (Spec Tech)

Position Description

Eighty percent of American women aren't bothering to wear at least a quarter of the clothes in their closets, according to a 2006 consumer survey conducted by clothing retailer Talbots. Of that group, 56 percent attributed the problem to one deciding factor: fit—or, more accurately, lack thereof.

An informal poll of visitors to About.com's "Women's Fashion" Web site revealed that 42 percent of respondents "never" find clothes that fit them; 40 percent "sometimes" do; and 14 percent "rarely" do. Only the remaining 4 percent said they "always" find clothes that fit.

The financial impact of this phenomenon on apparel manufacturers can be staggering. The National Retail Federation reports that due to poor fit, consumers return some $28 billion worth of merchandise to retail stores each year.

The Technical Designer's job is ultimately all about fit—and about making sure that apparel manufacturing staff and facilities have all the technical details they need to produce each garment accurately, so that it fits the buying consumer the way it's supposed to (and the way it was envisioned to by the fashion designer[s] who created it in the first place).

Once a fashion designer has come up with a prototype for a new garment, the Technical Designer steps into the process to develop specifications, or "specs," for the garment by carefully measuring it and having samples made. Once samples are available, the Technical Designer oversees a fitting process that involves putting the garment on a mannequin or, much more often, a live fit model whose body proportions match those the company uses to determine the various sizes of its clothing items. During the fitting process, the Technical Designer looks for fit problems and other discrepancies and makes note of them in careful detail so that alterations can be made to correct them.

Eventually, the Technical Designer is responsible for approving final fit of each garment and then developing a specification package (or "spec pack") that will be used by the manufacturing facility and its staff to create the garment in mass quantities. Along the way, the Technical Designer is often involved in key activities such as pattern making and grading, not to mention sketching—either by hand or, much more often these days, using computer software like Adobe Illustrator or Adobe Photoshop.

Most Technical Designers must also communicate frequently—often daily—with manufacturing personnel, who usually have questions or clarifications they must clear up before starting the production process for the garment. In today's global marketplace, such communication often means being fluent in a second language besides English, particularly Chinese or Spanish. It also means that the Technical Designer must be patient and flexible, yet thorough enough to ensure that the garment gets produced correctly and on time.

Salaries

Technical Designers are mid-level professionals who are paid comparatively well due to their education, experience, and—especially—their exacting skills and the direct impact they often have on a company's bottom line. Technical Designers typically make between $45,000 and $65,000 a year, depending on their exact duties and responsibilities. Once a Technical Designer advances to a senior Technical Designer or technical design manager role, however, he/she can make $100,000 a year or more.

Employment Prospects

Though they play an essential role in turning fashion designs into finished garments, Technical Designers have only fair employment prospects—despite the fact that companies sometimes have a difficult time finding skilled Technical Designers because their overall numbers are so small.

Most Technical Designers work full-time as employees for a specific fashion/apparel company. A few, however, become self-employed freelancers who are hired to oversee various technical design tasks for several or even many companies.

It's difficult to quantify just how many Technical Designers are working in the United States today. For the purposes of comparison, however, about 17,000 people worked as fashion designers in 2004, according to the U.S. Department of Labor.

Advancement Prospects

Once Technical Designers have accumulated several years of experience in the field, they can often advance to higher-level senior Technical Designer or technical design manager positions, either in their current companies or others. Some Technical Designers also move into the often more creative role of fashion designer, where they can come up with their own garment designs instead of executing the garment designs of others.

It's difficult to quantify growth prospects for Technical Designers. But for the purposes of comparison, employment of fashion designers is expected to grow more slowly than average between now and 2014, according to the U.S. Department of Labor.

Education and Training

At a minimum, Technical Designers generally need a two-year degree in pattern making or a closely related discipline. More often in today's global marketplace, however, Technical Designers need both the technical training and the soft skills (e.g., communication, teamwork) that come from a four-year degree, typically in fashion/apparel design, fashion/apparel technical design, or a closely related area.

Experience, Skills, and Personality Traits

Technical Designers need solid skills in key design-related tasks such as pattern making, grading, measuring and calculating (i.e., quantitative/numerical skills), and fitting, as well as thorough knowledge of garment design and construction techniques. Increasingly, they must also have exceptional computer skills, whether for tracking important data (e.g., Microsoft Excel, Microsoft Access) or sketching garments for production and/or recordkeeping purposes (e.g., Adobe Illustrator, Adobe Photoshop).

The most successful Technical Designers have essential soft skills and key personality traits to complement their sound technical knowledge. Among the most important soft skills and personality traits: written and verbal communication (so they can interact well with both on-site colleagues and, especially, off-site manufacturing personnel); solid organizational skills, attention to detail, thoroughness, and follow-through abilities; flexibility, adaptability, and multitasking skills; and outstanding teamwork skills.

Unions and Associations

While there are no specific unions or associations for the discipline, many Technical Designers keep current in the overall fashion industry by participating in organizations such as Fashion Group International (FGI) and the International Association of Clothing Designers and Executives (IACDE).

Tips for Entry

1. During college, gain some practical experience in technical design or a closely related discipline through an internship, a co-op program, or even volunteering.
2. Begin reading industry publications such as *Women's Wear Daily* and *DNR (Daily News Record),* along with consumer publications such as *Cosmopolitan* and *Vogue,* to learn about fashion trends and forecasts.
3. Do whatever you can to get to know some working Technical Designers in the industry. If possible, talk to some Technical Designers (i.e., informational interviewing) to learn more about what they do and how they got to where they are now. The more connections you can make with Technical Designers who are already in the field, the more potential opportunities you'll uncover for yourself.
4. Visit apparel company and job search Web sites to look for Technical Designer job listings. What key skills and abilities, experiences, education, and traits do companies seem to be looking for in the Technical Designers they want to hire?

RETAIL

BOUTIQUE OWNER

CAREER PROFILE

Duties: Owns and operates a small specialty store, which often features unique or hard-to-find fashions and accessories

Alternate Title(s): Store Owner, Owner

Salary Range: $0 to $100,000+

Employment Prospects: Limited

Advancement Prospects: Limited

Best Geographical Location(s): Large urban areas

Prerequisites:

Education or Training—A college degree is helpful, either in a business-related area (e.g., business administration, marketing, management) or a fashion-related area (e.g., fashion design, apparel merchandising)

Experience—Extensive and varied retail sales experience, in an apparel-related setting, is essential

Special Skills and Personality Traits—Entrepreneurial mind-set; business skills, including accounting, planning, marketing and advertising, market research, personnel management, and sales; extensive knowledge of trends and forecasts in apparel and accessories; ability to wear many "hats"; analytical skills; stamina and drive; self-motivation and discipline; detail and follow-through skills; creativity; willingness to take calculated risks; problem-solving skills; strong interpersonal skills and communication skills

CAREER LADDER

Boutique Owner

Mid- or High-Level Retail Manager

Buyer

Sales Associate

Position Description

People with extensive experience in retail apparel and accessories sometimes have the desire to call their own shots—to have their own store. One way for them to do that is to become Boutique Owners. Boutique Owners own and operate stores that often sell unique or hard-to-find merchandise. Their goal is to fill a specialized market niche and make money at the same time, all while creating an opportunity to make their own decisions about which products to sell, at what prices, where, and to whom.

The typical Boutique Owner is a jack of all trades. On the one hand, he or she is responsible for all of the business-related aspects of the store such as accounting and finances, employees, security, and cleanup. On the other hand, the Boutique Owner must oversee marketing and promotions, advertising, sales, merchandising, buying, visual displays, and the many other apparel-specific duties that go into operating a store that will be financially successful.

In many ways, the Boutique Owner's work begins even before the store exists. Starting any business often involves considerable financial investment, locating and securing a site, developing a sound business plan, and finding and ordering actual products to sell. Thus, the person who wants to become a Boutique Owner must first invest enormous time and energy in research. He or she needs to know which products are most likely to sell and at what price, and then determine how the store will provide those products and make prospective customers aware of them.

Boutique Owners can get or create stores in one of three ways. They might, for example, buy an existing store and then run it their own way in hopes that it will be more successful than in the past. Or, they might become a franchisee, owning and operating a "franchise" store that has similar outlets in many other locations. Or, they might simply start their own store from scratch, either on their own or with a group of partners or investors. Whatever the approach, the end goal is the same: develop a profitable operation and keep it profitable for many years to come.

Salaries

The profit Boutique Owners earn varies enormously. In most cases, Boutique Owners actually lose money in the first few years of operation, since they have to invest so much upfront to purchase merchandise, secure and pay for a store location, and advertise their products. Thus, the typical Boutique Owner has to have considerable money in the bank before starting his or her operation.

If all goes well in the first two or three years, Boutique Owners might start turning a small profit, which can then grow in the years that follow. Boutique Owners who succeed can thus sometimes earn six-figure salaries.

It's important to understand, however, that the majority of boutiques fail, often because of poor financial management, planning, or personnel management.

Employment Prospects

While, theoretically, anyone can become a Boutique Owner, only a few who try it succeed. So employment prospects for Boutique Owners are generally poor, though those who succeed can do quite well for themselves.

Advancement Prospects

The majority of boutiques fail, so in general advancement prospects for Boutique Owners are poor. However, those who do succeed can earn a considerable amount of money and open additional stores or start other businesses.

Education and Training

While it's not required, a college degree is a good idea for any prospective Boutique Owner. You can focus on a business-related major like business administration, management, or marketing, or on a fashion-related major like fashion design or apparel merchandising.

Experience, Skills, and Personality Traits

It's critical for Boutique Owners to have extensive and varied experience in retail apparel or accessory sales. Before starting their own businesses, almost all Boutique Owners first work in various positions for someone else's retail operation. The more knowledge a prospective Boutique Owner gains in someone else's company, the better the chance that person will succeed with his or her own store.

Boutique Owners need an enormous variety of business and apparel and accessories expertise and skills. On the business side, Boutique Owners need accounting, planning, marketing and advertising, market research, personnel management, and sales skills. On the apparel and accessories side, they must have extensive knowledge of trends and forecasts in the fashion industry.

In order to be successful, Boutique Owners must have analytical skills, stamina and drive, self-motivation and discipline, and detail and follow-through skills. They also need creativity and the willingness to take calculated risks. Problem-solving skills are critical, as are strong interpersonal skills and communication skills.

Unions and Associations

While there is no specific professional organization or labor union for Boutique Owners, the National Retail Federation (NRF) is an excellent resource for the retail industry.

Boutique Owners are also wise to participate in groups that will help them stay on top of industry trends and forecasts, like the International Textile and Apparel Association (ITAA) and the American Apparel and Footwear Association (AAFA). Many also take advantage of the resources and services of the U.S. Small Business Administration and related organizations for business owners.

Tips for Entry

1. Get as much retail apparel/accessory sales experience as you can, and try to gain knowledge of and experience in many different areas (e.g., merchandising, promotions, buying, sales, visual display).
2. Talk to one or more Boutique Owners to learn more about how they got to where they are now. Ask for their advice and suggestions on how you too can own your own store(s) someday.
3. Join apparel industry organizations and attend events, both to educate yourself about trends and forecasts

and to meet people who could potentially be helpful to you now or later on.

4. Read industry publications (in print and online) to stay on top of apparel and accessory developments, and to learn more about successful businesses of all sizes.
5. Research potential store locations and sites, as well as financing options, by working closely with a librarian or the U.S. Small Business Administration.
6. Set aside a substantial sum of money to help pay for the many startup costs that will emerge if and when you open your own store.

BUYER'S CLERICAL

CAREER PROFILE

Duties: Assists an apparel retailer's buyers, associate buyers, and/or assistant buyers with routine but important clerical and organizational tasks

Alternate Title(s): Buyer's Assistant, Assistant Buyer Trainee, Merchandise Clerical

Salary Range: $24,000 to $32,000+

Employment Prospects: Fair

Advancement Prospects: Good

Best Geographical Location(s): Large fashion centers across the United States where central buying offices are located, particularly New York City

Prerequisites:

Education or Training—A minimum of a two-year college degree is required, though a four-year degree is preferred, in an area like fashion buying, fashion merchandising, business administration, marketing, or the liberal arts; executive training programs are also available

Experience—Retail fashion sales experience and clerical administrative experience is very helpful

Special Skills and Personality Traits—Strong organizational skills; ability to work well with people of diverse backgrounds; ability to work well under pressure, prioritize, and meet deadlines; positive, outgoing personality; sound oral and written communication skills; mathematical abilities; typing and filing skills; accuracy and orderliness; patience and flexibility; willingness to learn from more experienced colleagues; computer skills; fashion knowledge and fashionable appearance; good follow-up skills

CAREER LADDER

Buyer

Assistant or Associate Buyer

Buyer's Clerical

Retail Sales Associate

Position Description

The Buyer's Clerical is typically the "right hand" of the assistant buyer, associate buyer, or buyer he or she works for, handling most or all of that person's routine but important clerical and organizational duties.

Most Buyer's Clericals are responsible for a huge variety of tasks, many of which their supervisors don't want to do or simply cannot do for lack of time. The Buyer's Clerical might arrange appointments for a buyer or associate buyer with one of the company's retail store managers, or they might type information into a computerized database so that their supervisors know the status of a certain shipment of clothes. Buyer's Clericals might respond to questions e-mailed by the buyer's contacts at apparel manufacturers, or they might arrange for the payment of an invoice that's been sent by one of those manufacturers.

Depending on their specific job descriptions and experiences, Buyer's Clericals may take on other tasks as well.

More experienced Buyer's Clericals, for example, might in some cases offer their opinions and suggestions on what types of merchandise the company ought to purchase for its retail stores. Other Buyer's Clericals might work closely with in-store stock clerks or heads of stock to track sales and inventories of certain items, or coordinate the transfer of merchandise from one store to another.

Most Buyer's Clericals work in large organizations, often "central buying offices" that purchase the merchandise for all of the retail stores in a chain. Some Buyer's Clericals, however, work for "resident buying offices," operations that consult with Buyers from many organizations to help them make sound purchasing decisions for their companies.

Salaries

Buyer's Clericals are entry-level employees and earn salaries on the low end of the range within the apparel industry in general and the buying sector in particular. Typically they start with salaries of around $24,000 a year, give or take a few thousand dollars. With experience, they can earn salaries in the low $30,000s before moving up to higher-level positions.

Employment Prospects

The number of job opportunities for Buyer's Clericals is somewhat limited, and competition for the available jobs is often keen. Employment prospects for potential Buyer's Clericals are therefore only fair. The best opportunities go to those who have experience in both retail sales and clerical/administrative positions, along with high degrees of both persistence and patience.

Advancement Prospects

Successful Buyer's Clericals have good opportunities to advance, particularly if they have a college degree and have participated in their companies' executive training programs.

Many Buyer's Clericals go on to become assistant buyers or associate buyers, and then on to full-fledged buyers. With even more experience, they can become senior buyers or head buyers for a store, a department within a store, or even an entire chain of stores.

Education and Training

In most cases, prospective Buyer's Clericals need at least a two-year degree, and preferably a four-year degree, in an area like fashion buying, fashion merchandising, business administration, marketing, or the liberal arts. Those whose degrees aren't fashion-specific benefit from at least having taken courses related to fashion merchandising and buying. Many Buyer's Clericals also participate in their companies' executive training programs, where they learn company buying operations from the ground up under the supervision of experienced buyers and other company leaders.

Experience, Skills, and Personality Traits

Many Buyer's Clericals begin their careers in fashion by working as retail sales associates, stock clerks, or cashiers, perhaps during college or even before. Those who want to become full-fledged buyers someday simply must understand customers and their buying habits, and working closely with consumers in a retail store setting is one of the best ways to gain that knowledge.

As their job title implies, Buyer's Clericals must have outstanding clerical skills, particularly with respect to organization. They must communicate well with a variety of other professionals inside and outside the company, whether via phone or fax or email. Often they are the "right hand" of their supervisors, so they must be detail-oriented and thorough, pleasant and approachable, and flexible.

In order to be successful, Buyer's Clericals also need to be good with numbers, able to work well with many different types of people, and able to prioritize, meet deadlines, and handle pressure. Perhaps most important of all, Buyer's Clericals must be willing to learn and have great patience; some of their tasks may seem boring and monotonous at times, but they're all important to the success of both their supervisor and the company.

Unions and Associations

While there are no unions or associations specifically for Buyer's Clericals in the apparel industry, smart Buyer's Clericals stay informed about the industry as a whole by participating in organizations like the American Apparel and Footwear Association (AAFA), Fashion Group International (FGI), and the International Textile and Apparel Association (ITAA).

Buyer's Clericals also benefit by monitoring the activities of general retail-oriented professional groups—for example, the National Retail Federation (NRF).

Tips for Entry

1. Get a job in retail fashion sales and hold on to it for several years. Pay close attention to how and why particular items sell, and ask your direct supervisor and the store's buyers to talk to you once in a while about how items are selected, ordered, received, and displayed for the best results.
2. Contact several Buyer's Clericals and ask them about how they got their jobs, and how you might get a similar job.
3. If you already have a college degree (or you're thinking about getting one), apply for executive training programs with various department or fashion stores or chains.
4. Read all you can about the fashion industry—designing, manufacturing, merchandising, distribution, marketing and sales, and advertising. Pick up copies of

consumer-oriented fashion magazines, and visit your library to see if it carries fashion trade publications like *Women's Wear Daily* or *DNR (Daily News Record).* Visit fashion-oriented Web sites as well.

5. If possible, work part- or full-time as an administrative assistant for an apparel-related company or another company. Use the job to polish your organizational, communication, and follow-up skills.

CASHIER

CAREER PROFILE

Duties: Checks out customers at a retail store by adding up their purchases on a cash register, taking their money, and bagging their merchandise

Alternate Title(s): Checkout Cashier

Salary Range: $2,000 to $20,000+

Employment Prospects: Excellent

Advancement Prospects: Excellent

Best Geographical Location(s): Large cities across the United States, though opportunities are available wherever retail stores exist

Prerequisites:

Education or Training—A high school diploma is helpful but not required; on-the-job training

Experience—No experience required, but previous cashiering or sales experience is helpful

Special Skills and Personality Traits—Trustworthiness and honesty; ability to work well with people from diverse backgrounds, particularly customers; patience and tact; efficiency and accuracy; ability to follow directions and store policies and procedures; ability to learn quickly; willingness and ability to be on one's feet or in one place for long periods of time; friendly, outgoing personality; basic computer skills; ability to deal with repetition; ability to deal with customer questions and complaints; ability and willingness to work evenings, weekends, and some holidays

CAREER LADDER

Department Manager

Sales Associate/Trainee

Head Cashier or Cashier Supervisor

Cashier

Position Description

Cashiers are among the employees at retail stores who interact with customers the most. When a customer is ready to check out, the Cashier scans each of the customer's items using an electronic scanner, which then automatically enters each item's price into a computerized cash register. The Cashier might also remove security-related items from certain pieces of merchandise so that the customer won't set off electronic alarms when leaving the store.

Once the Cashier has scanned all of the customer's items, he or she adds up the total cost of the items and then takes that amount of money from the customer, either in cash or check form or by scanning credit card information into the computerized cash register. Once the customer has successfully paid for his or her merchandise, the Cashier puts it all in bags or boxes so that the customer can leave the store.

Cashiers in the apparel or textile fields can work in one of several different settings. Many work in fashion-specific chain stores such as Abercrombie & Fitch, Men's Wearhouse, or Vanity. Some work for department stores such as Bloomingdale's, Macy's, or Kohl's. Others work for discount stores like Target, Wal-Mart, or K-mart. Still others work for newer factory outlet stores that manufacturers have established so that they can sell slightly (or not-so-slightly) damaged or "irregular" merchandise. Whatever the setting, the Cashier will always be working closely with customers, accommodating people's wants and needs.

Those customers often have needs beyond simply purchasing their merchandise, and Cashiers are expected to deal with them or at least guide them to others in the store who can. For example, customers will frequently ask Cashiers where merchandise is located in the store, or come to Cashiers with complaints or to return or exchange merchandise. It's critical for Cashiers to be able to handle these sometimes tense situations with tact and good humor, so that customers won't take their shopping elsewhere in the future.

In most cases, Cashiers are responsible for a certain drawer for several hours or an entire day. As such, they have to make sure that they collect the proper amount of money from each customer, and hand out the appropriate amount of change when necessary. At the end of a shift or day, managers check each Cashier's drawer to make sure that the money in the drawer matches the amount of merchandise sold that day. If it doesn't, the Cashier can get into trouble, particularly if the amount of money in the drawer is less than the amount of merchandise sold. In some cases, Cashiers lose their jobs for making this mistake too often.

About half of the Cashiers in the United States—in all types of stores across all industries—are part-timers who work fewer than 40 hours a week, according to the U.S. Department of Labor. Many Cashiers are young people who are in high school or college and are working to earn money for school or leisure activities. Increasingly, older people are taking cashiering jobs, to supplement their retirement income or to simply remain vital in their later years.

The Cashier's job can be repetitious, and most Cashiers are on their feet or sitting in one place for long periods of time. Most Cashiers must also work nonstandard, non–9-to-5 hours during evenings, weekends, and even some holidays. It can be easy for Cashiers, at times, to lose their patience with customers or with the job itself. It's important not to do so, however, since Cashiers are often the first people customers see when entering a store and the last people customers see when leaving. Thus, the impression a particular Cashier leaves on customers can be the difference between whether customers continue shopping in the store and, therefore, whether that store is financially successful or not.

Salaries

In general, salaries for Cashiers are relatively low. In 2004, the U.S. Department of Labor reports, the median hourly salary for Cashiers in all types of retail establishments (except gaming) was $7.81, which translates into an annual salary of about $16,240 based on a 40-hour workweek. Cashiers in department stores earned slightly more at $7.89 an hour, or about $16,410 a year based on a 40-hour workweek.

Some Cashiers start their jobs working for the federal minimum wage ($5.15 an hour as of 2006, which translates to an annual salary of about $10,700 based on a 40-hour workweek). However, the U.S. Department of Labor reports, other Cashiers—particularly those with previous experience—can earn up to $11.30 an hour, which translates into an annual salary of about $23,500 based on a 40-hour workweek.

Many full-time Cashiers are eligible for benefits such as health insurance as well, and some also receive discounts on merchandise they buy in their own stores. Other Cashiers, however, work only part time and may earn only a few thousand dollars a year, with no extra benefits like health insurance.

Employment Prospects

Because turnover among Cashiers is quite high and the number of retail establishments in the United States is also high, employment prospects for potential Cashiers are excellent. In 2004, about 3.5 million people worked as Cashiers in the United States, according to the U.S. Department of Labor. Applicants with some previous cashiering experience and flexibility in their schedules generally have the best opportunities.

Advancement Prospects

Cashiers in retail apparel or textile stores have excellent advancement potential. Some go on to become head cashiers or cashier supervisors, while many move into sales-oriented positions as sales associates or sales trainees. Eventually, Cashiers can move into even higher-level positions within their organizations, particularly if they pursue education beyond high school and gain experience in a variety of areas such as sales, merchandising, marketing, and promotions. They can become supervisors or go on to become an assistant manager or manager for their store or department.

Education and Training

Having a high school diploma is helpful to prospective Cashiers, but it's certainly not required. Many Cashiers, in fact, are high school students who haven't yet graduated, and who are working to save money for college or other pursuits. Cashiers are almost always trained on the job by more experienced Cashiers or cashier supervisors.

Experience, Skills, and Personality Traits

Previous sales or retail experience is helpful to prospective Cashiers. Since cashiering is almost always an entry-level job, applicants don't necessarily have to have previous experience of any kind.

Perhaps most important of all, Cashiers must be honest and trustworthy because they're the people who are on the front lines with customers, taking their money from purchases and making sure that money goes into the store's coffers. Similarly, Cashiers need to be accurate and follow store policies and procedures to the letter.

Cashiers need to be efficient as well, particularly during busy shopping periods when customer lines are long and customer patience is often short. Also, Cashiers must be outgoing, helpful, and tactful with customers so that those customers will get what they want and need and, thus, be less apt to take their shopping to other stores.

In order to be successful, Cashiers must be able to follow directions and work well under close supervision, deal with repetition and occasional monotony, and cope with being on their feet or in one place for long periods of time. They must also know about the merchandise in their stores and where that merchandise is located. Basic computer literacy is important as well, especially since most retail establishments today use electronic scanners and computerized cash registers to check customers out.

Unions and Associations

While there is no specific professional organization for Cashiers in retail apparel or textile establishments, the National Retail Federation (NRF) is an excellent resource for the retail industry in general.

Some Cashiers are members of the Retail, Wholesale, and Department Store Union (RWDSU), which represents workers in a wide variety of retail and related occupations.

Tips for Entry

1. Visit a nearby chain, discount, or department store or factory outlet store and ask how you can apply for a job as a Cashier. If possible, get a position that allows you to work for a store that sells apparel or fabric items and related accessories.
2. Talk to one or more Cashiers at nearby chain, discount, or department stores or factory outlet stores to see how they got their jobs and to learn how you can get a similar job.
3. Volunteer at a nonprofit organization to gain experience interacting with people from diverse backgrounds. People skills are essential to the success of any prospective Cashier.

DEPARTMENT MANAGER

CAREER PROFILE

Duties: Oversees the day-to-day operations for a department or group of departments in a retail store, focusing on sales, inventory, hiring, employee training, customer service, merchandising, and promotions

Alternate Title(s): Group Manager, Group Department Manager

Salary Range: $30,000 to $60,000+

Employment Prospects: Good

Advancement Prospects: Excellent

Best Geographical Location(s): Large urban areas across the United States

Prerequisites:

Education or Training—A bachelor's degree is generally required, in an area like business administration, management, or marketing; executive training programs are also common

Experience—Extensive experience in retail is required

Special Skills and Personality Traits—Thorough knowledge of retail store operations; ability to work well with diverse colleagues and customers; leadership skills; strong communication skills; supervisory skills; computer skills; accuracy and attention to detail; strong sense of fashion trends and forecasts; analytical skills; energy and an outgoing personality; self-motivation and initiative

CAREER LADDER

Assistant Store Manager or Group Manager

Department Manager

Assistant Department Manager

Sales Associate

Position Description

Department Managers, working under the supervision of the assistant store manager or store manager, are responsible for the day-to-day operations of a department or a group of departments in a retail store. Like their store management supervisors, Department Managers handle a wide variety of activities. They hire and train employees and schedule the days and times when those employees will be working. They open and close registers, make sure that the proper merchandise is on display and priced correctly, and answer questions from employees or customers. In essence, Department Managers are floor managers who are in the trenches with their sales associates each day, solving problems as they arise and ensuring that everything runs as smoothly as possible.

Department Managers often serve as liaisons to buyers because Department Managers have a good idea of what customers are buying or not buying and why. Some experts in the apparel retail field call Department Managers the eyes and ears of buyers because of the insight they can offer.

Department Managers are responsible for the sales success in their respective departments. They have to monitor product inventories, reorder merchandise when supplies run low, make recommendations about which products should be marked up or marked down, track down merchandise that is late in arriving, and oversee the design and implementation of visual displays. They also see that their employees are well trained and knowledgeable, so that they can answer customers' questions, deal with customers' complaints, and handle the many other problems that can develop during a typical day on the retail sales floor.

Indeed, people skills are perhaps the most important skills for any Department Manager. The typical Department Manager works closely with buyers, the store manager or the assistant store manager, assistant department managers, sales associates, customers, and vendors/suppliers, often all in one day. If those people fail to work well together, it may hurt the financial success of the Department Manager's area, and in extreme cases, lead to his/her termination.

Salaries

Retail managers across all fields earned a median salary of $32,720 in 2004, according to the U.S. Department of Labor. Department Managers in fashion/apparel retail settings, however, can often earn considerably more. Many Department Managers, particularly those who work in large, complex operations, can earn $50,000 to $60,000 a year.

Employment Prospects

While the number of job opportunities for Department Managers varies considerably with the state of the economy, prospective Department Managers have good employment prospects overall. The field is highly competitive, however, so the best opportunities will go to those who have extensive experience (particularly in fashion/apparel retail) and the willingness and ability to relocate. Retail managers across all fields held about 2.2 million jobs in the United States in 2004, according to the U.S. Department of Labor.

Advancement Prospects

Successful Department Managers have excellent opportunities for advancement. They may, for example, become assistant store managers and then store managers. Later on they might move into district manager or regional manager positions, in which they oversee the performance of many stores. With even more experience, Department Managers can advance to high-level leadership positions, many of them paying $100,000 a year or more.

Education and Training

Typically, Department Managers have at least a bachelor's degree, in an area like business administration, management, or marketing. Course work in fashion/apparel merchandising can also be helpful to prospective Department Managers. Most Department Managers participate in their organizations' executive training programs as well, so that they can gain experience in many retail areas like merchandising, marketing and promotions, sales, human resources, and public and community relations.

Experience, Skills, and Personality Traits

Since they play such an integral role in day-to-day activities, Department Managers must have a thorough knowledge of retail store operations. They must also be able to work well with many different types of people, including high-level managers, buyers, outside vendors/suppliers, sales associates, and store customers.

Department Managers need supervisory and leadership skills so that they can hire and train successful employees who will contribute positively to the bottom-line performance of the department. They also need strong communication skills, computer skills, and teaching and training skills. They must also be accurate and attentive to detail, and have a well developed sense of fashion trends and forecasts. Analytical skills are critical, particularly as they relate to putting out the right products on the selling floor, the right way, and at the right price.

Department Managers need considerable energy and an outgoing personality, along with self-motivation and initiative.

Unions and Associations

While there is no specific professional organization or labor union for Department Managers, the National Retail Federation (NRF) is an excellent resource for the retail industry in general. Many Department Managers also participate in professional organizations like the American Management Association (AMA), the Society for Human Resource Management (SHRM), and Sales and Marketing Executives International (SMEI), depending on their specific interests and responsibilities.

Tips for Entry

1. While in school, participate in a retail-focused internship or co-op program, preferably in the fashion/apparel industry.
2. Gain retail sales experience by taking a summer job or getting an entry-level position as a retail sales associate. It's important to understand how the retail industry works and how and why consumers decide to buy or not buy retail products.
3. Apply for a retailer's executive training program so that you can gain extensive experience in a wide variety of areas within fashion/apparel retail.
4. Identify and talk to some current Department Managers to determine how they got to where they are, and to find out how you can do the same.
5. Read fashion industry and consumer publications in print and online to learn about and stay on top of fashion trends and forecasts.
6. Read retail industry publications in print and online to better understand overall buying and selling trends and forecasts.

DISTRIBUTION PLANNER

CAREER PROFILE

Duties: Keeps track of a retail chain's merchandise; assures that the right apparel and accessory items get to the right retail store branches on time and in sufficient quantities

Alternate Title(s): Distributor, Planner, Distribution Engineer, Distribution Analyst, Allocations Planner/Analyst

Salary Range: $45,000 to $65,000+

Employment Prospects: Fair

Advancement Prospects: Good

Best Geographical Location(s): New York City and other major cities where large central buying offices or major retailers' headquarters are located

Prerequisites:

Education or Training—A bachelor's degree is generally required, in a field such as logistics, apparel merchandising, or business administration

Experience—At least five years of apparel-related experience is required, preferably in a distribution setting

Special Skills and Personality Traits—Strong research and analytical skills; computer skills; mathematical and problem-solving abilities; sound communication skills; budgeting skills; detail orientation; organization and orderliness; ability to meet deadlines; follow-through skills; self-motivation and initiative

CAREER LADDER

Distribution Manager or Director

Distribution Planner

Distribution Planner Trainee

Position Description

Large apparel retailers of all kinds can have dozens or even hundreds of different stores. It's the Distribution Planner's job to make sure that each store receives the proper amounts and types of garments and accessories to sell, on time and in good condition.

Distribution Planners typically work for large retailers or central buying operations. Often serving as liaisons among buyers, merchandise managers, and distribution centers, they keep track of their organizations' merchandise by using computerized databases. They then decide or help decide how that merchandise will be distributed among the individual stores in the chain.

To make these decisions, Distribution Planners study past sales records and other data on each store, then figure out which apparel styles, colors, and sizes should be shipped where and when and in what quantities. They also look at overall apparel and accessory industry trends, all the while keeping in mind their organizations' overall sales goals as well as the sales goals for each individual store.

Much of the Distribution Planner's work involves record-keeping and planning. The Distribution Planner must know how much of each item the company has and where the merchandise is located, typically in a distribution center. He or she must carefully plot how that merchandise is going to be divided up among the stores in the chain. Most often, different stores will receive slightly different merchandise in slightly different amounts. Each store's product "mix" will in many ways determine that store's financial success or failure, so the Distribution Planner's work is critical to the organization's bottom-line performance.

Salaries

Distribution Planners in the apparel industry can earn as little as $45,000 a year or as much as $65,000 a year, depending in great part on their experience and their performance. Those who advance into higher-level positions, such as distribution manager or distribution director, can earn even higher salaries.

Employment Prospects

While employment prospects for Distribution Planners in the fashion industry are relatively limited, there are so many fashion retailers and central buying offices that prospective Distribution Planners have at least a fair chance of finding a job in the field. The best opportunities go to candidates who already have apparel industry experience, especially if that experience relates to distribution and logistics or a similar area.

Advancement Prospects

Distribution Planners can advance to a variety of higher-level positions in their organizations, including the job of distribution director or distribution manager. Some Distribution Planners go on to work as buyers or head buyers, controllers, or high-level managers. Since Distribution Planners are so involved in the business-related operations of their companies, many of their skills, such as analysis, planning, budgeting, and research, transfer nicely into more advanced positions.

Education and Training

Most Distribution Planners have at least a bachelor's degree in a field like logistics, apparel merchandising, or business administration. Typically, prospective Distribution Planners also learn about the field by entering as distribution planner trainees and gaining relevant hands-on experience.

Experience, Skills, and Personality Traits

To be successful, Distribution Planners need to have sound knowledge of many aspects of the apparel industry, particularly sales, merchandising, logistics, and trend analysis. They must be highly organized and deadline-oriented, and capable of following through on plans and solving the inevitable problems that arise from the distribution process.

Distribution Planners must have strong mathematical, analytical, and research skills, as well as sound communication skills. Computer skills are critical as well, as Distribution Planners use complex computerized databases to guide their planning and decision-making activities.

Unions and Associations

Two main professional organizations serve Distribution Planners, in the apparel industry as well as other industries. The American Society of Transportation and Logistics (ASTL) offers information and guidance for individuals in the fields of traffic, transportation, logistics, and physical distribution management. The Council of Supply Chain Management Professionals (CSCMP), meanwhile, caters to professionals who work in logistics in any manner. Distribution Planners can also benefit by using the information and contacts they can find through the National Retail Federation (NRF).

Tips for Entry

1. While in school, participate in at least one logistics or distribution-related internship or co-op program, preferably within the apparel industry, so that you can gain hands-on experience and personal contacts in distribution planning.
2. Talk to one or more Distribution Planners in the apparel industry to get a better sense of the career itself as well as how you can pursue it someday.
3. Get a part-time or summer job in an apparel retailer's distribution center, so that you can learn firsthand about how the retail chain's merchandise is shipped to its various stores.
4. Look for an entry-level position as a distribution planner trainee so that you can learn about the career under the guidance of a more experienced Distribution Planner and/or distribution director/manager.

FABRIC STORE MANAGER

CAREER PROFILE

Duties: Oversees all aspects of a retail fabric store's operations, including sales, inventory, hiring and training of employees, customer service, promotions, merchandising, finances, and community relations and education

Alternate Title(s): None

Salary Range: $35,000 to $75,000+

Employment Prospects: Good

Advancement Prospects: Good

Best Geographical Location(s): Urban areas across the United States

Prerequisites:

Education or Training—A bachelor's degree is generally required, in an area like textile merchandising, textile management, business administration, management, or marketing; in-house training programs are also common

Experience—At least five years of varied experience in fabric retailing is required; sales experience is helpful

Special Skills and Personality Traits—Sound knowledge of retail fabric store operations; thorough knowledge of fabrics and their uses; sewing skills; ability to work well with diverse colleagues and customers; leadership skills; strong communication skills; sound budgeting and financial skills; supervisory skills; computer skills; willingness to relocate; attention to detail; energetic and outgoing personality; self-motivation and initiative; creativity; strong organizational skills; decisiveness; willingness to take calculated risks

CAREER LADDER

District Manager

Fabric Store Manager

Assistant Fabric Store Manager

Fabric Store Sales Associate or Trainee

Position Description

Fabric Store Managers oversee all the activities of a retail fabric store's operation. They're ultimately responsible for store sales, inventory, promotions, merchandising, and financial activities. They also manage their stores' customer service efforts and relationships with the surrounding community, and oversee the hiring and training of all store employees.

Fabric Store Managers may supervise a number of lower-level managers, who in turn supervise lower-level employees. The Fabric Store Manager, for example, might work closely with a human resources director to hire and train and sometimes fire employees. Similarly, the Fabric Store Manager may work with an assistant store manager to ensure that all areas of the store's sales operations are meeting their assigned responsibilities.

Most Fabric Store Managers must also take on some of the behind-the-scenes duties that are crucial to any retail store's success. For instance, the Fabric Store Manager hires store security personnel, either as employees or independent contractors, to prevent shoplifting and ensure customers' safety. The Fabric Store Manager also makes arrangements (with employees or outside contractors) to have the store thoroughly cleaned each night so that customers the next day will have a pleasant shopping experience and, hopefully, be more apt to buy.

Many Fabric Store Managers, particularly those who work for large chain operations, also oversee community education activities. Some fabric stores, for example, offer one-day or several-day short courses for customers, on everything from basic sewing to quilt-making. Sometimes these classes cover other craft-oriented activities as well. The Fabric Store Manager makes sure such classes are well attended and helpful, so that attendees will be more likely to become customers of the fabric store.

Since most fabric stores sell not only fabrics but other crafts as well, Fabric Store Managers must devote considerable time to learning about various crafts and deciding which types to stock. They must also be prepared to answer customers' questions about the different crafts available, and perhaps special order items for customers who want craft materials that aren't readily available in the store.

While in smaller stores, particularly non-chain stores, a Fabric Store Manager can be a one-person operation, in medium-sized and large stores the Fabric Store Manager supervises several other employees and must work with people of diverse backgrounds. It's not unusual for a Fabric Store Manager to deal with a high-level executive one minute and an irate store customer the next. The employees the Fabric Store Manager supervises usually have widely varying personal and career goals that must align with the store's mission and vision. The Fabric Store Manager must continuously assess whether employees' actions are contributing to or detracting from the store's overall objectives. The Fabric Store Manager is ultimately responsible if the employees aren't doing the things they need to do to make the store financially successful.

Most Fabric Store Managers work well over 40 hours a week. Weekend and holiday work is common for them, as is filling in when employees are sick or cannot make it to work for some other reason.

Salaries

Retail managers across all fields earned a median annual salary of $32,720 in 2004, according to the U.S. Department of Labor. Fabric Store Managers, however, can often earn considerably more, especially since many of them receive bonuses based on store performance. Most also receive commissions on sales (i.e., a percentage of each sale they make).

Some Fabric Store Managers, particularly those who work in large, complex operations and who have considerable experience in the field, earn $50,000 to $60,000 a year, and others can earn more than $75,000 a year. Beginning Fabric Store Managers, however, can expect to earn salaries in the $35,000 to $40,000 range.

Employment Prospects

While the number of job opportunities for Fabric Store Managers varies considerably with the state of the economy, prospective Fabric Store Managers have good employment prospects overall. The best opportunities will go to those who have extensive experience, particularly in fabric store retail or a similar field like apparel retail. Retail managers across all fields held 2.2 million jobs in the United States in 2004, according to the U.S. Department of Labor.

Advancement Prospects

Fabric Store Managers who oversee high-performing stores in a chain can become district managers or higher-level administrators who oversee the performance of many stores. They can also move into high-level executive positions. In any case, their salaries can increase substantially; earning more than $80,000 a year in one of these positions is common. It's important to keep in mind, however, that fewer of these positions are available, so competition for them is keen.

Education and Training

Many Fabric Store Managers have at least a bachelor's degree, in an area like textile merchandising, textile management, business administration, management, or marketing. Coursework in textile merchandising or apparel merchandising can also be helpful to prospective Fabric Store Managers, as can an advanced degree like a master of business administration (M.B.A.).

Most Fabric Store Managers participate in their organizations' in-house training programs as well, so that they can gain experience in many retail areas such as merchandising, marketing and promotions, sales, human resources, and public and community relations. Some prospective Fabric Store Managers use this experience exclusively, in lieu of a college degree, to become Fabric Store Managers, learning on the job instead of in a formal classroom.

Experience, Skills, and Personality Traits

Fabric Store Managers must be able to work well with many different types of people. They must also have supervisory, leadership, and delegation skills so that they can get the most out of their employees and make their stores financially successful.

Fabric Store Managers also need extensive knowledge of and experience in various retail operations areas, including sales, inventory, human resources, finance, public and community relations, marketing and promotions, and customer service. Additionally, of course, they need to have considerable expertise in fabrics, garment construction (especially for hand-sewn items), sewing, and, in many cases, other types of crafts.

Fabric Store Managers must have sound communication skills, budgeting and financial planning abilities, the willingness and ability to pay close attention to detail, and computer skills. They also need to be energetic and outgoing, self-motivated, friendly, creative, and decisive.

Fabric Store Managers for chain operations need to be flexible as well, particularly when their organizations ask them to relocate so that they can supervise underperforming stores. Similarly, Fabric Store Managers must be willing and able to put up with long hours and working nights, weekends, and holidays in some cases.

Unions and Associations

While there is no specific professional organization or labor union for Fabric Store Managers, the National Retail Federation (NRF) is an excellent resource for the retail industry in general.

Many Fabric Store Managers keep up with textile industry trends by joining groups like the International Textile and Apparel Association (ITAA). Others participate in professional organizations like the American Management Association (AMA), the Society for Human Resource Management (SHRM), and Sales and Marketing Executives International (SMEI), depending on their specific interests and responsibilities.

Tips for Entry

1. While in school, participate in at least one internship or co-op program, preferably in fabric retail.
2. Gain retail sales experience, preferably at a fabric store, by taking a summer job or getting an entry-level sales position. Learn how fabric retail works, and how and why consumers decide to buy or not buy certain fabrics and related products.
3. Identify and talk to some current Fabric Store Managers to determine how they got to where they are and to find out how you can do the same.
4. Read textile industry publications in print and online to stay on top of fabric trends. The more you know about what's going on in the textile world, the better you'll likely do as a Fabric Store Manager.
5. Learn how to sew your own garments so that you can better advise fabric store customers who are sewing garments of their own, and so that you can perhaps lead a fabric store's community education classes for customers.
6. Read apparel and retail industry publications in print and online to better understand overall buying and selling trends and forecasts.

FASHION BUYER

CAREER PROFILE

Duties: Selects and purchases apparel and accessories from manufacturers or wholesalers for retail resale to consumers; determines what consumers want and will buy and makes it available; watches finances, stays abreast of industry trends, and pays attention to competitors' offerings

Alternate Title(s): Buyer

Salary Range: $30,000 to $120,000+

Employment Prospects: Fair

Advancement Prospects: Good

Best Geographical Location(s): Large cities

Prerequisites:

Education or Training—A college degree is required

Experience—Retail sales experience is very helpful; some companies have an executive training program, composed of coursework and experiential activities with professional buyers who serve as teachers and mentors

Special Skills and Personality Traits—Love of fashion and ability to keep up with trends and forecasts in the industry; excellent mathematical, planning, and budgeting skills; decisiveness; ability to negotiate shrewdly (with manufacturers and wholesalers); willingness to work beyond the typical 9-to-5 schedule; openness to traveling

CAREER LADDER

Assistant or Associate Merchandising Manager

Fashion Buyer

Assistant/Associate Buyer

Executive Training Program Trainee

Position Description

No matter where you go to buy new clothes, you'll always find at least a little bit of selection, and often a great deal of selection. The person responsible for that selection of choices is the Fashion Buyer.

Fashion Buyers, often called buyers, shop for and buy clothes and accessories from manufacturers and wholesalers, in the hopes of reselling them to retail consumers at a profit. They can work for a department store, a retail chain, an independently owned store, or a wholesale distributor. The buyer's ultimate job is to predict what consumers will want and make sure it's available in sufficient quantities and at prices that will encourage buying.

Fashion Buyers are typically responsible for the profits of an entire store, a department within a store, or a chain of stores. Using their knowledge of industry trends and forecasts, their extensive research skills, and their instincts based on experience, they predict which fashions and accessories are likely to sell, often doing so a year or two years in advance. They then oversee the ordering, the receiving, and frequently the presentation of those fashions and accessories in stores.

The typical Fashion Buyer develops a plan that will be implemented months or even a year or two in the future. The plan must include what fashions will be purchased, in what quantities, and from whom. It must also outline the projected profits the buyer anticipates as a result of following the plan. This involves a certain amount of guesswork, but the more experienced a buyer becomes, the more educated his or her planning guesswork becomes.

To decide what to purchase for their organizations, buyers often travel to fashion showrooms and fashion industry shows in places like New York City. There, they get a sense of the apparel and accessories that manufacturers will be producing and selling in the coming year. Often, a buyer has to make his or her purchasing decision based only upon a black-and-white or color drawing of a particular item. Sometimes the buyer can look at small fabric samples or swatches to see what the item will be made of. Still, because the buyer often isn't able to see an actual sample of the item in question, he or she has to imagine how it will look, feel, and wear for the ultimate consumer.

When they're not shopping for clothing and accessories, buyers are often crunching numbers. They call upon their mathematical and budgeting skills almost daily as they track the sales of each item and determine which articles they need to order more of, and whether their plan is working or not working. As they track the performance of the current plan, they must simultaneously research and develop the plan for the following year. Buyers often find themselves thinking about the here and now one moment and about a year from now the next.

Since buyers are largely responsible for a department's or store's ultimate profit or loss, it's in their best interest to get the best prices possible when purchasing from manufacturers and wholesalers. Thus, buyers have to be exceptional negotiators who aren't afraid to push to get the prices they want for certain items. Sometimes that means taking calculated risks—for example, threatening to take the store's business elsewhere if it doesn't get the right price from a particular vendor.

It's also in the buyer's best interest to maintain close contact with his or her retail salespeople and, especially, the organization's customers. Most buyers spend a healthy chunk of their time and energy talking to their sales personnel and, sometimes, directly to customers as well. It's important for Fashion Buyers to be aware of how their customers make their purchasing decisions. A middle-income customer in Minnesota, for example, is likely to have very different spending habits than a high-income customer in California. Fashion Buyers need to know their customers well, and the only way to do so is to communicate with them (and their stores' salespeople) regularly.

Salaries

Assistant buyers in the fashion industry can earn salaries as low as $30,000 or as high as $50,000 a year. If and when they become associate buyers, they can expect to earn $60,000 a year or more. The salaries of full-fledged Fashion Buyers top $100,000 in some cases, though it's more common for buyers to earn $60,000 to $80,000 a year. Meanwhile, senior buyers, divisional merchandise managers, and general merchandise managers can easily make over $100,000 a year—and often substantially more than that if bonuses are included in the compensation.

Employment Prospects

Employment of buyers across all industries (including fashion and apparel) is expected to grow more slowly than average between now and 2014, according to the U.S. Department of Labor. However, plenty of employment opportunities are and will be available where Fashion Buyers are concerned, particularly in larger cities that have central buying offices for retail stores or chains. The best opportunities will go to those who are willing to start as retail salespeople or buyer's assistants/clericals and participate in corporate executive training programs leading to assistant buyer and, ultimately, buyer positions.

Advancement Prospects

Once someone has broken into the field at the trainee or assistant buyer level, he or she can advance within three to five years to the full-fledged buyer position. He or she can then move on to become the senior-level buyer for a store, a department within a store, or a chain; the purchasing manager or merchandising manager, who supervises and mentors a large group of subordinate buyers; the division merchandise manager (DMM), who oversees all buying and merchandising personnel, budgets, and purchasing selections for an entire company division; or the general merchandise manager (GMM), who heads an entire company's buying functions.

Education and Training

Those who want to pursue a career as a Fashion Buyer should earn a college degree in a business-oriented major like business administration, marketing, or management. Participation in a company's or chain's executive training program—which allows participants to learn how to become an assistant buyer over a period of months or several years—is also an excellent idea (if not required).

College or community education in some area of fashion, particularly fashion merchandising, is also quite helpful, as is immersion in fashion industry trends and forecasts through reading industry publications.

Experience, Skills, and Personality Traits

The most successful and respected Fashion Buyers began their careers by gaining experience on the retail sales side of the fashion business. There they learned what apparel customers like and don't like, what fashions and accessories sold best and worst, ways to best present and sell various fashions in the store, and the intricacies of the buying and selling process. All of this is critical to a Fashion Buyer's personal and professional success.

Being a Fashion Buyer demands an extremely diverse skill set. Fashion Buyers must be knowledgeable about the fashion industry as a whole and be able to predict what fashions will be hot a year or even two years ahead of time.

Every day they must tap their skills in research, analysis, financial and inventory planning, and inventory control to make buying decisions that will add profits to the company's bottom line.

Fashion Buyers must also be conscious of their various customers, consumers, vendors, and colleagues. They must be willing to listen to and provide what consumers want instead of what their own fashion tastes might dictate. They should be open to negotiating with wholesalers and manufacturers. They must talk frequently to their colleagues, especially in retail sales, to get their insights and suggestions on what items to buy and in what quantities.

Long hours, travel, stress, and deadlines are all part of the Fashion Buyer's daily worklife, so patience, the ability to deal with pressure and ambiguity, and strong organizational skills are also key to the Fashion Buyer's success. The Fashion Buyer must be able to deal with budget concerns one moment, plans for the upcoming year the next, and dwindling inventories for hot-selling items the next. If a Fashion Buyer cannot easily bounce back and forth between the big picture and the pesky details, he or she will burn out quickly.

Unions and Associations

Fashion Buyers involve themselves in any apparel- or textile-related organizations that allow them to keep abreast of industry trends and forecasts, including the American Apparel and Footwear Association (AAFA), Fashion Group International (FGI), and the International Textile and Apparel Association (ITAA). Many Fashion Buyers also participate in organizations geared toward their specific areas of interest—for example, the National Association of Men's Sportswear Buyers (NAMSB).

Fashion Buyers also benefit from monitoring the activities of general retail-oriented professional groups like the National Retail Federation (NRF) and the International Mass Retail Association (IMRA).

Tips for Entry

1. Get a job in retail fashion sales and hold on to it for several years. Pay close attention to how and why particular items sell, and ask your direct supervisor and the store's buyers to talk to you once in a while about how items are selected, ordered, received, and displayed for the best results.
2. Contact several Fashion Buyers in your city or area and ask them for 20 minutes of their time so that you might ask them about their careers. This informational interviewing approach can help you learn about fashion buying from people who are actually doing it. It might also lead to job or internship opportunities in the field.
3. If you have a college degree or you're thinking about getting one, look for executive training programs with various department or fashion stores or chains. Often, the programs will be highlighted on company Web sites (usually within a "Careers" or "Training Opportunities" section). By getting into an executive training program, you can learn the ropes of fashion buying from people who are already doing it. You can also put yourself in position to be groomed for an assistant buyer position and, eventually, a buyer position and even higher-level positions.
4. Read all you can about the fashion industry—designing, manufacturing, merchandising, distribution, marketing and sales, and advertising. Pick up copies of consumer-oriented fashion magazines, and visit your library to see if it carries fashion trade publications like *Women's Wear Daily* or *DNR (Daily News Record)*. Visit fashion-oriented Web sites as well. The more you can learn about all aspects of the fashion industry, the better prepared you'll be to start pursuing fashion buying as a career.
5. If possible, participate in an activity or organization that allows you to oversee a group of people and manage a budget. If you're a college student, for example, run for the leadership of a student organization. Fashion Buyers deal with both budget issues and people issues almost every working day. Whatever you can do to grow accustomed to dealing with financial issues and communications will only help you as you consider or pursue a career as a Fashion Buyer.

FASHION COORDINATOR

CAREER PROFILE

Duties: Coordinates the various departments, particularly the fashion buyers and salespeople, of a retail store or chain to ensure that all departments and stores offer consumers a consistent fashion look

Alternate Title(s): Fashion Director

Salary Range: $50,000 to $100,000+

Employment Prospects: Limited

Advancement Prospects: Limited

Best Geographical Location(s): Urban areas or wherever large retailers or centralized retail buying offices are located

Prerequisites:

Education or Training—A minimum of a bachelor's degree, preferably in a field such as fashion merchandising or fashion design, is required; on-the-job training through fashion retailing and merchandising jobs and, often, by first being an assistant fashion coordinator is helpful

Experience—Extensive experience in fashion in general, and fashion merchandising and sales in particular

Special Skills and Personality Traits—Ability to handle a diverse range of tasks and work with different types of people; knowledge of industry trends and forecasts; ability to guide buyers, advertising and promotions personnel, salespeople, marketing staff, and visual merchandising staff; excellent communication and organization skills; a strong interest in fashion design, colors, styles, and fabrics; a well-developed fashion sense; keen understanding of consumers; adaptability and resourcefulness; the ability to handle stress and pressure; strong time management skills; public speaking skills; ability to predict fashion and accessory trends before they begin to reveal themselves in the consumer marketplace.

CAREER LADDER

Fashion Coordinator

Assistant Fashion Coordinator

Fashion Buyer

Retail Sales Associate or Manager

Position Description

In any major department store, you'll find a variety of different fashion-related departments. Chances are, however, that the apparel and accessories in those various departments share a common look or feel with each changing fashion season. The Fashion Coordinator is the retail management professional who works to create that effect.

In many cases, Fashion Coordinators are concerned with ensuring that the various fashion departments within a store go together, even though those departments might be serving different subsets of the consumer population, such as women, men, children, or young adults. In other cases, Fashion Coordinators work with centralized buying offices to ensure a consistent look for a whole group of stores. In either case, the wide-ranging basics of the job are similar.

Fashion Coordinators work closely with other retail staff, particularly fashion buyers and retail salespeople. Using their knowledge of industry trends and forecasts, Fashion Coordinators educate the fashion buyers and retail salespeople on what's hot and what's expected to be hot six months or even a year down the road. With this knowledge, the various Fashion Buyers can make purchasing decisions for their stores that are consistent with both consumer expectations and the decisions of their fellow buyers. This ensures that all of the buyers are on the same page when it comes to the types of apparel and accessories they're procuring. Retail salespeople use the knowledge they gain from the Fashion Coordinator to better understand current and emerging trends in apparel silhouettes (i.e., outlines or forms), colors, fabrics, and styles so that they can more effectively assist their customers and, hopefully, sell them more items.

Fashion Coordinators devote a considerable part of their time to researching the apparel, accessory, and textile markets. They often must travel to industry trade shows, where they can both see new apparel items and confer with designers, manufacturers, industry media members, and others who can give them helpful trend and forecast information. Fashion Coordinators also work with fashion information services, independent companies that monitor trends and forecasts in colors, fabrics, and styles. Of course, Fashion Coordinators also must spend significant time monitoring industry publications in print or online.

Fashion Coordinators are typically closely involved in marketing, advertising, and promotional activities as well. They often help choose the garments and accessories that will appear in window and in-store displays, and they usually work closely with store advertising and public relations staff. Additionally, they might plan and implement fashion shows, either for the general public or, in the case of centralized buying operations, fashion buyers from member stores. They might speak at public events or offer educational seminars to consumers, with the goal of teaching people about the latest fashion styles and, hopefully, coaxing them into the stores to buy those styles.

The Fashion Coordinator's job is highly diverse and ever changing. His or her duties will probably vary significantly from company to company, but the overarching goal is generally the same: to make sure that the apparel and accessories a retail store or group of stores are selling harmonize with each other and consistently grab the consumer's attention.

Salaries

Since their work is so complex and diverse, Fashion Coordinators can sometimes make $100,000 a year or more. At lower levels or in smaller companies, though, Fashion Coordinators typically make $50,000 to $60,000 a year. Fashion Coordinators might also receive bonuses for consistently outstanding performance.

Employment Prospects

Competition for the small number of Fashion Coordinator jobs that exist is stiff, so employment prospects are limited, generally speaking. The person who lands this type of job will be someone who has the appropriate education and, probably more important, extensive experience and contacts in the fashion world.

Advancement Prospects

Since there aren't many Fashion Coordinator jobs in the first place, and since the job itself is a high-level position, advancement prospects for Fashion Coordinators are limited. Some may go on to take high-level executive positions in merchandising or sales, or advance by moving to larger or more prestigious companies.

Education and Training

The vast majority of Fashion Coordinators have at least a bachelor's degree, in a field like fashion merchandising, fashion marketing, or fashion design. Most have also received considerable on-the-job training by working in other fashion-related jobs, like fashion buying or fashion merchandising.

All Fashion Coordinators benefit from the training they receive through retail sales experience, which gives them a basic understanding of how apparel buying decisions are made, whether by corporate buyers or consumers.

Experience, Skills, and Personality Traits

Retail sales experience is essential for Fashion Coordinators, as is extensive experience in one or more related areas, such as fashion buying, fashion merchandising, or fashion marketing. Fashion Coordinators need a broad knowledge of the full spectrum of apparel development and merchandising functions, best gained through actual experience.

Fashion Coordinators must know the fashion industry inside and out. They need to consistently stay on top of apparel and accessory trends and forecasts by using their research skills. This can mean interviewing designers or manufacturers at industry trade shows, monitoring industry publications in print or online, or visiting with consumers right in their stores to get a sense of their likes and dislikes.

Fashion Coordinators must also have superior communication skills so that they can successfully work with a diverse range of people, including everyone from fashion buyers and fashion merchandisers to advertising and public relations staff and marketing or promotions personnel. They need to be well organized and able to manage their time, yet flexible and adaptable enough to deal with the inevitable changes each day in both their job tasks and the world of fashion in general.

The Fashion Coordinator's job is a stressful one that involves considerable responsibility for whether a retail store or chain does well. Long hours are common, as are making important decisions, supervising other staff, and dealing with volumes of information, particularly with the recent explosive growth of Internet Web sites and online communities. So Fashion Coordinators must be self-motivated and enthusiastic as well. If a Fashion Coordinator doesn't have a passion for fashion, he or she won't go far.

Unions and Associations

Fashion Coordinators generally participate in a wide variety of professional organizations because their job responsibilities are so diverse. Among the most popular associations for Fashion Coordinators are Fashion Group International (FGI), the American Apparel and Footwear Association (AAFA), the Clothing Manufacturers Association of the U.S.A. (CMAUSA), the Color Association of the United States (CAUS), and the International Textile and Apparel Association (ITAA).

Tips for Entry

1. Monitor apparel and accessory industry publications in print and online very closely. Fashion Coordinators need to have extensive and current knowledge about practically all aspects of the apparel industry. You can start developing that knowledge and expertise by reading about the field and monitoring trends and forecasts.
2. Get some retail sales experience. Fashion Coordinators are ultimately concerned with sales. Retail experience will help you get to know customers and their likes and dislikes in a hands-on way.
3. Get a bachelor's degree in fashion merchandising, fashion design, fashion marketing, or a related field. While you're in college, pursue internships or co-op programs that will give you experience in one or more of these areas.
4. Contact one or more Fashion Coordinators and talk to them in person or via e-mail or phone about the work they do. Ask them to advise you on how you might break into a Fashion Coordinator's job someday.
5. If possible, attend one or more industry trade shows or similar events where you might run into Fashion Coordinators and related professionals. If you do, ask about entry-level job or internship and co-op opportunities with their companies.
6. Pursue jobs in fashion buying or fashion merchandising to begin gaining the experience you'll need to become a Fashion Coordinator someday. While you're working in these jobs, try to develop a strong relationship with the Fashion Coordinators in your company. Express your interest in their work and ask them if they'll serve as mentors to you as you work toward your career goals.

LOSS PREVENTION MANAGER

CAREER PROFILE

Duties: Oversees theft/fraud prevention, detection, and enforcement for a retail apparel store or a group of retail apparel stores

Alternate Title(s): None

Salary Range: $30,000 to $120,000+

Employment Prospects: Good

Advancement Prospects: Good

Best Geographical Location(s): Large cities across the United States that are home to retail apparel stores or the headquarters of retail apparel stores.

Prerequisites:

Education or Training—A bachelor's degree is generally required, in a security- or law enforcement–oriented discipline such as criminal justice; often, specialized training in interviewing and interrogation techniques is required as well

Experience—Two to five years of experience are generally required for a mid-level position such as a Loss Prevention Manager; higher-level positions typically call for five to 10 years of experience

Special Skills and Personality Traits—Background in law enforcement or security; extensive knowledge of the law and the legal process, particularly regarding crimes like shoplifting and fraud; proven abilities in interviewing and interrogating people suspected of crimes; exceptional analytical and problem-solving skills; sound interpersonal and leadership abilities; good communication skills (written and verbal); well-developed computer skills, especially using spreadsheet and database software; experience with and knowledge of surveillance systems and techniques; ability to work independently and as a member or leader of a team; high ethical standards; ability to work well under pressure; solid time management and project management skills; training and advising capabilities

CAREER LADDER

Regional or District Loss Prevention Director

Loss Prevention Director

Loss Prevention Manager

Loss Prevention Agent or Security Officer/Specialist

Position Description

In 2004, American retailers lost some $31.3 billion to inventory shrinkage—a combination of employee theft, shoplifting by consumers, administrative errors, and vendor fraud—according to the University of Florida's "National Retail Security Survey." As a result, "An average family of four will spend more than $440 this year in higher prices because of inventory theft," noted survey director Richard

Hollinger. "Thieves also generally target hot-selling items, which means that those must-have toys on your child's holiday wish list are less likely to be available on the store shelves."

It is the Loss Prevention Manager's job to ensure that a retail apparel store (or a group of retail apparel stores) loses as little merchandise—and therefore money—as possible to theft and fraud.

Using their experience and skills in security and law enforcement strategies, Loss Prevention Managers develop comprehensive loss prevention strategies for the companies that employ them. Their duties break down into three main categories: 1) prevention—setting up policies, procedures, and tools with the goal of preventing theft and fraud in the first place; 2) detection—using surveillance systems and monitoring tactics to catch employees or consumers who are committing theft or fraud in a store or a group of stores; and 3) enforcement—apprehending, detaining, and interviewing/interrogating suspects; turning them over to law enforcement and prosecution authorities; and participating as a witness in court trials.

Depending on the work setting and the scope of their specific jobs, Loss Prevention Managers can be involved in any number of activities on a day-to-day basis. Among them: training staff members in loss prevention and detection techniques; developing and implementing loss prevention policies and procedures; advising executives on ways to handle loss prevention matters; creating solid working relationships with outside law enforcement and prosecution personnel; procuring and setting up surveillance equipment; writing and presenting loss prevention reports; and conducting field audits in various stores to identify and address potential loss prevention–related problems.

Interestingly, while shoplifting by consumers is the loss prevention–related crime that tends to get the most attention among members of the public and the media, Loss Prevention Managers know that they must keep an eye on their own company's employees as well. In the 2004 University of Florida study, shoplifting accounted for only about 32 percent of the $31.3 billion inventory shrinkage figure; employee theft accounted for nearly half (48.5 percent).

Salaries

The Loss Prevention Manager job is not an entry-level position, so salaries for Loss Prevention Managers are comparatively high. According to compensation Web site Salary.com, Loss Prevention Managers across the entire retail sector earned a median annual salary of $64,117 in 2006. Lower-level loss prevention representatives (e.g., loss prevention agents or security officers) earned significantly less—a median of $26,812, Salary.com notes—while higher-level professionals earned much more—a median of $120,889.

Employment Prospects

Given the number of retail establishments (apparel-related and other) in the United States, along with the scope of the inventory shrinkage problem, employment prospects for Loss Prevention Managers are quite good. The best opportunities will go to those who have extensive law enforcement and/or security experience in the apparel retailing industry, as well as demonstrated ability to reduce inventory shrinkage levels to acceptable levels.

Advancement Prospects

Loss Prevention Managers who prove themselves in overseeing one store or a small group of stores can frequently advance to become regional Loss Prevention Managers or district Loss Prevention Managers overseeing a larger "territory" of stores and their associated personnel. Later, they can be promoted into high-level executive positions. So advancement prospects for Loss Prevention Managers are good, despite the fact that most are already working in relatively high-level positions.

Education and Training

Most apparel retailers require their Loss Prevention Managers to have a bachelor's degree in a law enforcement or security-related discipline such as criminal justice (though in some cases, extensive experience in the field can partially or fully substitute for a four-year college degree). In many cases, Loss Prevention Managers must also complete specialized training in suspect interviewing and interrogation techniques. Typically, these courses are offered by private training companies staffed by industry experts.

Experience, Skills, and Personality Traits

Loss Prevention Managers generally need to have an educational and/or experiential background in law enforcement or security, along with a mastery of suspect interviewing and interrogation techniques. They must also have exceptional knowledge of various laws, the criminal justice system, and the legal process. Indeed, one slipup—for example, not following proper procedures—can potentially result in an apparel retailer not only losing a prosecution against someone it has accused of theft or fraud but also facing the possibility of a civil lawsuit by the "wrongly accused" suspect.

To be successful, Loss Prevention Managers need good analytical skills; sound interpersonal and leadership abilities; and strong communication skills (written and verbal) so they can train others in essential loss prevention strategies and explain loss prevention plans to executives who typically don't have law enforcement or security backgrounds. Loss Prevention Managers must also have well-developed computer skills, especially those necessary for using spreadsheet and database software; experience with and knowledge of surveillance systems and techniques; high ethical standards; solid time and project management abilities; and proven problem-solving capabilities.

Unions and Associations

The National Retail Federation (an umbrella group for the entire retail industry) has several advisory boards, councils, and committees devoted to loss prevention. The "Investigator's Network," for example, is made up of more than 500 loss prevention professionals from across the United States who can "network with each other on critical issues and cases," according to the NRF Web site.

Loss Prevention Managers who work for apparel retailers can also keep current on overall apparel industry trends by participating in organizations such as the American Apparel and Footwear Association (AAFA) and the International Textile and Apparel Association (ITAA).

Tips for Entry

1. Complete at least a bachelor's degree in criminal justice or a similar law enforcement or security-related discipline.
2. During college, gain some practical experience in loss prevention through an internship or a co-op assignment within an apparel retailer's loss prevention department/division.
3. Get a part-time job as a security officer, for an apparel retailer or another organization, to accumulate experience in the broad security field.
4. If possible, talk to some Loss Prevention Managers (i.e., informational interviewing) to learn more about what they do and how they got to where they are now.
5. Visit apparel retailer and job search Web sites to look for Loss Prevention Manager job listings. What key skills and abilities, experiences, education, and traits do companies seem to be looking for in the Loss Prevention Managers they want to hire?

MERCHANDISE MANAGER

CAREER PROFILE

Duties: Oversees the buying and distribution of apparel and accessories for a retail store, department, division, or chain

Alternate Title(s): None

Salary Range: $75,000 to $200,000+

Employment Prospects: Fair

Advancement Prospects: Fair

Best Geographical Location(s): Urban centers throughout the United States

Prerequisites:

Education or Training—A bachelor's degree in an area like fashion merchandising, retail merchandising, business, or marketing is required; a master of business administration (M.B.A.) is helpful

Experience—At least five to 10 years of experience in the retail apparel industry; fashion buying and fashion retailing experience is essential

Special Skills and Personality Traits—Problem-solving and interpersonal skills; ability to forecast apparel sales and profits; ability to effectively recruit, train, coach, and supervise employees; knowledge of the broad fashion marketplace, customers, competitors, and new and existing products; solid analytical skills; planning skills; top-notch research skills; expertise in the areas of pricing, planning, forecasting, product development, and sales

CAREER LADDER

General Merchandise Manager

Divisional Merchandise Manager

Merchandise Manager

Assistant or Associate Merchandise Manager

Position Description

Merchandise Managers supervise the buying and distribution of apparel and accessories for a retail store, department, division, or chain. In collaboration with fashion buyers, merchandisers, marketing and promotions professionals, and senior executives, they work toward maximizing sales of apparel and accessory items, and, thus, increasing profits and minimizing their companies' losses.

The Merchandise Manager's role is one of enormous responsibility. Merchandise Managers spend considerable time researching the apparel and accessory marketplace. More specifically, they have to study what their companies' competitors are doing, what their companies' customers and other companies' customers are buying and not buying and why, and what the overall trends and forecasts are in the apparel and accessory markets. As one apparel company job advertisement described, the Merchandise Manager needs an exceptionally accurate "fashion radar" that he or she uses in almost every part of the job.

A large part of the Merchandise Manager's job involves overseeing the efforts of fashion buyers, the people who select and purchase apparel and accessories from manufacturers or wholesalers. Many Merchandise Managers, in fact, are former fashion buyers themselves, and they must closely monitor the entire buying process and the fashion buyers responsible for it. Merchandise Managers serve, in many ways, as coaches or mentors to fashion buyers, establishing their budgets and advising them on purchases. They might also teach the fashion buyers about new and different sources of merchandise, analyze sales records with them, work with them to develop new store areas or departments within a store, and review their apparel and accessory selections.

Merchandise Managers have considerable responsibilities in the areas of product distribution and inventory. For example, if sales of a certain garment skyrocket, the Merchandise Manager must obtain more quantities of that particular garment for their company's stores. Conversely, if an item isn't selling well, the Merchandise Manager makes sure that fewer or no additional quantities of the garment show up in the company's stores. Different stores often have different rates of success with different items, so the Merchandise Manager determines how much of each product should be available for sale in each store or department. It is a continuous game of analysis and adjustments.

Most Merchandise Managers travel frequently to apparel showrooms and trade shows or to industry events where they can keep up-to-date with fashion and accessory trends and forecasts. This is a critical part of their job, since they're ultimately responsible for ensuring that profits are as high as possible. The Merchandise Manager must also be in constant communication with an assortment of other professionals within the company, such as merchandisers, marketing and advertising personnel, sales staff, manufacturing staff, and senior executives, all of whom need and can share insights and information that contribute to the company's success.

Salaries

Even the lowest-paid Merchandise Managers in the retail apparel industry earn $75,000 to $80,000 a year. Many Merchandise Managers, however, earn even more. A salary of $100,000 a year is not uncommon, and highly experienced Merchandise Managers with a solid track record sometimes make $200,000 a year at the highest levels—especially if they earn bonuses and other incentives based on performance.

Employment Prospects

Prospective Merchandise Managers who come through the ranks often start their careers as retail sales associates, eventually advancing to the level of fashion buyer or senior fashion buyer. Once there, they'll typically find a fair number of employment opportunities at the Merchandise Manager level and even higher levels, either within their own organizations or in other organizations.

As companies continue to merge with other companies and closures occur among department stores, retail chains, independently owned stores, and wholesale distributors, the number of jobs for prospective Merchandise Managers drops. Plenty of employment opportunities are still available, though, particularly in larger cities and in circumstances when the economy is thriving and retail sales in all sectors are strong.

Advancement Prospects

Merchandise Managers can advance to higher-level positions. For example, some go on to become Divisional Merchandise Managers (DMM), who oversee all of the buying and merchandising personnel, budgets, and purchasing selections for an entire company division. Later, they can advance to become General Merchandise Managers (GMM), the professionals who head buying and related functions for an entire organization.

Some Merchandise Managers advance even further to take senior-level executive positions in the merchandising area or a related area. Some seek advancement by moving to higher-level positions with other companies.

All along the advancement path, of course, salaries continue to increase. Divisional Merchandise Managers routinely make $120,000 or more a year, and salaries for General Merchandise Managers can go even higher.

Education and Training

Merchandise Managers almost always have at least a bachelor's degree, in an area like fashion merchandising, retail merchandising, business, or marketing. Many Merchandise Managers hold an advanced degree as well, for example, a master of business administration (M.B.A.).

Since many Merchandise Managers are former fashion buyers, they may also have participated in a company's executive training program to prepare first for entry-level buying positions and later for higher-level buying and related jobs.

Experience, Skills, and Personality Traits

Merchandise Managers need extensive industry knowledge and experience in order to do their jobs well. Most Merchandise Managers have at least five years of experience, and often they have 10 or more years of experience. Most often, they've developed expertise by working as Fashion Buyers and in various other retail sales-oriented positions.

To be successful, Merchandise Managers need a wide array of skills. Perhaps most important among them are people skills and the ability to collaborate with others toward the common goal of increasing sales and profits. Coaching, mentoring, training, and hiring skills are crucial as well, since the typical Merchandise Manager supervises at least a small group of fashion buyers who need guidance in their purchasing decisions.

Merchandise Managers need to be highly analytical. They must use their data-gathering and synthesizing abilities to clearly understand their competitors, their customers, and the apparel industry in general, particularly the retail sector but also the manufacturing sector. The Merchandise Manager is largely responsible for bottom-line profits. In that regard, knowledge is power; so the more the Merchandise Manager knows about apparel industry trends and forecasts, consumer buying tendencies, and competitor merchandising and product development plans, the greater the chance he or she will oversee a store, department, division, or chain that is highly profitable.

Merchandise Managers need well-developed skills in teaching, coaching, and leading others; communicating effectively with fellow professionals at all levels, including professionals outside the organization; researching and analyzing consumer preferences; planning, developing, and implementing merchandising strategies; and continuously following up on their efforts to determine what's working and what isn't. Merchandise Managers also need a bit of an independent or entrepreneurial streak; they must be willing to compete with both themselves and others to ensure that the organizations they oversee continuously improve.

Unions and Associations

While there are no unions or associations specifically for Merchandise Managers in the apparel industry, most Merchandise Managers stay informed about the industry as a whole by participating in organizations like the American Apparel and Footwear Association (AAFA), Fashion Group International (FGI), and the International Textile and Apparel Association (ITAA).

Some Merchandise Managers participate in general retail-oriented professional groups as well—for example, the National Retail Federation (NRF).

Tips for Entry

1. Get a job in retail fashion sales and hold on to it for several years. Pay close attention to how and why particular items sell, and ask your direct supervisor and the store's buyers to talk to you about how items are selected, ordered, received, and displayed for the best results. Knowing why some items sell and some don't will be critical to you later in your career when you attempt to move into a Merchandise Manager or higher position.
2. While you're in school, participate in internships or co-op programs to gain hands-on experience in the apparel field. In particular, look for internship or co-op opportunities in fashion buying, fashion merchandising, or sales.
3. If you have a college degree or you're thinking about getting one, look for executive training programs with various department or fashion stores or chains. Often, the programs will be highlighted on company Web sites (usually within a "Careers" or "Training Opportunities" section). By getting into an executive training program, you can learn the ropes of fashion, which will be essential to your future success as a Merchandise Manager who supervises fashion buyers.
4. Monitor industry publications in print and online so that you can learn as much as possible about the broad fashion industry, particularly the areas of design, manufacturing, merchandising, distribution, marketing and sales, and advertising. Pick up copies of consumer-oriented fashion magazines, and visit your library to see if it carries fashion trade publications like *Women's Wear Daily* or *DNR (Daily News Record)*. Visit fashion-oriented Web sites as well.
5. If possible, participate in an activity or organization that allows you to oversee a group of people and perhaps a budget as well. If you're a college student, for example, run for the leadership of a student organization. Merchandise Managers need wide-ranging skills in personnel supervision, budget management, and sales, all of which you can learn in a student leadership role.
6. Contact one or more Merchandise Managers and talk to them about how they advanced to their current positions. Seek their advice on how you might break into the fashion field and, more specifically, become a Merchandise Manager someday.

RETAIL SALES ASSOCIATE

CAREER PROFILE

Duties: Oversees retail apparel and accessory sales to consumers; shows customers merchandise; conducts purchases

Alternate Title(s): Retail Salesperson, Retail Sales Clerk

Salary Range: A few thousand dollars to $50,000+

Employment Prospects: Excellent

Advancement Prospects: Excellent

Best Geographical Location(s): Large, urban areas, though opportunities exist in all locations

Prerequisites:

Education or Training—A high school diploma or general educational development (GED) certificate is often required; on-the-job training is common

Experience—Any type of sales experience is helpful

Special Skills and Personality Traits—Willingness and ability to help people (i.e., customers) by suggesting apparel or accessories they might like; knowledge of fashion trends and forecasts; good sense of color and style; enthusiasm and self-motivation; outstanding listening, speaking, and presenting skills; courtesy and honesty

CAREER LADDER

Department Manager

Assistant Department Manager

Retail Sales Associate

Position Description

A fashion industry insider once called the fashion retail sector "the center of the retail universe." Perhaps it's no wonder, then, that many of the estimated 1.8 million Americans who work as Retail Sales Associates do so in apparel- and/or accessory-related settings. And the stores they work for rang up an estimated $525 billion in sales in 2005, according to the U.S. Census Bureau.

If the fashion retail sector is "the center of the retail universe," the Retail Sales Associate is certainly the first "planet" revolving around that center. Untold numbers of high-level fashion industry professionals got their start in the business as Retail Sales Associates. Because the retail store is the place where most customers do their apparel and accessory buying, it provides the ultimate test of whether a garment or an accessory is successful or not based on its sales.

Retail Sales Associates have three basic responsibilities. First, they must know the merchandise in their stores and be able to present that merchandise effectively to visiting customers. Next, they must assist customers in making their purchases by using a cash register, often equipped with an electronic scanner as well, to ring up the items customers want to buy. Finally, they must take payments from customers—cash, check, or credit card—and make sure those payments get into the cash register so that they can be included with the day's tally of purchases.

Retail Sales Associates must invest considerable time, especially in the beginning days and weeks of their jobs, getting to know the merchandise in their stores as well as the layout of those stores. When customers come in, Sales Associates need to be able to quickly and easily guide them to the merchandise they're interested in perusing. If questions arise, as they often do, Sales Associates need to be ready, with either direct answers or ways consumers can find answers on their own.

Retail Sales Associates might spend time interacting with customers, taking inventory, restocking shelves or racks, handling merchandise returns and exchanges, setting up attractive displays in the store or in-store windows, or even receiving merchandise orders from wholesalers and distributors. Sometimes Retail Sales Associates handle bigger responsibilities as well, such as adding up the store's or department's purchases at the end of the day and making sure the total matches the totals from cash, checks, and credit card receipts in the cash register.

Retail Sales Associates can work in a variety of settings. Many work in fashion-specific chain stores such as Abercrombie & Fitch, Men's Wearhouse, or Vanity. Some work for department stores such as Bloomingdale's, Macy's, or Kohl's. Others work for discount stores like Target, Wal-Mart, or K-mart. And still others work for factory outlet stores that manufacturers have established so that they can sell slightly (or not-so-slightly) damaged or "irregular" merchandise. Whatever the setting, the Retail Sales Associate will always be working closely with customers.

The Retail Sales Associate position is an excellent one for anyone who wants to test the waters of the retail world in general and fashion retailing in particular. It's also a flexible position that typically offers part- or full-time working hours. Employees may work during the morning, afternoon, or evening, or work additional hours to earn more money during special sales or around various holidays, particularly Christmas. In the case of high school and college students, it offers an opportunity to work during summer or semester breaks.

Salaries

Salaries for beginning Retail Sales Associates can be quite low, starting at the federal minimum wage ($5.15 an hour as of 2006). In many cases, however, Retail Sales Associates can earn much more, especially if the economy is robust and consumer spending is strong.

The median hourly salary for Retail Sales Associates in apparel and accessory stores was $8.44 in 2004, according to the U.S. Department of Labor. That works out to an annual salary of about $17,500 based on a 40-hour workweek. However, Retail Sales Associates who are effective sellers can earn more money when their sales commissions (a percentage of each sale they make) are taken into account. Indeed, top-performing Retail Sales Associates can earn $30,000 to $50,000 a year—and occasionally even more.

Often, Retail Sales Associates will receive additional compensation in the form of discounts (10 percent to 25 percent) on the clothing and accessories they buy from their own stores. Some retail companies offer partial or full tuition reimbursement for their full-time Retail Sales Associates who are attending college, a perk that could easily add up to several thousand dollars in extra salary.

Employment Prospects

It's relatively easy to get a job as a Retail Sales Associate, in part because it's an entry-level position and in part because there are so many positions available, especially when the economy is strong. The U.S. Department of Labor predicts that the number of retail sales jobs in all industries will grow about as fast as average between now and 2014, creating even more job opportunities.

Advancement Prospects

Retail Sales Associates can go on to do almost anything in the world of fashion. Indeed, many of today's top fashion designers and fashion industry leaders got their start by working as Retail Sales Associates, perhaps starting in college or even in high school. Sales associates who accumulate a year or more of experience can often move up into an assistant department manager role and, later, a department manager role. From there, they can pursue opportunities as store managers or area managers, or even move on to take jobs in fashion merchandising or fashion marketing/promotion. Retail sales, as an occupation, ultimately connects to every other part of the fashion industry—in an indisputably important way—through its direct link to the consumer.

Education and Training

Typically, Retail Sales Associates need at least a high school diploma or general educational development (GED) certificate. Most training for the position itself, however, happens on the job, under the direction of a more experienced Retail Sales Associate or a department or store manager.

Experience, Skills, and Personality Traits

While previous experience isn't a necessity for this entry-level job, it's always helpful if prospective Retail Sales Associates have at least some sales-related experience, even if it's only from selling Girl Scout cookies or candy bars for the school fundraiser. Previous jobs or leisure activities that have involved interacting with diverse people are also an asset.

To do their jobs well, Retail Sales Associates must be people-oriented first and foremost. They have to genuinely like interacting with people and helping them make purchasing decisions. Good listening skills are critical, as are strong speaking and presentation skills, the willingness and ability to answer customers' questions, and a gift or knack for being informative and persuasive without being pushy.

Retail Sales Associates must have basic computer skills as well. They're benefiting from speaking and understanding a language besides English, particularly Spanish, as America becomes more racially and ethnically diverse.

The successful Retail Sales Associate is organized and reliable, outgoing and courteous, and knowledgeable about the merchandise in his or her store as well as apparel and accessories in general, particularly when it comes to fashion trends. He or she is also detail-oriented and accurate, honest and dependable, and skilled in problem solving. Perhaps most important of all, the successful Retail Associate is able to think like customers think and carry himself or herself accordingly.

Unions and Associations

While there is no specific professional organization or labor union for Retail Sales Associates, the National Retail Federation (NRF) is an excellent resource for the retail industry in general. On its Web site at www.nrf.com, it offers an extensive "Retail Careers & Advancement" section for anyone interested in learning more about the field.

Tips for Entry

1. Visit retail stores in your area and ask for a job application at each one. See what types of Retail Sales Associate and related jobs are available, and how you can learn more about them.
2. If you're a high school or college student, take some courses in marketing, fashion merchandising, mathematics, business, and computer applications so that you can pick up some basic knowledge and skills you can use in a Retail Sales Associate's role.
3. Watch your local newspaper classifieds, Internet job sites, and specific retailers' Web sites for Retail Sales Associate job listings.
4. Go into a retail store when it doesn't appear to be too busy and ask one of the Retail Sales Associates about the job. You might even want to spend some time "shadowing" the person as he or she assists customers and goes about other job-related tasks.
5. Read fashion industry and consumer publications in print and online to learn about and stay on top of fashion trends. The more you know about what's going on in the fashion world, the better you'll likely do as a Retail Sales Associate.

STOCK CLERK

CAREER PROFILE

Duties: Unpacks a retail store's apparel items and accessories from boxes; sorts and inspects them, marks them for sale, and places them on shelves and/or racks

Alternate Title(s): Stocking Clerk, Stock Associate, Stocker, Inventory Clerk, Stockperson, Merchandise Clerical

Salary Range: A few thousand dollars to $25,000+

Employment Prospects: Fair

Advancement Prospects: Good

Best Geographical Location(s): Large cities across the United States, though opportunities are available wherever retail stores exist

Prerequisites:

Education or Training—A high school diploma or general educational development (GED) certificate is helpful but not required; on-the-job-training is common

Experience—Previous stocking or inventory experience is helpful

Special Skills and Personality Traits—Strong organizational and record-keeping skills; attentiveness to detail; efficiency and accuracy; ability to follow directions and store policies and procedures; ability to learn quickly; mathematical abilities; physical strength; typing and filing skills; dependability and trustworthiness; basic computer skills; ability to deal with repetition

CAREER LADDER

Buyer

Assistant Buyer

Head of Stock

Stock Clerk

Position Description

The apparel items and accessories you see on store shelves everywhere don't get there by magic. Instead, they were most likely received from shippers, sorted, inspected, marked with price tags, and put out for display by one or more Stock Clerks.

Stock Clerks are retail employees who make sure that a store's merchandise gets onto the shelves or racks. Stock Clerks first receive the merchandise that has been shipped and begin sorting it. They have to ensure that the store has received the right items, in the right quantities, and in the right styles and colors. Stock Clerks have to inspect the merchandise to make sure it isn't damaged or dirty. Next, Stock Clerks mark the merchandise with price tags containing electronic scanning information, which is then used by the store's cashiers to ring up consumers' purchases. Finally, Stock Clerks put the merchandise out in the store on shelves and racks so that customers can look at it, inspect it, and decide if they want to buy it.

Throughout this process, Stock Clerks have to keep a number of detailed records. For starters, they have to document, for each shipment of goods, that the appropriate quantities of items have been received; determine how many are damaged or dirty; and perhaps arrange to have damaged merchandise replaced. Then, when items are placed on shelves or racks for sale, Stock Clerks document how many items have left the stockroom, and when, so that the store knows exactly how much merchandise is left to be sold and how much is immediately available for customers to purchase.

In previous years, Stock Clerks did much of their record-keeping using pencil and paper. Today, however, almost all of their records are computerized. In either case, Stock Clerks must be highly accurate and detail-oriented, since mistakes can be costly to the store.

Periodically throughout the year, Stock Clerks will generally participate in inventorying activities, during which the store determines how much of each item it has sold and how much is still on hand and available for sale to the public. Throughout the year, meanwhile, Stock Clerks are also responsible for keeping merchandise from getting dirty, damaged, or even stolen.

Stock Clerks in the retail apparel and accessories sector can work in a variety of settings. Many work in fashion-specific chain stores such as Abercrombie & Fitch, Men's Wearhouse, or Vanity. Some work for department stores such as Bloomingdale's, Macy's, or Kohl's. Others work for discount stores such as Target, Wal-Mart, or K-mart. And still others work for factory outlet stores that manufacturers have established so that they can sell slightly (or not-so-slightly) damaged or "irregular" merchandise.

Salaries

In general, salaries for Stock Clerks are relatively low. In 2004, the median annual salary for Stock Clerks across all industries was $20,100, according to the U.S. Department of Labor. The median hourly salary for Stock Clerks in apparel and accessory stores was $8.70 in 2004, which translates into an annual salary of about $18,100 based on a 40-hour workweek. Some Stock Clerks start their jobs working for the federal minimum wage of $5.15 an hour (as of 2006), which translates into an annual salary of about $10,700 based on a 40-hour workweek.

Most full-time Stock Clerks are eligible for various benefits like health insurance, and many also receive discounts on merchandise they buy in their own stores. Other Stock Clerks, however, work only part-time and may earn only a few thousand dollars a year, with no extra benefits like health insurance.

Employment Prospects

The U.S. Department of Labor (DOL) predicts that employment of Stock Clerks across all industries will decline between now and 2014, largely as a result of automation and computerization. However, the DOL notes that because the occupation is large and many jobs are entry level, many job openings will occur each year to replace those who transfer to other jobs or leave the labor force.

In 2004, about 429,000 people worked as Stock Clerks in the United States, the DOL says.

Advancement Prospects

Stock Clerks in retail apparel stores have good advancement potential. Some go on to become head of stock, while others advance to become assistant buyers and, eventually, head buyers. Eventually, Stock Clerks can sometimes move into higher-level positions within their organizations, particularly if they pursue education beyond high school and gain experience in a variety of areas like sales, merchandising, marketing, and promotions.

Education and Training

Having a high school diploma or general educational development (GED) certificate is helpful for anyone who wants to become a Stock Clerk, but it's certainly not required. Some Stock Clerks, in fact, are high school students who haven't graduated yet and who are working to save money for college or other pursuits. Stock Clerks are almost always trained on the job by more experienced Stock Clerks or the head of stock.

Experience, Skills, and Personality Traits

While prospective Stock Clerks don't necessarily need previous experience, it can certainly help, particularly if that experience relates to stocking or inventorying activities.

To be successful, Stock Clerks must have strong organizational and record-keeping skills. They have to be efficient and accurate, attentive to detail, and able to deal with unforeseen problems quickly and thoroughly.

Stock Clerks must be able to follow directions and abide by store policies and procedures, particularly when it comes to inspecting and inventorying merchandise. Stock Clerks also need the ability to learn quickly, along with strong mathematical skills, some physical strength (e.g., the ability to lift heavy boxes), typing and filing skills, basic computer skills, and the willingness and ability to deal with repetition.

Perhaps most important of all, Stock Clerks must be dependable, helpful, and knowledgeable so that they effectively contribute to the financial success of their stores.

Unions and Associations

While there is no specific professional organization for Stock Clerks in retail apparel or textile establishments, the National Retail Federation (NRF) is an excellent resource for the retail industry in general. Some Stock Clerks are members of the Retail, Wholesale, and Department Store Union (RWDSU), which represents workers in a wide variety of retail and related occupations.

Tips for Entry

1. Visit a nearby chain, discount or department store or factory outlet store and ask how you can apply for a job as a Stock Clerk. If possible, get a position that allows you to work for a store that sells apparel or fabric items and related accessories.
2. Talk to one or more Stock Clerks at nearby chain, discount, or department stores or factory outlet stores to see how they got their jobs, and to learn how you can get a similar job.
3. Ask if you can "shadow" a working Stock Clerk for a day or two to learn more about his or her job and whether it might be a good fit for you.

STORE MANAGER

CAREER PROFILE

Duties: Oversees all aspects of a retail store's operations, including sales, inventory, hiring and training of employees, customer service, promotions, merchandising, finances, and community relations

Alternate Title(s): None

Salary Range: $30,000 to $100,000+

Employment Prospects: Good

Advancement Prospects: Good

Best Geographical Location(s): Large urban areas all across the United States, though opportunities exist everywhere

Prerequisites:

Education or Training—A bachelor's degree is generally required, in an area like business administration, management, or marketing; executive training programs are common

Experience—Extensive experience in retail is required

Special Skills and Personality Traits—Thorough knowledge of retail store operations; ability to work well with diverse colleagues and customers; leadership skills; strong communication skills; sound budgeting and financial skills; supervisory skills; computer skills; willingness to relocate to stores in other locations; attention to detail; strong sense of fashion; energy and an outgoing personality; self-motivation and initiative

CAREER LADDER

Store Manager

Assistant/Associate Store Manager

Department Manager

Retail Sales Associate

Position Description

Store Managers are high-level administrators who oversee all of the various activities that make up a retail store's operation. They're ultimately responsible for sales, inventory, promotions and merchandising, and financial activities. They also manage their stores' customer service efforts and relationships with the surrounding community, plus oversee the hiring and training of all store employees.

Of course, Store Managers cannot do all of these activities by themselves. Instead, they supervise a number of lower-level managers, who in turn supervise lower-level employees. The Store Manager might work closely with a human resources director to hire and train and sometimes fire employees. Similarly, the Store Manager will work with an assistant Store Manager and department managers to ensure that all areas of the store's sales operations are meeting their assigned responsibilities.

Store Managers must also take on some of the behind-the-scenes activities that are crucial to a retail store's success. In most cases, for instance, the Store Manager is the person who hires store security personnel, either as employees or independent contractors, to prevent shoplifting and to ensure customers' safety. The Store Manager also makes arrangements—with employees or outside contractors—to have the store thoroughly cleaned each night so that the next day's customers will have a pleasant shopping experience and, hopefully, be more apt to buy.

One of the typical Store Manager's daily tasks is problem solving, sometimes referred to as "putting out fires." If a shipment of new jeans fails to arrive, for example, the Store Manager must figure out why the jeans haven't shown up and how to get the jeans to the store quickly. On a broader level, if a store is losing too much merchandise and, thus, money to shoplifting, the Store Manager is ultimately responsible for developing and implementing new procedures, policies, or tools to reduce or eliminate the problem.

It is necessary for Store Managers to work with people of diverse backgrounds who do diverse tasks. It's not unusual for a Store Manager to deal with a high-level retail executive one minute and an irate store customer the next. All the while, the employees the Store Manager supervises, whether directly or indirectly, usually have widely varying personal and career goals that must align (to some degree at least) with the store's mission and vision. The Store Manager has to continuously assess whether employees' actions are contributing to or detracting from the store's overall objectives.

While in smaller operations the Store Manager can literally be a one-person show, in medium- and large-sized stores the Store Manager supervises dozens of employees. No matter what area those employees focus on, the Store Manager will be held accountable by high-level executives if the employees aren't doing the things they need to do to make the store financially successful, so pressure and stress are part of the job for all Store Managers. With their many responsibilities come many worries, but also, potentially, many rewards.

Salaries

Retail managers across all fields earned a median annual salary of $32,720 in 2004, according to the U.S. Department of Labor. Store Managers in the retail apparel and accessories sector, however, often earn considerably more, especially since many of them are eligible to receive bonuses based on individual and/or store performance. Many Store Managers, particularly those who work in large, complex operations, earn $60,000 to $70,000 a year, and some even earn more than $100,000 a year.

Employment Prospects

While the number of job opportunities for Store Managers varies considerably with the state of the economy, prospective Store Managers have good employment prospects overall. The field is highly competitive, however, so the best opportunities will go to those who have extensive and varied experience, particularly in fashion and apparel retail.

Retail managers across all fields held about 2.2 million jobs in 2004, according to the U.S. Department of Labor. The DOL predicts that employment of retail managers will grow (although more slowly than average) between now and 2014.

Advancement Prospects

Store Managers who oversee high-performing stores can become district managers or regional managers who oversee the performance of many stores. They can also move into high-level management positions. In any case, their salaries can increase substantially; earning more than $100,000 a year in one of these positions is quite common.

Education and Training

Almost all Store Managers have at least a bachelor's degree, in an area like business administration, management, or marketing. Course work in fashion/apparel merchandising can also be helpful to prospective Store Managers, as can an advanced degree like a master of business administration (M.B.A.).

Most Store Managers participate in their organizations' executive training programs as well, so that they gain experience in many retail areas, such as merchandising, marketing and promotions, sales, human resources, and public and community relations.

Experience, Skills, and Personality Traits

Store Managers must be able to work well with many different types of people. They must also have supervisory and leadership skills so that they can get the most out of their employees and make their stores financially successful.

Store Managers also need extensive knowledge of and experience in various retail operations areas, including sales, inventory, human resources, finance, public and community relations, marketing and promotions, and customer service.

The best Store Managers have sound communication skills, budgeting and financial planning abilities, the willingness and skills to pay close attention to detail, and computer skills. They're also energetic and outgoing, fashionable and well groomed, and self-motivated.

Store Managers need to be flexible as well, particularly when their organizations ask them to relocate so that they can supervise underperforming stores. Similarly, Store Managers must be willing and able to put up with long hours and working nights, weekends, and holidays in some cases.

Unions and Associations

While there is no specific professional organization or labor union for Store Managers, the National Retail Federation (NRF) is an excellent resource for the retail industry in general.

Many Store Managers also participate in professional organizations like the American Management Association (AMA), the Society for Human Resource Management (SHRM), and Sales and Marketing Executives International (SMEI), depending on their specific interests and responsibilities.

Tips for Entry

1. While in school, participate in at least one retail-focused internship or co-op program, preferably in the fashion/apparel industry.
2. Gain retail sales experience by taking a summer job or getting an entry-level position as a retail sales associate. It's important to understand both how the retail industry

works and how and why consumers decide to buy or not buy retail products.

3. Apply for a retailer's executive training program so that you can gain extensive experience in a wide variety of areas within fashion/apparel retail.
4. Identify and talk to some current Store Managers to determine how they got to where they are and to find out how you can do the same.
5. Read fashion industry and consumer publications in print and online to learn about and stay on top of fashion trends. The more you know about what's going on in the fashion world, the better you'll likely do as a Store Manager.
6. Read retail industry publications in print and online to better understand overall buying and selling trends and forecasts.

VISUAL MERCHANDISER

CAREER PROFILE

Duties: Oversees the conceptualization, design, and execution of visual displays of apparel in stores, at trade shows, and in fashion showrooms

Alternate Title(s): Visual Display Artist/Coordinator/Director/Supervisor, Merchandise Displayer, Merchandise Display Artist/Coordinator/Director/Supervisor, Window Display Designer/Artist/Coordinator/Director/Supervisor

Salary Range: $15,000 to $60,000+

Employment Prospects: Fair/Good

Advancement Prospects: Good

Best Geographical Location(s): Opportunities exist everywhere, but particularly in fashion centers like New York City

Prerequisites:

Education or Training—A bachelor's degree is generally helpful, in a field that combines creativity and technical abilities, such as applied design, fashion merchandising, interior design, or architecture; some Visual Merchandisers major in psychology (with an emphasis in consumer psychology), marketing, or graphic design

Experience—Gaining experience through a part-time job or an internship is essential to breaking into the field

Special Skills and Personality Traits—Artistic and creative abilities combined with technical skills; solid organizational skills; ability to collaborate with other people; capability of not only conceptualizing visual displays but also creating them with hands-on construction and carpentry work

CAREER LADDER

Visual Merchandise Supervisor or Director

Visual Merchandise Coordinator

Visual Merchandiser or Visual Merchandise Artist

Visual Merchandise Assistant

Position Description

Whenever you stop to admire the clothes in a store window or on the mannequins that make up an eye-catching in-store display, you're likely seeing the finished work of the Visual Merchandiser. Visual Merchandisers combine their creativity and artistic abilities with their design and technical skills to conceptualize, design, and execute store window displays and in-store displays wherever fashion is sold. Often, they're also involved in planning and designing the layout of a particular store department, or even of the store itself, so that customers can easily make their way around the store and will be more likely to notice and, hopefully, buy the clothing and accessories on display. In some cases, Visual Merchandisers are also involved with designing displays and exhibits for fashion manufacturers' showrooms or fashion trade shows, where the ultimate customer isn't the average, everyday consumer but rather the professional fashion buyer, who represents a particular store or chain of stores.

Visual Merchandisers are designers first and foremost and often collaborate with other fashion professionals, including buyers, managers, and salespeople. They spend much of their time and effort developing display concepts that will grab the attention of consumers or buyers. Their goal, in many cases, is to create an image for the store or the manufacturer and then maintain that image in the minds of consumers. How they decide to display the store's or manufacturer's fashion items can make a considerable difference in whether that image will be established and maintained and, as a result, whether sales will increase and the organization's bottom line will improve.

When developing displays, Visual Merchandisers tap into their knowledge of color, lighting, theatrical staging, and forms and lines. They also draw from the expertise they've gained by keeping up with fashion industry trends in general and visual display trends in particular, typically by reading industry publications, attending industry conferences and seminars, and talking to colleagues in the field. While the art of developing exciting displays attracts almost every Visual Merchandiser, all professionals in the field must constantly keep in mind their real reason for existing: to increase revenue. Thus, the conflict between artistic expression and maximizing sales can be troublesome at times for some Visual Merchandisers.

Visual Merchandisers must also have technical interests, skills, and aptitudes, so that they can actually carry out the visual presentation plans they develop. They often need to construct and perhaps paint props, install lights and other presentation equipment, and fix items that may need minor repairs. Sometimes they must even bring in additional tools, such as mirrors, to create the unique visual effects they have in their mind's eye.

When they're not conceptualizing or building displays or floor plans, Visual Merchandisers are usually selecting and ordering props and mannequins, creating signage for displays or entire departments or stores, meeting with colleagues to discuss future ideas or review the strengths and weaknesses of previous displays, and, in the case of supervisory personnel, training subordinates. Whatever the particular task, the goal of the Visual Merchandiser is, ultimately, always the same: to help his or her organization make money from the purchases of consumers or professional buyers. As one experienced professional put it, the Visual Merchandiser is "the silent salesperson" whose behind-the-scenes efforts turn into front-and-center displays that build the organization's image and positively influence customers' buying habits.

Salaries

Salaries among Visual Merchandisers vary widely, but generally an entry-level visual merchandising assistant can expect to earn a salary in the low to mid-$20,000s, especially if he or she is employed by a smaller store or a chain. (Note: That salary figure may be lower if the visual merchandising assistant is working only part time.) With a few years of experience, however, a Visual Merchandiser can earn a salary in the $30,000 to $40,000 range, while senior-level Visual Merchandisers in supervisory roles can earn $60,000 a year or more—especially if they garner a solid reputation in the field.

Employment Prospects

While the number of Visual Merchandiser jobs will always depend somewhat on the state of the economy and how fashion retailers are doing, employment prospects for Visual Merchandisers (and other design professionals in general) are expected to grow about as fast as average between now and 2014, according to the U.S. Department of Labor. Visual Merchandisers held about 86,000 jobs in the United States in 2004, the DOL notes—compared with just 77,000 in 2002—as retail administrators apparently continued to acknowledge the positive effects that well-designed displays and stores can have on the bottom line.

As is the case in many fashion-related occupations, the best opportunities for Visual Merchandisers exist in large urban areas, where there are many retail stores and, often, many fashion manufacturers and independent visual merchandising firms as well.

Advancement Prospects

The opportunities for advancement in the Visual Merchandising field are good, especially for those Visual Merchandisers who prove themselves by designing displays or store layouts that increase customer traffic and drive up sales.

After breaking into the field as a visual merchandise assistant or trainee, you can move into a full-fledged Visual Merchandiser or visual merchandising artist job, in which you'll assume more overall conceptualization and design responsibilities. From there, you can advance to a visual merchandise coordinator role in which you might oversee visual merchandising for an entire department or store. And after several years in a coordinating position, you can move into the visual merchandise supervisor or director role, in which you'll manage the visual merchandising for perhaps an entire chain of stores.

If you have an entrepreneurial bent, you might also consider becoming a freelance Visual Merchandiser, either for your own company or another visual merchandising consulting firm. This path can be somewhat riskier than the traditional path up the company ladder, but it can also offer better financial rewards and more opportunities to be creative and to work with diverse clients.

Education and Training

While there is no set academic path that leads to a career in visual merchandising, a bachelor's degree in a field that combines creativity and technical abilities is a good bet. It's best to explore a college major such as applied design, fashion merchandising, interior design, or architecture. Some Visual Merchandisers major in psychology (with an emphasis in consumer psychology), marketing, or graphic design.

Experience, Skills, and Personality Traits

Gaining experience through a part-time job or an internship is essential to breaking into the visual merchandising field. Experience offers the opportunity to develop the appropriate skills for the field and, importantly, the chance to meet people working in the field already and learn from their successes and mistakes.

One of the keys to being a successful Visual Merchandiser is having interests and skills that lie in both the artistic/creative and hands-on, technical domains. All Visual Merchandisers must be able to dream up imaginative but effective displays and designs. But typically, they must also be able to execute their plans by installing and using appropriate lighting, building and painting props and background sets, setting up and dressing mannequins, creating appropriate signage (often using computer graphics programs), and perhaps even physically modifying display items so that they fit the overall image the Visual Merchandiser is trying to create. It's not an understatement to say that a Visual Merchandiser must be able to work with his or her hands as well as his or her imagination.

Visual Merchandisers must also be highly organized and able to collaborate with other people. Often, they must work with other professionals, such as fashion buyers, store managers, and members of the sales and promotion or advertising staffs, to come up with displays and designs that meet the needs of the department, store, or manufacturer for which they're working.

Visual Merchandisers who decide to pursue freelance careers must also be willing to take calculated risks and continually market themselves to potential new clients. Unlike those who work full time for stores or manufacturers, freelancers can't necessarily look forward to the next job automatically. Instead, their performance for previous clients and their ongoing self-marketing efforts must be good enough to keep attracting new projects and, thus, new revenues.

Unions and Associations

Many Visual Merchandisers belong to the National Association of Visual Merchandisers (NAVM), a Texas-based trade organization intended to help people in the field network with each other and promote themselves within the overall retail industry. Some Visual Merchandisers are also involved with the Institute of Store Planners (ISP), a New York-based trade association that offers professional growth and education opportunities for Visual Merchandisers, store planners, and related professionals.

Tips for Entry

1. Gain retail experience by working as a salesperson in a fashion store or department. It's important for all Visual Merchandisers to understand consumers' buying habits and preferences. Working with the customer one on one is perhaps the best way to gain this type of knowledge.
2. Read fashion trade publications like *Women's Wear Daily* to keep up with trends in the broad fashion and apparel industry. It's critical for Visual Merchandisers to stay on top of what's working and what's not working, not only in their specific field but in fashion retailing in general.
3. Supplement your education with practical experience gained through an internship or a part-time job with a fashion retailer's visual merchandising department.
4. Develop your mechanical and hands-on building/repairing skills as well as your design/creative skills.
5. Offer to volunteer your services to a Visual Merchandiser or visual merchandising department at a store in your city or area. Be willing to start small if you must, running errands, repairing props, or simply being a "gofer." Ask questions and try to learn more about how your colleagues and supervisors do their jobs, both from an artistic and a hands-on perspective. The more knowledge and personal connections you can gain through experience, the better your opportunities will be to break into and advance within the field.

MEDIA

FASHION EDITOR

CAREER PROFILE

Duties: Oversees the development and presentation of fashion-related content in fashion-specific magazines and trade publications, the fashion sections of consumer-oriented newspapers and magazines, fashion- and consumer-oriented Web sites, and/or fashion-oriented television programs and segments

Alternate Title(s): Editor in Chief, Editorial Director, Content Editor, Content Producer, Producer

Salary Range: $40,000 to $100,000+

Employment Prospects: Fair/Good

Advancement Prospects: Fair/Limited (for print and online publications); Limited (for television programs and segments)

Best Geographical Location(s): Large cities, especially New York City, that are centers for fashion-oriented publishing and information and media companies

Prerequisites:

Education or Training—A college degree in communications or mass communications, journalism, English, or the liberal arts is required; a degree or course work in fashion design or fashion merchandising is a plus

Experience—Extensive experience in the field of fashion journalism

Special Skills and Personality Traits—Top-notch writing skills and a passion for the field of fashion; comfort with big-picture content planning; ability to interact and build relationships with various people who serve as story sources; ability to work well with other professionals, such as stylists, photographers, and advertising personnel; ability to motivate and encourage staff members; willingness and ability to deal with often fierce competition; ability to cope with a sometimes breakneck pace that includes constant stress and deadlines

CAREER LADDER

Editor in Chief

Fashion Editor

Senior Editor

Assistant Editor

Position Description

Fashion Editors are experienced, senior-level staffers who oversee the production and presentation of fashion-oriented content for various print and online publications and, in a few cases, for television programs or segments.

Fashion Editors work in a variety of settings. Many of them, particularly the most well known, who often become celebrities in the fashion world, work for fashion-specific print publications like *Harper's Bazaar, Vogue,* and *Glamour.* Others work for publications whose content focuses moderately or heavily, but not exclusively, on fashion—for example, print magazines like *Cosmopolitan* or Web sites like iVillage.com. Other Fashion Editors work for online or print trade publications such as *Women's Wear Daily, DNR* (*Daily News Record,* which covers men's fashion and retail), or FashionWireDaily.com. Still other Fashion Editors work for large general-interest newspapers and magazines, like *The New York Times,* or nationwide or worldwide news services offering fashion-related articles to their corporate subscribers.

As senior-level professionals, Fashion Editors are typically responsible for their publications' overall content, look, production, and distribution. As such, they manage large groups of other professionals, including fashion writers (whether on staff or freelance), the editors of various portions or sections of the publication, photographers and stylists, graphic artists, and marketing and public relations personnel.

Fashion Editors must also be able to plan what their publications or programs will be covering and how, either months in advance or mere hours before a newsworthy event happens. Fashion Editors working for magazines, for instance, generally have months of lead time they can use to conceptualize what content they want to cover in a particular magazine issue and how they want to cover it. Fashion Editors for trade newspapers or daily general-interest newspapers, on the other hand, typically don't have the luxury of time when it comes to making decisions about content; instead, they have to see that their publications cover important fashion-related events and news in a timely way, so that their readers are among the first to know about trends and happenings in the world of fashion.

The life of the Fashion Editor can be glamorous and fast-paced or mundane. Many Fashion Editors travel to cities like London or Paris or New York to cover fashion shows and similar events. They also have the opportunity to interact with celebrities from the worlds of fashion and show business. But Fashion Editors will often find themselves stuck in the office too—planning future editions of their publications, handling correspondence and returning phone calls and e-mails, dealing with the inevitable problems that emerge in the day-to-day life of producing publications, meeting with other editors and staff, assigning articles to staff writers and freelancers, and perhaps carving out time to do what they often like to do most but usually get to do the least: write, be it for a personal column or a more news-oriented article or feature.

Fashion Editors and their staffs are constantly battling deadlines and the stress those deadlines create. While they're competing against the clock, they're also competing with other publications. Fashion is an intensely competitive business in general, and Fashion Editors feel the pressure daily (but often thrive on it as well). The race to be the first to report on a trend or to produce the best feature article on a designer's new line is never-ending. Yet many Fashion Editors wouldn't have it any other way.

Interestingly, Fashion Editors wield a great deal of power, with consumers, fashion designers, and manufacturers. A positive mention in a magazine, on a Web site, or on a television segment can create a "buzz" around a particular piece of fashion and mean lucrative opportunities for the designer who created it and the company that manufactures it. In turn, that mention can convince ordinary consumers to go out and buy the piece and wear it themselves. As such, Fashion Editors are always being approached by manufacturers' publicists who want to gain media coverage for their fashion lines. In some ways, industry insiders say, whether the coverage is positive or negative doesn't matter; the harshest blow to designers and manufacturers is getting no coverage whatsoever.

Perhaps most important of all, Fashion Editors must know the fashion world inside and out. In order to cover the industry well, Fashion Editors need to understand how the industry works, which means being knowledgeable about fashion design, manufacturing, merchandising, retail sales, and trends and forecasts. Much of this knowledge is gained through experience, by working directly in the fashion industry, by pursuing fashion-related degrees or coursework, by constantly reading competing publications and Web sites, and, especially, by talking to people in the fashion field. If a Fashion Editor doesn't truly know fashion, he or she won't be a Fashion Editor for very long, and he or she most certainly won't be a successful one.

Salaries

Depending on their level of responsibility and the medium they work for, Fashion Editors can make anywhere from $40,000 to $100,000 a year or more. In general, lower-level assistant and associate editors earn salaries on the lower end of the scale, while higher-level editors with managerial and content direction responsibilities command the highest salaries.

The U.S. Department of Labor reports that the median annual salary for editors across all fields and levels was $43,890 in 2004. In its 2005 "Editorial Management Salary Survey," *Folio* magazine found that managing editors earned an average salary of about $49,000 a year, whether they worked for business-to-business or consumer publications. Higher-level editorial directors, meanwhile, earned an average salary of between $86,000 (business-to-business publications) and $97,000 (consumer publications), the *Folio* study found.

Employment Prospects

Editors held about 127,000 jobs across the United States in 2004, according to the U.S. Department of Labor, and employment of editors and writers in general is expected to grow about as fast as average between now and 2014. However, only a fraction of editors specialize in fashion, making the job tougher to land than most.

Still, the fashion world does offer some opportunities for Fashion Editors, especially with the advent and growth of Web-based publications. Fashion-specific and consumer-oriented magazines and newspapers, fashion trade publications, and fashion- and consumer-oriented Web sites all hold job possibilities for Fashion Editors, especially if the people competing for such jobs are willing to gain experience in lower-level positions first.

Advancement Prospects

Fashion Editors are already at or near the top of the profession by the time they reach their positions. However, Fashion Editors who are serving in more of an assistant's or associate's role can move up to become editors who have not only writing and newsgathering duties, but planning, managerial, and budgeting duties as well. From there, they can advance to become editors in chief or even publishers of their magazines, newspapers, or Web sites.

Education and Training

Most industry insiders and publications agree that a Fashion Editor needs a college degree, be it in a field like journalism or mass communications, an area like fashion design or fashion merchandising, or both. The Fashion Editor is as much fashion professional as editorial professional, and vice versa. An understanding of the entire fashion industry—design, manufacturing, merchandising, marketing, and budgeting—is also essential.

Experience, Skills, and Personality Traits

It's critical for aspiring Fashion Editors to start at the bottom of the profession and work their way up. That means interning at least once (if not more) in college, taking an entry-level job as a writer or an editorial assistant to gain experience in and knowledge of the field, and being willing to do almost anything with a good attitude. As one now fashion editor in chief described her internship experience on the Fashion.net Web site: "To me, that job was like saving lives. I did it with a real vengeance." That tenacity and determination, she said, helped her start building a reputation as a hard-working, enthusiastic professional.

The two key skills every Fashion Editor must have are writing talent and wide-ranging knowledge of the fashion industry. Fashion Editors use their writing skills daily, either to pen their own articles or, perhaps more often in the case of senior-level Fashion Editors, to edit the work of others and hand out writing assignments. People skills, tact, and the willingness to offer both praise and constructive criticism are thus essential to the success of any Fashion Editor. Without extensive knowledge of the fashion industry, however, a prospective Fashion Editor can't and won't go far. He or she simply must be knowledgeable about fashion trends and forecasts, the various emphases (e.g., design, manufacturing, merchandising, marketing) that comprise the fashion industry, and the key players who either currently drive the industry or are likely to dominate it in the near future.

Passion for fashion is another key trait of all successful Fashion Editors. They should also have a competitive spirit, the ability to work well with employees or industry professionals, and a knack for coping with constant deadlines and highly stressful workdays. They should be able to think about a publication from a big-picture standpoint, and possess a willingness to deal with the mundane one minute and hop aboard a plane to London the next to cover a major fashion show.

Unions and Associations

Most Fashion Editors are involved in both media- and fashion-related organizations. On the media side, Fashion Editors often participate in groups such as the American Society of Magazine Editors (ASME), while on the fashion side they usually monitor industry trends and forecasts by getting involved in organizations like Fashion Group International (FGI) and The Fashion Association.

Tips for Entry

1. While in college, be sure to participate in at least one internship and, if possible, more than one, no matter what the pay, the hours, or the tasks assigned. Gaining experience in the fashion field early on in your career is critical, especially if you have visions of working up to a senior-level Fashion Editor position someday.
2. Talk to as many people as you can in the fashion industry to see what they do on a day-to-day basis, get their career advice, learn about their specific roles in fashion, and gain knowledge about various aspects of the industry. Fashion Editors need to have a grasp on how the entire industry works, not just parts of it.
3. Start writing fashion-related articles, either on your own or for a college or local newspaper or Web site. The sooner you can begin building a portfolio of your writing clips, even if you don't get paid for your articles at first, the sooner you'll be able to start pursuing internships and entry-level editorial opportunities in the fashion world.
4. Read every fashion-related magazine, newspaper, and trade publication you can, and visit fashion-related Web sites as well. The more you can learn about fashion industry processes, trends, and forecasts, the

better prepared you'll be to assume a senior role with a fashion-oriented publication in the future.

5. As you read fashion-related publications and visit fashion Web sites, think about how the articles/content you examine come to be in the first place. What articles did the editor have to plan, and to whom did she or he assign those articles? What was likely the editor's role in the "look" and content of the layouts and photographs? How many advertisements are featured in the publication, and what was the editor's probable role in their inclusion and placement?
6. Get involved in team-oriented projects of all kinds. Fashion Editors must manage others and delegate tasks as often as they pursue their own writing-oriented projects. If possible, participate in projects that allow you to manage a budget as well. Fashion Editors must do everything with the bottom line in mind.

FASHION ILLUSTRATOR

CAREER PROFILE

Duties: Conceptualizes and draws apparel items and accessories, by hand or with a computer, for use by magazines, newspapers, advertising agencies, fashion-oriented Web sites, pattern companies, fashion forecasting firms, retail stores, apparel manufacturers, design companies, or textile and fiber companies

Alternate Title(s): Fashion Artist

Salary Range: $0 to $60,000+

Employment Prospects: Limited

Advancement Prospects: Limited

Best Geographical Location(s): Large cities, especially fashion centers like New York City, London, Milan, and Paris

Prerequisites:

Education or Training—A college degree with coursework in fashion illustration, art, drawing, or fashion design is important though not always required; additional training as an apprentice or volunteer with an established Fashion Illustrator is helpful

Experience—Drawing experience of any kind is helpful

Special Skills and Personality Traits—Artistic and drawing skills; ability to work with a variety of media (e.g., ink, paints, pencils, brushes); ability to carry out the visions of various clients; ability to produce drawings that meet clients' wants and needs; strong computer skills, particularly involving software such as Adobe Illustrator, Adobe Freehand, and Adobe Photoshop; sound business and self-marketing skills; ability to handle stress and work under pressure to meet deadlines

CAREER LADDER

Fashion Illustrator, Staff or Freelance

Volunteer or Trainee

Position Description

Fashion Illustrators conceptualize and draw men's, women's, and children's apparel items and accessories. They use a variety of tools in their work. Most have expertise using different media, such as pen and ink, brushes, watercolors, and pencils, to develop their drawings. Today's Fashion Illustrators use computers and design software (e.g., Adobe Illustrator, Adobe Freehand, Adobe Photoshop) as well, both to develop their drawings and to market themselves online via electronic portfolios of their work.

The drawings that Fashion Illustrators create are used in a variety of media and by an assortment of companies. Often, the Fashion Illustrator's work appears in magazines, in print or online, or newspapers, sometimes accompanying an article by a fashion writer. In other instances, Fashion Illustrators work for advertising agencies to come up with drawings for ads in print publications. Pattern companies use Fashion Illustrators to show consumers who buy their patterns what the various garments are supposed to look like when sewn; often, the Fashion Illustrator is asked to emphasize seams and trimming details on these patterns so that sewers will clearly understand the construction of the finished garment.

Still other Fashion Illustrators do work for fashion forecasting firms that make predictions about fashion trends one or two years into the future. Because the fashions these companies are describing don't yet exist, it is often up to the Fashion Illustrator to render drawings of the predicted styles so that retailers and fashion buyers will have a clear sense of what clothing and accessories will look like.

Some Fashion Illustrators do work for apparel manufacturers and design companies as well, often doing rough drawings or sketches of several finished garments or a whole line of finished garments for a company's records. On occasion, Fashion Illustrators will work with fashion designers, to help illustrate their apparel and accessory ideas for others (e.g., prospective buyers, retailers).

The majority of Fashion Illustrators are independent freelancers who own their own companies and work on projects for many different clients. As such, these professionals must have artistic and creative skills as well as business skills. They spend at least some of their time running their businesses, setting rates, developing contracts, marketing themselves and their services, keeping careful records of their income and expenses, and updating their portfolios of presentations of their past work for various clients. Fashion Illustrators of all kinds must devote time to keeping up with fashion trends and forecasts, whether that means reading industry publications and visiting industry Web sites, attending fashion shows and visiting fashion showrooms and retail centers, or meeting with fashion industry professionals.

In recent years, some Fashion Illustrators have expressed concern that theirs is a dying craft, especially as more and more companies and media outlets have decided to use photographs instead of illustrations to highlight various fashion items and accessories. With the growth of the Internet, however—along with the fashion world's continuing reliance on forecasting companies, as well as the constant need among fashion media, manufacturers, retailers, and advertising agencies to stand out—Fashion Illustrators are holding their own, though their numbers are still small compared with those of other fashion-related professions.

Salaries

Salaries for Fashion Illustrators vary widely, depending on for whom they're working, where they're living, their experience and reputation in the field, and whether they work for a company full time as an employee versus on their own as an independent freelancer. Fashion Illustrators can make as little as a few thousand dollars a year, especially if they're new to the field or do fashion illustration only part time. In a paid staff position, a Fashion Illustrator might start out making a salary that's only in the low to mid-$20,000s. If, on the other hand, a Fashion Illustrator decides to become an independent freelancer who works for a variety of clients, he or she could make $60,000 a year or more, especially if he or she gains a solid reputation in the field.

Employment Prospects

Employment prospects for Fashion Illustrators are quite limited. Indeed, there were only 29,000 illustrators, sculptors, and painters across all fields in the United States in 2004, according to the U.S. Department of Labor. Some full-time positions do exist for Fashion Illustrators, but most of the people who work in the field are independent freelancers who must constantly market themselves and their services in order to land projects and make money.

Advancement Prospects

Fashion Illustrators who establish a positive reputation with their clients and among the fashion industry as a whole can, theoretically, attract more clients than they could possibly handle on their own. But most Fashion Illustrators who are independent freelancers must constantly look for new clients, especially early on in their careers. Only the best of the best reach a point where they no longer have to market themselves and their services to others, but instead simply choose which work offers they want to pursue.

Education and Training

Many Fashion Illustrators have a two- or four-year college degree in fashion illustration, art, drawing, or fashion design. Some Fashion Illustrators pursue additional training by becoming apprentices or volunteers for established Fashion Illustrators.

Most Fashion Illustrators agree that education and/or training in both business processes (marketing, accounting, recordkeeping) and computer applications is also important.

Experience, Skills, and Personality Traits

To break into the fashion illustration field, you need to find a way to gain some sort of drawing experience, even if it means doing it for no pay. The key is to find ways to do drawings so that you can build up a portfolio of the projects you've done. Employers or, more likely, prospective clients will expect to see a portfolio and will use it to evaluate whether your previous experiences and your style meet their wants and needs.

It's important to have excellent drawing abilities if you want to become a successful Fashion Illustrator. You must be skilled in using a variety of media, such as pen and ink, brushes and watercolors, and pencil and have the imagination and creativity every professional artist needs to thrive. In today's computerized world, you must also be proficient with illustration-oriented computer software, such as Adobe Illustrator, Adobe Freehand, or Adobe Photoshop.

Artistic skills alone aren't enough, especially if you're an independent freelancer. You must be willing to constantly market yourself and your previous work. You must also be deadline-oriented and capable of working to meet your clients' wants and needs rather than insisting on doing things your way. Since your work is constantly evaluated by other people, you also need to be able to handle criticism and feedback without sacrificing your own personal drawing and presentation style.

Increasingly, computer skills are essential as well, both for completing drawings and for marketing yourself and your work via, for example, a Web site featuring your electronic portfolio. You'll also need perseverance, a competitive spirit, excellent communication and presentation skills, and knowledge of fashion trends and forecasts.

Unions and Associations

Some Fashion Illustrators belong to the Society of Illustrators, a trade organization made up of professional illustrators in a variety of specialty areas, including fashion.

Tips for Entry

1. If you aren't already doing so, start drawing. Practice doing fashion drawings by looking at items you see in stores or in the pages of magazines. Try to get a sense of what your drawing style is, and then see if you can incorporate aspects of other illustrators' styles to create a brand-new style.
2. Contact (in person or via the Internet) some practicing Fashion Illustrators who are making at least part of their living through this craft. Ask them how they got started in the field, what advice they have for you to help you get started, and what job or project leads they might have for you, even if it means working for free.
3. Develop a portfolio of your work. If possible, create a printed version of your portfolio, which you can show to people during in-person meetings, as well as a Web-based electronic portfolio, which you can show to people no matter where they might be.
4. Contact local retailers and ask if they have any volunteer opportunities for which you could work on your fashion illustration skills. Would they like to use some illustrations in their print advertisements? Do they need some illustrations to help publicize upcoming in-store fashion presentations?
5. Read fashion industry trade publications and visit fashion industry Web sites often so that you can better understand the industry as a whole, particularly fashion trends and forecasts.
6. If you're a college student, visit the Web sites of major designers, manufacturers, and fashion media to see if any of them offer internships in fashion illustration or a related field. Gaining practical, hands-on experience is key to future success in the industry, whether you decide to work in a full-time staff position or become an independent freelancer.

FASHION PHOTOGRAPHER

CAREER PROFILE

Duties: Conceptualizes, shoots, develops, and prints still and sometimes moving pictures to depict apparel and accessories in an eye-catching, creative, and artistic way

Alternate Title(s): None

Salary Range: $0 to $100,000+

Employment Prospects: Limited

Advancement Prospects: Limited

Best Geographical Location(s): Large cities, particularly major fashion centers like New York City, Paris, Milan, and London

Prerequisites:

Education or Training—No formal education is required; postsecondary course work or a college degree in photography, design, or art is very helpful

Experience—Work experience as a fashion photographer's assistant is essential; must have a portfolio or book of sample photographs demonstrating one's style, techniques, and previous assignments

Special Skills and Personality Traits—A combination of creative skills and artistic abilities, technical skills, and people skills; sound business, marketing, and financial abilities

CAREER LADDER

Photo Editor or Director of Photography

Staff or Freelance Fashion Photographer

Fashion Photographer's Assistant

Position Description

When you glance at pictures of glamorous models in magazines, spot a television ad marketing the hottest blue jeans, or look at pictures of yesterday's fashion show in today's newspaper, you're seeing the fruits of a Fashion Photographer's labor.

Fashion Photographers shoot pictures—using traditional film-based still cameras, electronic still cameras, or video cameras—to present a selected garment (or line of garments) in a creative, eye-catching way that reflects the designer's style and the manufacturer's wants and needs.

One of the biggest misconceptions about fashion photography is that people in the field spend most of their time on sunny, tropical beaches shooting pictures of beautiful models wearing the latest fashions. While some Fashion Photographers do get such assignments, most Fashion Photographers spend the bulk of their time preparing for shoots, creating the finished product after shoots, and, especially in the case of independent or freelance photographers, looking for other jobs.

For a typical print shoot, a Fashion Photographer must land the assignment in the first place through his or her marketing efforts and develop a concept for the shoot. Once the concept is approved, the photographer must locate and hire models and assistants, book a studio or an outdoor site, make travel and accommodation arrangements, and determine what film and equipment will be needed. Once this is done he or she must make sure everyone and everything gets to the shoot location on time, and in one piece. All of this must be done before the shoot even occurs! Once the shoot is over—a process that can take hours if not days—the Fashion Photographer must either develop the film or download the electronic files of the shots, determine which of the shots have turned out best, and in many cases print the photos using a variety of darkroom and/or image-editing techniques (using software such as Adobe Photoshop). The photos must then be submitted to the photo editor or contracting clients to determine that they meet their needs.

Once the shoot is over, the Fashion Photographer will have to move on to another assignment. If the photographer is a salaried staff member of a magazine, the next project will simply be assigned by the photo editor. If the photographer is a freelancer, however, he or she will have to find the next project and client through his or her own marketing efforts and networking connections.

Fashion Photographers work in a variety of settings. Many are on the staffs of or are hired on a freelance or contract basis by fashion-oriented consumer and trade publications to produce photos that will accompany editorial articles or advertisements. Some work for newspapers, magazines, and television networks that cover fashion shows and similar fashion-oriented events—for example, the Academy Awards ceremonies. Other Fashion Photographers are employed or hired to photograph fashions for publicity brochures, retailers' and manufacturers' catalogs (both print and online), and ad agency projects. And still other Fashion Photographers specialize in videotape or motion film work for television commercials and programs.

While salaried staff photographers either develop their own assignments or, much more often, receive assignments from their photo editors, freelance photographers must invest considerable time and energy marketing themselves, their services, and, especially, their photographs. Thus, freelance Fashion Photographers spend as much time, or perhaps more, on sales and business activities as they do on actually taking pictures. By making phone calls and sending e-mails, setting up meetings with photo editors, constantly working on their portfolios, and networking with colleagues, they attempt to ensure that the current project won't be the last (i.e., that they can continue to make a living in the field). They must also deal with the various other duties that might accompany running any business: keeping track of expenditures and income; identifying, interviewing, and hiring assistants and models for various projects; ensuring that their photography equipment is up to date and in working order; and keeping up with news and trends in both the photography field in general and the fashion industry in particular.

Salaries

To gain experience and contacts in the fashion field, beginning Fashion Photographers may be forced to work for little or no pay at first and earn virtually nothing for their efforts. With experience and, especially, a strong reputation in the field, the best Fashion Photographers can easily land enough projects to earn $100,000 a year or more. The median annual salary for photographers across all fields was just over $26,000 in 2004, according to the U.S. Department of Labor.

Employment Prospects

Becoming a successful Fashion Photographer isn't easy. There are many more people who want to work in the field than there are positions and projects to sustain them. Still, jobs are available, especially for those who are willing to work on a freelance or contract basis versus a full-time employee basis.

Photographers across all fields held about 129,000 jobs in the United States in 2004, according to the U.S. Department of Labor. However, only a fraction of photographers work exclusively in the fashion industry, and more than half are self-employed freelancers or independent business owners.

The best employment prospects are reserved for people who are willing to start out as fashion photographer's assistants, perhaps working for little or no pay for several years, to gain hands-on experience in the field and develop a portfolio or book of samples. With increased experience will come opportunities to take responsibility for easier or routine shoots. Most important, you will make the all-important personal connections in the fashion and fashion photography industries that often spell the difference between working and not working.

Advancement Prospects

Once someone has broken into the fashion photography field as an assistant, he or she can, with time, experience, patience, and persistence, land opportunities for some initial professional photography projects. In some cases, the projects may be ones the Fashion Photographer doesn't have time for. In other cases, the projects will emerge as a result of the assistant making a positive connection with someone in the fashion industry. As the opportunities to take photographs and organize and supervise real shoots grow, the photographer's portfolio and reputation grow as well, and, hopefully, the number of assignments and the amounts on paychecks begin to grow too.

Many Fashion Photographers who are freelancers choose to remain freelancers, preferring the flexibility, independence, and creative freedom it allows them. Other Fashion Photographers, however, move into staff photography positions with magazines, advertising agencies, and television and commercial production facilities. Eventually, Fashion Photographers can advance to become photo editors or directors of photography, who spend most of their time managing other photographers, identifying and hiring freelancers, and supervising major photography-related projects.

Education and Training

No formal education is required to become a Fashion Photographer. However, pursuing postsecondary course work or a bachelor's degree in photography, photojournalism, design, or art can be helpful.

Perhaps more important than formal education is gaining experience working under a professional Fashion Photographer and developing a portfolio or book of photographs to show to prospective employers. Without a book featuring his or her best work and style, the prospective Fashion Photographer is unlikely to get very far in the industry.

Experience, Skills, and Personality Traits

Almost all people who go on to succeed as professional Fashion Photographers start out as assistants for established Fashion Photographers. In the assistant's role, they often take responsibility for the detail-oriented tasks that might otherwise take up too much of the Fashion Photographer's time—for example, setting up equipment for shoots, developing film and photographs, identifying and contacting prospective models, looking for studios and on-site locations for shoots, and perhaps even keeping the Fashion Photographer's studio and darkroom clean. Being an assistant is hardly glamorous, and often the pay isn't great, but it's a form of apprenticeship that is common in the field; and with so many people interested in pursuing the field, there are plenty willing to take on these responsibilities with a smile.

Fashion Photographers need to have a unique combination of creative, technical, and business skills. On the creative side, they must be able to envision and execute the best ways to make apparel look good. They must also understand how lighting and composition impact finished photographs, and how to place models and the fashions they're wearing for maximum visual impact. From a technical standpoint, Fashion Photographers need to know how to use many types of cameras, films, lights (artificial and natural), darkroom strategies, and electronic image-editing techniques (using complex software programs such as Adobe Photoshop) to produce superior photographs. On the business side, Fashion Photographers need to understand not only how the fashion industry operates, but also how they will be able to continue landing assignments and pay the bills.

Fashion Photographers must have excellent people skills too. Working with models, for example, can be difficult at times, as can trying to please fussy clients or land assignments in the first place. So a good attitude, tact, a sense of humor, and the ability to roll with changes are all essential personality traits for Fashion Photographers. The same is true for competitive spirit, the ability to deal with stress and deadlines, and a willingness to constantly hustle to meet new people in the industry and land new assignments.

Unions and Associations

Depending on their interests, Fashion Photographers can be involved in any number of professional organizations. Many are photography-specific—for example, the American Society of Media Photographers (ASMP), Advertising Photographers of America (APA), and Professional Photographers of America (PPA).

Sometimes Fashion Photographers participate in apparel-related groups like Fashion Group International (FGI) and the Fashion Association, in great part to develop industry contacts in the hopes of landing future projects.

Tips for Entry

1. Do whatever you can to gain experience taking still or motion photographs. Find some friends who are interested in being models and ask them to model for you for free. In return, you can give them copies of your photos. The sooner you can begin accumulating samples of your work, the sooner you'll be able to start pursuing entry-level professional assignments.
2. Talk to professional photographers in your area, whether they specialize in fashion or not, and see if they'd be willing to hire you as an assistant, either for pay or on a volunteer basis. Almost all of today's successful Fashion Photographers started out as assistants for someone else so that they could gain the experience, skills, education, and professional contacts necessary to succeed in the industry.
3. Ask some professional photographers in your area if you could meet with them to learn more about what they do and how they got to where they are now. This informational interviewing approach can be extremely useful in helping you understand what professional photographers do. (Note: With the growth of the Internet, it's now possible for you to interview photographers anywhere in the world, as long as they have an e-mail address.)
4. Start reading fashion magazines and photography magazines. Pay close attention to general trends and the styles of various Fashion Photographers. Also, try to imagine the techniques and strategies photographers have used to produce the high-quality photographs you're looking at.
5. If possible, take some photography courses at a local college/university or community center. Learn about the basics of photography composition, film development and darkroom skills, electronic image-editing strategies (using software packages like Adobe Photoshop), and photographic printing techniques. (Note: Often, by taking such courses, you can gain access to a darkroom, which you can use to develop film and print photographs; and/or to computers equipped with electronic image-editing software like Adobe Photoshop, which you can use to manipulate electronic files of photographs you've shot.)
6. Visit Web sites of professional Fashion Photographers and look at the photos they've posted there.

Pay attention as well to any advice the photographers offer about breaking into the fashion photography field.

7. Invest significant time and energy getting to know some professional Fashion Photographers, if only by e-mail or phone. Fashion photography is a business of personal connections. As Fashion Photographer Jeff Berlin told the Web site Monster.com: "This business is so much about who you know. You can walk in with the best portfolio, but if you aren't hanging out with the right people, you don't get the job."

FASHION STYLIST

CAREER PROFILE

Duties: Works with photographers, fashion directors, art directors, and editors to conceptualize and help execute photo shoots for print publications, television shows and music videos, and commercials

Alternate Title(s): Stylist

Salary Range: 0 to $100,000+

Employment Prospects: Limited

Advancement Prospects: Limited

Best Geographical Location(s): Large cities, especially fashion centers like New York City and television/production hubs like Los Angeles

Prerequisites:

Education or Training—A college degree in art, design, or fashion history is helpful but not essential

Experience—Working as an assistant stylist or apprentice for a practicing Fashion Stylist is essential; a position in an editorial or advertising capacity for a fashion-oriented magazine may also be helpful

Special Skills and Personality Traits—A combination of creative, big-picture skills and organizational, detail-oriented abilities; flexibility; creativity; resourcefulness; imagination; knowledge of fashion trends and forecasts; outgoing personality

CAREER LADDER

Fashion Stylist

Assistant Fashion Stylist

Apprentice or Volunteer Assistant

Position Description

Fashion Stylists, often referred to simply as stylists, work to create the appropriate look or statement for fashion items and accessories that are used in print advertisements, magazine editorial spreads, television commercials, and even music videos.

A Fashion Stylist's duties are extremely diverse. On the creative side, stylists often work with photographers, fashion directors, art directors, and editors to select the clothing and accessories that will be used for a particular photo shoot. They also play a key role in determining how the clothing and accessories will be presented. This involves deciding who will model the items, where the shoot will take place, what mood or tone will be created, what makeup and hairstyles will be most effective, and how the entire project will make the statement or create the look a particular client is seeking.

To perform this creative work effectively, Fashion Stylists need to be highly knowledgeable about fashion trends and forecasts as well as fashion history. If, for example, a photographer says he wants to create a look resembling the Old South in the late 1800s, the stylist has to have some idea of what the clothing and styles were at that time so that he or she can recreate them for the photo shoot. Stylists also need to have expertise in current styles, colors, and fabrics, since they often must choose and then find the appropriate garments and accessories for a shoot.

However, creativity and imagination are only a part of the stylist's job. Stylists must also have an assortment of nitty-gritty detail skills in order to do their jobs effectively. For example, in many cases the Fashion Stylist is responsible for finding and booking models for a particular shoot. So he or she must be both skilled in choosing people who have the right look and connected enough within the industry to find those people and hire them.

Stylists are also typically responsible for obtaining the clothing items and accessories that will be used. They often borrow them from manufacturers and retailers, and make sure they reach the shoot location, prepare them for the shoot, fit them on the models, and ensure the items are cleaned and returned promptly.

Often Fashion Stylists must use their ingenuity and resourcefulness to locate or build props and sets for the shoot. Many stylists make a habit of visiting secondhand stores and even yard sales in the hopes of finding items they might need for a shoot someday or immediately.

On top of all their other duties, Fashion Stylists are typically juggling many other tasks too. So they quickly become effective multitaskers. Since many of them work for independent freelancers or as independent freelancers themselves, stylists are constantly thinking about the next project, even while the current project is in progress. As such, they must invest time and energy developing and maintaining a portfolio of their previous work, which might include tearsheets—pages of printed articles or advertisements they've worked on—and perhaps even videotapes.

While most stylists are independent freelancers, some find full-time staff positions with magazines, catalog companies, or even retailers. Increasingly, Fashion Stylists are also finding freelance and staff work with Web sites and electronic magazines. In most cases, finding a job as a stylist means going to a large city, especially a fashion center like New York City or a television and video production hub like Los Angeles. While, theoretically, a stylist could find work anywhere, most stylists end up working for local clients who have used them once with success in the past and who want to continue the productive working relationship that was formed.

Salaries

It's difficult to pinpoint specific salaries for Fashion Stylists. Many people who are trying to break into the field wind up working for free (or close to it), simply to gain experience and make personal connections in the industry. Eventually, though, experienced volunteers who land jobs as assistant stylists might start getting paid on the order of $200 to $250 a day. Later, if they become independent stylists, they can earn more—anywhere from $300 to $850 a day. A few stylists eventually garner the experience and reputation they need to command fees of $5,000 a day or more, which can sometimes result in annual earnings exceeding $100,000.

Stylists who work full time for a particular company can sometimes earn more than $100,000 a year, depending on their clientele and the demand for their services.

Employment Prospects

Opportunities for budding Fashion Stylists and assistant stylists are limited. In most cases, you must be willing to work for a stylist for little or no pay to gain experience, skills, and industry contacts you'll need either to move into an assistant stylist position or start your own styling business.

Since most stylists are independent freelancers, the next project is always of the utmost importance. The most successful stylists are the ones who have a combination of creative skills and business acumen that will help them perform effectively for a particular project and ensure they continue landing projects in the future.

Advancement Prospects

Once you have a few years of experience as a volunteer or as an assistant stylist, you put yourself in a position to either take a full-time Fashion Stylist position with a magazine, catalog house, or retailer, or pursue your own independent business. In either case, you'll only advance if you have creativity, imagination, excellent people and communication skills, and business savvy.

Education and Training

A college degree can be helpful for getting a job in the styling industry, though it isn't essential. If you do pursue college, a degree in art, design, fashion history, or another liberal arts major is your best bet.

More important is your willingness to receive appropriate training by starting out as a volunteer or assistant stylist for a working stylist. You may or may not get paid in this role, but the experiential "salary" you'll earn on the job is essential if you really want to become a full-time, working stylist someday.

Finally, knowing about fashion industry trends and forecasts, and fashion history, is critical. Reading industry trade publications and consumer magazines is essential. You might also want to visit fashion-oriented Web sites and participate in message boards and discussion groups hosted by those sites so that you can better understand the broad fashion industry and the styling niche.

Experience, Skills, and Personality Traits

Along with working for a practicing Fashion Stylist, perhaps the most essential piece of experience you can pursue, it can be helpful to gain some retail fashion experience as well so that you better understand the fashion industry and, especially, the buying habits of consumers. Working in an editorial or advertising capacity for a fashion or consumer magazine can also be helpful, in that such a job will allow you to meet public relations professionals in the industry and perhaps even assist with some of the styling duties that might pop up for particular projects.

Stylists need to be able to handle many tasks at once, whether planned or unplanned. Just when you think you have everything figured out, a problem will crop up, and you need to deal with it quickly and effectively without neglecting your other duties. Stylists also need strong artistic and creative skills, organizational and follow-through skills, perseverance, and outstanding people skills.

The most effective stylists also have the unique ability to keep everyone in a large group of people happy, and to be diplomatic with rabble-rousers and troublemakers. Stylists also thrive when they're resourceful, flexible, energetic, detail-oriented, and outgoing, and when they're able to inject humor and playfulness into situations that could otherwise turn into disasters.

Unions and Associations

The Association of Stylists and Coordinators is a New York-based nonprofit organization made up of stylists whose specialties include fashion as well as a host of other niches. The group is intended to be a resource for art directors, photographers, and advertising agencies around the world that need to hire and work with talented stylists and related professionals.

Tips for Entry

1. Locate some professional Fashion Stylists, either in your area or elsewhere, and talk to them in person or via e-mail or phone about what they do and how they got to where they are. Ask especially how they got started in the business, and how you might do the same.
2. Get a job in retail fashion so that you can learn about the fashion industry as a whole and observe how consumers make their buying decisions when it comes to apparel and accessories.
3. Either on your own or, if you're in college, with the help of a career counselor, pursue an internship or a part-time job with the editorial department of a fashion magazine or a consumer magazine with a strong fashion focus. In many cases, you'll be able to meet and interact with public relations professionals and others in the fashion field who regularly work with stylists in some capacity. You might also get the opportunity to assist with shoots, and either learn how stylists work by watching them or actually help them with some of their work.
4. Read fashion industry trade publications and consumer magazines to keep abreast of fashion trends and forecasts.
5. If you're in college, pursue coursework in fashion history, fashion design, or fashion merchandising, or similar courses in art and design so that you can understand the fashion industry as a whole and, in particular, fashion styles and looks from various time periods.
6. Find some way to work with an experienced professional stylist, even if it means doing so for free. The experience and personal contacts you'll gain are essential to both breaking into the field and succeeding within it later on.

FASHION WRITER

CAREER PROFILE

Duties: Conceptualizes, researches, and writes fashion-related articles for fashion-specific magazines and trade publications, the fashion sections of consumer-oriented newspapers and magazines, fashion and consumer-oriented Web sites, and/or fashion-oriented television programs and segments

Alternate Title(s): Fashion Journalist, Fashion Critic, Freelance/Contributing Fashion Writer

Salary Range: $30,000 to $55,000+

Employment Prospects: Fair/Limited (for print and online publications); Limited (for television programs and segments)

Advancement Prospects: Fair/Limited (for print and online publications); Limited (for television programs and segments)

Best Geographical Location(s): Large cities, especially New York City

Prerequisites:

Education or Training—A college degree in communications, journalism, English, or the liberal arts is almost always required; course work in fashion design or fashion merchandising is a plus

Experience—Internship experience is critical for developing a portfolio of published articles, making contacts, and gaining the fashion and journalistic expertise necessary to advance; other writing experience is helpful, preferably for a fashion-oriented publication; a broad understanding of and passion for the various aspects of the fashion industry is essential

Special Skills and Personality Traits—Top-notch writing skills and a broad knowledge of the field of fashion; ability to cope with a breakneck pace and constant stress and deadlines; ability to spot fashion news and generate ideas for articles

CAREER LADDER

Staff or Freelance Fashion Writer or Journalist

Editorial Assistant

Intern

Position Description

Fashion Writers conceptualize, research, and write articles for magazines, newspapers, Web sites, and television programs and segments covering the often glamorous, but also hectic and ever-changing, world of fashion.

Every day, Fashion Writers tap into their expertise in two broad areas: fashion and journalism. To determine what articles they should write and how, they first call upon their knowledge of fashion industry trends, people, and happenings, and attempt to identify those developments that are newsworthy. Once the writer decides to put together an article on a certain topic, he or she must then conduct extensive research. This often includes interviewing people in the field (in person or via phone or e-mail), attending fashion shows and similar events, and using Web-based search tools and electronic research databases. When the writer feels he or she has the information necessary to complete the article, he or she must then actually outline and write the article—a sometimes painstaking and frustrating process—under the stress of a pressing deadline and hard-to-please editors, who will likely demand minor or major revisions.

Fashion Writers work for a variety of different print, electronic, and online publications. Many write for fashion-specific print publications geared toward consumers—for example, *Harper's Bazaar, Vogue,* and *Glamour.* Others write for publications whose content focuses moderately or heavily, but not exclusively, on fashion—for example, print magazines like *Cosmopolitan* or Web sites like iVillage.com. Other Fashion Writers develop articles for online or print trade publications such as *Women's Wear Daily, DNR* (*Daily News Record,* which covers men's fashion and retail), or Fashion WireDaily.com. Other Fashion Writers work for large general-interest newspapers and magazines, like *The New York Times,* or nationwide or worldwide news services offering fashion-related articles to their corporate subscribers.

Many Fashion Writers are professional staff members of their publications, drawing a full-time salary with benefits for their work. Many other Fashion Writers, however, are freelancers who market and sell their work to a variety of publications on an article-by-article basis. Staff Fashion Writers generally enjoy more job security than do freelancers, although both types of writers can fall victim to cuts when the publications they work for are struggling financially.

Fashion Writers can also specialize in several different ways. Some cover only a particular area of fashion, such as women's wear or children's wear. Other Fashion Writers concentrate on feature articles, such as pieces on rising fashion design stars or fashion manufacturers. Others might focus more on the business side of the fashion industry by covering mergers and acquisitions within the industry or styles that are expected to be hot in coming months.

Often, Fashion Writers, especially those at the senior level, are instrumental in determining how their articles will look in their publications. They might, for instance, get involved in choosing photos of fashion items or events that will accompany their finished pieces. On some smaller newspapers, magazines, and Web sites, the Fashion Writer might also be responsible for physically designing and laying out his or her articles so that they appear with photographs, headlines, and other design elements.

Fashion Writers may find themselves attending many team meetings as well, usually with other writers and editors, to decide what stories they should cover in their publications (and why and how). Especially at higher levels where they might assume more managerial duties while cutting back on their actual writing duties, Fashion Writers have to be able to focus on the big picture of a publication's overall presentation and coverage as well as the small picture of their own articles.

Fashion Writers often go on the road. Travel is a big part of the job, whether it means jetting to Paris to cover the latest fashion show or driving to the site of the local apparel manufacturer to participate in the news conference on its latest spring line of fashions. Many Fashion Writers caution that, while travel may seem glamorous and exciting, it can also become tiring and draining, especially since it often involves competing with other writers and publications once the Fashion Writer has reached his or her destination.

Salaries

Entry-level Fashion Writers can expect to make about $30,000 a year to start, give or take a few thousand dollars—though that number might be slightly higher in fashion centers like New York City. Experienced Fashion Writers, particularly those with managerial responsibilities, can earn $55,000 a year or more, depending on their exact duties, experience, and skills.

The median annual salary for writers across all fields was $44,350 in 2004, according to the U.S. Department of Labor.

Employment Prospects

Becoming a Fashion Writer isn't easy, and job prospects are somewhat limited. While the U.S. Department of Labor reports that writers across all fields held about 142,000 jobs in the United States in 2004, only a fraction of those professionals specialize in fashion.

Still, the fashion world does offer some opportunities for Fashion Writers, especially with the advent and growth of Web-based publications. Fashion-specific and consumer-oriented magazines and newspapers, fashion trade publications, and fashion- and consumer-oriented Web sites all hold job possibilities for Fashion Writers, especially if the people competing for such jobs are willing to gain experience in lower-level positions first.

Contributing articles on a freelance or contract basis, even if it means doing so for little or no pay at first, is an effective way to break into fashion writing. Some freelancers find that they can market and sell more than enough articles to various publications to make a good living. More often than not, however, freelancers must subsidize their fashion writing with other jobs or use their freelance clips and connections to pursue full-time staff positions with publications.

Advancement Prospects

Once a beginning Fashion Writer has gained some experience in the field, and developed a strong portfolio of published clips, either as a freelancer or as an entry-level intern or editorial assistant, he or she can become a full-time Fashion

Writer. This also requires sufficient knowledge of fashion industry players, news, and trends. From there, Fashion Writers can move into roles that call for more news judgment and content planning. These include market editors, who oversee a publication's coverage of a particular fashion market or specialty area; senior editors, who manage a publication's staff of writers and offer the final okay to all of the publication's content; and editors or editors-in-chief, who oversee all aspects of content for their publications.

Education and Training

Most industry insiders and publications agree that a Fashion Writer needs a college degree, be it in a field like journalism or mass communications, an area like fashion design or fashion merchandising, or, the perfect scenario, both. A broad liberal arts degree is another good educational choice, especially if it's combined with a fashion writing internship or similar experience.

Experience, Skills, and Personality Traits

It's critical for aspiring Fashion Writers to start at the bottom of the profession and work their way up. That means interning at least once in college, taking an entry-level job as an editorial assistant or trainee to gain both experience in and knowledge of the field, and being willing to do almost anything with a good attitude.

It is essential to compile a list of published writing clips. Many successful Fashion Writers began their careers by writing articles for their college newspapers or magazines, volunteering to write fashion articles for local freebie newspapers, or taking magazine or newspaper internships that allowed them to write small "filler" articles related to the fashion industry.

The two key skills every Fashion Writer needs are writing talent and a wide-ranging knowledge of the fashion industry. Fashion Writers may use their writing skills daily, but without extensive knowledge of the fashion industry, a prospective Fashion Writer won't be able to decide what to write about or how to write about it. He or she must be knowledgeable about fashion trends and forecasts, the various emphases (e.g., design, manufacturing, merchandising, marketing) that comprise the fashion industry, and the key players who either currently drive the industry or are likely to dominate it in the near future.

Fashion Writers must also have a nose for news and the ability to gather information from a variety of sources by interviewing people in the industry, attending fashion shows and press conferences, using electronic and Web-based research tools, and constantly reading competing and complementary publications.

Passion for fashion is another key trait of the successful Fashion Writer, as are a competitive spirit, the ability to work well with industry professionals, a knack for coping with constant deadlines and often highly stressful workdays, and written communication skills. After all, an unread or misunderstood article is as bad as, or worse than, no article at all.

Unions and Associations

Like their fashion editor colleagues, many Fashion Writers are involved in both media and fashion-related organizations. On the media side, Fashion Writers often participate in groups such as the Society of Professional Journalists (SPJ), while on the fashion side they usually monitor industry trends and forecasts by getting involved in organizations like Fashion Group International (FGI) and the Fashion Association.

Tips for Entry

1. While in college, be sure to participate in at least one internship related to fashion writing and, if possible, more than one, no matter what the pay, the hours, or the tasks assigned.
2. Talk to some Fashion Writers to see what they do on a day-to-day basis, get their career advice, learn about their specific roles with their publications, and gain knowledge about various aspects of the industry.
3. Read the work of various Fashion Writers closely. Try to get a sense of their writing styles, the issues and events they tend to write about most, and what research they've had to conduct to develop their pieces.
4. Start writing fashion-related articles, either on your own or for a college or local newspaper or Web site. The sooner you can begin building a portfolio of your writing clips, the sooner you'll be able to start pursuing internships and entry-level editorial opportunities in the fashion world.
5. Read every fashion-related magazine, newspaper, and trade publication you can, and visit fashion-related Web sites as well. The more you can learn about fashion industry processes, trends, and forecasts, the better prepared you'll be to write about news, trends, and people in the fashion world.
6. Consider attempting to market and sell one or more fashion-related articles on a freelance basis. What fashion-related events, news, or people would you like to write about, and for whom? While you probably won't be able to get something accepted and published in a major magazine like *Glamour* or *Vogue* right away, you might very well be able to pitch an article to a local or regional publication. Be sure, too, to approach fashion-oriented Web sites and e-zines as well, many of which welcome working with new and somewhat inexperienced Fashion Writers.

WEB CONTENT PRODUCER

CAREER PROFILE

Duties: Oversees the development and presentation of high-quality content for a fashion- or apparel-related Web site

Alternate Title(s): Online Content Producer, Content Producer, Producer, Content Specialist

Salary Range: $30,000 to $70,000+

Employment Prospects: Fair

Advancement Prospects: Good

Best Geographical Location(s): Fashion centers like New York City and Los Angeles, as well as other large cities that are home to apparel-related companies or media organizations that cover some aspect(s) of the apparel industry

Prerequisites:

Education or Training—A bachelor's degree in journalism, mass communications, English, communication, or a liberal arts discipline (e.g., psychology) is typically required

Experience—Two to five years of experience are usually required for mid- and high-level positions; entry-level positions often require only a year or two of experience (which can include internships or co-ops during college)

Special Skills and Personality Traits—Exceptional writing and editing skills; mastery of the rules of grammar, punctuation, and usage; ability to work well individually and with others (including internal colleagues and external contractors/freelancers); solid organizational skills; willingness and ability to multitask, prioritize, and set and meet often stringent deadlines; outstanding computer skills; comfort with Internet technologies like HTML, Web content management software, search engine optimization strategies, online message boards, and Web logs (blogs); ability to continuously learn new technologies; solid research and conceptualization skills; expertise in apparel-related news and trends

CAREER LADDER

Content Manager

Senior Content Producer/Specialist

Content Producer/Specialist

Content Production Intern or Assistant

Position Description

Whenever you visit a fashion-related Web site—particularly one that features lots of news and stories on industry trends, key industry players, and the like—it's easy to fall into the trap of believing that what you're seeing just sort of magically showed up out of nowhere. It didn't. All of that great information—and the way it's presented to you on screen—represents the comprehensive, fast-paced job of a Web Content Producer.

Content producers in most organizations have two main responsibilities: developing Web site content (by writing it themselves, having others [such as freelancers] write it, or both) and making sure the final content actually gets put onto the site, and in a way that is graphically pleasing and compelling to the end user. Given this unique editorial/technological combination, then, it's no surprise that successful Web Content Producers have a unique combination of communication and technical skills.

In some ways, Web Content Producers are simply print journalists who are working in an online medium. Like journalists, content producers typically must come up with article ideas that their Web site's users will find interesting and useful. They then must either research and write those articles themselves or assign them to colleagues or freelancers whose pieces must then be edited for clarity and content.

In other ways, Web Content Producers are more like Web designers or multimedia specialists, using their knowledge of HTML and, much more important these days, content management software to make sure finished articles (and, often, other elements such as photos or even audio or video clips) actually get onto the Web site for users to see.

Depending on the specific sites for which they're responsible, Web Content Producers might also manage online message boards (where site users can "talk" with each other electronically); oversee Web logs (blogs) where they and/or others can write in depth about topics of special interest; and assist with the actual design or redesign of the Web site itself so that its users will be able to find what they need quickly and easily.

Salaries

Compensation Web site Salary.com notes that mid-level content specialists across all fields earned a median annual salary of $44,500 in 2006. Senior content specialists earned $57,900, and content managers earned $73,900.

At the entry level, meanwhile, content specialists across all fields earned a median annual salary of about $32,000 in 2005, according to a study of 2,412 bachelor's degree recipients conducted by the University of Georgia's Grady College of Journalism & Mass Communication.

Employment Prospects

Since the Internet itself—particularly the Web—is a comparatively young medium, the job of Web Content Producer is in many ways still evolving. So while job opportunities do exist for people who want to become Web Content Producers for apparel-related Web sites, employment prospects can only be characterized as fair.

The 2005 University of Georgia study found that only 1.1 percent of the 2,412 college graduates surveyed were working in communication-related jobs involving the Web. However, the same study revealed, 30.3 percent of the survey respondents said they did "writing and editing for the Web" as at least part of their job in the journalism/communications sector.

Advancement Prospects

Web Content Producers have a unique combination of editorial and technical skills, making their advancement prospects good—whether they want to remain in the online communication realm or move into higher-level jobs in print journalism, broadcast journalism, or even marketing or advertising.

As content-driven Web sites become more complex, companies must hire not only Web Content Producers but also higher-level employees who oversee content producers and the entire content development process. Thus, Web Content Producers who prove themselves can advance to become content managers with more responsibilities and higher salaries.

Education and Training

Most Web Content Producers have at least a bachelor's degree in a field such as journalism, mass communications, English, communications, or a liberal arts field like psychology. Today, a bachelor's degree tends to be the minimum educational requirement for the job. Some Web Content Producers also pursue additional education (through certificate programs, private courses, and the like) on Internet technologies like HTML, Cascading Style Sheets, and software packages like Macromedia Dreamweaver.

Experience, Skills, and Personality Traits

First and foremost, Web Content Producers must be exceptional writers and editors who have solid command of the rules of grammar, punctuation, and usage. Content producers are the last (and sometimes only) line of defense between content as it's originally written and that same content when it's actually posted on the Web site. Clear, error-free writing is paramount to the credibility of a content-driven Web site, and it is the Web Content Producer's job to make it happen.

Content Producers must also be able to work well both individually and with others—especially outside contractors or freelancers who might be asked to provide some or all of a site's content. The best Content Producers have solid organizational and computer skills; the ability to multitask and prioritize; a dedication to deadlines; and solid research and article conceptualization abilities. Those who want to work for fashion-related Web sites in particular must also have fashion industry expertise and/or experience in many cases.

Unions and Associations

While there are no specific unions or associations for the profession, Web Content Producers can and do participate in a variety of industry organizations, depending on their interests. Some Content Producers, for instance, are members of the Society of Professional Journalists (SPJ), an association for journalists working in print, broadcast, or online media. Other Web Content Producers join groups ranging from the Association for Women in Communications (AWC) to the International Association of Business Communicators (IABC).

Web Content Producers who work for fashion-related Web sites can keep current in the overall fashion industry by participating in organizations like Fashion Group International (FGI), the American Apparel and Footwear Association (AAFA), and the International Textile and Apparel Association (ITAA).

Tips for Entry

1. Complete at least a bachelor's degree in journalism, mass communications, English, communications, or a liberal arts discipline like psychology.
2. During college, gain some practical writing and/or editing experience through an internship or a co-op assignment—with an apparel-related Web site if possible (though *any* setting would be helpful). Consider writing for the school's student newspaper as well—or, better yet, producing its Web site.
3. Talk to some Web Content Producers (i.e., informational interviewing) of fashion-related Web sites to learn more about what they do and how they got to where they are now. (Note: Even if you can't find such a Web Content Producer in your own immediate geographic area, you can talk to one elsewhere via e-mail or phone.)
4. Visit apparel company and job search Web sites to look for Web Content Producer job listings. What key skills and abilities, experiences, education, and traits do companies seem to be looking for in the content producers they want to hire?
5. Visit content-heavy fashion Web sites regularly to see what they're publishing. Look for opportunities to contribute content on a freelance/contract basis so that you can build your portfolio of published writing and start developing networking relationships with people who might one day hire you for a full-time, permanent job in the field.

PROMOTIONS

ADVERTISING PROFESSIONAL

CAREER PROFILE

Duties: Oversees paid promotional activities for a fashion retailer or manufacturer to raise consumer awareness of the firm's products and entice consumers to buy them

Alternate Title(s): Account Executive

Salary Range: $30,000 to $100,000+

Employment Prospects: Good

Advancement Prospects: Good

Best Geographical Location(s): Fashion centers like New York City, Los Angeles, Chicago, Dallas, and Philadelphia; other large, urban areas

Prerequisites:

Education or Training—A bachelor's degree is usually required, with a concentration in advertising, journalism, public relations, mass communications, marketing, fashion merchandising, or a related field; course work in graphic design, photography, computer applications, and English is helpful

Experience—College internship or co-op experience; higher-level positions require several years of professional advertising industry experience

Special Skills and Personality Traits—Excellent oral and written communication skills; ability to conceptualize, develop, and execute promotional concepts that are convincing and persuasive; ability to work effectively with other members of the advertising team (e.g., artists, writers, photographers, clients); an understanding of fashion trends and forecasts and consumer buying habits; ability to juggle many activities at once, and meet deadlines

Special Requirements—Possible certification through advertising-related professional organizations

CAREER LADDER

Vice President of Promotions

Advertising Manager

Advertising Coordinator or Assistant Advertising Manager

Advertising Trainee or Account Executive

Position Description

Advertising Professionals in general, and those working in or with the fashion industry in particular, oversee paid promotional activities for apparel retailers and manufacturers. They conceptualize, develop, and execute advertising campaigns through various media that will raise consumer awareness of a company's fashions and accessories and convince consumers to buy those products.

Some Advertising Professionals in the fashion industry work in house as employees of the advertising department of an apparel manufacturer or retailer. Other fashion Advertising Professionals work for outside advertising agencies, which oversee some or all of the advertising-related activities for one or more apparel manufacturers and/or retailers.

Depending on their work setting, their job level, their training, and their experience, Advertising Professionals in the fashion industry are involved in any number of wide-ranging activities. Almost all Advertising Professionals devote considerable time and energy to generating new promotional ideas, either on their own or, much more often, in collaboration with colleagues. Advertising Professionals also participate in market research, consumer surveys, and other activities that allow advertisers to take the pulse of a fashion retailer's or manufacturer's customers and develop an accurate picture of their wants and needs.

Advertising Professionals are also involved in a great deal of creative work. Writing is a big part of the job, whether that means coming up with the text that will appear in a catalog or accompany a print or an online ad; developing the dialogue and camera shots for a television commercial; or writing the script for a radio ad. Some Advertising Professionals, particularly those with training and experience in graphic design or a similar field, devote most of their time to the artistic side of the business, perhaps using a computer graphics program to design a magazine ad or a banner ad for a Web site. Other Advertising Professionals are responsible for media buying, determining which medium (e.g., print publications, Internet sites, radio, television, billboards) an ad should go into and which particular companies within that medium should get the fashion company's advertising dollars. Still other Advertising Professionals are upper-level managers or directors who oversee all of these activities along with many more—for example, budgeting, hiring, or, in the case of outside ad agencies, cultivating and retaining new clients.

Whatever their activities and wherever they work (in house or for an outside agency), Advertising Professionals combine their people skills, their creativity, their artistic and communication skills, and their fashion industry expertise to pursue one overriding goal: increased sales for their companies and clients. If they succeed, they will often continue running with the campaigns that have worked. If they don't, it's usually back to the drawing board, whether that means coming up with new ideas in the case of in-house Advertising Professionals, or hiring a new outside promotional firm in the case of fashion companies that outsource some or all of their advertising activities to advertising agencies. A particular advertising campaign may be highly creative and innovative, but if it doesn't result in increased sales, the fashion company isn't getting what it paid for—and thus it must take its advertising strategy in a new direction.

Salaries

On average, entry-level Advertising Professionals earned starting salaries of just over $34,000 as of spring 2006, according to a survey conducted by the National Association of Colleges and Employers.

As Advertising Professionals gain experience, however, their salaries tend to go up significantly. The median salary for Advertising Professionals in all fields was $63,610 in 2004, according to the U.S. Department of Labor. And highly experienced Advertising Professionals—particularly those who earn a solid reputation of success—can easily earn $100,000 a year or more.

Employment Prospects

Employment of Advertising Professionals and related personnel (e.g., marketing professionals, public relations professionals) across all fields is expected to increase faster than average between now and 2014, according to the U.S. Department of Labor. Still, the competition for available jobs—especially at the entry level as well as the highest levels—is often keen. The best opportunities will go to college graduates who have not only an appropriate degree(s) but also advertising-related experience gained through college internship or co-op programs.

Advancement Prospects

Advancement opportunities for Advertising Professionals, whether they work in or for the fashion industry or another industry, are generally good. Once they've gained several years of experience, many Advertising Professionals move into higher-level positions within their organizations or new organizations. Some also pursue related careers in fashion merchandising or public relations.

Advertising Professionals who earn advanced degrees (e.g., a master of business administration [M.B.A.] degree) can often assume managerial or directorial positions that offer substantial salary increases and more varied and complex job responsibilities.

Education and Training

A bachelor's degree is generally required to break into the advertising field. The best opportunities typically go to applicants who have a degree in advertising, journalism, public relations, mass communications, marketing, fashion merchandising, or a related field. Advertising Professionals typically find it helpful to have additional course work or training in areas like graphic design, photography, computer applications, and/or English.

Many Advertising Professionals complete additional training and receive various industry certifications from professional organizations.

The Promotional Products Association International (PPAI) offers master advertising specialist (MAS) and certified advertising specialist (CAS) certification. To earn either of these designations, Advertising Professionals must work in the field a certain number of years, take courses, make significant contributions to the industry, and pass a written exam.

Sales and Marketing Executives International (SMEI) offers three certifications: certified marketing executive (CME), certified sales executive (CSE), and SMEI-certified professional salesperson (SCPS). To earn any of these, Advertising Professionals must meet an experience requirement plus pass a written exam.

The Public Relations Society of America (PRSA) provides certification as accredited in public relations (APR) to Advertising Professionals who meet an experience requirement and pass a written exam.

The American Marketing Association (AMA) offers the Professional Certified Marketer (PCM) credential. To become a PCM, an Advertising Professional must meet an experience requirement of two or four years (two years with a master's degree or four years with a bachelor's degree) and pass an exam.

A portfolio highlighting previous writing- and design-related projects is essential for grabbing the attention of prospective employers.

Experience, Skills, and Personality Traits

Most people who want to become Advertising Professionals participate in one or more college internships or co-op programs to gain some entry-level experience and, importantly, cultivate contacts in the advertising industry. Many gain additional experience and skills by participating in advertising-related professional organizations on campus or in the community.

Advertising Professionals in all fields need myriad skills to be successful. Among the most important for Advertising Professionals in the fashion industry are excellent oral and written communication skills, outstanding creativity and conceptualization abilities, strong analytical and problem-solving skills, and extensive knowledge of the fashion industry as a whole and fashion consumers in particular. Advertising Professionals must also have proven skills in planning and organizing, juggling many projects at once under the pressure of deadlines, assessing the success of advertising campaigns, and working well with an assortment of different people (e.g., artists, writers, photographers, media professionals).

At the managerial or directorial level, Advertising Professionals need to have sound supervisory, training, budgeting, and big picture abilities as well. Advertising Professionals at all levels must now be proficient with a variety of computer applications and Internet advertising and marketing strategies.

Unions and Associations

Many Advertising Professionals are members of the American Advertising Federation (AAF), an industry trade organization. Others participate in the professional development activities of similar organizations like the American Marketing Association (AMA), the Public Relations Society of America (PRSA), and Sales and Marketing Executives International (SMEI).

Advertising Professionals in the fashion industry often supplement their participation in these organizations by participating in fashion-oriented trade associations as well.

Tips for Entry

1. While you're in school, be sure to pursue one or more advertising-related internships or co-ops so that you can gain practical, hands-on experience in the field. If possible, target your internship or co-op efforts toward in-house advertising departments within fashion companies or outside advertising agencies serving the fashion industry.
2. Contact one or more Advertising Professionals who work in or for the fashion industry and ask them to tell you more about their careers and how they got into them.
3. Gain as much writing experience as you can by, for example, working for your school's student newspaper. Advertising Professionals at all levels spend considerable time writing, whether for catalog blurbs, radio scripts, or television ad dialogue.
4. Develop your computer skills, particularly your graphic design and Web design skills. Not only will this help you grow in your creativity, but it will also teach you skills that will be highly desirable to advertising professionals you approach about jobs and internships.
5. Monitor fashion industry publications in print and online so that you continuously develop broad knowledge of the industry as a whole. Pay particular attention to the advertisements you see. Study the copy and graphics used in the ads and try to assess what messages the ads are attempting to communicate.
6. Start developing a portfolio, a three-ring binder or folder made up of your best writing- and design-related projects from school, part-time jobs, or internships. Prospective employers in the advertising field will expect and need to see your portfolio when they're interviewing you for an internship or entry-level position.

COPYWRITER

CAREER PROFILE

Duties: Writes text that accompanies fashion-related advertisements in print or electronic media, in catalogs, on Web sites, or in direct-mail pieces

Alternate Title(s): None

Salary Range: $0 to $80,000+

Employment Prospects: Good

Advancement Prospects: Good

Best Geographical Location(s): Major cities across the United States, particularly fashion centers like New York City and Los Angeles

Prerequisites:

Education or Training—A bachelor's degree is generally required, in an area like advertising, marketing, public relations, journalism, communications, English, or the liberal arts; course work in fashion design and apparel merchandising is helpful

Experience—College internship or co-op experience under a veteran Copywriter is highly recommended; a portfolio demonstrating previous work samples is required; summer or part-time job experience in sales or market research is helpful

Special Skills and Personality Traits—Strong writing skills; knowledge of fashion industry trends and consumer buying psychology and habits; creativity; ability to put complex ideas into concise words; organizational skills; ability to manage multiple projects at once and meet deadlines; knowledge of print and electronic media; strong computer skills; ability to collaborate well with others; thoroughness; flexibility; ability to work well under pressure

CAREER LADDER

Senior Copywriter

Copywriter

Junior Copywriter

Copywriting Intern

Position Description

Copywriters are wordsmiths who write the text that accompanies fashion-related advertisements, whether those advertisements appear in print media (i.e., magazines and newspapers), on radio or television, in catalogs, on Web sites, or in direct-mail pieces that arrive in consumers' mailboxes.

However, copywriters don't just pen words. Their goal is to write text that sells. The words accompanying an advertisement must grab the attention of the reader, viewer, or listener and compel him or her to buy the product described, or, at the very least, to remember the company or organization behind the product. As such, the Copywriter's words must be easy to understand, concise, and benefit-focused.

In most cases, Copywriters collaborate with many other professionals in their work. They may, for example, consult with graphic designers about the look of an advertisement and the type of overall message to be communicated by the ad. Or, they may collaborate with Web developers to determine whether the words they write for an Internet ad can be flashed across the screen at different times or in different places. In some cases—particularly when they work for advertising agencies—Copywriters must also collaborate closely with clients to ensure that the ad copy they're writing meets the client's wants and needs.

Copywriters can work for a variety of organizations. Many work for advertising agencies, which are hired by apparel manufacturers, retailers, and other organizations to oversee part or all of a company's advertising efforts. Other Copywriters work in house for apparel manufacturers' or retailers' own advertising departments. Still other Copywriters are self-employed freelancers who solicit and work for their own clients, whether those clients are apparel manufacturers and retailers or advertising agencies that need additional copywriting help for certain projects.

Copywriters have to constantly think about the audiences for their writing, so it's important for Copywriters to continually analyze their target readers, viewers, or listeners and to understand them in great detail. Often Copywriters will study a population's or subpopulation's demographics (e.g., age, gender, income) so that they can better predict which words will grab their attention and nudge them toward buying the product or service an ad is promoting.

Often, Copywriters work on several projects at once, all with different deadlines, so their days can sometimes be quite hectic, especially when deadlines coincide. A Copywriter might easily be working on new ad copy one minute, answering a client's question the next, meeting about an upcoming ad campaign the next, and then editing previously written copy. The work is almost always diverse, and it usually requires both strong writing skills and good people skills.

Salaries

Depending on who they work for and how much work they do, Copywriters can earn as little as a few thousand dollars a year or as much as $80,000. Self-employed freelancers who are just starting their businesses often need time to build up enough income to live on. Experienced, senior-level Copywriters, on the other hand, can sometimes make $100,000 a year or more, particularly if they've developed a reputation for writing ad copy that substantially increases sales.

The median annual salary for writers across all fields was $44,350 in 2004, according to the U.S. Department of Labor. Writers who work in advertising (i.e., Copywriters and similar professionals) fared considerably better, earning a median annual salary of $54,410 in 2004, the DOL notes.

Employment Prospects

Writers across all fields in the United States held about 142,000 jobs in 2004, according to the U.S. Department of Labor. The DOL predicts that the number of jobs for writers (and editors) will grow about as fast as average between now and 2014.

Competition for copywriting jobs and related jobs, however, is often keen, especially for those interested in fashion and/or textiles in particular. But given the sheer number of jobs already available, plus the continuing growth of the Internet as a medium, employment prospects for Copywriters are good.

Advancement Prospects

Copywriters who gain experience and, especially, a strong reputation based on their performance can advance to a variety of higher-level positions, including senior Copywriter, advertising manager or director, or even creative director.

Many Copywriters start their own single-person or several-person companies, capitalizing on their contacts and past performance to grow their own successful firms. Often, their old employers and clients are among their first customers.

Education and Training

Generally speaking, Copywriters need at least a bachelor's degree, in a field like advertising, marketing, public relations, journalism, communications, English, or the liberal arts. Course work or a minor in apparel merchandising or fashion design is also quite helpful to those who want to work in apparel or textiles in particular, as are business-related courses, especially for Copywriters who plan to start their own companies someday.

Experience, Skills, and Personality Traits

College internship or co-op experience under a veteran Copywriter is highly recommended for anyone who wants to get into copywriting. Such activities offer hands-on, real-world experience in the field, not to mention important contacts that can be invaluable in the job hunt.

Prospective Copywriters also need to put together a portfolio demonstrating their skills and showing their previous work samples and clips. Many of these samples can come from summer or part-time jobs, internships, and even volunteer activities.

Copywriters with experience in sales and/or market research will have an edge over other candidates in most cases because they'll have a better understanding of consumers and how they make their purchasing decisions.

To be successful, Copywriters need to be exceptional writers who can develop concise, attention-grabbing text. They must be creative and imaginative, and have thorough knowledge of the fashion industry, consumer buying habits, and consumer psychology.

Collaboration skills are also essential to all Copywriters. Rarely do Copywriters work alone; instead, they work in teams made up of other Copywriters, graphic designers, clients, and others. They must be able to not only contribute ideas, but also listen to and evaluate the ideas of others. They need to be flexible, willing and able to accept constructive criticism, and capable of dealing with change as well.

Copywriters must be able to manage many projects at once and meet deadlines, often under pressure that is beyond their immediate control.

Unions and Associations

Most Copywriters and similar professionals are members of the American Advertising Federation (AAF), an umbrella trade association for the advertising industry. Some are also involved with industry groups like the American Marketing Association (AMA), the Public Relations Society of America (PRSA), and Sales and Marketing Executives International (SMEI).

Copywriters can keep up with industry trends by getting involved with fashion-specific organizations like the American Apparel and Footwear Association (AAFA) and Fashion Group International (FGI).

Tips for Entry

1. Participate in one or more college internships or co-op programs so that you can get some practical, hands-on experience in copywriting before you graduate. If possible, get into an internship or a co-op program at a fashion-oriented firm—for example, a fashion manufacturer or retailer, or a fashion-oriented advertising agency.
2. Develop a portfolio showcasing some specific examples of your work. Volunteer to write for college organizations (e.g., the student newspaper) or local nonprofit groups so that you can get some practical writing experience and add published pieces to your portfolio.
3. Talk to one or more Copywriters who work in the fashion industry in some way, so that you can learn how you too can work in the field someday.
4. Join a professional organization like the American Advertising Federation or the American Marketing Association so that you can meet Copywriters in a variety of fields, including fashion, and learn about job and internship opportunities.

EVENT PLANNER

CAREER PROFILE

Duties: Plans and executes special events (e.g., store openings, trunk shows, new product launches) for a retail apparel company in order to boost the company's visibility and increase sales

Alternate Title(s): Event Coordinator, Event Planning Coordinator, Event Planning Specialist

Salary Range: $30,000 to $70,000+

Employment Prospects: Fair

Advancement Prospects: Good

Best Geographical Location(s): Large cities across the United States that are home to retail apparel companies

Prerequisites:

Education or Training—A bachelor's degree in marketing, communications, or a related discipline is generally preferred

Experience—Two to three years of event planning and/or general public relations experience, particularly in an apparel retail setting, is typically required

Special Skills and Personality Traits—Outstanding creativity and imagination; excellent written and verbal communication skills; planning, coordinating, and scheduling abilities; follow-through and exceptional attention to detail; ability to set and meet deadlines; ability to perform well under pressure; ability to build solid working relationships with colleagues, potential corporate sponsors, and members of the media; flexibility, adaptability, and problem-solving capabilities

CAREER LADDER

Public Relations Manager or Fashion Coordinator

Director of Special Events

Event Planner

Event Planning Assistant

Position Description

Retail fashion and apparel establishments—particularly those in large cities with competitive markets—have to constantly come up with ways to stand out in an often crowded field of players. One way they do just that is to hold a variety of special events for their current and prospective customers. It is the Event Planner's job to conceptualize, develop, and implement these visibility-enhancing activities, either alone or, often, in collaboration with colleagues such as public relations staff, marketing staff, or company fashion coordinators.

Depending on the size and goals of the companies for whom they work, Event Planners can be involved in setting up a variety of different events throughout the course of a year or even a season. Among the most common types of activities: store openings, trunk shows (during which a fashion designer visits a store to personally show his/her latest collection), bridal shows, new product launches, educational classes/seminars, and holiday-related events. The goal is to boost the store's visibility—among both consumers and members of the media—so that, ultimately, more customers will shop at the store and buy merchandise there, thus boosting the store's sales.

Event Planners can break their jobs down into four main activities: 1) conceptualizing—coming up with event ideas that are not merely creative and fun but that will also contribute to the company's bottom line; 2) planning—determining what needs to be done for each event, along with who will do it and by when; 3) executing—taking care of all the details before the event (e.g., contacting the media, making arrangements for food and/or entertainment, securing a venue, hiring models) as well as running the show on the day of the event itself; and 4) evaluating—assessing afterward what went well at the event, what didn't go so well, and what the specific results were in terms of store visibility and sales.

Sometimes Event Planners also build connections with local or national charity and nonprofit organizations so that they, too, might benefit from a fashion retailer's special events—by, for instance, receiving a portion of sales proceeds or a boost in their own visibility thanks to a celebrity visit.

Salaries

Event Planners who work for apparel-related retail companies can expect to earn about $30,000 a year to start, give or take a few thousand dollars. Those who have a solid track record of experience and results, and who perhaps oversee other public relations or promotional activities as well (which is fairly common), can earn considerably more—perhaps $45,000 to $50,000 a year.

Mid-level Event Planners across all industries earned a median annual salary of $51,319 in 2006, according to compensation Web site Salary.com, while event planning assistants earned a median annual salary of $42,835.

Employment Prospects

Relatively few retail fashion companies employ people who are strictly Event Planners. Indeed, in many companies, event planning is overseen not as someone's entire job but instead part of the job of, for example, a public relations professional or company fashion coordinators. So employment prospects for Event Planners in retail fashion can only be characterized as fair.

Opportunities do exist, though, especially for people who have event planning experience (through other jobs or internships/co-ops) and who are open to working for larger organizations that have the resources necessary to hire full-time event planning staff.

Advancement Prospects

Event planning isn't easy. Event Planners who prove themselves to company decision makers—especially in terms of key results like company visibility and sales—are likely to move up to higher-level positions, not only in event planning but also in the expanded realm of public relations and the even broader realm of marketing. So advancement prospects for Event Planners are good, particularly if they have the willingness and ability to take calculated risks and perhaps relocate when a higher-level position becomes available.

Education and Training

Though it's not necessarily required, most Event Planners today have at least a bachelor's degree in a field such as marketing, communications, public relations, or journalism. Those who work for apparel retailing companies also benefit from having apparel industry experience of some sort, be it in retail store sales or another closely related area like merchandising or fashion coordination.

Experience, Skills, and Personality Traits

More than anything else, Event Planners in the retail apparel field (and all other industries, for that matter) must be creative and imaginative. The pressure to come up with the most memorable (and most original) events is constant, as is the pressure to actually pull them off successfully. To do their jobs well, Event Planners must have exceptional written and verbal communication skills, proven planning and coordinating abilities, and the relatively rare combination of being able to envision the big picture and attend to all the important details at the same time.

The most successful Event Planners are detail-oriented, capable of setting and meeting deadlines, and able to perform well under pressure. They also have—or can easily create—solid working relationships with both internal colleagues and outsiders, such as members of the media. Perhaps most important of all, Event Planners must be flexible and adaptable, easily rolling with changes and solving problems as they occur—because as any experienced Event Planner will attest, there's no such thing as the perfectly executed event.

Unions and Associations

Event Planners across all industries can get involved in several professional organizations in the field, including the International Special Events Society (ISES) or the slightly broader Meeting Professionals International (MPI). Since many of the people who oversee event planning in retail apparel are also responsible for a broader range of public relations–related activities, the Public Relations Society of America (PRSA) is another good professional resource.

Event Planners in fashion/apparel retail can also keep current on trends by tapping the resources of the National Retail Federation (NRF) and/or organizations like Fashion Group International (FGI), the American Apparel and

Footwear Association (AAFA), and the International Textile and Apparel Association (ITAA).

Tips for Entry

1. Complete at least a bachelor's degree in a discipline like marketing, communications, or mass communications. Consider pursuing a minor (or a double major) in an apparel-related discipline such as fashion merchandising.
2. During college, gain some practical experience in event planning through an internship or a co-op assignment, either with an apparel retailer or perhaps an outside company that specializes in event planning.
3. Do whatever you can to get to know some working Event Planners in the apparel retailing field. If possible, talk to some Event Planners (i.e., informational interviewing) to learn more about what they do and how they got to where they are now.
4. Visit the Web sites of apparel retailers, as well as general job search Web sites, to look for Event Planner job listings. What key skills and abilities, experiences, education, and traits do companies seem to be looking for in the Event Planners they want to hire?
5. Whenever possible, attend special events held by fashion/apparel retailers in your city or nearby. What went into that four-hour seminar . . . or that trunk show . . . or that exciting product launch you witnessed? How can you learn more?

FASHION PUBLIC RELATIONS SPECIALIST

CAREER PROFILE

Duties: Works to keep an apparel company's name in the public eye and develop a favorable corporate image; writes news releases, arranges media interviews and special events, and develops strong professional working relationships with members of the media

Alternate Title(s): Publicist (Fashion), Media Relations Specialist (Fashion), Communications Specialist (Fashion), Promotions Specialist (Fashion)

Salary Range: $25,000 to $100,000+

Employment Prospects: Fair/Good

Advancement Prospects: Fair/Good

Best Geographical Location(s): Fashion centers like New York City and other large cities, especially where the headquarters of major apparel manufacturers, retail stores, and department stores are located

Prerequisites:

Education or Training—A bachelor's degree in public relations or a similar field is usually required

Experience—Related internship or co-op experience; experience working as a journalist or reporter, either for fashion-specific publications or for more general publications, is helpful

Special Skills and Personality Traits—Excellent oral and written communication skills; solid interpersonal skills; advanced computer skills, particularly those involving design and database management; strong public speaking and presenting skills; ability to multitask and manage time effectively; energy and flexibility; versatility; attention to detail

CAREER LADDER

Public Relations or Promotions Director

Public Relations or Promotions Coordinator

Fashion Publicist

Publicity or Promotions Assistant

Position Description

Fashion Public Relations (PR) Specialists have one of the most diverse job descriptions in the entire fashion industry. Apparel companies hire them to develop and maintain a positive image among the media, consumers, investors, employees, and even competitors. They do that through a wide variety of communication-oriented activities.

One of the Fashion PR Specialist's most important tasks is developing strong working relationships with members of the media, such as magazine or newspaper reporters, television or radio producers, or Web site producers. Media members are always looking for news to feature in their publications or on their programs. Fashion PR Specialists, on the other hand, are always looking to make news about the products and companies they represent. Such coverage is often seen as better than the coverage the company would have received through advertising, since it hasn't been paid for and it carries an editorial versus an advertising voice.

Fashion PR Specialists provide—or, some would say, create—news in a variety of ways. They often write and distribute news releases to members of the media. Each news release highlights what the Fashion PR Specialist believes to be a product, event, or person worthy of the recipient's attention. Their hope is that the reporter or producer who receives the news release will use it verbatim in his or her publication, or, as more commonly happens, use it as the springboard for an article or program. If that happens, the Fashion PR Specialist has successfully put his or her company and its products and people in the public eye.

Fashion PR Specialists perform many other tasks in pursuit of this same goal. They arrange or help to arrange fashion shows, product shoots for fashion magazines, or celebrity endorsements of their company's products. They also wine and dine members of the media—for example, by inviting them out for lunch or dinner so that they can build strong professional working relationships with them. Occasionally, Fashion PR Specialists will also arrange news conferences, media gatherings where a company may make a major announcement about a new product line or the hiring of a significant new staff member. Similarly, Fashion PR Specialists are responsible for arranging media interviews with company presidents, fashion designers, merchandisers, and other high-level personnel in their companies who have the expertise media members sometimes seek.

In addition to their media-related tasks, many Fashion PR Specialists also write and produce publications for employees and investors. These might include a weekly or monthly employee newsletter or the company's annual report, documenting for stockholders the company's performance over the previous year and its plans and goals for the year ahead. Fashion PR Specialists are also called upon to develop and maintain PR-related Web sites for their companies. The sites often include archives of previous news releases, electronic versions of various publications (e.g., newsletters, reports, bulletins, announcements), and key company contacts for the media.

Fashion PR Specialists also must maintain clip files of the diverse coverage they secure for their companies in various media. They may keep an eye on industry publications, programs, and Web sites themselves to stay abreast of where they're being covered and how, but more often they enlist the help of outside clipping services that specialize in monitoring a company's media coverage.

Fashion PR Specialists can work on staff for apparel manufacturers, fashion or general retailers, or even fashion-related media outlets. Many also work for independent firms that specialize in fashion public relations. In New York City alone there are more than 20 such firms. Whatever the work setting, the Fashion PR Specialist's overriding goal remains the same: to promote a company's products, events, and people in as many diverse ways as possible so that the consuming public views the company favorably and consistently buys its products.

Salaries

Starting salaries for Fashion PR Specialists, and for entry-level PR specialists in general, can be somewhat low—perhaps as low as $25,000 a year—although the figure can range up to $30,000 or even $35,000 a year, depending on the company, the company's location, and the job duties and requirements. As Fashion PR Specialists progress in their careers and gain more experience and expertise, however, their salaries can increase substantially. Compensation Web site Salary.com reports that experienced public relations directors earned a median annual salary of about $116,000 in 2006.

The median annual salary for PR professionals across all fields and levels was $43,830 in 2004, according to the U.S. Department of Labor.

Fashion PR Specialists who work on staff for their companies generally receive an annual salary with benefits. Those who work for independent PR firms with fashion industry clients may also receive salaries, but may receive project-oriented fees instead, especially if their firms are small one- or two- or three-person operations.

Employment Prospects

Prospective Fashion PR Specialists have a relatively good chance of breaking into the field, despite somewhat stiff competition for entry-level jobs, especially if they're willing to start at the bottom to gain experience and make contacts. PR specialists across all fields and levels held about 188,000 jobs in 2004, according to the U.S. Department of Labor, and their employment prospects are expected to grow faster than average between now and 2014, the DOL says.

Those who have volunteer or internship/co-op experience through their colleges/universities will likely have the best opportunities, as will those who have fashion-related education or experience. Having reporting-related experience is also a highly valued asset, since so much of the Fashion PR Specialist's job centers around understanding and meeting media wants and needs.

Advancement Prospects

Once a Fashion PR Specialist has gained three to five years of experience and cultivated substantial contacts in the fashion PR and fashion media areas, he or she may advance to a PR coordinator's or even a PR director's role, which entails supervision of employees and the entire public relations operation.

Many experienced Fashion PR Specialists also start their own PR companies, landing immediate clients as a result of the industry contacts they've already made working for someone else. As their fledgling companies gain a positive reputation within the industry, they can continue to grow, bringing in even more clients and more money. The entrepreneurial road can be risky, though, for it's never certain whether current clients will stay or new clients will sign on.

Education and Training

Most Fashion PR Specialists have a bachelor's degree in public relations or a related field like mass communications, journalism, communications, advertising, or marketing. Many also have degrees in fashion merchandising, fashion design, or a similar field.

To create better future job opportunities for themselves, many college students who want to get into fashion PR pursue an internship, co-op experience, or even a volunteership, so that they can start gaining the experience, contacts, and skills they'll need to succeed in an entry-level position after graduation.

Some college students also wisely decide to gain editorial/ journalism experience by, for example, writing for their college newspapers, or writing freelance articles for their community newspapers or magazines.

Experience, Skills, and Personality Traits

To be successful, Fashion PR Specialists need a wide range of skills. Perhaps most important, they need to be excellent communicators, in writing and in person, and be personable and social enough to develop positive working relationships with other people, especially members of the media. If a Fashion PR Specialist has poor relationships with most or all members of the media, he or she will rarely be successful in getting his or her company in the public eye.

Fashion PR Specialists also greatly benefit by having media experience of their own. Journalists and reporters often complain that "PR flaks" don't understand what media members do. The Fashion PR Specialist who has been a journalist or reporter, however, will gain an appreciation for the stresses, constraints, and deadlines that journalists face each day. Very likely, he or she will command more respect from the media members as a result.

Fashion PR Specialists have to understand what makes a product, event, person, or company newsworthy in the eyes of the media and others. They have to continuously search for a story angle that will grab the media's attention. As such, they must be analytical problem-solvers who are also persuasive, assertive, persistent, and creative.

Since their jobs are so diverse, Fashion PR Specialists must also be master jugglers who manage their time well, consistently meet their deadlines, and successfully take care of the many minor and major details their jobs entail. While a good deal of their job involves planning, they must also be able to deal with unplanned situations. These might include a reporter who needs to interview a company spokesperson before 5 P.M. that day, a magazine editor who wants to include a certain dress the company produces in a photo shoot the next day, or a technical problem that makes the news release archives on the PR Web site inaccessible.

Unions and Associations

Many Fashion PR Specialists and public relations practitioners in other industries belong to the Public Relations Society of America (PRSA), a New York City–based professional trade organization. College students who want to pursue a career in fashion PR can also get involved with their school's chapter of the Public Relations Student Society of America (PRSSA), the PRSA's college affiliate.

Some Fashion PR Specialists are also members of the International Association of Business Communicators (IABC), a San Francisco–based trade group made up of professionals in public relations, employee communications, marketing communications, public affairs, and related fields.

Tips for Entry

1. Contact one or more Fashion PR Specialists and ask to meet with them so that you can learn more about what they do. You might also be able to land an internship or a volunteership using this approach.
2. Visit the Web sites of apparel manufacturers and public relations firms with apparel-related clients. Study the news releases and other materials on the site so that you can begin to understand the amount and content of the news each apparel company is attempting to generate.
3. If you're a college student, write articles for your school's student newspaper. Perhaps you could even write a fashion column. It's important to understand how journalists think and do their jobs.
4. Contact professional associations like the Public Relations Society of America (PRSA) and the International Association of Business Communicators (IABC) to learn more about the public relations field in general and fashion PR in particular. See if these and similar organizations can help you identify people you can talk to in the fashion PR field.
5. Read fashion industry publications in print or on the Internet to see what kind of news items they feature. What seems to make each item newsworthy?
6. Begin developing a portfolio showing some of your best writing samples and other examples of your work. Most PR departments and independent firms will want to see your portfolio when they consider you for internships or entry-level jobs.

FASHION SHOW PRODUCER

CAREER PROFILE

Duties: Plans and implements fashion shows, whether they're glamorous designer shows, charity shows for nonprofit fundraising, or trunk shows that travel to different retail stores

Alternate Title(s): Fashion Show Director, Promotion Director

Salary Range: $0 to $100,000+

Employment Prospects: Limited

Advancement Prospects: Limited

Best Geographical Location(s): Fashion centers like New York City, Milan, and Paris for designer shows, and smaller cities for trunk shows and charity shows

Prerequisites:

Education or Training—While there are no specific educational requirements, a college degree in fashion design, fashion marketing/promotion, or theater is helpful

Experience—Extensive fashion industry experience, often in design, merchandising, or marketing, is required

Special Skills and Personality Traits—Organizational skills; creativity; decisiveness; solid interpersonal skills; ability to conceptualize an entire show and oversee the hundreds of details involved in executing it successfully; well-developed marketing and public relations skills

CAREER LADDER

Fashion Show Producer, Independent

Fashion Show Producer, In-house

Various positions

Position Description

If you've ever seen highlights of the latest highbrow fashion show on television, you've seen the fruits of the Fashion Show Producer's labor. Fashion Show Producers, whether they work in-house for a particular apparel designer, manufacturer, or retailer, or on their own as independent freelancers, handle the hundreds of details that go into the planning and implementation of every fashion show.

Fashion Show Producers can work on several different types of shows. The most well-known type of show is the designer show, the elaborate, glamorous production in which a top-name designer shows his or her latest collection to guests like industry media, celebrities and other socialites, and top fashion buyers and fashion directors. Sometimes, the person who produces this type of show is an in-house employee of the designer or his or her manufacturer. But much more often these days, the person is an independent Fashion Show Producer whose sole business revolves around producing fashion shows for the top designers.

Other Fashion Show Producers oversee charity shows held to raise money for nonprofit agencies. Again, these producers can be in-house employees of the retail or department store hosting the show, or they can be independents who specialize in putting on such shows for a variety of clients. During charity shows, the Fashion Show Producer does many of the same things he or she might do for a more elaborate show, but often takes on unique tasks, such as teaching volunteer models from the nonprofit agency how to do their work in the show.

Still other Fashion Show Producers handle trunk shows, in which designers or manufacturers assemble one or more fashion lines for travel to different stores around a city or in different cities. These types of shows are generally easier and less expensive to produce, but even so they can be complex. Thus, they too might be handled either by an in-house person or an independent freelancer.

Different types of shows call for different types of activities on the part of the Fashion Show Producer, but in general he or she must handle an array of details before, during, and even after the show. Fashion Show Producers typically have to handle some or all of the following tasks:

- Secure a date and time for the show
- Secure a venue
- Work with the designer, manufacturer, or retailer to determine what clothing items will be modeled
- Locate and book models, some of whom are very expensive
- Oversee preshow promotional activities, like sending out news releases to industry media, celebrities, and other potential guests
- Determine the lighting, staging, music, and commentary for the show, and hire people to oversee each
- Locate and hire makeup and hair stylists for the show, along with "dressers" who will help the models get into and out of their clothes quickly
- Develop a sort of "script" for the show, describing who will model what and when
- Send out attention-grabbing invitations to prospective guests
- Ensure that the clothing to be worn gets to the show venue on time, and that it gets returned on time and in good condition
- Check in models and others on the day of the show
- Welcome guests and introduce the designer if he or she is in attendance
- Manage the actual show while it's going on
- Interact with guests and participants after the show, often at parties or similar events

Interestingly, the producer of the highbrow designer fashion show usually has one other key responsibility: deciding which guests will sit where for the event, and with or near whom. There's a certain status conferred upon guests who get front-row seats, and a corresponding lack of status among those who get poorer seats. Fashion Show Producers often agonize over whom to seat in the first row, the second row, etc., for fear of angering someone who might retaliate with, say, a poor review of the show or the collection featured. Producers also have to make sure that guests who are known to dislike each other—for example, the editors of two competing fashion publications—aren't seated next to each other, and yet still get the appropriate seating treatment.

Salaries

Salaries for Fashion Show Producers vary enormously, depending on their level of experience and, especially, their reputations in the field. Beginning fashion show production assistants might earn only a few thousand dollars a year helping with elaborate productions or coordinating small, local shows. Experienced, well-known Fashion Show Producers, on the other hand, can easily make $100,000 a year or more, depending on the number of shows they oversee, especially if they work in major fashion centers like New York City, London, Paris, or Milan.

Employment Prospects

Opportunities for Fashion Show Producers are quite limited. There are very few people who work full time in fashion show production; in fact, many people responsible for producing charity or trunk shows do so in addition to other job responsibilities. Still, opportunities do exist, especially if you're persistent and willing to work for free in the beginning to gain experience.

Advancement Prospects

It's difficult to advance in the fashion show production field, although independent freelancers who build a strong reputation by putting on quality shows need not fear lack of work. Still, the average person will find it difficult to advance in the fashion show production realm, though advancement is certainly possible, particularly for those who aren't willing to take no for an answer.

Education and Training

There is no set educational path for Fashion Show Producers. Some, however, have college degrees in fashion design, fashion marketing/promotion, theater, or a related field. Most have also received on-the-job training by volunteering for fashion show producers or similar professionals.

Experience, Skills, and Personality Traits

The Fashion Show Producer's job isn't an entry-level position. To be successful, Fashion Show Producers need extensive fashion industry experience, particularly in marketing, promotions, or actual fashion show productions. Independent Fashion Show Producers must also have many personal contacts in the industry who know them and their work well enough to entrust their fashion show productions to them, despite the often high financial costs.

Outstanding people skills are essential to every Fashion Show Producer, since they are constantly hiring personnel and dealing with sometimes egotistical members of the fashion media and other highbrow guests. Organizational and big-picture skills are also keys to succeeding. Fashion Show Producers have to be able to conceptualize a show that will garner positive attention from guests. On the other hand, however, they need to deal with the nitty-gritty details as well, since there are hundreds of decisions to make in putting a show together and hundreds of small but important tasks to be completed correctly.

Creativity, flexibility, originality, and knowledge of music, theater, and staging strategies are critical to the Fashion Show Producer's success. So are strong troubleshooting and problem-solving abilities and, perhaps above all, nerves of steel to deal with the inevitable problems that will emerge before, during, and even after a fashion show without compromising the production.

Unions and Associations

There are no specific unions or associations for Fashion Show Producers, but most are involved in groups that allow them to establish and maintain personal connections with fashion designers and other VIPs in the field. These might include Fashion Group International (FGI), the Fashion Association, and the Council of Fashion Designers of America (CFDA).

Tips for Entry

1. While it's quite difficult to do so, try to land a volunteer position with either an independent Fashion Show Producer or an in-house show production staff. Landing one of these positions will help you learn the business from the inside and, most important, meet the wide range of people you'll need to know to pursue the career someday.
2. Try to talk to one or more Fashion Show Producers, either in person or via phone or e-mail. Even a 15-minute chat will give you an enormous amount of useful information about how to get into the field, the pluses and minuses of the work, and the types of tasks various Fashion Show Producers work on each day.
3. Attend fashion shows whenever you can. Pay close attention to the music, the staging, the lighting, the models, the choreography, and the way guests are treated. Identify ways you would change each show if you were in charge of producing it, and consider approaching the producer of the show with your ideas. It's a bold move, but it may be just what you need to do to get noticed and, perhaps, land a volunteer position or even a part-time job.
4. Consider pursuing a college degree in fashion merchandising, fashion design, or theater so that you can gain the basic skills and knowledge the Fashion Show Producer needs.
5. Closely monitor industry publications in print or online, and watch television programs featuring fashion-related news. Extensive industry knowledge is critical to every Fashion Show Producer, as are wide-ranging industry contacts.

GRAPHIC DESIGNER

CAREER PROFILE

Duties: Designs advertisements, logos, brochures, annual reports, magazine layouts, Web sites, and other materials for various fashion and/or textile businesses

Alternate Title(s): Graphic Artist, Layout Artist

Salary Range: $0 to $80,000+

Employment Prospects: Good

Advancement Prospects: Good

Best Geographical Location(s): Major cities across the United States, particularly fashion centers like New York City and Los Angeles, or cities where apparel manufacturers' and retailers' headquarters are located

Prerequisites:

Education or Training—A bachelor's degree is required, in an area like graphic design, art, or advertising

Experience—College internship or co-op experience is highly recommended, and a portfolio demonstrating previous work samples is required

Special Skills and Personality Traits—Strong sense of design, color, and style; strong computer skills; creativity and imagination; ability to implement the ideas of others; ability to work well in teams; sound communication skills; problem-solving ability; resourcefulness; patience; accuracy and attention to detail; knowledge of printing processes; knowledge of Internet and Web applications and processes; ability to handle constructive criticism

CAREER LADDER

Art Director

Assistant Art Director/ Senior Graphic Designer

Graphic Designer/Artist

Junior Graphic Designer/Artist

Position Description

Graphic Designers can work in a wide variety of settings in the apparel or textile industries. Some Graphic Designers work for advertising agencies or corporate advertising departments, designing ads for print publications, electronic media, or the Internet. Other Graphic Designers work for manufacturers' or retailers' corporate headquarters, designing annual reports, brochures, logos, packaging, and an assortment of similar materials. Still other Graphic Designers work for media companies, perhaps designing the layouts for fashion magazines or fashion-oriented Web sites. Other Graphic Designers work for industry trade associations, buying offices, and other organizations that have a variety of design-related needs.

Most Graphic Designers need a combination of artistic and technical skills in order to succeed. On the artistic side, Graphic Designers will be required to develop their own ideas and concepts and, often, carry out the ideas and concepts of others. They use their knowledge of color, proportions, visual balance, and printing and Internet processes to create designs that will attract attention for the right reasons. From a technical standpoint, meanwhile, Graphic Designers must understand the printing process. They spend considerable time dealing with printers to make sure a particular piece's colors are right, for example, or that its overall look will be the same in print as it is on the computer screen. Graphic Designers must understand Internet applications and strategies as well, since they're often involved in developing fashion- or textile-oriented Web sites. They have to take an eye-opening visual and make it work from a technical standpoint so that visitors to the Web site won't be distracted by a poor layout or, worse, be frustrated when parts of the Web site don't work.

Many Graphic Designers are self-employed as freelancers. Instead of working full-time for one particular company, they independently offer their skills and services to a variety of companies, getting paid by the hour or by the project. Self-employed Graphic Designers, then, have to worry about additional business-related activities, like keeping accurate records of their income and expenses, marketing themselves so that they continue getting new clients, maintaining and updating their equipment (especially their computer hardware and software), and sending out invoices so that they get paid.

One of the most difficult aspects of the Graphic Designer's work is turning the ideas of many people into a finished product that satisfies everyone. Graphic Designers almost never work by themselves on a project; instead, they collaborate with a host of other professionals in their organizations—and, in the case of ad agencies, with client companies as well—to come up with their designs. Rarely does a Graphic Designer's initial concept become the final concept. Instead, he or she has to be able to accept feedback and constructive criticism from others, and then use that information to improve the initial design idea until it becomes the final concept that pleases everyone involved in the process.

Salaries

Salaries for Graphic Designers in the fashion and apparel industry vary widely. Beginning freelancers, for example, might earn only a few thousand dollars a year, especially if they aren't able to devote all of their work time to designing. Successful Graphic Designers in the industry, however, whether employed or self-employed, can sometimes earn $80,000 a year or more, depending on their track records and their reputations in their respective fields.

The median annual salary for Graphic Designers across all fields and levels was $38,030 in 2004, according to the U.S. Department of Labor. Meanwhile, a 2006 survey by the American Institute of Graphic Arts revealed a median annual salary of $39,000 for mid-level Graphic Designers and $52,000 for senior Graphic Designers across all fields.

Employment Prospects

Opportunities for Graphic Designers who want to work in the fashion industry are good, though competition for the available jobs can often be quite intense, particularly for freelancers. Graphic Designers across all fields held about 228,000 jobs in the United States in 2004, according to the U.S. Department of Labor. Seventy percent were salaried employees while the remaining 30 percent were self-employed freelancers.

Employment of Graphic Designers across all fields is expected to grow about as fast as average between now and 2014, the DOL notes.

Advancement Prospects

Successful Graphic Designers may advance in a number of ways. Some working on staff can move up to senior design positions, or possibly become art directors or even creative directors for some companies. They can also advance their career by moving to larger or more prestigious companies. Freelance designers advance as they build their reputation and acquire more work and bigger and better clients. Highly successful freelance designers might even open their own design business and employ two or three or more designers to handle a heavy workload.

Education and Training

In almost all cases, Graphic Designers need at least a bachelor's degree in an area like graphic design, art, or advertising. A bachelor of fine arts or master of fine arts degree in one of these areas is particularly impressive to employers and prospective clients. Just as important, however, is having practical, hands-on experience. Most prospective Graphic Designers get this experience by participating in college internships or co-op programs, which give them the opportunity to work in real companies under the guidance of more experienced graphic design professionals.

All prospective Graphic Designers must develop a portfolio of their previous work as well. The portfolio shows prospective employers or clients actual examples of the Graphic Designer's work, giving the employers or clients an idea of the designer's style and the types of projects the designer has successfully completed in the past.

Experience, Skills, and Personality Traits

Graphic Designers who want to work in the fashion and apparel industry need to gain practical experience through a college internship or co-op program. Employers appreciate the design skills one learns in class, but they also expect prospective Graphic Designers to be able to prove they can use those skills in the real world, with all of its pressures, deadlines, and interpersonal relationships.

To be successful, Graphic Designers must have strong design skills, creativity, and imagination, along with well-developed computer skills. Their job typically requires both artistic abilities and technical know-how. Graphic Designers also need to understand the printing process and the technical aspects of developing designs for the Web.

The best Graphic Designers are detail-oriented and accurate, resourceful, and able to communicate effectively. They can work well with other people and incorporate other people's ideas with their own. Often that means being able to handle constructive criticism without taking it personally, and being willing to allow for some give and take in the design process.

Unions and Associations

Many Graphic Designers in all fields are members of the American Institute of Graphic Arts (AIGA), a trade organization for the entire graphic design field. Others, depending on their area(s) of emphasis, might participate in organizations like the American Advertising Federation (AAF), the American Marketing Association (AMA), or the Public Relations Society of America (PRSA).

Tips for Entry

1. Participate in one or more college internships or co-op programs so that you can get some practical experience in graphic design before you graduate. If possible, get into an internship or co-op at a fashion-oriented firm, a fashion magazine, or a fashion-oriented advertising agency.
2. Develop a portfolio showcasing some specific examples of your work. Volunteer to design print publications for a college organization, perhaps, or a local nonprofit group to get some hands-on design experience and develop real-world pieces for your portfolio.
3. Talk to other Graphic Designers who work in the fashion industry in some way, so that you can learn more about what they do and how you too can work in the field someday.
4. Join a professional organization like the American Institute of Graphic Arts so that you can meet Graphic Designers in a variety of fields, including fashion, and learn about job and internship opportunities.

MARKETING MANAGER

CAREER PROFILE

Duties: Develops and executes comprehensive marketing strategies for an apparel manufacturer or retailer, with the goals of increasing profits, boosting the company's visibility and market penetration, and promoting the company's brand(s)

Alternate Title(s): None

Salary Range: $50,000 to $100,000+

Employment Prospects: Fair

Advancement Prospects: Fair

Best Geographical Location(s): Fashion centers like New York City and Los Angeles, as well as other large cities that are home to apparel-related manufacturing or retail companies

Prerequisites:

Education or Training—A bachelor's degree in marketing or a closely related field (e.g., communications, mass communications) is required; often, a graduate degree—particularly the master of business administration (M.B.A.)—is preferred

Experience—At least five years of experience are generally required, and often employers prefer candidates with seven to 10 years of experience

Special Skills and Personality Traits—Extensive background in apparel manufacturing or apparel retailing; exceptional marketing, promotion, and persuasion abilities; solid written and verbal communication skills; expertise in apparel industry trends and forecasts; proven skills in leadership, management, employee hiring and retention, and employee development; good computer skills, particularly with respect to spreadsheet, database, and presentation applications; ability to work well with a variety of people, ranging from entry-level employees to high-level executives; outstanding research and competitive intelligence abilities; ability to coordinate many projects at once while dealing with pressure and meeting associated deadlines; creativity combined with the ability to take calculated risks; knack for spotting new business opportunities and developing ways to take advantage of them

CAREER LADDER

Vice President of Marketing

Director of Marketing or Senior Marketing Manager

Marketing Manager

Assistant or Associate Marketing Manager

Marketing Specialist or Assistant

Position Description

Without Marketing Managers and the many apparel industry professionals who work under and with them, you'd probably never find out about new fashion companies, new fashion products, or new fashion trends. For without Marketing Managers, you'd probably never see any television or print advertisements for new clothing lines, never receive any direct-mail fliers publicizing special events at the nearby major department store, or never be able to participate in any online promotions in which you have a chance to win a free apparel makeover from a world-renowned fashion designer.

Marketing Managers—whether they work for apparel manufacturing companies or apparel-related retailers—are messengers at their core. Their job: to plan and implement as many different strategies as they can think of to get you, the consumer, to buy their company's products.

Usually, Marketing Managers oversee (or work with) several related professionals or departments, including those involved with publicity, advertising, merchandising, online promotion, special events, and market research. Through their collaborative efforts with these workers/departments as well as with their own staffs, they guide the company's efforts to sell more of its products to consumers, thereby increasing profits, boosting the company's visibility and market penetration, and promoting the company's brand(s).

The typical Marketing Manager can break his/her job down into several key areas of emphasis: 1) research—determining what consumers want in the way of new products, identifying and monitoring what competing apparel-related companies are doing, and analyzing quantitative (often financial) and qualitative data to uncover trends and make predictions for the future; 2) planning—using the results of research as well as past experience to come up with a comprehensive marketing plan for the season or the year; 3) executing—overseeing the creation and distribution of advertisements and collateral materials (e.g., brochures); undertaking media relations and publicity activities; and launching various special events and other promotional activities; and 4) evaluating—determining which of the various marketing and promotion strategies paid off and which ones didn't, then adjusting accordingly for future efforts.

Marketing Managers, as well as higher-level marketing directors and marketing vice presidents, have critical responsibilities that are reflected in both their salaries and the stresses they often face on the job. Well-thought-out marketing plans that are flawlessly executed and wildly successful make the Marketing Manager look good—thanks in no small part to the money the company makes in the process. Ill-conceived marketing plans that fail, on the other hand, might cost the Marketing Manager his/her job. So while many of the Marketing Manager's activities are intellectually challenging and often highly creative, they can also be quite stressful—especially if they don't achieve the company's desired results.

Salaries

Marketing Managers are high-level professionals whose salaries are relatively good. Depending on the size of the company for whom he/she works and his/her specific responsibilities, a Marketing Manager in the apparel industry can make anywhere from $50,000 a year to $100,000 a year or more. Many Marketing Managers are also eligible for bonuses—sometimes handsome ones—based on exceptional performance (as measured by the company's sales, profits, brand recognition, and the like).

Marketing Managers across all fields earned a median annual salary of $87,640 in 2004, according to the U.S. Department of Labor.

Employment Prospects

Opportunities for Marketing Managers in general (across all industries) tend to be abundant, since every organization in existence (for-profit or nonprofit) ultimately has to sell its products, services, or cause(s). But Marketing Managers who want to work for apparel manufacturers or apparel-related retail companies are hindered to some degree by the natural limitations inherent in focusing on one particular sector of the overall marketplace and the relatively high level of the job itself. So employment prospects for those who want to become Marketing Managers in the fashion/apparel field can only be characterized as fair.

Indeed, the U.S. Department of Labor notes that there were only 188,000 Marketing Managers nationwide (across all industries) as of 2004. (For the purposes of comparison, there were 2.2 million retail store managers in 2004, according to the Department of Labor.)

Advancement Prospects

Marketing Managers in the fashion/apparel industry who accumulate a solid track record of success can move into higher-level marketing jobs (e.g., director of marketing or vice president for marketing) or even high-level executive leadership positions (e.g., chief executive officer), in their own companies or elsewhere. However, because the prevalence of these higher-level positions is comparatively low, advancement prospects for Marketing Managers in fashion/apparel can only be characterized as fair; they have room to grow, but there aren't many jobs for them to grow into.

Education and Training

At a minimum, Marketing Managers in the fashion/apparel industry need to have a bachelor's degree in marketing or a closely related field (e.g., communications, mass communications). Today, however, many apparel manufacturers and fashion retailers expect their Marketing Managers to have graduate-level degrees—typically, the master of business administration (M.B.A.), which gives Marketing Managers educational background in essential areas like planning, finance, staffing, and assessment.

Some Marketing Managers advance to their positions not with marketing degrees but instead with degrees in fashion-related disciplines such as apparel merchandising combined with extensive marketing experience.

Experience, Skills, and Personality Traits

Marketing Managers who work for apparel manufacturing or apparel-related retail companies won't survive (or probably even be hired) without extensive apparel industry experience, particularly in a marketing-related discipline such as advertising, public relations, promotions, or event planning, or a similar discipline such as merchandising. To be successful, Marketing Managers need outstanding persuasive and communication skills (both written and verbal), not to mention expertise in industry trends and forecasts, solid analytical and planning skills, and the ability to take calculated risks (and explain why to sometimes skeptical higher-ups).

Marketing Managers must also be able to lead and manage others, and hire and train employees who have both the skills and the drive to make the company successful in its marketing efforts. Moreover, Marketing Managers need good computer skills, particularly with respect to spreadsheet, database, and presentation applications; the ability to work well with a variety of people, ranging from entry-level employees to high-level executives; and outstanding research and competitive intelligence abilities.

Perhaps most important of all, Marketing Managers need to have an inherent ability to spot new business opportunities—for example, products the company can develop or services the company can provide—and turn them into reality.

Unions and Associations

Many Marketing Managers across all fields (including apparel manufacturing and retail) are members of the American Marketing Association (AMA), a professional organization with some 38,000 members worldwide. Depending on their specific interests and responsibilities, Marketing Managers in the field might also participate in other professional groups ranging from the Association for Women in Communications (AWC) and the American Advertising Federation (AAF) to the International Association of Business Communicators (IABC) and Sales and Marketing Executives International (SMEI).

Marketing Managers in fashion/apparel can also keep current on the industry in general by participating in organizations like Fashion Group International (FGI), the American Apparel and Footwear Association (AAFA), the International Textile and Apparel Association (ITAA), and the National Retail Federation (NRF).

Tips for Entry

1. Complete at least a bachelor's degree in a discipline like marketing, communications, or mass communications. Consider pursuing an advanced degree (particularly a master of business administration [M.B.A.]) as well.
2. During college, gain some practical experience in marketing or a closely related discipline (e.g., advertising, public relations, promotion, event planning) through an internship or a co-op assignment within an apparel manufacturing or retail firm.
3. Do whatever you can to get to know some working Marketing Managers in the apparel industry. If possible, talk to some Marketing Managers (i.e., informational interviewing) to learn more about what they do and how they got to where they are now.
4. Visit the Web sites of apparel manufacturers and retailers, as well as general job search Web sites, to look for Marketing Manager job listings. What key skills and abilities, experiences, education, and traits do companies seem to be looking for in the Marketing Managers they want to hire?
5. Begin reading industry publications such as *Women's Wear Daily* and *DNR (Daily News Record),* along with consumer publications like *Cosmopolitan* and *Vogue,* to learn about fashion trends and forecasts.

MEDIA BUYER

CAREER PROFILE

Duties: Determines which media (e.g., print publications, Internet sites, radio, television, billboards, direct mail) apparel or textile companies should use to advertise their products, then arranges to buy appropriate space or time in those media

Alternate Title(s): Media Researcher, Media Planner

Salary Range: $30,000 to $100,000+

Employment Prospects: Fair

Advancement Prospects: Good

Best Geographical Location(s): Large urban areas across the United States, particularly fashion centers like New York City, Los Angeles, Chicago, and Dallas, as well as cities where apparel or textile company headquarters are located

Prerequisites:

Education or Training—A bachelor's degree is generally required, in an area like advertising, marketing, public relations, journalism, business administration, or the liberal arts; sometimes a graduate degree, such as a master of business administration (M.B.A.), is required as well; coursework in apparel merchandising and/or textile merchandising is helpful, as is certification from advertising-related professional organizations

Experience—College internship or co-op experience is essential for entry-level positions, while mid-level positions require three to five years of lower-level media buying experience

Special Skills and Personality Traits—Extensive knowledge of various media (print publications, Internet sites, radio, television, billboards, direct mail) and their advertising offerings; strong research and analytical skills; sound negotiation skills; knowledge of apparel and/or textile industry trends and forecasts; ability to work well with people of diverse backgrounds, including clients and media professionals; organizational and follow-through skills; computer skills; strong interpersonal, communication, and presentation skills; ability to manage many tasks at once; ability to meet deadlines; creativity

CAREER LADDER

Media Director

Media Buyer

Media Coordinator

Advertising Assistant

Position Description

Media Buyers work either in-house, for the internal advertising departments within textile- or apparel-related companies, or for outside advertising agencies. Their job is to determine which media (e.g., print publications, Internet sites, radio, television, billboards, direct mail) apparel or textile companies should use to advertise their products most effectively, and then arrange to buy appropriate space or time in those media.

Much of the Media Buyer's job involves research and analysis. Media Buyers must study various types of media and various media outlets to determine what they have to offer advertisers, especially in the way of audiences, whether those audiences are readers, viewers, listeners, or Web site visitors. Media Buyers then analyze the information they've gathered to predict which media will be most effective in helping the companies they work for reach consumers and convince them to buy. If, for example, a Media Buyer works for an advertising agency representing an apparel manufacturer targeting teenagers, he or she will likely purchase media time or space on television shows or magazines watched or read by teenagers. If, on the other hand, that Media Buyer works for a fabric retailer whose customers are generally women over the age of 50, he or she will instead purchase media space or time from other outlets, such as quilting magazines or radio programs aimed at seniors.

Media Buyers work closely with media sales representatives, who work for print and electronic media outlets and attempt to sell space or time with those outlets. Media Buyers typically study a media outlet's demographic data—information about its readers/viewers/listeners, such as their average age and income, or their interests—and use data to determine if the outlet is a good fit for a textile or apparel company's advertisements. If it is, the Media Buyer then secures space or time with that outlet, typically negotiating for the best price and the best placement or time slot.

In larger companies and advertising agencies, Media Buyers oversee only the actual media buying activities needed by the companies they work for or with. In smaller organizations, however, Media Buyers are also responsible for handling traffic issues—that is, making sure ad copy or tapes physically get to the appropriate media outlets on time. A Media Buyer who purchases 10 radio spots on a local station, for example, and who wants two different spots to air, needs to make sure that high-quality copies of each ad get into the hands of the program director at the radio station, so that they can air at the proper times.

In most cases, Media Buyers collaborate closely with account executives, art directors, and market researchers, offering their expertise on various media and the audiences those media tend to reach best. The advertising team develops the best ads they can, leaving the Media Buyer to ensure that those ads actually make it into print or on to radio, television, or the Internet.

Salaries

Entry-level Media Buyers across all fields can expect to earn about $30,000 a year to start, give or take a few thousand dollars. More experienced Media Buyers, however, can earn much higher salaries—more than $100,000 a year at the highest levels.

The median annual salary for advertising professionals in general in the United States was $63,610 in 2004, according to the U.S. Department of Labor. Compensation Web site Salary.com notes that, as of 2006, media coordinators earned a median annual salary of $30,100; Media Buyers $56,804; and media directors $109,122.

Employment Prospects

Advertising and promotions managers held about 64,000 jobs in the United States in 2004, according to the U.S. Department of Labor. However, only a small subset of that population work as Media Buyers, and an even smaller subset work as Media Buyers in or for apparel- or textile-related companies. So employment prospects are only fair for prospective Media Buyers who want to work in a capacity that has a fashion-industry link.

Advancement Prospects

The U.S. Department of Labor predicts that employment of advertising and related professionals will grow much faster than average between now and 2014, especially among professionals who are willing and able to take on contract or freelance work. So in general, advancement prospects for Media Buyers are good.

Media Buyers who work in or for apparel- or textile-related companies can advance to higher-level positions as media buying managers or media directors, or move into other high-level advertising positions, many of them paying $100,000 a year or more.

Education and Training

A bachelor's degree is required to break into the advertising field in general and media buying in particular. The best job opportunities for prospective Media Buyers in apparel or textiles typically go to applicants who have a degree in advertising, marketing, public relations, journalism, business administration, or the liberal arts. Course work in apparel merchandising and/or textile merchandising is helpful as well.

Many Media Buyers and other advertising professionals complete additional training and receive various industry certifications from professional organizations.

Experience, Skills, and Personality Traits

Media Buyers need to have extensive knowledge of various media, including print publications, Web sites, radio, television, billboards, and direct mail. Media Buyers must also understand each medium's advertising offerings and how those offerings will benefit their clients' advertising campaigns. To gain that understanding, Media Buyers must employ their research and analytical skills to objectively evaluate whether a prospective media purchase is worth the money or not.

Media Buyers also need sound negotiation skills, both for price-setting purposes and for securing the best space or time slots for their clients. Knowledge of apparel and/or textile industry trends and forecasts is also critical to the Media Buyer's success, as is the ability to work well with people of diverse backgrounds, including clients and media professionals.

The best Media Buyers are highly creative and have strong organizational and follow-through skills; good computer skills; and sound interpersonal, communication, and presentation skills. They also have the ability to manage many tasks at once and meet deadlines.

Unions and Associations

Many Media Buyers are members of the American Advertising Federation (AAF), an industry trade organization. Others participate in the professional development activities of similar organizations like the American Marketing Association (AMA), the Public Relations Society of America (PRSA), and Sales and Marketing Executives International (SMEI).

Media Buyers who work in or for textile- or apparel-related companies often supplement their participation in advertising-centered organizations by tapping the resources of organizations like the American Apparel and Footwear Association (AAFA) or the International Textile and Apparel Association (ITAA), particularly to keep abreast of industry trends and forecasts.

Tips for Entry

1. While in school, pursue one or more media buying or related internships or co-ops so that you can gain practical, hands-on experience in the field. If possible, target your internship or co-op efforts toward in-house advertising departments within fashion or textile companies or outside advertising agencies serving the fashion or textile industries.
2. Consider pursing a master's degree in business administration (M.B.A.), particularly after you've worked as a Media Buyer in apparel or textiles for a few years. An advanced degree can help you secure a high-level position in media buying or other areas of advertising.
3. Contact one or more Media Buyers who work in or for the apparel or textile industry and ask them to tell you more about their careers and how they got into them.
4. Monitor fashion and textile industry publications in print and online so that you can continuously develop broad knowledge of the industries as a whole. Pay particular attention to the advertisements you see and study the copy and graphics used in the ads. Try to assess what messages the ads are attempting to communicate, and try to pinpoint the audiences each advertiser is trying to reach.

PRINT MODEL

CAREER PROFILE

Duties: Models new clothing designs and accessories for still photographs used in magazines, newspapers, advertisements, press kits, and other media

Alternate Title(s): Photographic Model, Editorial Model

Salary Range: $0 to $500,000+

Employment Prospects: Limited

Advancement Prospects: Limited

Best Geographical Location(s): Large cities, particularly fashion centers like New York City, Los Angeles, Chicago, Dallas, and Atlanta

Prerequisites:

Education or Training—No specific education is required, though some industry insiders recommend modeling school training

Experience—Some modeling experience is quite helpful

Special Skills and Personality Traits—Physical attractiveness; an appearance within certain limits with respect to height, weight, and body measurements; physical fitness; outgoing/extroverted personality; ambition; intelligence; fashion consciousness and style; self-confidence and poise; willingness and ability to work long hours; willingness and ability to follow directions; adaptability

CAREER LADDER

Supermodel

Runway Model

Print Model, Full-Time

Print Model, Part-Time

Position Description

Print Models model clothing such as dresses, coats, undergarments, swimwear, suits, and accessories so that new designs can be photographed for various print media. The Print Model's goal is to help create public interest in buying the new fashion products presented by Fashion Designers or the manufacturer employing him or her.

Under the direction of a still photographer, Print Models pose for photos that will eventually appear in consumer fashion magazines, fashion industry trade publications, newspaper articles and advertisements, catalogs, direct-mail fliers, billboards, and Web sites. Print Models can work either indoors or outdoors, depending on the photographer's wants and needs, and under a variety of conditions. They may, for example, work outside in a cold, snowy climate to model new winter coats, or work inside under hot lights with an ocean backdrop to model the latest swimsuit designs for a manufacturer's summer catalog.

Many Print Models work only sporadically or part time. A Print Model who works with a certain photographer, for example, may be asked to work only a few weeks out of an entire year. He or she then has to find other work with other photographers to make more money. Full-time Print Models, on the other hand, almost always work with a variety of photographers and for a variety of clients. Typically, the Print Model's job is far from nine to five. Instead, Print Models can work at almost any hour of the day, for almost any number of hours per week, depending on who they're working for, how much money they want to earn, and how much work they're willing to accept.

When Print Models are between jobs, they typically spend much of their time promoting and developing themselves, often with the assistance of an agent or a modeling agency. The Print Model maintains a portfolio of photos, and travels to "go and sees" (interviews for modeling jobs). Because they are almost always self-employed, Print Models must constantly be on the lookout for new work. They must also keep detailed records of their income and tax-deductible expenses, either on their own or with the help of an accountant or financial adviser.

Print Models need to stay in excellent physical condition, so they devote considerable time and effort to fitness. They must also maintain their physical body proportions, especially their weight, and thus they are quite careful when it comes to nutrition and eating. In some cases, Print Models can take this focus on weight and body image too far and develop an eating disorder, a potentially life-threatening condition for which they must seek medical and psychological treatment.

Salaries

Salaries for Print Models vary widely. A Print Model may start out working for local publications, stores, or manufacturers for little or even no pay, simply to gain experience and get some photographs for her or his portfolio. With experience, however, Print Models begin to earn more money, perhaps $200 to $500 an hour or more.

The most established and famous Print Models can make hundreds of thousands of dollars per year, not only from modeling but also from personal appearances and merchandise, such as calendars or exercise videos.

If a Print Model works with an agent, the agent will generally expect to receive 15 percent to 20 percent of the model's earnings.

Employment Prospects

There are many more aspiring Print Models than there are jobs, so employment prospects, on the whole, are limited. The U.S. Department of Labor reports that models held just 2,200 jobs in the United States in 2004, so anyone who wants to break into the field must be prepared for keen competition.

The job seekers with the best prospects will have the most widely demanded physical features (i.e., the look currently being sought) along with extensive modeling experience for a variety of clients.

Advancement Prospects

Advancement Prospects for Print Models are limited, for the most part, due to the small number of jobs that exist in the first place. However, since the typical print modeling career is relatively short—an average of 10 years for men and 20 years for women—opportunities do emerge from time to time. Those models who succeed can advance quickly by obtaining higher-profile assignments, working with influential photographers and designers, or even launching their own line of merchandise, such as clothing, cosmetics, or books. Some successful models go on to careers in film and television as actors or actresses or spokespersons. Much of a model's success relies on his or her popularity with the general public and ability to promote himself or herself.

Education and Training

There are no formal educational or training requirements for Print Models. Many modeling schools exist in the United States and around the world, but industry insiders have mixed views of such schools. Some say the schools provide valuable training in posing, walking, makeup application, and other basic modeling tasks. Others, however, say they prefer working with clients who have no previous training at all.

Experience, Skills, and Personality Traits

Perhaps the most unusual requirement for Print Models is that, in most cases, they need to be of a specific size, depending on the needs of their employer. Typically, they have to be physically attractive and photogenic, with an appearance that is within certain limits with respect to height, weight, and body measurements.

Print Models also need to be physically fit, and have a good sense of fashion and style, with outstanding features and grooming.

People skills are critical to the Print Model's success. Print Models must be willing to follow a photographer's directions, for example, and be able to adapt to a variety of working conditions determined by the photographer and others. Adaptability is an essential asset for Print Models.

The most successful Print Models are outgoing and extroverted, ambitious and self-starting, intelligent (especially with respect to their business affairs and finances), and willing to take calculated risks. They also know how to promote themselves well, either on their own or, more often, with the help of an agent or a modeling agency.

Unions and Associations

The primary union in the modeling field is The Model's Guild, based in New York City. The Guild represents both models and modeling-related professionals.

Tips for Entry

1. Think about attending modeling school to learn modeling basics. Also, consider pursuing course work or a two- or four-year degree in fashion design or a related field.

2. Volunteer to do some modeling for a local publication, or even for a local fashion show or nearby retail store. Get some photos from each of your modeling experiences so that you can develop a portfolio of your work.
3. Meet with some representatives of modeling agencies to see what sort of print modeling opportunities they can offer you.
4. Talk to working Print Models for advice on preparing for and entering the industry. If possible, talk to modeling agents as well to get their insights and suggestions.
5. Read books and magazines on modeling and visit modeling-oriented Web sites to educate yourself about the industry.

RUNWAY MODEL

CAREER PROFILE

Duties: Models new clothing designs for fashion industry media, fashion industry professionals and buyers, and, in some cases, consumers

Alternate Title(s): Live Model

Salary Range: $0 to $500,000+

Employment Prospects: Limited

Advancement Prospects: Limited

Best Geographical Locations(s): Large cities, particularly fashion centers like New York City, Miami, Paris, Milan, and London

Prerequisites:

Education or Training—No formal education or training is required

Experience—Runway Models often begin as Print Models appearing in fashion magazines

Special Skills and Personality Traits—Physical attractiveness; an appearance within certain limits with respect to height, weight, and body measurements; physical fitness; outgoing/extroverted personality; ambition; intelligence; fashion consciousness and style; self-confidence and poise; willingness and ability to work long hours; willingness and ability to follow directions; adaptability

CAREER LADDER

Supermodel

Runway Model

Print Model

Position Description

Runway Models display clothing such as dresses, coats, undergarments, swimwear, suits, and accessories for various audiences, including fashion industry media, fashion industry professionals, particularly fashion buyers, and in some cases, the end consumer. The Runway Model's goal is to help create public interest in buying the fashion products presented by the designer and manufacturer.

In displaying fashions, the Runway Model walks, stands, and turns to demonstrate each garment's key features. All the while, she or he is often being photographed by still and video photographers representing fashion magazines and other fashion media.

Runway Models work in a variety of locations. The most famous and familiar Runway Models can be seen "strutting the catwalk" in twice-yearly fashion shows in such major cities as New York, London, Milan, and Paris. During these shows, a Runway Model may wear as many as 10 different outfits, all the while walking and being photographed in front of a large audience.

Many other Runway Models, however, live and work on a much smaller scale, displaying fashions in shows held at apparel marts and department stores.

A Runway Model's work life can be both glamorous and stressful. On the one hand, she or he generally thrives on the idea of wearing the latest in fashion and performing before an audience. However, she or he must also be prepared to be busy, both during and in between fashion shows.

During a fashion show, the Runway Model will often have to change clothes and makeup and hairstyles in just minutes, usually with the help of an assistant, and then return to the stage. The Runway Model must also participate in preshow rehearsals so that the fashion designer and others can make sure that all the models, fashions, and show logistics are properly in place.

When Runway Models aren't working at fashion shows, they typically spend much of their time promoting and developing themselves, almost always with the assistance of an agent. The Runway Model maintains a portfolio of photos, and travels to "go and sees" (interviews for modeling jobs). Because they are often self-employed, Runway Models must constantly be on the lookout for new work. They must also keep detailed records of their income and tax-deductible expenses.

Often, Runway Models are called upon to work in distant cities or countries, so travel—which means being away from family and friends—is a major part of their work. Many Runway Models enjoy it because it takes them to beautiful and often exotic locations.

Runway Models need to stay in excellent physical condition, so they devote considerable time and effort to fitness. They must also maintain their physical body proportions (especially their weight) and they are quite careful when it comes to nutrition and eating. In some cases, Runway Models can take this focus on weight and body image too far and develop an eating disorder, a potentially life-threatening condition for which they must seek medical and psychological treatment.

Salaries

Salaries for Runway Models vary widely. A Runway Model may start out working in local fashion shows for little or even no pay, simply to gain experience and get some photographs for her or his portfolio. With experience, a Runway Model begins to earn more money, perhaps $500 to $5,000 per show. The most established and famous Runway Models can make hundreds of thousands or even millions of dollars per year. If a Runway Model works with an agent, the agent will generally expect to receive 15 percent to 20 percent of the model's earnings.

Employment Prospects

There are many more aspiring Runway Models than there are jobs, so employment prospects, on the whole, are limited. The U.S. Department of Labor reports that models held just 2,200 jobs in the United States in 2004, so anyone who wants to break into the field must be prepared for keen competition. The best jobs will go to Runway Models who have the most widely sought physical features, along with the willingness and ability to work in the major fashion centers of the world—sometimes on a moment's notice.

Advancement Prospects

Advancement Prospects for Runway Models are also limited, mostly due to the small number of jobs that exist in the first place. However, since the typical Runway Modeling career is relatively short, opportunities do emerge from time to time, especially as Runway Models retire or move on to other careers. Those models who succeed can advance quickly by obtaining higher-profile assignments, working with influential photographers and designers, or even launching their own line of merchandise, such as clothing, cosmetics, or books. Some successful models go on to careers in film and television as actors or actresses or spokespersons. Much of a model's success relies on his or her popularity with the general public and ability to promote himself or herself.

Education and Training

There are no formal educational or training requirements for Runway Models. There are many modeling schools in the United States and around the world, but industry insiders have mixed views of such schools. Some say the schools provide valuable training in posing, walking, makeup application, and other basic modeling tasks. Others, however, say they prefer working with clients who have no previous training at all.

Experience, Skills, and Personality Traits

Before becoming Runway Models, many of the professionals in this field begin by modeling fashions for magazines.

Many of the skills and personality traits necessary for Runway Models focus upon physical attributes. Women who become Runway Models generally must be about 5-feet-9-inches tall and of slender build. Men must generally be around 6 feet tall, and also of slender, "chiseled" build. Runway Models of both genders also need flawless skin, healthy hair, and attractive facial features.

The most successful Runway Models are outgoing and extroverted, ambitious and self-starting, intelligent (especially with respect to their business affairs and finances), and willing to take calculated risks.

Unions and Associations

The primary union in the Runway Modeling field is The Models Guild, based in New York City. The Guild represents both models and modeling-related professionals.

Tips for Entry

1. Volunteer to model for local fashion shows in department stores or malls, or to work behind the scenes for one of these events so that you can meet working models.
2. Develop a portfolio of photos so that you can meet with agents about representation possibilities.
3. Participate in "go and sees" and "open calls."
4. Talk to working Runway Models for advice on preparing for and entering the industry. If possible, talk to modeling agents as well to get their insights and suggestions.
5. Read books and magazines on modeling and visit modeling-oriented Web sites to educate yourself about the industry.

EDUCATION

COLLEGE PROFESSOR

CAREER PROFILE

Duties: Teaches college students about apparel- or textile-related subjects, based on industry experience and/or extensive field-specific education

Alternate Title(s): Faculty Member, Instructor, Adjunct Instructor

Salary Range: $5,000 to $90,000+

Employment Prospects: Fair

Advancement Prospects: Fair

Best Geographical Location(s): Large cities that have colleges and universities, particularly schools with apparel- or textile-related academic programs

Prerequisites:

Education or Training—A master's degree in a fashion- or textile-related discipline is almost always required; a doctoral degree in a fashion- or textile-related discipline is preferred and often required

Experience—Extensive apparel and/or textile industry experience is highly recommended, if not required

Special Skills and Personality Traits—Extensive knowledge of the apparel and/or textile industries; extensive knowledge of specialty areas within the apparel and/or textile fields; excellent teaching skills; strong written and oral communication skills; listening skills; creativity; knowledge of new developments, trends, and forecasts in the apparel and/or textile industries; planning skills; ability to work well with people of diverse backgrounds; knack for communicating complex information to others, including beginners; self-motivation; patience; analytical and research skills; curiosity; computer skills; flexibility; ability to work without close supervision

CAREER LADDER

Department Chair

Professor

Assistant or Associate Professor

Instructor or Adjunct Instructor

Position Description

College Professors—in particular, those in the apparel and textiles disciplines—teach college students about apparel- or textile-related subjects, using their own extensive educational background and, very often, drawing from their considerable experience working in the fashion or textile industries. Depending on their school, their academic department, and their area of expertise, College Professors might teach a wide variety of courses. A Professor whose specialty is fashion design, for example, will probably teach introductory, intermediate, and advanced fashion design courses, or perhaps related courses in illustration and drawing, pattern making, and sample making. Meanwhile, a Professor specializing in textile engineering will likely teach scientifically complex courses on topics like textile dyeing and finishing, fabric design, and fiber and yarn engineering.

Still other Professors might teach courses on everything from apparel merchandising and fashion promotion to retail store operations and human resource management.

College Professors don't spend all of their time in the classroom. Instead, they must manage an assortment of other activities as well. Most Professors, for example, advise a certain number of students, known as advisees, to help them choose their academic courses and majors as well as their career paths. Most Professors also devote considerable time to working on committees with other institutional faculty and staff, where they make important decisions about academic curricula and institutional direction.

Most College Professors must also commit time to research activities. They conduct studies related to their academic disciplines and then write papers that are published in academic journals. They also read academic journals and other print and online publications so that they can stay current in their disciplines—and within the broader textile and apparel industries—thus becoming better, more-informed teachers for their students.

Many College Professors in the apparel and textile disciplines are part-time adjunct instructors who teach only a class or two each semester. For these instructors, teaching is a side activity that complements their full-time work in the apparel or textile industry. While adjunct instructors aren't on campus full time, they typically offer their students a real-world perspective that some full-time Professors cannot.

Full-time College Professors sometimes work in the textile or apparel industry as their side activity, serving as consultants to various companies and organizations, or perhaps even running businesses of their own.

Most College Professors have to work some odd hours. Sometimes, for example, they teach courses in the evening or on the weekend, or take their students on visits to nearby cities so that the students can visit apparel- or textile-related companies. Most Professors don't have a standard nine-to-five work day. On the plus side, however, many Professors appreciate the flexibility they usually have in their schedules, which gives them time to do research, develop new courses or parts of courses, and even spend time with family and friends.

Salaries

Salaries for College Professors vary significantly depending on one's discipline, the institution for which he/she works, and his/her specific skills and experience. An adjunct instructor who teaches only one course per semester, for example, might make only $5,000 or $6,000 a year. A full-time Professor with extensive experience, on the other hand, can easily earn $75,000 a year and occasionally more.

The median annual salary for College Professors across all disciplines and levels in the United States was $51,800 in 2004, according to the U.S. Department of Labor.

The American Association of University Professors (AAUP), a professional organization for College Professors, found that the average salary for full-time Professors across all disciplines and levels was $68,505 during the 2004–05 academic year.

Employment Prospects

The U.S. Department of Labor reports that College Professors held about 1.6 million jobs in the United States in 2004 and that about 30 percent of those workers were part-time, adjunct faculty members.

The number of College Professors whose disciplines are specifically related to textiles or apparel, however, is much smaller. So while the Department of Labor predicts that employment of College Professors in general will grow much faster than average between now and 2014, prospects for those who want to land an apparel- or textile-specific professorial job can only be characterized as fair. Those who have the appropriate academic credentials, along with extensive fashion or textile industry experience, will have the best chance of landing one of the comparatively few professorial jobs that will be available in the coming years.

Advancement Prospects

Advancement prospects for textile- or apparel-oriented College Professors are only fair, since the total number of jobs in the field is relatively small. Those with extensive academic and industry experience have the best chance of advancing to higher-level academic positions (e.g., academic dean, institutional president) and/or earning tenure (i.e., lifetime appointment) and promotion to full professor.

Education and Training

In most cases, College Professors need at least a master's degree in their field of expertise, though a Ph.D. in the field is almost always preferred and is often required. College Professors who teach in textile- or apparel-related disciplines typically need to have extensive industry experience as well, particularly if they want to get full-time academic positions. In rare cases, hands-on experience in the industry can substitute for academic credentials, but a combination of the two is always most desirable.

Experience, Skills, and Personality Traits

Above all, College Professors need to be good teachers. They must be able to take often complex information and communicate it in a way that students will understand and benefit from. Professors also need to be excellent researchers, since they typically devote considerable time to research-related activities.

To be successful, College Professors in textile- or apparel-related disciplines must have extensive industry knowledge and experience, as well as the ability to pursue continuing educational opportunities so that they remain current in their fields. Professors in textiles and apparel must also know industry trends and forecasts—particularly as they relate to technological advances—so that they can communicate key information to their students and effectively prepare those students for their future careers.

All College Professors must be analytical and curious, self-motivated and creative, and able to work with people from diverse backgrounds. They also need strong computer skills and, increasingly, the ability to use online and video-based tools to teach their students. Patience is also a key attribute of Professors; without it, they will have difficulty with the often long-term activities involved in both teaching and research.

Unions and Associations

The American Association of University Professors (AAUP) is an umbrella organization for College Professors, offering information and advice for Professors in all academic disciplines.

College Professors in textile- or apparel-related disciplines can also benefit from involvement with industry-specific organizations like the American Apparel and Footwear Association (AAFA), the International Textile and Apparel Association (ITAA), and the Textile Society of America (TSA).

Tips for Entry

1. Gain textile or fashion industry experience by working in one or more jobs in the field. The best College Professors can offer their students not only academic knowledge, but expertise they've gained through hands-on experience.
2. Talk to one or more College Professors in a textile- or apparel-related discipline to get their advice and suggestions on how you can pursue a college teaching career in the field someday.
3. Read industry publications in print and online to gain a broad understanding of the textile and apparel industries. Try to develop a specific area of interest or specialty within textiles or apparel, so that you can focus on it in depth as part of your postgraduate studies and your college teaching and research career.

CONSULTANT

CAREER PROFILE

Duties: Sells expertise to textile- and/or apparel-related companies to help them improve their performance

Alternate Title(s): Management Consultant, Management Analyst

Salary Range: $0 to $200,000+

Employment Prospects: Fair

Advancement Prospects: Fair

Best Geographical Location(s): Large cities across the United States, especially fashion centers like New York City, as well as cities where textile or apparel companies have corporate headquarters, production facilities, and/or retail operations

Prerequisites:

Education or Training—A bachelor's degree is generally required, in a field closely related to the Consultant's areas of expertise; a master's degree is often required as well, either in business administration (M.B.A.) or a field closely related to the Consultant's areas of expertise

Experience—At least five years of experience is required, in a field closely related to the Consultant's areas of expertise, and 10 or more years of experience is helpful

Special Skills and Personality Traits—Strong data-gathering, research, and analytical skills; ability to think creatively and "out of the box"; sound written and oral communication skills; expertise in one or more specific areas; excellent listening skills and tact; self-confidence and self-motivation; good planning and organizational skills; ability to self-promote and market one's skills and expertise; ability to set and meet goals; ability to meet deadlines; presentation skills; honesty and trustworthiness; ability to work well with people of diverse backgrounds; adaptability and flexibility; business-related skills (e.g., accounting, finance)

Special Requirements—Certified Management Consultant certification from the Institute of Management Consultants is helpful

CAREER LADDER

Consultant

Extensive Related Experience

Position Description

Consultants sell their expertise to client companies so that those companies can improve their performance. Some Consultants, for example, might help textile manufacturers improve their production processes, thus saving the companies time and/or reducing waste. Other Consultants might assist apparel retailers that have acquired other companies by helping to merge the companies successfully, eliminating redundant jobs, and streamlining the combined organizations' operations.

Still other Consultants might work with apparel manufacturers' public relations personnel, developing sound publicity campaigns for new apparel lines or boosting coverage of the manufacturers' products in various media. Meantime, still other Consultants could be involved in revamping computer systems, improving company hiring efforts and employee retention efforts, or changing an organization's merchandising tactics.

In short, Consultants specializing in textiles and/or apparel can be involved with a huge variety of activities, such as management issues, marketing, strategic planning, merchandising, information technology, personnel issues, product development, logistics, production planning, and a host of other possibilities.

Some Consultants specialize by function. A Consultant may, for example, focus solely on logistical issues, whether he or she works for apparel- or textile-related companies or other types of companies. Other Consultants specialize by industry. Another Consultant may, for instance, do color forecasting work only for textile manufacturers.

More than half of all Consultants (across all industries) are self-employed. Consultants who own their own businesses need to focus upon business- and marketing-related tasks as well. They must be sure, for example, to keep accurate records of their earnings and expenditures, and to continuously market themselves so that they attract business from new clients.

Consultants in general must also have strong research, analysis, and communication skills so that they can develop proposals for companies they hope to work for. A proposal outlines the work the Consultant believes must be done, how much that work will cost the client company, when and how the work will be completed, and when and how that work will be evaluated. In most cases, Consultants are forced to compete for business with other Consultants, so the more persuasive the proposals they write, the better the chance they will land a company's business.

Salaries

Salaries for Consultants vary enormously, depending on how much work they do, who they work for, and where they do that work. Consultants who dabble in consulting, for example, while keeping their day jobs, may earn only a few thousand dollars a year. Full-time Consultants who successfully cultivate relationships with a variety of clients, on the other hand, can earn salaries well into the six figures, depending on their hourly, daily, or project-based rates.

Management analysts across all fields and levels in the United States earned a median annual salary of $63,450 in 2004, according to the U.S. Department of Labor.

Employment Prospects

Management analysts across all fields and levels held about 605,000 jobs in 2004, according to the U.S. Department of Labor. The number of Consultants who specialize in apparel- or textile-related activities, however, is comparatively small, so employment prospects for Consultants in apparel and/or textiles can only be characterized as fair.

The best opportunities go to Consultants who have not only the expertise they need, but also the self-promotion and marketing skills necessary to continuously attract new clients and develop strong relationships in the apparel and/or textile industries. Between 30 and 50 percent of Consultants (depending on the field) are self-employed.

Advancement Prospects

The U.S. Department of Labor predicts that the number of jobs for management analysts in the United States will grow faster than average between now and 2014, especially as companies in all fields continue to seek cost-effective ways to improve their performance.

The landscape for Consultants, however, is always highly competitive, particularly for those who specialize in helping textile- and/or apparel-related companies. The state of the economy also makes a considerable difference where Consultants' job and advancement prospects are concerned. So in general, Consultants specializing in textiles and/or apparel should expect only fair prospects for advancement.

Education and Training

Consultants specializing in textiles and/or apparel need at least a bachelor's degree in most cases, in a field closely related to their specific areas of expertise. A master's degree is often a respected credential to have as well, again in a field closely related to the Consultant's specific areas of expertise, or in business administration (M.B.A.).

Often, Consultants pursue certification as well. Some management consultants, for example, hold the Certified Management Consultant certification from the Institute of Management Consultants, an industry trade organization.

Experience, Skills, and Personality Traits

Consultants across all industries must have at least five years of experience in a field closely related to their areas of expertise. Often, however, Consultants have 10 or more years of related experience, which usually increases their credibility among prospective client companies.

Consultants in textiles and/or apparel must have extensive knowledge within their areas of expertise, as well as a successful track record of helping companies improve their performance. Consultants must be able to work well with people of diverse backgrounds, whether those people are colleagues, a company's employees, or a company's managers and executives. Written and oral communication skills are essential to the Consultant's success, as are strong listening skills and the ability to gather information, analyze it, and synthesize it into helpful recommendations and action plans for their client companies.

Consultants need good organizational and time management skills as well, along with tact, self-confidence, and self-motivation. The many Consultants who are self-employed must have self-promotion and marketing skills too, not to mention business-related skills so that they can, for example, keep accurate financial records and pay appropriate taxes on their earnings.

Unions and Associations

Many Consultants are involved in the Institute of Management Consultants (IMC), a trade organization representing Consultants across all industries. Depending on their specific areas of expertise, Consultants usually participate in other professional organizations as well, including associations related to the textile and/or apparel industries.

Consultants in textiles or apparel are also wise to participate in groups that will help them stay on top of industry trends and forecasts, like the International Textile and Apparel Association (ITAA), the American Apparel and Footwear Association (AAFA), and Fashion Group International (FGI). Many Consultants, particularly those who are self-employed, also take advantage of the resources and services of the U.S. Small Business Administration and related organizations for business owners.

Tips for Entry

1. Get involved in professional organizations, in both consulting and your specific areas of expertise, so that you can develop relationships with consulting colleagues and company representatives. The more "known" you are in the consulting field—particularly if you target apparel and/or textile companies specifically—the better the chances that you'll continuously attract clients.
2. Pursue entry- and mid-level jobs within the textile and/or apparel industries so that you can gain professional, hands-on experience in your field of interest. All Consultants need extensive industry experience to gain the trust and business of corporate clients.
3. Talk to other Consultants to get a better sense of what they do and how they got to where they are in their careers. Ask them how you, too, can become a successful Consultant.
4. If you have a day job, consider using your current expertise to do some part-time consulting for one or more apparel or textile companies, for low or no fees. The experience and contacts you gain will more than make up for your investment of time, energy, and perhaps money.

WARDROBE CONSULTANT

CAREER PROFILE

Duties: Works with individual clients, small groups or classes, or corporations to educate people about fashions and accessories; helps people make fashion and accessory choices reflecting their needs, lifestyles, and personalities

Alternate Title(s): Fashion Consultant, Image Consultant

Salary Range: $8 an hour to $50,000+

Employment Prospects: Limited

Advancement Prospects: Fair

Best Geographical Location(s): Large cities and upscale communities

Prerequisites:

Education or Training—No specific education is required, but a college degree in an area such as fashion merchandising or fashion design is helpful; attending seminars on business strategies like marketing, promotions, accounting, and finance is helpful

Experience—Previous experience as a fashion buyer, fashion merchandiser, or fashion designer is helpful

Special Skills and Personality Traits—Knowledge of fashion industry trends and forecasts; ability to successfully gauge clients' wants and needs; marketing skills and savvy; self-reliance; self-motivation; self-confidence

CAREER LADDER

Wardrobe Consultant, Independent

Wardrobe Consultant, Staff

Related Fashion Position

Position Description

If you've ever looked in the mirror and wished the clothes you were wearing—and, indeed, the entire image you were projecting—was better, then you'd probably benefit greatly from the services of a Wardrobe Consultant.

Wardrobe Consultants work with individuals, small groups of people, or the staff members of organizations to help them look and feel better. Wardrobe Consultants interview clients about their image-oriented wants and needs and then help them create that image by purchasing and wearing the appropriate apparel and accessories.

To do their work effectively, Wardrobe Consultants will typically engage their clients in several activities. They may, for example, analyze a client's colors, styles, current wardrobe, and grooming to look for ways to improve some or all of those aspects of the client's image. They might also examine the client's body structure and stature, along with his or her silhouette (i.e., body outline or form), and then advise the client about ways to enhance certain features while minimizing others.

Many Wardrobe Consultants go even further in their services. Some, for example, will go to a client's home and help the client sort through his or her closet. Together, the Wardrobe Consultant and the client will decide what stays and what has to go, and talk about why in both cases. Other Wardrobe Consultants will go on apparel and accessory shopping outings with or for their clients, so that each client can buy items that will fit into his or her new or updated fashion image.

By necessity, the Wardrobe Consultant's work involves a great deal of information gathering and analysis. Most Wardrobe Consultants will interview their clients for at least 20 to 30 minutes to determine what they want and need to get out of the consulting experience. Other Wardrobe Consultants do even more in the way of research: they may walk their clients through elaborate (and often computer-based) assessments of their color and style preferences and dislikes, their fashion- or image-related goals, and even their spending habits. Additionally—particularly in the case of professional presenters or entertainment celebrities—Wardrobe Consultants might also study what others in the client's field or area of interest are wearing, so that they can advise the client with field-specific and current fashion trends in mind.

Some Wardrobe Consultants work on staff for retail stores, e.g., the Men's Wearhouse or Nordstrom Department Stores. They help customers who come into the stores by going beyond mere selling to offer fashion consulting services. Many other Wardrobe Consultants work as independent freelancers, either on their own or with a handful of other colleagues or employees. Some independent Wardrobe Consultants even work from home offices, where they can meet their clients or work on other activities related to their businesses.

Beyond their direct wardrobe consulting activities, independent Wardrobe Consultants must also manage a wide range of business-related activities. They need to keep careful records of their income and expenses, and continually market themselves and their services by attending professional meetings, designing and mailing brochures, and developing and updating their company Web sites. Many Wardrobe Consultants also invest time and energy into setting up and conducting community "image building" seminars, where they can serve several clients at one time, earn some money for their efforts, and, most important, gain some new individual clients.

Wardrobe Consultants also need to spend time keeping up with fashion and accessory trends and forecasts, attending fashion shows and similar events, monitoring industry and consumer publications in print or online, and chatting with colleagues at professional meetings (local, state, or national). A few develop such a high level of expertise that they're asked to write newspaper or magazine articles, or to appear on television or radio programs—all of which can increase their public exposure and, potentially, their income as well.

Salaries

Salaries for Wardrobe Consultants vary widely, depending on their work setting, the services they provide, their education and experience, their geographic area, and the clients they target and serve.

Retail store Wardrobe Consultants, who typically function more as salespeople and less as actual consultants, might earn as little as $8 an hour to start. It's important to keep in mind, however, that in most cases commissions and bonuses are part of the salary package. More experienced Wardrobe Consultants—especially those who are self-employed—can earn $50,000 a year or more, especially if they develop a solid reputation among clients and prospective clients.

Independent Wardrobe Consultants have widely varying earnings also, but it isn't unusual for them to earn $100 an hour for their services. It's important to put that figure in context, however, since it covers only the time the consultant actually works with a client and not the hours spent on business-related activities and other non-billable activities.

Employment Prospects

There aren't many jobs for Wardrobe Consultants, so employment opportunities are quite limited. However, jobs do exist, both in retail settings and, much more often, in independent freelance settings. Landing a retail Wardrobe Consultant job is a good first step for breaking into the field, although many have eventually pursued the field after having jobs and careers in related areas like fashion buying or fashion merchandising.

Advancement Prospects

Once you become a Wardrobe Consultant, your advancement prospects are slightly better. In a retail setting, for example, you might be able to move into a supervisory position, or perhaps into another part of the company's operations, like fashion merchandising or fashion marketing. Independent Wardrobe Consultants, meanwhile, can often become as big or as small as they'd like, depending on the number and types of clients they pursue and their success in landing those clients as customers.

Education and Training

While there is no set educational or training path for Wardrobe Consultants, many have college degrees and experience in an area like fashion buying or fashion merchandising. Some have also studied the fine arts so that they can learn extensively about color, form, and styles. Many who pursue work as independent Wardrobe Consultants participate in business-related workshops and seminars as well, so that they can learn about the nuances of accounting and record-keeping, finance and tax issues, and marketing and promotion.

Experience, Skills, and Personality Traits

Most Wardrobe Consultants have considerable experience, either in a fashion-related field like fashion buying or fashion merchandising or in the world of business. Whatever their previous experience, it's essential that they have vast knowledge of fashion and accessory trends and forecasts. It's also quite helpful, particularly for independent Wardrobe Consultants, to have wide-ranging industry contacts who can either refer potential clients or become clients themselves.

Perhaps the most critical skill Wardrobe Consultants need is the ability to listen to and understand their clients' wants and needs. The recent college graduate who has little money but a strong need to look good in his or her first workplace will likely have vastly different concerns compared to the experienced corporate executive who is moving into a new corporate officer role and is willing to spend top dollar to make himself or herself look right for the job. The Wardrobe Consultant needs to be able to easily discern these differences and, as importantly, respect them.

Wardrobe Consultants must also be self-motivated and self-reliant since, in most cases, their salaries depend on their ability to attract clients and truly help them. Additionally, Wardrobe Consultants must be flexible, comfortable with an ever-changing and rather fast-paced environment, and able to sell their products, their services, and even themselves.

Independent Wardrobe Consultants also need a variety of business-related skills—for example, the ability to keep good records, promote themselves and their services, and manage activities as simple as answering the phone or as complex as developing a company Web site. Through it all, they must honestly enjoy working with people and helping them feel more pleased with and confident in their appearances.

Unions and Associations

Many independent Wardrobe Consultants are members of the Association of Image Consultants International (AICI), an Iowa-based organization for Wardrobe Consultants and others who specialize in visual appearance issues.

Tips for Entry

1. Get a summer or part-time job in the fashion retail industry to see how and why consumers choose the fashions and accessories they do. Pay attention to how you might help them make better choices for their wants and needs, and practice not only selling to your customers but also educating them about fashion and fashion trends.
2. Work with a Wardrobe Consultant yourself to see what it's like from a client's perspective. Ask questions about why the consultant is recommending certain items, how the consultant is evaluating your wants and needs, and which colors and styles fit you best.
3. Arrange to talk to one or more Wardrobe Consultants to learn more about their jobs and how they got them. In particular, ask the consultants you meet with how they broke into the field, and how you might do the same.
4. Monitor fashion-related publications in print and online to stay on top of fashion trends and heighten your awareness of forecasted trends. The more general knowledge you have about the fashion industry and how its products are developed, manufactured, marketed, and sold, the more valuable you'll be to clients.
5. Use an Internet search tool like Yahoo! (http://www.yahoo.com) or Google (http://www.google.com) to locate the Web sites of independent Wardrobe Consultants. (Search using the terms "wardrobe consultant," "fashion consultant," and/or "image consultant.") Gain a sense of the services the consultants provide, the fees they charge, and the types of clients they target.

OTHER FASHION CAREERS

ADMINISTRATIVE ASSISTANT

CAREER PROFILE

Duties: Handles administrative tasks—from the routine to the complex—for a middle or executive manager (or an entire department/office) within the fashion/apparel industry

Alternate Title(s): Office Manager, Assistant, Receptionist

Salary Range: $21,000 to $60,000+

Employment Prospects: Excellent

Advancement Prospects: Good

Best Geographical Location(s): Fashion centers like New York City and Los Angeles, as well as other large cities where apparel companies' or fashion retailers' headquarters are located

Prerequisites:

Education or Training—Most organizations require at least an associate degree, though many require a bachelor's degree; a high school diploma combined with extensive experience may suffice in some cases

Experience—One to two years of experience are typically required for entry-level jobs, while higher-level positions usually demand three to five years of experience (and occasionally more, especially when they involve working for a high-level executive)

Special Skills and Personality Traits—Exceptional written and verbal communication skills; outstanding computer skills, particularly with Microsoft Office applications; solid time management, scheduling, organizing, and follow-through abilities; ability to type quickly and accurately; good customer service and listening skills; ability to manage many tasks at once and see all of them through to completion; patience, tact, and grace under pressure; ability to handle a variety of tasks large and small; flexibility and adaptability; ability to work well both individually and as part of a team; trustworthiness, reliability, and the ability to maintain confidentiality

CAREER LADDER

Various fashion jobs, depending on education and skills

Executive Assistant

Administrative Assistant

Position Description

In a 2006 Swingline survey of 2,300 American adults (including more than 1,000 who said they worked in office settings), 78 percent said the role of administrative professionals—Administrative Assistants and the like—is "absolutely essential," "very important," or "important" to an organization's success.

No wonder the fashion industry, like so many other fields, employs thousands of Administrative Assistants.

But the Administrative Assistants of today do much more than make coffee, answer phones, and file documents (though all three of these activities still have their place in an Administrative Assistant's world). In the fast-paced fashion world in particular, Administrative Assistants must have extremely diverse skill sets. After all, in many ways they're the people running the professional lives of their bosses or departments!

It's not unreasonable to think of the Administrative Assistant's job description as encompassing "everything the boss can't or won't do or doesn't have time to do." Among the essential tasks: answering the phone, reading and responding to e-mail messages and faxes, and handling formal written correspondence; scheduling meetings, making travel arrangements, and managing schedules (the boss's and/or those of other employees in the office); using various computer software packages to create everything from product spreadsheets to invoices to client databases; ordering equipment and supplies, troubleshooting technological problems, and keeping the staff lounge well stocked with food and drink; and, in many cases, serving as a sort of "line of defense" for the boss by handling tasks alone or delegating them to others who can complete them.

It isn't difficult to find a manager or an executive in the fashion industry or elsewhere who might say, "I don't know what I'd do without my assistant." And it isn't difficult to find an Administrative Assistant who might say, "I love my job for the variety, the responsibility, the chance to grow, and the opportunity to see the industry from the inside."

Salaries

Most Administrative Assistants in the fashion industry earn between $20,000 and $30,000 a year at the entry level. However, as they accumulate experience, new skills, and—especially—the trust of the people for whom they work, they can often earn considerably more. In fact, it's not unusual for an Administrative Assistant who works for a high-level fashion industry executive to make $60,000 a year or more.

Administrative Assistants across all industries earned a median annual salary of $34,970 in 2004, according to the U.S. Department of Labor. A 2006 study by the International Association of Administrative Professionals (a professional organization for Administrative Assistants and related workers) revealed that starting salaries for Administrative Assistants ranged between $26,000 and $31,750 that year.

Employment Prospects

Administrative Assistants make up one of the largest employment sectors in the American economy, according to the U.S. Department of Labor, accounting for about 3.5 million jobs in 2004. In the fashion industry, the Administrative Assistant position is one of the most common entry-level jobs available. So employment prospects are excellent for people who want to become Administrative Assistants in a fashion-oriented setting, be it for an apparel manufacturer or a clothing retailer.

Employment of Administrative Assistants is expected to grow more slowly than average between now and 2014, the Department of Labor notes. But the sheer number of positions available means opportunities abound.

Advancement Prospects

Job ads for Administrative Assistants in the fashion industry will often include a statement like this one from a 2006 listing: "This is an excellent opportunity to get your foot in the door and learn about the fashion industry." Indeed, Administrative Assistants who work in apparel-oriented settings can advance in any number of ways—into either higher-level administrative positions or, in some cases, other positions within the industry (e.g., buying, design, merchandising, marketing). Thus, advancement prospects are good for Administrative Assistants who work in fashion-related organizations.

Education and Training

In previous decades, a high school diploma was enough to land an Administrative Assistant job, be it in the fashion industry or elsewhere—and on occasion today, a high school diploma combined with extensive administrative experience is still enough to win the position. Increasingly, however, employers are seeking applicants who have at least a two-year (associate) college degree, if not a bachelor's degree. The reason? Applicants with two- or four-year degrees are often perceived as having stronger communication skills and, especially, better computer skills.

Experience, Skills, and Personality Traits

The typical Administrative Assistant, in the fashion industry or elsewhere, needs a diverse skill set to be successful. Exceptional written and verbal communication skills—including a solid command of grammar, punctuation, and usage—are essential, as are outstanding computer skills (particularly when it comes to Microsoft Office applications and desktop publishing software).

Administrative Assistants must also be good time managers who know how to prioritize, schedule, and meet deadlines. Moreover, they need to be able to type quickly (usually at least 50 words per minute) and accurately, provide outstanding service (to both internal and external customers), and take on a variety of tasks at once.

The best Administrative Assistants are good listeners who are flexible and adaptable, capable of working well both alone and on teams, reliable under pressure, and trustworthy to the fullest (especially when dealing with confidential information).

Unions and Associations

While there are no unions or associations geared specifically to Administrative Assistants in the fashion industry, some Administrative Assistants in the field are members of the International Association of Administrative Professionals

(IAAP), a professional organization with some 40,000 members worldwide.

Administrative Assistants who eventually want to move into other jobs in the fashion industry can keep current by participating in organizations like Fashion Group International (FGI).

Tips for Entry

1. Complete at least an associate degree in a fashion-related discipline or, better yet, a bachelor's degree.
2. During college, gain some practical administrative experience through an internship or a co-op assignment in an apparel manufacturing or retail firm.
3. Investigate the possibility of working for a temporary employment (temp) agency, particularly one that specializes in placing people into short-term administrative jobs (in the fashion industry, if possible). Many of today's employers view temp assignments as extended job interviews. Do good work, and you may be hired for a permanent, full-time position with a fashion-related company.
4. Talk to some Administrative Assistants (i.e., informational interviewing) in fashion-related jobs to learn more about what they do and how they got to where they are now.
5. Visit apparel company and job search Web sites to look for fashion-related Administrative Assistant job listings. What key skills and abilities, experiences, education, and traits do companies seem to be looking for in the Administrative Assistants they want to hire?

CONTROLLER

CAREER PROFILE

Duties: Oversees financial planning, budgeting, cash management, record-keeping, and other financial activities for textile- or apparel-related companies

Alternate Title(s): Financial Manager

Salary Range: $50,000 to $150,000+

Employment Prospects: Fair

Advancement Prospects: Fair

Best Geographical Location(s): Large cities across the United States, particularly those where textile or apparel companies have their corporate headquarters

Prerequisites:

Education or Training—A bachelor's degree is required, in a field like accounting, finance, economics, mathematics, or business administration. Often, a master's degree is preferred, in a field like business administration (M.B.A.) or risk management; fashion- or textile-related course work is helpful

Experience—At least five years of accounting- or finance-related experience—preferably in a textile- or apparel-related setting—are required

Special Skills and Personality Traits—Strong financial planning and budgeting skills; accuracy and precision; trustworthiness and honesty; knowledge of various tax and finance laws and regulations, both domestic and foreign; strong numerical abilities; good organizational skills; research and analytical skills; problem-solving skills; ability to interpret and clearly explain complex financial data; strong computer skills; sound oral and written communication skills; ability to write and speak in a language besides English (particularly Spanish or Chinese); ability to work well with people of diverse backgrounds

Special Requirements—Professional certification—most often the CPA (Certified Public Accountant) designation—is always recommended and frequently required

CAREER LADDER

Chief Financial Officer or Vice President for Finance

Controller

Assistant Controller

Financial Analyst or Accountant

Position Description

Controllers are the financial eyes and ears of their companies. They oversee the management of their organizations' finances and financial activities so that those organizations are or become profitable and then remain consistently profitable year after year.

Controllers are involved in many activities. Among the most important are budgeting and financial planning—predicting what their companies will earn and spend over the course of an upcoming period of time (for example, one year) and then making financial plans in accordance with those estimates. A Controller for an apparel retailer, for example, will likely analyze company sales and expenditures from previous years, and then combine that information with his or her knowledge of industry trends and forecasts to develop a comprehensive budget or financial plan for the company. Usually the Controller will collaborate with many other mid- and high-level professionals in this process, which many in the field view as an art as well as a science.

Controllers are also involved in day-to-day activities, such as overseeing accounts receivable (i.e., money owed to the company) and accounts payable (i.e., money the company owes to other organizations), and developing various reports for company officers and outside groups (e.g., stockholders or government regulatory agencies). They must also monitor income and expenses to track whether both are on budget or not. Other duties might include researching whether their companies should proceed with activities like hiring new employees or cutting employees.

Occasionally, Controllers are asked to prepare research for company mergers or acquisitions as well. An apparel manufacturer that wants to merge with another company, for example, needs to know ahead of time whether the merger will be financially viable. The same is true for an apparel manufacturer that is interested in buying another company, either to expand its own operations or eliminate a competitor. In these and other situations, the Controller's input is essential.

While most Controllers work as employees for their respective companies, some with extensive experience start their own consulting companies, which allows them to work for many different companies on an independent contract basis. Controllers who go into the consulting business and succeed can earn annual salaries well into the six figures, though such opportunities are relatively few.

Salaries

Controllers in small textile or apparel companies might earn as little as $50,000 a year, while Controllers in larger organizations often earn $100,000 a year and sometimes $150,000 a year or more—along with performance-based bonuses in some cases.

Financial managers across all fields earned a median annual salary of $81,880 in 2004, according to the U.S. Department of Labor. Controllers in particular, however, earned an average annual salary of nearly $114,000 in 2005, according to a study conducted by the Association for Financial Professionals, a trade organization for professionals in financial disciplines.

Employment Prospects

Financial Managers across all fields held about 528,000 jobs in 2004, according to the U.S. Department of Labor. The number of Controllers, however, is considerably smaller, and the number of Controllers working specifically for textile- or apparel-related companies is smaller still. So employment prospects for Controllers in textiles or apparel are only fair. The best opportunities go to those who have five or more years of financial experience in textiles and/or apparel, along with an advanced degree and various certifications.

Advancement Prospects

The number of jobs for financial managers across all fields and levels is expected to grow about as fast as average between now and 2014, according to the U.S. Department of Labor. The number of opportunities for Controllers will be considerably smaller, however, as will the number of opportunities for Controllers working specifically for textile- or apparel-related companies.

Furthermore, Controllers are already in fairly high-level positions within their companies, a situation that leaves them with limited room for growth. So advancement opportunities for Controllers in textiles or apparel are only fair.

Controllers with extensive experience and a strong track record of performance can, however, advance to become chief financial officers or even chief executive officers of their companies, both positions that can pay annual salaries well into six figures.

Education and Training

At minimum, Controllers need a bachelor's degree in a field such as accounting, finance, economics, mathematics, or business administration. Often, a master's degree is preferred, in a field like business administration (M.B.A.) or risk management. Professional certification—most often the CPA (Certified Public Accountant) designation—is always preferred and frequently required.

Those who want to become Controllers in the textile or apparel industry in particular also benefit from having course work or an academic minor in a textile- or apparel-related field, such as apparel merchandising or textile merchandising.

Experience, Skills, and Personality Traits

Controllers in all industries, including apparel and textiles, need at least five years of accounting- and/or finance-related experience to succeed in their high-level positions. They also need strong financial planning and budgeting skills in order to guide their companies to profitability and growth, year in and year out.

To be successful, Controllers need to be exact in their work, not to mention trustworthy and honest. Mistakes can be enormously costly, as can poor or rash decisions and attempts to cut corners.

Controllers also need to thoroughly understand various tax and finance laws and regulations, both domestically and overseas. Additionally, they must have strong numerical abilities, good organizational skills, research and analytical skills, and problem-solving skills.

Controllers must also be able to interpret and then clearly explain complex financial data, often to other senior-level executives who may not have financial backgrounds. As such, sound oral and written communication skills are essential, as are strong computer skills.

Increasingly, Controllers need to be able to write and speak in a language besides English (particularly Spanish or Chinese) when dealing with overseas clients and suppliers. As is the case in many jobs, the ability to work well with people of diverse backgrounds is critical.

Unions and Associations

Controllers and related professionals are generally involved in a variety of professional organizations. Among the most popular are the Association for Financial Professionals (AFP), Financial Executives International (FEI), and the Financial Management Association International (FMAI).

Controllers who work for apparel or textile manufacturers might tap the resources of organizations like the American Apparel and Footwear Association (AAFA) or the International Textile and Apparel Association (ITAA), to keep abreast of industry trends and forecasts. Controllers who work for retail companies may also use the resources of the National Retail Federation (NRF).

Tips for Entry

1. Start building accounting- and/or finance-related experience by working in entry- and mid-level financial positions, preferably within textile- or apparel-related companies.
2. Join professional organizations like the Association for Financial Professionals (AFP) or Financial Executives International (FEI), especially at the local level, so that you can meet working Controllers and related professionals, learn about their companies, and uncover job leads.
3. Consider taking courses or obtaining an academic minor in a textile- or apparel-related field, so that you gain a basic understanding of fashion and textiles and, especially, start building your knowledge base where industry trends and forecasts are concerned.
4. Talk to one or more Controllers who work for fashion- or textile-related companies so that you can learn how they got their jobs and find out how you can do the same thing.

COSTUME DESIGNER

CAREER PROFILE

Duties: Conceptualizes, designs, creates, and maintains costumes for theater, film, and television productions

Alternate Title(s): None

Salary Range: $0 to $150,000+

Employment Prospects: Limited

Advancement Prospects: Limited

Best Geographical Location(s): Major cultural centers like New York, Los Angeles, and Chicago; college/university cities; cities with regional/community theater groups

Prerequisites:

Education or Training—A college degree in costume design, fashion design, or theater is helpful; some Costume Designer positions require an advanced degree

Experience—Experience designing clothes is essential; experience assisting with costume design and production is very helpful

Special Skills and Personality Traits—Creativity; ability to work well with other professionals; research skills (e.g., using library databases, historical documents, and the Internet); knowledge of fashion history, art history, and history in general; knowledge of dressmaking and fabrics; ability to work well under pressure and within budget restrictions; willingness to work long hours; willingness to take calculated risks

CAREER LADDER

Costume Designer, Television and Films

Costume Designer, Broadway and Off-Broadway

Costume Designer, College/ University or Regional Theater

Costume Design Assistant, College/ University or Regional Theater

Position Description

Costume Designers are responsible for conceptualizing, designing, creating, and maintaining the characters' costumes for theatrical productions, whether those productions are stage plays, musicals, or ballets; television programs; or motion pictures. A skilled Costume Designer plays a key role in helping the production's characters come to life in the minds of the audience.

A Costume Designer's work starts long before the production begins. It involves collaboration with a number of other professionals, including the director, producers, and set designers. Typically, the Costume Designer first reads the production's script to get a sense of the overall story, the characters, and the time period in which the story is set. Then he or she spends considerable time doing historical research to get a better idea of how people actually dressed in the story's time period, the types of materials that were used for clothing of the time, and the types of accessories (e.g., jewelry, hats, shoes) people wore at the time.

The Costume Designer then begins calculating how many costumes will be needed for the production, how many times the actors will need to change costumes, and how they will do so, especially in the case of a live stage play, where time is of the essence.

Once the Costume Designer and the other production leaders agree on a costuming plan and a costuming budget, the Costume Designer begins sketching what each costume will look like. The sketches are then approved by the director or, as the case may be, sent back for revisions, so that the Costume Designer can move on to the next step: creating the costumes, which can involve many hours of long, painstaking work.

When all of the costumes are completed, the Costume Designer will often oversee a walk-through of sorts in which the actors and actresses in the production try on the costumes to see how well they fit and whether they need any adjustments or additions. The walk-through also serves as a test to determine how well the costumes coordinate with set lighting and scenery.

In large productions, the Costume Designer's work is often finished once the costumes have been finalized. But in many small productions, Costume Designers must also oversee the day-to-day use of the costumes, and make sure they're repaired and cleaned.

Once a production is over, the Costume Designer must begin readying for the next production, or, in the case of independent Costume Designers, find another job.

Some Costume Designers complement their hands-on work with other duties, such as teaching costume design at colleges/universities or working in other areas of fashion design or theater.

Salaries

Salaries for Costume Designers vary widely, depending on the type of production (e.g., theater, film, TV), the Costume Designer's reputation, and the production venue (e.g., college/university theater, Broadway play, Hollywood film). Beginning Costume Designers or assistants may work for free at the start of their careers, simply to gain experience. With time and experience, Costume Designers can earn more money—anywhere from $500 to $20,000 or more per production. Union status plays a key role in industry salaries. For example, according to 2006 figures, Costume Designers who are members of United Scenic Artists—one of the industry's key labor unions, affiliated with the International Alliance of Theatrical Stage Employees—can expect to make, at a minimum, just over $32,000 for their work on a Broadway musical that has a cast of 36 people or more. Top Costume Designers can make $150,000 a year or more.

Employment Prospects

Employment opportunities for Costume Designers are limited since there are more people interested in the career than there are jobs in the field. With appropriate experience, however, Costume Designers can find work, particularly in the movie and television industries.

Many Costume Designers work on a per-project basis versus a full-time employment basis. As such, when they finish one project they must work to find another in order to continue earning a living. Competition for jobs in the field is strong, and it may be difficult for newcomers to overcome such obstacles as lack of experience and limited personal contacts.

Advancement Prospects

The field of costume design is characterized by a fairly rigid hierarchy. At the bottom of the hierarchy are volunteers, assistants, and apprentices who do much of the hands-on work. Once someone in the field has gained experience—and, perhaps, obtained a college degree in costume design, fashion or textile design, or theater—she or he is eligible to move up and take on greater responsibilities.

Often, a Costume Designer who begins her or his career in smaller productions will advance to take on Broadway or off-Broadway plays and musicals, or perhaps higher still to design costumes for television programs and movies.

Education and Training

A college degree in costume design, fashion or textile design, or theater is a helpful credential for the Costume Designer, though it's not required. Studying costume design or a similar field and assisting with college/university theater and film productions is one good way to gain practical experience through internships.

Aspiring Costume Designers might also benefit from taking courses in sewing, drawing, art history, general history (particularly relating to a specific time period), and psychology.

Experience, Skills, and Personality Traits

Previous experience is a must for the Costume Designer whose goal is to work in regional productions or at even higher levels.

Costume Designers must also possess creativity, a flair for fashion design, a sense of style, the ability to draw and sketch, the nerve to work well under pressure, and the discipline to stay within budgets and meet deadlines.

Since they work with and rely upon many other people, among them directors, producers, actors, and assistants, Costume Designers must also have good communication and delegation skills, tact and diplomacy, patience, and grace under pressure.

Unions and Associations

Costume Designers who work in unionized settings must belong to United Scenic Artists, a union representing not only Costume Designers but also costume stylists and their assistants and a host of other professionals.

Many Costume Designers are also members of the Costume Designers Guild, an affiliate of the International

Alliance of Theatrical Stage Employees. The guild's more than 650 members include Costume Designers, assistant Costume Designers, and illustrators working in film and television, as well as stylists and commercial Costume Designers working in commercials and music videos.

Tips for Entry

1. Learn how to sew well, so that once you become a Costume Designer you can handle any last-minute sewing jobs yourself.
2. Pursue a college degree in costume design, fashion or textile design, or theater so that you can get both education and hands-on experience in the field.
3. Volunteer to help with costume design and creation for a local high school or college production, a community theater production, or a similar production so that you can get hands-on experience in the field.
4. Watch lots of movies, television programs, and plays so that you can study the costumes in those productions and analyze how they work with the actors, the scenery, and the theme.
5. Be willing to work for low or no pay at first, and to put in long hours, so that you can accumulate both the experience and personal contacts you need to play a bigger role in the industry.
6. Talk to people in your city or area who are involved with costume design. You'll find them in community/regional theaters and at colleges/universities, among other places. Your local newspaper's theater critic can also help you identify some Costume Designers in your area.

DATABASE MANAGER

CAREER PROFILE

Duties: Oversees the design, programming, development, analysis, and maintenance of complex information databases for apparel- or textile-related organizations

Alternate Title(s): Database Administrator

Salary Range: $55,000 to $100,000+

Employment Prospects: Good

Advancement Prospects: Good

Best Geographical Location(s): Large cities across the United States, particularly those where the headquarters of apparel manufacturers and retailers are located

Prerequisites:

Education or Training—A bachelor's degree is almost always required, in an area such as computer science, management information systems, computer information systems, computer engineering, or electrical engineering; in some cases a master's degree in a similar field is also required; course work or an academic minor in an apparel- or textile-related field is helpful

Experience—At least three, and often five or more, years of related experience in database programming, design, development, and maintenance are required

Special Skills, and Personality Traits—Exceptional computer skills, particularly in the areas of database design, programming, development, analysis, and maintenance; proficiency with various computer languages and software programs; computer hardware knowledge; troubleshooting skills; conceptualization skills and creativity; patience and persistence; problem-solving abilities and technical savvy; mathematical abilities; logical reasoning skills; ability to work well with people of diverse backgrounds; ability to take projects from start to finish; good communication skills; willingness and ability to continuously learn new skills and technologies

Special Requirements—Various certifications may be required or helpful

CAREER LADDER

Information Systems Manager or Director

Database Manager

Database Designer or Analyst

Database Programmer

Position Description

Database Managers oversee the design, programming, development, analysis, and maintenance of complex databases for apparel- or textile-related organizations. The information in these databases, whether it relates to the company's customers, orders, vendors, or products and services, is one of the most critical organizational assets, and thus must be well maintained, protected, and utilized. The Database Manager is the person who holds this responsibility, usually with a group of other professionals who assist with various database operations.

Most Database Managers are involved with a wide variety of activities. Sometimes, for example, the Database Manager will oversee technical support for databases that already exist, recommending ways to modify those databases so that they function more efficiently and effectively. In other cases, the Database Manager will oversee the creation of brand new databases for the company, which involves not only technical savvy but also big-picture and conceptualization skills. And in almost all cases, Database Managers are responsible for protection of the data in company databases, which might include developing information backup and recovery strategies or creating security systems that allow only certain individuals to make changes to company databases.

Database Managers are heavily involved with corporate Web site design and development as well, particularly when it comes to e-commerce, promotion, research, and publicity activities. Many retailers, for example, sell merchandise via their Web sites—a complex undertaking. Database Managers must collaborate with company Web developers and designers on activities such as making the firm's product catalog available and searchable online and gathering sensitive customer information securely so that consumers can make purchases with the assurance that the information they provide won't ultimately fall into the wrong hands.

Database Managers can work for apparel retailers of all kinds, apparel and textile manufacturers, and other fashion- and/or textile-related entities, such as fashion magazines and technology consulting companies that specialize in helping apparel and textile clients.

Salaries

Database Managers across all fields and levels in the United States earned a median annual salary of $60,650 in 2004, according to the U.S. Department of Labor. More recent figures, however, reflect a continuing trend of steady annual salary increases for Database Managers.

A spring 2005 survey by *Computerworld* magazine, for example, revealed that Database Managers earned an average salary of about $87,700 at that time. The Web site Salary.com, meanwhile, noted a median annual salary for Database Administrators of about $84,400 in summer 2006.

The highest salaries go to Database Managers who have extensive experience and knowledge of key programs and programming languages, as well as sound leadership and management abilities.

Employment Prospects

The U.S. Department of Labor predicts that the number of Database Managers will grow much faster than average between now and 2014. In 2004, Database Managers across all fields and levels in the United States held about 104,000 jobs.

Prospective Database Managers who want to work for apparel- or textile-related companies may have slightly fewer opportunities (since they are looking for jobs in a narrower field, and since they hold relatively high-level positions), but will still have many jobs to pursue.

Advancement Prospects

The computer system design and related services sector—which includes Database Managers—is currently one of the fastest-growing parts of the American economy, according to the U.S. Department of Labor. With e-commerce activities continuing to expand and computer security becoming more complex, Database Managers have plenty of options when it comes to both lateral and upward career movement.

Database Managers who gain several years of experience, sound technical skills, and leadership expertise can advance to become higher-paid information systems managers or even chief information officers, both of whom can easily earn over $100,000 a year.

Education and Training

Prospective Database Managers need at least a bachelor's degree in a field like computer science, management information systems, computer information systems, electrical engineering, or computer engineering. Often, they also need to pursue a master's degree in a related field, as well as various certifications documenting their technical knowledge and skills.

Database Managers who would like to somehow work in the fashion and apparel industry benefit from having courses or an academic minor in a fashion- or textile-related field, so that they understand apparel and textiles in general and business-related concepts in particular.

Database Managers must also participate in continuing education and training programs, since the technologies they work with change rapidly and new technologies emerge constantly.

Special Requirements

Database Managers may earn certifications from companies, such as the following:

Microsoft offers the Microsoft Certified Database Administrator (MCDBA) certification for Database Managers who oversee Microsoft SQL Server databases. Applicants must "pass three core exams and one elective exam that provide a valid and reliable measure of technical proficiency and expertise in the implementation and administration of SQL Server databases."

Oracle offers three certifications for both its Oracle Database 10g and Oracle9i Database; Sybase offers several certifications for professionals who use Sybase products; and IBM offers certification for its DB2 database program.

Experience, Skills, and Personality Traits

Database Managers need exceptional computer skills, particularly in the areas of database design, programming, development, analysis, and maintenance. They must also be proficient with various computer languages and software programs, and be willing to continuously learn about new languages and programs so that their companies remain on the cutting edge.

Troubleshooting skills are essential to the Database Manager's success, as are patience, persistence, problem-solving abilities, and technical savvy. Database Managers must also be strong communicators who can work well with others in small teams, even if they aren't always involved in the hands-on technical aspects of the database systems they oversee.

Database Managers must also have mathematical abilities, logical reasoning and analytical skills, and a solid background in the theory of database design. Those who want to work for an apparel- or textile-related organization also benefit from having general knowledge of fashions and textiles.

Unions and Associations

Depending on their specific jobs and interests, Database Managers can be involved in a host of professional organizations. Among the most popular are the Association for Computing Machinery (ACM), the Association of Information Technology Professionals (AITP), and the Institute of Electrical and Electronics Engineers (IEEE).

Database Managers who work for apparel or textile manufacturers might tap the resources of organizations like the American Apparel and Footwear Association (AAFA) or the International Textile and Apparel Association (ITAA), while those who work for retail companies may use the resources of the National Retail Federation (NRF).

Tips for Entry

1. While in school, be sure to gain database experience through an internship or a co-op program, preferably with a company that somehow relates to fashion or textiles.
2. Explore and pursue certifications that can help you gain an edge in the employment market. Today's hot certification is tomorrow's "no big deal," so be sure to talk to industry experts, counselors, employers, and others to get a sense of which certifications make the most sense for you to obtain.
3. Consider taking courses or obtaining an academic minor in a fashion- or textile-related field, so that you gain a basic understanding of apparel and textiles.
4. Talk to one or more Database Managers who work for fashion- or textile-related companies so that you can learn how they got their jobs and find out how you can do the same thing.
5. Look for entry-level contract or temporary positions that will allow you to gain some hands-on experience with database programming, design, development, analysis, and/or maintenance.

HUMAN RESOURCES ADMINISTRATOR

CAREER PROFILE

Duties: Oversees various employee-related activities for a textile or apparel company, including recruitment and selection, training and development, performance appraisals, and administration of salary and benefits

Alternate Title(s): Personnel Administrator, Human Resources Coordinator, Personnel Coordinator

Salary Range: $50,000 to $120,000+

Employment Prospects: Fair

Advancement Prospects: Fair

Best Geographical Location(s): Large cities across the United States, particularly those where textile or apparel companies have corporate headquarters, production facilities, and/or retail operations

Prerequisites:

Education or Training—A minimum of a bachelor's degree is generally required, usually in an area like human resource management, psychology, or the liberal arts

Experience—Three to five years of human resources experience, preferably with an apparel or textile company, are required

Special Skills and Personality Traits—Outstanding people skills; strong communication skills; outgoing, friendly personality; sound research and analytical skills; good judgment; knowledge of employment laws and regulations; basic understanding of textiles and/or apparel; good decision-making skills; trustworthiness; organizational skills; computer skills; ability to manage multiple projects at once and meet associated deadlines; teaching and training skills; knowledge of human resources functions; fluency in a language besides English (particularly Spanish or Chinese)

Special Requirements—Certification by human resource-related professional organizations may be required

CAREER LADDER

Human Resources Director

Human Resources Administrator

Human Resources Assistant or Specialist

Position Description

Human Resources Administrators are professionals within textile and apparel organizations who ensure that the right people are hired as employees, that those people are trained well, and that those people are then paid on time and evaluated periodically.

Like their counterparts in other fields, Human Resources Administrators in textiles and apparel oversee four broad areas of concern. First and foremost, they're responsible—directly or indirectly—for recruiting and selecting employees for their companies. So they must advertise job listings—often in newspapers but also on Web sites—and then determine which applicants to interview and, ultimately, hire for different jobs.

Next, once employees have been hired, Human Resources Administrators are often involved in training them for their various job duties. The Human Resources Administrator for a retail apparel store, for example, might train new sales associates on company policies and selling strategies. Increasingly, Human Resources Administrators are involved in training employees for the future as well. Many companies are beginning to realize that employees who receive regular training to improve their skills are more likely to remain with their companies.

The third main function of Human Resources Administrators is to manage or assist with employee performance appraisals, so that the company can inform each employee of what he or she is doing well and what he or she can do better. Typically, these performance appraisals have a direct impact on each employee's compensation. An employee who receives an excellent review, for example, will generally receive a larger pay raise than an employee who receives a poor review.

Finally, Human Resources Administrators also oversee the processes ensuring that employees are paid correctly and on time, and that they receive benefits such as health care insurance, disability insurance, and money for retirement plans. New employees in particular are concerned about getting paid and receiving their benefits. The Human Resources Administrator guides employees through the various paperwork to make it all happen.

Depending on the job and the company, Human Resources Administrators may be involved in a variety of other activities as well. Some Human Resources Administrators, for example, oversee employee assistance programs that offer help to employees who may be experiencing personal problems of some sort, and who may need counseling or other services. Other Human Resources Administrators are closely involved with labor relations—developing and maintaining strong working relationships between corporate management and unionized employees. Still other Human Resources Administrators oversee dispute resolution among employees, for example, or between an employee and his or her manager.

The chances are good that if a company issue or problem has something to do with employees, or is likely to affect employees somehow, the Human Resources Administrator will be involved in trying to resolve it.

Salaries

Human resources managers across all fields and levels in the United States earned a median annual salary of $81,810 in 2004, according to the U.S. Department of Labor. Depending on the size of the organization, the job duties, the geographic location of the organization, and one's background, Human Resources Administrators can typically earn anywhere from $50,000 to $120,000 a year—and occasionally more.

Employment Prospects

Human resources managers across all fields and levels held about 157,000 jobs in the United States in 2004, according to the U.S. Department of Labor, and the DOL predicts that employment of human resources professionals will grow faster than average between now and 2014. So employment prospects for the human resources field in general are good, particularly as more companies begin to recognize the long-term benefits of having sound human resources programs in place for their employees. The number of positions for Human Resources Administrators and other human resources professionals in textiles and apparel, however, is somewhat limited, so employment prospects for human resources professionals within these industries are only fair.

Advancement Prospects

Since the number of human resources professionals in textiles or apparel is relatively small compared with the number of human resources professionals across all fields, advancement prospects for Human Resources Administrators in textiles or apparel are only fair. Additionally Human Resources Administrators are already mid to high-level managers in most cases, so advancement sometimes comes from moving to the same position at a larger company.

Education and Training

In almost all cases, Human Resources Administrators in textiles or apparel need at least a bachelor's degree, usually in an area like human resource management or a similar field like psychology or even the liberal arts. For higher-level positions, a master's degree (often in business administration [M.B.A.] or human resources) is often required as well.

Human Resources Administrators in textiles or apparel also benefit from fashion- and/or textile-related coursework, as well as classes in employment law.

In some cases, Human Resources Administrators must have certain certifications as well, from professional organizations like the Society for Human Resource Management (SHRM) or the American Society for Training and Development (ASTD). SHRM offers two certifications: the Professional in Human Resources (PHR) and the Senior Professional in Human Resources (SPHR). ASTD offers the Human Performance Improvement (HPI) certification.

Experience, Skills, and Personality Traits

Above all, Human Resources Administrators need to have excellent people skills. They have to be able to judge and then wisely select people for employment, help employees develop their skills and perhaps deal with various personal problems, see to it that employees' problems with compensation and/or benefits are rectified, and evaluate employees' performance. All of these activities require sound communication skills, strong listening skills, and, often, tact.

The most successful Human Resources Administrators are outgoing, friendly, and personable managers and leaders who are well organized and trustworthy. They know their organizations and the specific divisions and jobs within those organizations extremely well, and they have a solid understanding of what their companies do and why. They also have thorough knowledge of employment laws and regulations, good decision-making skills, and strong research and analytical skills.

Human Resources Administrators need above-average computer skills as well, whether they use computers for recruiting purposes, for salary and benefits administration, or for training and development activities.

Unions and Associations

The primary professional organization for Human Resources Administrators and related professionals is the Society for Human Resource Management (SHRM). Human Resources Administrators who are involved in training activities often belong to the American Society for Training and Development (ASTD), while those who work with compensation and benefits often join WorldatWork (formerly called the American Compensation Association).

Human Resources Administrators who work for apparel or textile manufacturers might tap the resources of organizations like the American Apparel and Footwear Association (AAFA) or the International Textile and Apparel Association (ITAA), while those who work for retail companies may use the resources of the National Retail Federation (NRF).

Tips for Entry

1. While in school, participate in one or more internships or co-ops in human resources—preferably at a textile- or apparel-related company—to gain hands-on experience in the field before you graduate.
2. Join professional organizations like the Society for Human Resource Management (SHRM), especially at the local level, so that you can meet working human resources professionals, learn about their companies, and uncover job leads.
3. Consider taking courses or obtaining an academic minor in a textile- or apparel-related field, so that you gain a basic understanding of fashion and textiles. Consider taking business and employment law courses as well.
4. Talk to one or more Human Resources Administrators who work for fashion- or textile-related companies so that you can learn how they got their jobs and find out how you can do the same thing.

RECRUITER

CAREER PROFILE

Duties: Identifies, screens, interviews, and selects candidates to fill job openings (current or anticipated) in apparel-related companies

Alternate Title(s): Corporate Recruiter, Personnel Recruiter, Placement Specialist

Salary Range: $30,000 to $100,000+

Employment Prospects: Fair

Advancement Prospects: Good

Best Geographical Location(s): Fashion centers like New York City and Los Angeles, as well as other large cities that are home to apparel-related companies (or placement firms that serve apparel-related companies)

Prerequisites:

Education or Training—A bachelor's degree in an apparel- or textile-related discipline, or in human resource management or business administration, is generally required; in certain cases, extensive apparel industry experience can substitute for a bachelor's degree

Experience—Two to three years of recruiting experience are usually required, with higher-level positions requiring five to 10 years of experience; a background in fashion/apparel is often required as well

Special Skills and Personality Traits—Ability to identify potential job candidates using personal networking, print advertising, and online advertising strategies; solid interviewing skills; outstanding communication (written and verbal) and interpersonal (i.e., "people") skills; customer service focus; sound judgment; expertise in employment laws and regulations; good sales and persuasion skills; ability to create and maintain large personal/professional networking relationships; exceptional listening and questioning abilities

CAREER LADDER

Director of Recruitment

Senior Recruiter

Recruiter

Recruiting Assistant

Position Description

An apparel-related company isn't a company at all if it doesn't have employees; and if those employees aren't skilled and capable, the company won't be around for very long.

It's the Recruiter's job to make sure his/her company (or the company his/her third-party staffing firm represents) has the employees it needs to achieve its goals.

Recruiters are responsible for four basic tasks. First, they must find potential job candidates for the company to consider, by tapping their own professional relationships, developing and posting job announcements in print and/or online media outlets, and searching online résumé databases. Second, Recruiters must screen candidates, evaluating résumés and cover letters (and perhaps conducting various background checks—e.g., criminal or credit history, education) to choose which candidates should be contacted for interviews. Third, Recruiters must conduct job interviews with candidates, asking them questions and evaluating their responses. Finally, Recruiters use their analytical skills and experience to choose the best candidate(s) for the job(s) at hand and create an offer package (i.e., salary, benefits) for that person.

Recruiters have a critical job in any company—especially considering the fact that, according to various studies, replacing an employee who does not work out can cost thousands of dollars. Recruiters must have a solid grasp of the various techniques used to identify, screen, interview, and select job candidates. Just as important, Recruiters who work for or on behalf of apparel-related companies need to understand the apparel industry itself so that they can make intelligent decisions about whom to hire—and whom not to hire, as the case may be.

Many Recruiters are employed by apparel manufacturing firms or apparel retail companies (usually within an organization's broader human resources function). Some Recruiters, however, work for outside firms called placement agencies that are hired by apparel-related companies to fill job openings.

Salaries

Most Recruiters have at least several years of experience under their belts, which is reflected in their salaries. While entry-level recruiting assistants might make only about $30,000 a year or so to start, it's not unusual for Recruiters to earn significantly more—indeed, $100,000 or more in some cases (especially if they work for a placement firm that recruits high-level executives). Recruiters who work for placement firms in particular typically receive a base salary along with commissions (based on a percentage of the salary of each person placed).

Employment, recruitment, and placement specialists across all industries earned a median annual salary of $41,190 in 2004, according to the U.S. Department of Labor.

Employment Prospects

While employment of human resources, training, and labor relations managers and specialists is projected to grow faster than average between now and 2014, according to the U.S. Department of Labor, the number of Recruiters who work for or on behalf of apparel-related companies is comparatively small. So employment prospects for Recruiters who want to work in the fashion industry can only be characterized as fair.

Jobs are available with apparel manufacturers, apparel retail companies, and the placement firms that serve both.

Advancement Prospects

Recruiters who work for or on behalf of apparel-related companies can advance in several ways. They can move into higher-level positions within their own companies—to become senior Recruiters or directors of recruitment, for instance; they can take on executive-level positions, either in human resources or another area of the company; or they can join (or even start) outside placement firms.

Education and Training

Most Recruiters in the fashion industry need at least a bachelor's degree, either in an apparel- or textile-related discipline or in an area like human resources or business administration. Sometimes, Recruiters with extensive (10 years or more) experience can still advance in their careers without a bachelor's degree, especially if they have a solid network of contacts and a proven track record of identifying and hiring solid employees.

Experience, Skills, and Personality Traits

To be successful, Recruiters must have the analytical skills necessary to identify good candidates and the interviewing skills necessary to pick the best person for the job. Solid communication and interpersonal (i.e., "people") skills are paramount, as is having a customer service focus that addresses the wants/needs of both job candidates and company managers.

The best Recruiters are good listeners and questioners who can demonstrate both sound judgment and good decision-making abilities. Today's Recruiters also need strong computer skills, especially when it comes to using online résumé databases and Web sites to search for potential job candidates. And to protect both themselves and the companies they work for or represent, they must also understand—and abide by—employment laws and regulations.

Unions and Associations

Many Recruiters are members of the Society for Human Resource Management (SHRM), a professional association for human resources professionals across all industries and disciplines. Recruiters can also find and join various other organizations, depending on their responsibilities and interests. Those who recruit new college graduates for entry-level positions, for instance, can participate in the National Association of Colleges and Employers (NACE). Those who recruit executive-level candidates, on the other hand, might tap the resources of the National Association of Executive Recruiters (NAER).

Recruiters who work for or on behalf of apparel-related companies can keep current on the overall fashion industry and its employment trends and forecasts by participating in organizations like Fashion Group International (FGI), the American Apparel and Footwear Association (AAFA), and the International Textile and Apparel Association (ITAA).

Tips for Entry

1. Complete at least a bachelor's degree in either a fashion-related discipline or a business discipline

like human resources management or business administration.

2. During college, gain some practical recruiting (or broader human resources) experience through an internship or a co-op assignment—either with an apparel-related company or a placement agency that serves apparel-related firms.
3. Work somewhere within the apparel industry (in a non-recruiting job) for a few years to get a sense of what the career is like in the trenches. That way, if and when you become a Recruiter later in your career, you'll have a better understanding of the types of jobs you're trying to fill.
4. Talk to some Recruiters (i.e., informational interviewing) who work for or on behalf of apparel-related companies to learn more about what they do and how they got to where they are now.
5. Visit apparel company and job search Web sites to look for Recruiter job listings. What key skills and abilities, experiences, education, and traits do companies seem to be looking for in the Recruiters they want to hire?

TAILOR

CAREER PROFILE

Duties: Creates custom-made garments and/or alters mass-produced garments for individual customers

Alternate Title(s): Custom Tailor, Dressmaker, Seamstress

Salary Range: $0 to $100,000+

Employment Prospects: Limited

Advancement Prospects: Fair

Best Geographical Location(s): Large urban areas all across the United States

Prerequisites:

Education or Training—Though not required, a high school diploma is very helpful, as is a two- or four-year college degree in fashion design, apparel production, pattern making, textile design, or a related field

Experience—Extensive sewing and garment creation experience is required; apprenticeship experience under an expert Tailor highly recommended

Special Skills and Personality Traits—Well-developed sense of fashion; sound knowledge of garment construction; knowledge of form, fit, proportion, and color; excellent sewing skills; skills in pattern making and draping; expertise in fabric design and durability; good hand-eye coordination and finger dexterity; neatness and accuracy; ability to work well with people and identify and meet their wants and needs; business skills

CAREER LADDER

Tailor, Self-Employed

Tailor, Retail Outlet

Sewing Machine Operator

Position Description

Tailors are masters at sewing and garment creation, and they use their skills to either create custom-made garments (e.g., suits, dresses) from scratch or to alter mass-produced garments for individual customers.

Many tailors in the United States work in retail outlets, especially department stores. When customers buy garments from these stores, they often want those garments to be altered in some way—for example, pants shortened, dresses lengthened, etc. Tailors do this work, quickly and accurately, in the hopes that satisfied customers will become repeat customers in their stores.

More than half of all Tailors in the United States are self-employed, according to the U.S. Department of Labor, working either from their own storefront shops or home offices. Often these Tailors work closely with individual customers to conceptualize, design, create, and, if necessary, alter garments suiting customers' individual tastes. In some cases, Tailors earn excellent money for this type of work. It's not uncommon, for example, for a celebrity to pay several thousand dollars for a custom-made suit. Even noncelebrities who are relatively well-off are often willing and able to spend several hundred dollars for just the right dress.

Most Tailors specialize in a certain type of clothing. Some Tailors, for example, work exclusively on wedding gowns for women, while others work only on suits for very tall men. Once these Tailors develop a niche by using their special expertise to serve a specific group of customers, they can often count on having those customers return for other garments and bringing in new business.

Tailors have to be good with both people and their hands. Whether they're altering a pair of pants or creating a wedding gown from scratch, Tailors deal with different people who have different wants and needs, and different expectations. Tailors must be able to determine what their customers want, and then keep their promises by using their sewing skills and knowledge of garment construction to actually deliver the goods on time, at the agreed-upon price.

Tailors who are self-employed must also invest considerable time and energy in business-related tasks—for example, keeping track of finances, promoting their businesses, perhaps hiring and supervising employees, taking care of their places of operation, and following up with customers to ensure they're satisfied.

Salaries

Salaries for Tailors vary widely. Self-employed, part-time, home-based Tailors might earn only a few hundred or a few thousand dollars a year, depending on the number of customers they seek and find. On the other hand, self-employed Tailors who devote all of their energy to their businesses can occasionally make $100,000 a year or more, particularly if they work in large, urban areas and they're able to attract celebrity or well-off customers. Tailors as a whole earned a median hourly salary of $10.79 in 2004, according to the U.S. Department of Labor, which translates to an annual salary of about $22,450 based on a 40-hour workweek.

Employment Prospects

Employment of Tailors (and dressmakers and sewers) is expected to decline between now and 2014, according to the U.S. Department of Labor. In 2004, there were only 85,000 people working as Tailors (or dressmakers or sewers) in the United States.

Employment prospects are the toughest for those who want to become self-employed Tailors, in part because many new businesses fail, and in part because the number of potential customers is relatively small and often confined to people who have a considerable amount of disposable income.

Advancement Prospects

Tailors who start out working for retail outlets are sometimes able to start their own businesses, often on the side at first. As they gain a positive reputation and pick up customers, they can go on to make their businesses larger and serve more clients.

Still, generally speaking, advancement prospects for Tailors are fair at best, particularly if the economy is weak and consumers cut back on perceived luxuries such as custom-made clothing and alterations.

Education and Training

Generally speaking, Tailors don't need to follow a specific, prescribed educational path. Most, however, have at least a high school diploma, and many have earned two- or four-year college degrees in an area like fashion design, apparel production, pattern making, or textile design. Self-employed Tailors are also well served by having experience or education in business-related areas like accounting, finance, promotions and advertising, public relations, and human resources.

Almost all Tailors have worked as apprentices under more experienced Tailors so that they could develop sewing expertise and sound knowledge of garment construction techniques. Much of a Tailor's training comes from actually creating and/or altering garments under the supervision of an expert.

Experience, Skills, and Personality Traits

Tailors need extensive experience in creating custom garments from start to finish and in altering existing garments. In most cases, Tailors gain this experience through apprenticeships under more experienced Tailors.

To be successful, Tailors need a strong sense of fashion and thorough knowledge of garment conceptualization and construction. They must be experts on form, fit, proportion, and color, and have a sound understanding of fabric design and uses.

Tailors need plenty of hands-on skills. They have to be able to sew difficult items quickly and accurately, which calls for excellent finger dexterity and hand-eye coordination. They also need to be skilled in patternmaking, draping, and measuring techniques.

People skills are essential for Tailors in all settings, whether they're employed by another organization or self-employed. Tailors have to be able to communicate well with customers, determine what those customers want and need in their clothes, and then ensure that those customers are satisfied with the finished products they receive.

Self-employed Tailors must have additional skills related to business functions. They have to be able to manage their businesses' accounting and financial concerns, advertising and promotion activities, and human resources if they hope to stay in business and be financially successful.

Unions and Associations

Many Tailors are members of the Custom Tailors and Designers Association of America, a professional organization made up of Tailors, designers, custom clothiers, and direct sellers.

Tailors, especially those who are self-employed, are also wise to participate in groups that will help them stay on top of apparel industry trends and forecasts, like the International Textile and Apparel Association (ITAA), the American Apparel and Footwear Association (AAFA), and Fashion Group International (FGI). Many also take advantage of the resources and services of the U.S. Small Business Administration and related organizations for business owners.

Tips for Entry

1. Practice designing and sewing garments from start to finish so that you become a highly skilled, accurate, and fast sewer.
2. Get a job or an apprenticeship that will allow you to perfect your conceptual and sewing skills. Work under an experienced Tailor who can teach you how to create garments that meet customers' wants and needs.
3. Talk to some working Tailors—either in person or via phone or e-mail—to learn how they got to where they are now and how you can do the same.

TRAINER

CAREER PROFILE

Duties: Designs, develops, and implements training programs for various employees of apparel manufacturing or apparel retail companies

Alternate Title(s): Training Specialist, Training and Development Specialist, Learning Specialist, Learning and Development Specialist

Salary Range: $30,000 to $75,000+

Employment Prospects: Fair

Advancement Prospects: Good

Best Geographical Location(s): Fashion centers like New York City and Los Angeles, as well as other large cities that are home to apparel-related manufacturing or retail companies

Prerequisites:

Education or Training—A bachelor's degree in human resources management, training, education, or a closely related field is generally required; some higher-level positions require a graduate degree, such as the master of business administration (M.B.A.)

Experience—Two to five years of training experience are generally preferred for lower- and mid-level training positions, while higher-level jobs (e.g., director of learning and development) typically require five to 10 years of experience; professional experience in apparel manufacturing or retail apparel is also quite helpful, if not required

Special Skills and Personality Traits—Exceptional teaching and training skills; solid listening capabilities; ability to develop educational curricula and associated training materials (print, video, and online); good communication (written and verbal) and presentation skills; command of computer software applications, particularly presentation programs like Microsoft PowerPoint; research and analytical skills; conceptualization abilities; knowledge of adult learning theories and techniques as well as instructional design strategies; solid organizational and time management abilities; ability to assess training needs (via one-on-one interviews with employees and executives, surveys, and the like) and then create programs to meet those needs

CAREER LADDER

Vice President for Learning and Development

Director of Training or Director of Learning and Development

Trainer or Training Specialist

Training Assistant

Position Description

No new employee comes into an apparel manufacturing or apparel retail company knowing exactly what to do (and why) from day one. Each new employee needs some training. Often that training is informal and handled by the employee's own supervisor or colleagues. But sometimes—particularly in larger, more complex organizations—that training is handled by a professional Trainer who understands not only what has to be taught but also how best to teach it.

Trainers are educators by nature. Most hold a bachelor's degree in a discipline such as human resources management, training and development, or education, and they use that background in several ways: 1) to identify the types of training employees need—by, for example, conducting employee interviews or designing and administering surveys to assess training needs; 2) to conceptualize and design training programs (e.g., individual training sessions, in-person or online seminars); 3) to deliver training through effective presentations that cater to participants' usually diverse learning styles and experiences; and 4) to evaluate both the training efforts themselves and the people who have participated in those programs (to measure what they've learned).

Trainers can work in a variety of settings and tackle diverse tasks. A Trainer who works for an apparel retailer, for example, might oversee educational sessions for loss prevention personnel and/or other employees so that they all understand the company's loss prevention policies, procedures, and strategies. A Trainer who works for an apparel manufacturing firm, meanwhile, might lead educational sessions on a particular software program that merchandising staff must know and use. In short, wherever and whenever there is something that employees need to learn, Trainers are responsible for making it happen.

Most Trainers focus not only on teaching hard skills (e.g., mastery of a piece of software, knowledge of loss prevention techniques) but also soft skills, such as being a reliable team member or communicating more effectively with colleagues. Trainers must also be able to create and present educational programs using a variety of formats, ranging from one-on-one and group presentations to video-based approaches to interactive multimedia programs available online.

Salaries

While salaries for Trainers often start out relatively low (around $30,000 a year in many cases), they do tend to rise as Trainers accumulate more experience and expertise. At high levels (e.g., vice president for learning and development), a salary of $100,000 a year is not out of the question.

Most Trainers, though, earn considerably less than that. In 2004, Trainers across all industries earned a median annual salary of $44,570, according to the U.S. Department of Labor.

Employment Prospects

Relatively few apparel manufacturing and apparel retailing companies have personnel and/or departments devoted strictly to employee training, and even those that do tend to have comparatively small staffs. Training itself can be difficult (though not impossible) to tie to a company's bottom line, so some high-level executives question its value and, on occasion, its very existence as a stand-alone function.

Still, some apparel manufacturers and larger apparel retailers do indeed have training divisions and staffs. So employment prospects for Trainers who want to get into some aspect of the apparel industry are fair.

Advancement Prospects

Trainers who prove themselves can advance to higher-level training positions in their companies or, perhaps more often, seek out higher-level jobs elsewhere within the broader human resources function (e.g., human resources manager, human resources administrator), either in their current companies or elsewhere. So once a Trainer lands a job in the field and begins accumulating experience, expertise, and credibility, his/her chances for advancement are quite good.

Education and Training

Most Trainers (in the apparel industry and elsewhere) have at least a bachelor's degree in human resources management, training and development, education, or a closely related field. Those who eventually want to move into higher-level jobs often pursue a graduate degree as well, such as the master of business administration (M.B.A.).

Experience, Skills, and Personality Traits

First and foremost, Trainers need to be outstanding teachers. They must be capable of identifying training needs, creating approaches and materials to meet those needs, and delivering training programs in a way that will have a long-term impact on participants in terms of their skills and knowledge.

Strong communication and presentation abilities are essential to the Trainer's success, as is the ability to develop educational curricula and associated training materials (print, video, and online). Expertise in adult learning theories and techniques is critical. Trainers must also have solid command of computer software applications (particularly presentation programs such as Microsoft PowerPoint); good organizational and time management skills; the ability to formally assess training needs (instead of merely guessing at what they "should" be); and a knack for demonstrating to higher-ups and other potential skeptics that a company's investment in training its employees is, indeed, an investment—and not merely another expenditure that has no return.

Unions and Associations

Many Trainers (in fashion/apparel and elsewhere) are members of the American Society for Training and Development (ASTD), a professional association for training specialists across all organizational settings. Some Trainers also participate in the activities of the Society for Human Resource Management (SHRM).

Trainers in fashion/apparel can also keep current on trends by tapping the resources of the National Retail Federation (NRF) and/or organizations like Fashion Group International (FGI), the American Apparel and Footwear Association (AAFA), and the International Textile and Apparel Association (ITAA).

Tips for Entry

1. Complete at least a bachelor's degree in a discipline like human resource management, training and development, or education. Consider pursuing a minor (or a double major) in an apparel-related discipline as well (e.g., apparel merchandising, fashion marketing).
2. During college, gain some practical experience in training through an internship or a co-op assignment, with an apparel retailer or an apparel manufacturing firm.
3. Do whatever you can to get to know some working Trainers in the apparel field. If possible, talk to some Trainers (i.e., informational interviewing) to learn more about what they do and how they got to where they are now.
4. Visit the Web sites of apparel retailers and manufacturers, as well as general job search Web sites, to look for Trainer job listings. What key skills and abilities, experiences, education, and traits do companies seem to be looking for in the Trainers they want to hire?
5. If your community has a chapter of the American Society for Training and Development (ASTD), join it and get involved. Use it to meet Trainers who work in apparel-related jobs and/or to identify potential internship, co-op, or job possibilities.

WEB DESIGNER

CAREER PROFILE

Duties: Designs, implements, and maintains complex Web sites for apparel- and textile-related manufacturers and retailers, as well as other apparel- and textile-related organizations

Alternate Title(s): Web Site Designer, Webmaster, Web Developer

Salary Range: $50,000 to $90,000+

Employment Prospects: Good

Advancement Prospects: Good

Best Geographical Location(s): Large cities across the United States, particularly those where the headquarters of apparel manufacturers and retailers are located

Prerequisites:

Education or Training—A bachelor's degree is almost always required, in an area such as computer science, management information systems, computer information systems, computer engineering, or electrical engineering; in some cases a master's degree in a similar field is also required; course work or an academic minor in apparel merchandising or another apparel- or textile-related field is helpful, as is course work in graphic design

Experience—At least two years of related experience in Web site design and development, either through college internships or co-ops or entry-level jobs

Special Skills and Personality Traits—Exceptional computer skills; proficiency with various computer languages and software programs; computer hardware knowledge; troubleshooting skills; conceptualization skills and creativity; patience and persistence; problem-solving abilities and technical savvy; mathematical abilities; logical reasoning skills; general knowledge of fashion and textiles; ability to work well with people of diverse backgrounds; ability to explain complex technical ideas to people with little or no technical expertise; ability to take projects from start to finish; willingness and ability to continuously learn new skills and technologies

Special Requirements—Various certifications may be required

CAREER LADDER

Web Operations Manager

Web Developer

Web Designer

Web Design Assistant

Position Description

Just a few short years ago, the Internet and, in particular, the World Wide Web were in their infancy, and organizations could only imagine how they could harness the Web's reach and power. Today, companies of all kinds, including many in the fashion and apparel industry, are using the Web routinely, most often in their marketing, sales, and promotional efforts. Web Designers are the professionals who conceptualize these Web sites, implement them, and maintain them so that users who visit the sites have a pleasant experience and, hopefully, come back.

Depending on their specific job duties and the companies they work for, Web Designers can participate in a wide range of activities. Most Web Designers, for example, are involved in conceptualizing the Web sites they work on. This includes collaborating with others to determine what sort of content, tools, and features the site should present and how, as well as how the site should look and feel to the user. Many Web Designers are also involved in the actual implementation of their companies' sites, using their computer software, hardware, and programming language skills to turn the Web site idea into a reality. Additionally, most Web Designers are responsible for maintaining their companies' Web sites once those sites are live, and troubleshooting the inevitable problems that arise. This might mean, for example, intervening when users are having trouble accessing the site for some reason, or making changes when pieces of code or software conflict with each other and wreak havoc on the site.

Web Designers generally work with a host of other professionals, some of whom are themselves technically savvy but many of whom are not. In the latter case, the Web Designer has to be able to explain complex technical information and terms in a way the nontechnical people, who may be company decision makers, can understand. In many cases, the Web Designer must also tactfully explain to decision makers the Web site's limits with respect to tools and features, and then help those decision makers come up with alternatives that can more readily be implemented.

In large companies, Web Designers might specialize and focus on only one or two specific tasks, such as developing Web graphics or interactive tools such as message boards or chat rooms. In smaller companies, however, there may be only one or a handful of Web Designers, each of whom must assume much more technical, creative, and daily maintenance responsibilities. Some Web Designers prefer working in smaller companies for the opportunity to wear many hats in their day-to-day activities. Others, however, prefer to specialize in a larger organization so that they can become experts in their assigned areas.

Web Designers and related professionals are also expected to stay on top of new technologies, which can literally change by the day or the week. Smart Web Designers enroll in continuing education programs, through their companies or local institutions, so that they can learn about the constantly expanding range of tools they can use in their work and how those tools can benefit the companies for which they work.

Salaries

Web Designers across all industries and levels earned a median annual salary of about $61,000 in 2006, according to compensation Web site Salary.com. Depending on their specific job titles and duties, however, Web Designers can earn slightly less or significantly more.

A spring 2006 survey by *InformationWeek* magazine found that Web Designers/Developers at the staff level earned a median annual salary of $63,000, while those at the managerial level earned a median annual salary of $80,000.

Employment Prospects

The U.S. Department of Labor reports that "the expanding integration of Internet technologies into businesses . . . has resulted in a growing need for specialists who can develop and support Internet and intranet applications." In all, computer scientists and database administrators held about 507,000 jobs in the United States in 2004, the DOL notes. So employment prospects for Web Designers appear to be good.

Advancement Prospects

Advancement prospects for Web Designers in general are excellent, especially as technology continues to move forward and companies expand their use of the Internet and the Web.

Web Designers who gain several years of experience and have sound technical skills can advance to become higher-paid Web developers (who oversee the technical implementation of Web sites) and Web operations managers (who oversee the entire Web design, development, and maintenance function). Web operations managers can easily earn more than $100,000 a year.

Education and Training

Prospective Web Designers need at least a bachelor's degree in a field like computer science, management information systems, computer information systems, electrical engineering, or computer engineering. Often, they also need to pursue a master's degree in a related field, as well as various certifications documenting their technical knowledge and skills.

Web Designers who would like to somehow work in the fashion and apparel industry benefit from having courses or an academic minor in apparel merchandising or another fashion- or textile-related field, so that they understand apparel and textiles in general and business-related concepts (e.g., marketing, advertising, promotions) in particular.

Graphic design courses or experience can also be beneficial, particularly for Web Designers who work in smaller organizations and who may be asked to develop graphics for company Web sites.

Special Requirements

Various certifications may be helpful or required. For example, the International Webmasters Association (IWA) offers Certified Web Professional (CWP) certification, while ProSoft Training offers the Certified Internet Web Professional (CIW) certification.

Experience, Skills, and Personality Traits

Web Designers need exceptional computer skills as well as a strong interest in working with computers and, more specifically, the Internet and the Web. Web Designers must also be proficient with various computer languages and software programs, and be willing to continuously learn about new langauges and programs so that their companies remain on the cutting edge.

Troubleshooting skills are essential to the Web Designer's success, since no Web site works flawlessly the first time. Web Designers also need to be creative and able to conceptualize new ideas and systems from scratch. Often that calls for both patience and persistence, not to mention problem-solving abilities and technical savvy.

Web Designers must also have mathematical abilities, logical reasoning and analytical skills, and the ability to explain complex technical ideas to people with little or no technical expertise. Web Designers who want to work for an apparel- or textile-related organization also need to have general knowledge of fashion and/or textiles, as well as the ability to work well with people of diverse backgrounds.

Unions and Associations

Depending on their specific jobs and interests, Web Designers can be involved in a host of different professional organizations. Among the most popular are the Association for Computing Machinery (ACM), the Association of Information Technology Professionals (AITP), and the Institute of Electrical and Electronics Engineers (IEEE).

Web Designers who work for apparel or textile manufacturers might tap the resources of organizations like the American Apparel and Footwear Association (AAFA) or the International Textile and Apparel Association (ITAA), while those who work for retail companies may use the resources of the National Retail Federation (NRF).

Tips for Entry

1. While in school, be sure to gain Web design or similar experience through an internship or co-op program, preferably with a company that somehow relates to apparel or textiles.
2. Explore and pursue certifications that can help you gain an edge in the employment market. Today's hot certification is tomorrow's "no big deal," so be sure to talk to industry experts, counselors, employers, and others to get a sense of which certifications make the most sense for you to obtain.
3. Consider taking courses or obtaining an academic minor in apparel merchandising or another fashion- or textile-related field, so that you gain a basic understanding of fashions and textiles. Consider taking business, marketing, advertising, or public relations courses as well, since company Web sites are often used for sales, marketing, and promotion purposes.
4. Talk to one or more Web Designers who work for a fashion- or textile-related company so that you can learn how they got their jobs and find out how you can do the same thing.
5. Build one or more Web sites, on your own or for, perhaps, a local nonprofit organization, so that you will have a portfolio of Web sites you can show to prospective employers. If possible, develop a site that is somehow related to fashions or textiles.

APPENDIXES

APPENDIX I
EDUCATIONAL INSTITUTIONS

The following is a list of American colleges, universities, and other insitutions offering educational programs related to fashion and apparel, textiles, and/or fiber sciences. To learn about specific programs at specific schools, contact the institutions at the phone numbers listed or visit their accompanying websites.

When inquiring about schools and programs, be sure to be thorough in your research. Talking to admissions representatives is a good start, but talk to others as well—especially career counselors, professors, students, and recent graduates. In particular, find out what graduates of the various programs have gone on to do with their degrees, and ask for specifics when you do. The more information you gather, the better prepared you will be to decide your educational path.

ALABAMA

Alabama Agricultural & Mechanical University
Normal, AL 35762
Phone: (256) 851-5000
http://www.aamu.edu

Alabama Southern Community College
Monroeville, AL 36461
Phone: (334) 575-3156
http://www.ascc.edu

Auburn University
Auburn, AL 36849
Phone: (334) 844-4000
http://www.auburn.edu

Bishop State Community College
Mobile, AL 36603
Phone: (251) 690-6801
http://www.bishop.edu

Faulkner State Community College
Bay Minette, AL 36507
Phone: (800) 231-3752
http://www.faulkner.cc.al.us

Judson College
Marion, AL 36756
Phone: (800) 447-9472
http://www.judson.edu

Lawson State Community College
Birmingham, AL 35221
Phone: (205) 925-2515
http://www.ls.cc.al.us

Samford University
Birmingham, AL 35229
Phone: (205) 726-2011
http://www.samford.edu

Shelton State Community College
Tuscaloosa, AL 35405
Phone: (205) 391-2211
http://www.shelton.cc.al.us

Trenholm State Technical College
Montgomery, AL 36108
Phone: (334) 420-4200
http://www.trenholmtech.cc.al.us

University of Alabama at Tuscaloosa
Tuscaloosa, AL 35487
Phone: (205) 348-6010
http://www.ua.edu

Wallace State Community College–Hanceville
Hanceville, AL 35077
Phone: (866) 350-9722
http://www.wallacestatehanceville.edu

ARIZONA

Arizona State University
Tempe, AZ 85287
Phone: (480) 965-9011
http://www.asu.edu

Mesa Community College
Mesa, AZ 85202
Phone: (480) 461-7000
http://www.mc.maricopa.edu

Northern Arizona University
Flagstaff, AZ 86011
Phone: (928) 523-9011
http://www.nau.edu

Phoenix College
Phoenix, AZ 85013
Phone: (602) 285-7800
http://www.pc.maricopa.edu

Scottsdale Community College
Scottsdale, AZ 85256
Phone: (480) 423-6000
http://www.sc.maricopa.edu

University of Arizona
Tucson, AZ 85721
Phone: (520) 621-2211
http://www.arizona.edu

ARKANSAS

Harding University
Searcy, AR 72149
Phone: (501) 279-4000
http://www.harding.edu

University of Arkansas–Fayetteville
Fayetteville, AR 72701
Phone: (479) 575-2000
http://www.uark.edu

University of Arkansas–Fort Smith
Fort Smith, AR 72913
Phone: (479) 788-7000
http://www.uafortsmith.edu

University of Arkansas–Pine Bluff
Pine Bluff, AR 71601
Phone: (870) 575-8000
http://www.uapb.edu

University of Central Arkansas
Conway, AR 72035
Phone: (501) 450-5000
http://www.uca.edu

CALIFORNIA

Academy of Art College
San Francisco, CA 94105
Phone: (800) 544-2787
http://www.academyart.edu

Allan Hancock College
Santa Maria, CA 93454
Phone: (805) 922-6966
http://www.hancock.cc.ca.us

American Intercontinental University–Los Angeles
Los Angeles, CA 90066
Phone: (888) 594-9888
http://www.aiula.com

American River College
Sacramento, CA 95841
Phone: (916) 484-8011
http://www.arc.losrios.edu

Art Center College of Design
Pasadena, CA 91103
Phone: (626) 396-2200
http://www.artcenter.edu

The Art Institutes International–San Francisco
San Francisco, CA 94102
Phone: (415) 865-0198
http://www.artinstitutes.edu/sanfrancisco

Brooks College
Long Beach, CA 90804
Phone: (866) 746-5711
http://www.brookscollege.edu

Butte College
Oroville, CA 95965
Phone: (530) 895-2511
http://www.butte.cc.ca.us

California College of Arts
San Francisco, CA 94107
Phone: (800) 447-1278
http://www.cca.edu

California Design College
Los Angeles, CA 90010
Phone: (213) 251-3636
http://www.cdc.edu

California State Polytechnic University–Pomona
Pomona, CA 91768
Phone: (909) 869-7659
http://www.csupomona.edu

California State University–Long Beach
Long Beach, CA 90840
Phone: (562) 985-4111
http://www.csulb.edu

California State University–Northridge
Northridge, CA 91330
Phone: (818) 677-1200
http://www.csun.edu

Canada College
Redwood City, CA 94061
Phone: (650) 306-3100
http://www.canadacollege.net

Cerritos Community College
Norwalk, CA 90650
Phone: (562) 860-2451
http://www.cerritos.edu

Chabot College
Hayward, CA 94545
Phone: (510) 723-6600
http://www.chabotcollege.edu

Chaffey College
Rancho Cucamonga, CA 91737
Phone: (909) 987-1737
http://www.chaffey.edu

City College of San Francisco
San Francisco, CA 94112
Phone: (415) 239-3000
http://www.ccsf.cc.ca.us

College of Alameda
Alameda, CA 94501
Phone: (510) 522-7221
http://www.alameda.peralta.edu

College of San Mateo
San Mateo, CA 94402
Phone: (650) 574-6161
http://www.collegeofsanmateo.edu

College of the Desert
Palm Desert, CA 92260
Phone: (760) 346-8041
http://www.desert.cc.ca.us

College of the Sequoias
Visalia, CA 93277
Phone: (559) 730-3700
http://www.cos.edu

Compton Community College
Compton, CA 90221
Phone: (310) 900-1600
http://www.compton.cc.ca.us

Diablo Valley College
Pleasant Hill, CA 94523
Phone: (925) 685-1230
http://www.dvc.edu

El Camino College
Torrance, CA 90506
Phone: (866) 352-2646
http://www.elcamino.cc.ca.us

Evergreen Valley College
San Jose, CA 95135
Phone: (408) 274-7900
http://www.evc.edu

Fashion Careers of California College
San Diego, CA 92110
Phone: (619) 275-4700
http://www.fashioncollege.com

Fashion Institute of Design and Merchandising
Los Angeles, CA 90015
Phone: (800) 624-1200
http://www.fidm.edu

Fresno City College
Fresno, CA 93741
Phone: (559) 442-4600
http://www.fresnocitycollege.edu

Fullerton College
Fullerton, CA 92832
Phone: (714) 992-7000
http://www.fullcoll.edu

Glendale Community College
Glendale, CA 91208
Phone: (818) 240-1000
http://www.glendale.cc.ca.us

Las Positas College
Livermore, CA 94550
Phone: (925) 424-1000
http://www.laspositascollege.edu

Long Beach City College
Long Beach, CA 90808
Phone: (562) 938-4353
http://www.lbcc.cc.ca.us

Los Angeles Mission College
Sylmar, CA 91342
Phone: (818) 364-7600
http://www.lamission.edu

Los Angeles Southwest College
Los Angeles, CA 90047
Phone: (323) 241-5225
http://www.lasc.edu

Los Angeles Trade-Technical College
Los Angeles, CA 90015
Phone: (213) 763-7000
http://www.lattc.cc.ca.us

Los Angeles Valley College
Valley Glen, CA 91401
Phone: (818) 947-2600
http://www.lavc.cc.ca.us

Marymount College
Rancho Palos Verdes, CA 90275
Phone: (310) 377-5501
http://www.marymountpv.edu

Mendocino College
Ukiah, CA 95482
Phone: (707) 468-3000
http://www.mendocino.edu

Merced College
Merced, CA 95348
Phone: (209) 384-6000
http://www.merced.cc.ca.us

Modesto Junior College
Modesto, CA 95350
Phone: (209) 575-6550
http://www.mjc.edu

Mt. San Antonio College
Walnut, CA 91789
Phone: (909) 594-5611
http://www.mtsac.edu

Orange Coast College
Costa Mesa, CA 92626
Phone: (714) 432-0202
http://www.occ.cccd.edu

Otis College of Art and Design
Los Angeles, CA 90045
Phone: (800) 527-6847
http://www.otis.edu

Pacific Union College
Angwin, CA 94508
Phone: (800) 862-7080
http://www.puc.edu

Palomar College
San Marcos, CA 92069
Phone: (760) 744-1150
http://www.palomar.edu

Pasadena City College
Pasadena, CA 91106
Phone: (626) 585-7123
http://www.pasadena.edu

Sacramento City College
Sacramento, CA 95822
Phone: (916) 558-2111
http://www.scc.losrios.edu

Saddleback College
Mission Viejo, CA 92692
Phone: (949) 582-4500
http://www.saddleback.cc.ca.us

San Diego Mesa College
San Diego, CA 92111
Phone: (619) 388-2600
http://www.sdmesa.sdccd.cc.ca.us

San Francisco State University
San Francisco, CA 94132
Phone: (415) 338-1111
http://www.sfsu.edu

San Joaquin Delta College
Stockton, CA 95207
Phone: (209) 954-5151
http://www.deltacollege.org

Santa Ana College
Santa Ana, CA 92706
Phone: (714) 564-6000
http://www.sac.edu

Santa Rosa Junior College
Santa Rosa, CA 95401
Phone: (707) 527-4011
http://www.santarosa.edu

Shasta College
Redding, CA 96049
Phone: (530) 225-4600
http://www.shastacollege.edu

Sierra College
Rocklin, CA 95677
Phone: (916) 624-3333
http://www.sierra.cc.ca.us

Solano Community College
Suisun, CA 94585
Phone: (707) 864-7000
http://www.solano.edu

University of California–Davis
Davis, CA 95616
Phone: (530) 752-1011
http://www.ucdavis.edu

University of San Francisco
San Francisco, CA 94117
Phone: (415) 422-5555
http://www.usfca.edu

West Valley College
Saratoga, CA 95070
Phone: (408) 741-2000
http://www.westvalley.edu

Woodbury University
Burbank, CA 91510
Phone: (818) 767-0888
http://www.woodbury.edu

Yuba College
Marysville, CA 95901
Phone: (530) 741-6700
http://www.yccd.edu/yuba

COLORADO

Colorado State University
Fort Collins, CO 80523
Phone: (970) 491-1101
http://www.colostate.edu

CONNECTICUT

Asnuntuck Community-Technical College
Enfield, CT 06082
Phone: (860) 253-3000
http://www.acc.commnet.edu

Briarwood College
Southington, CT 06489
Phone: (860) 628-4751
http://www.briarwood.edu

Gateway Community College
New Haven, CT 06511
Phone: (203) 285-2000
http://www.gwctc.commnet.edu

University of Bridgeport
Bridgeport, CT 06601
Phone: (800) 392-3582
http://www.bridgeport.edu

University of Connecticut–Storrs
Storrs, CT 06269
Phone: (860) 486-2000
http://www.uconn.edu

University of New Haven
West Haven, CT 06516
Phone: (203) 932-7000
http://www.newhaven.edu

DELAWARE

Delaware State University
Dover, DE 19901

Phone: (302) 857-6060
http://www.desu.edu

University of Delaware
Newark, DE 19716
Phone: (302) 831-2792
http://www.udel.edu

DISTRICT OF COLUMBIA

Howard University
Washington, DC 20059
Phone: (202) 806-6100
http://www.howard.edu

University of the District of Columbia
Washington, DC 20008
Phone: (202) 274-5000
http://www.udc.edu

FLORIDA

Art Institute of Fort Lauderdale
Fort Lauderdale, FL 33316
Phone: (800) 275-7603
http://www.aifl.artinstitutes.edu

Brevard Community College
Cocoa, FL 32922
Phone: (321) 632-1111
http://www.brevard.cc.fl.us

Flagler College
St. Augustine, FL 32084
Phone: (904) 829-6481
http://www.flagler.edu

Florida Community College–Jacksonville
Jacksonville, FL 32202
Phone: (904) 646-2300
http://www.fccj.org

Florida State University
Tallahassee, FL 32306
Phone: (850) 644-2525
http://www.fsu.edu

Gulf Coast Community College
Panama City, FL 32401
Phone: (850) 769-1551
http://www.gc.cc.fl.us

Indian River Community College
Ft. Pierce, FL 34981
Phone: (866) 866-4722
http://www.ircc.edu

International Academy of Design & Technology
Tampa, FL 33609
Phone: (813) 881-0007
http://www.academy.edu

Lynn University
Boca Raton, FL 33431
Phone: (561) 237-7000
http://www.lynn.edu

Manatee Community College
Venice, FL 34293
Phone: (941) 408-1300
http://www.mccfl.edu

Miami-Dade College
Homestead, FL 33030
Phone: (305) 237-5000
http://www.mdc.edu

Miami International University of Art and Design
Miami, FL 33132
Phone: (800) 225-9023
http://www.artinstitutes.edu/miami

Okaloosa-Walton Community College
Niceville, FL 32578
Phone: (850) 678-5111
http://www.owcc.cc.fl.us

Santa Fe Community College
Gainesville, FL 32606
Phone: (352) 395-5000
http://www.santafe.cc.fl.us

St. Petersburg College
St. Petersburg, FL 33733
Phone: (727) 341-4772
http://www.spcollege.edu

University of Miami
Coral Gables, FL 33124
Phone: (305) 284-2211
http://www.miami.edu

GEORGIA

Abraham Baldwin Agricultural College
Tifton, GA 31794
Phone: (800) 733-3653
http://www.abac.peachnet.edu

American Intercontinental University–Buckhead
Atlanta, GA 30326
Phone: (888) 591-7888
http://www.aiubuckhead.com

Art Institute of Atlanta
Atlanta, GA 30326
Phone: (800) 275-4242
http://www.artinstitutes.edu/atlanta

Bauder College
Atlanta, GA 30326
Phone: (404) 237-7573
http://www.bauder.edu

Brenau University
Gainesville, GA 30501
Phone: (800) 252-5119
http://www.brenau.edu

Clark Atlanta University
Atlanta, GA 30314
Phone: (404) 880-8000
http://www.cau.edu

Georgia Institute of Technology
Atlanta, GA 30332
Phone: (404) 894-2000
http://www.gatech.edu

Georgia Southern University
Statesboro, GA 30460
Phone: (912) 681-5611
http://www.georgiasouthern.edu

Gwinnet Technical College
Lawrenceville, GA 30043
Phone: (770) 962-7580
http://www.gwinnettechnicalcollege.com

Middle Georgia College
Cochran, GA 31014
Phone: (478) 934-6221
http://www.mgc.edu

Morris Brown College
Atlanta, GA 30314
Phone: (404) 739-1000
http://www.morrisbrown.edu

Savannah College of Art and Design
Savannah, GA 31402
Phone: (800) 869-7223
http://www.scad.edu

University of Georgia
Athens, GA 30602
Phone: (706) 542-3000
http://www.uga.edu

HAWAII

Honolulu Community College
Honolulu, HI 96817

Phone: (808) 845-9211
http://www.honolulu.hawaii.edu

University of Hawaii–Manoa
Honolulu, HI 96822
Phone: (808) 956-8111
http://www.uhm.hawaii.edu

IDAHO

Brigham Young University–Idaho
Rexburg, ID 83460
Phone: (208) 496-2411
http://www.byui.edu

University of Idaho
Moscow, ID 83844
Phone: (888) 884-3246
http://www.uidaho.edu

ILLINOIS

Black Hawk College–East Campus
Kewanee, IL 61443
Phone: (309) 852-5671
http://www.bhc.edu

Black Hawk College–Quad Cities Campus
Moline, IL 61265
Phone: (309) 796-5000
http://www.bhc.edu

Chicago State University
Chicago, IL 60628
Phone: (773) 995-2000
http://www.csu.edu

College of DuPage
Glen Ellyn, IL 60137
Phone: (630) 942-2800
http://www.cod.edu

Columbia College
Chicago, IL 60605
Phone: (312) 663-1600
http://www.colum.edu

Dominican University
River Forest, IL 60305
Phone: (708) 366-2490
http://www.dom.edu

Harper College
Palatine, IL 60067
Phone: (847) 925-6707
http://goforward.harpercollege.edu

Illinois State University
Normal, IL 61790
Phone: (309) 438-2181
http://www.ilstu.edu

International Academy of Design and Technology
Chicago, IL 60602
Phone: (312) 980-9200
http://www.iadt-schools.com

John A. Logan College
Carterville, IL 62918
Phone: (618) 985-3741
http://www.jalc.edu

Joliet Junior College
Joliet, IL 60431
Phone: (815) 729-9020
http://www.jjc.cc.il.us

Kaskaskia College
Centralia, IL 62801
Phone: (618) 545-3000
http://www.kc.cc.il.us

Moraine Valley Community College
Palos Hills, IL 60465
Phone: (708) 974-4300
http://www.mv.cc.il.us

Northern Illinois University
DeKalb, IL 60115
Phone: (800) 892-3050
http://www.niu.edu

Olivet Nazarene University
Bourbonnais, IL 60914
Phone: (815) 939-5011
http://www.olivet.edu

School of the Art Institute of Chicago
Chicago, IL 60603
Phone: (312) 899-5100
http://www.artic.edu

South Suburban College of Cook County
South Holland, IL 60473
Phone: (708) 596-2000
http://www.ssc.cc.il.us

Southern Illinois University–Carbondale
Carbondale, IL 62901
Phone: (618) 453-2121
http://www.siuc.edu

Triton College
River Grove, IL 60171
Phone: (708) 456-0300
http://www.triton.edu

University of Illinois at Urbana-Champaign
Urbana, IL 61801
Phone: (217) 333-4666
http://www.uiuc.edu

Waubonsee Community College
Sugar Grove, IL 60554
Phone: (630) 466-7900
http://www.wcc.cc.il.us

INDIANA

Ball State University
Muncie, IN 47306
Phone: (800) 382-8540
http://www.bsu.edu

Indiana State University
Terre Haute, IN 47809
Phone: (800) 468-6478
http://www.indstate.edu

Indiana University–Bloomington
Bloomington, IN 47405
Phone: (812) 855-4848
http://www.iub.edu

Purdue University
West Lafayette, IN 47907
Phone: (765) 494-4600
http://www.purdue.edu

Vincennes University
Vincennes, IN 47592
Phone: (812) 888-8888
http://www.vinu.edu

IOWA

Des Moines Area Community College
Ankeny, IA 50021
Phone: (515) 964-6200
http://www.dmacc.cc.ia.us

Hawkeye Community College
Waterloo, IA 50704
Phone: (319) 296-2320
http://www.hawkeye.cc.ia.us

Iowa State University
Ames, IA 50011
Phone: (515) 294-4111
http://www.iastate.edu

Kirkwood Community College
Cedar Rapids, IA 52404
Phone: (319) 398-5517
http://www.kirkwood.cc.ia.us

North Iowa Area Community College
Mason City, IA 50401
Phone: (641) 423-1264
http://www.niacc.cc.ia.us

University of Northern Iowa
Cedar Falls, IA 50614
Phone: (319) 273-2311
http://www.uni.edu

KANSAS

Central College
McPherson, KS 67460
Phone: (620) 241-0723
http://www.centralcollege.edu

Johnson County Community College
Overland Park, KS 66210
Phone: (913) 469-8500
http://www.jccc.net

Kansas State University
Manhattan, KS 66506
Phone: (785) 532-6011
http://www.k-state.edu

Pittsburg State University
Pittsburg, KS 66762
Phone: (620) 231-7000
http://www.pittstate.edu

University of Kansas
Lawrence, KS 66045
Phone: (785) 864-2700
http://www.ku.edu

KENTUCKY

Eastern Kentucky University
Richmond, KY 40475
Phone: (859) 622-1000
http://www.eku.edu

Kentucky State University
Frankfort, KY 40601
Phone: (502) 597-6000
http://www.kysu.edu

Murray State University
Murray, KY 42071
Phone: (800) 272-4678
http://www.murraystate.edu

University of Kentucky
Lexington, KY 40506
Phone: (859) 257-9000
http://www.uky.edu

Western Kentucky University
Bowling Green, KY 42101
Phone: (270) 745-0111
http://www.wku.edu

LOUISIANA

Louisiana State University
Baton Rouge, LA 70803
Phone: (225) 578-1175
http://www.lsu.edu

Southern University
Baton Rouge, LA 70813
Phone: (225) 771-4500
http://www.subr.edu

University of Louisiana–Lafayette
Lafayette, LA 70504
Phone: (337) 482-1000
http://www.louisiana.edu

MAINE

Thomas College
Waterville, ME 04901
Phone: (207) 859-1111
http://www.thomas.edu

MARYLAND

Baltimore City Community College
Baltimore, MD 21215
Phone: (410) 462-8000
http://www.bccc.edu

Maryland Institute College of Art
Baltimore, MD 21217
Phone: (410) 669-9200
http://www.mica.edu

University of Maryland–Eastern Shore
Princess Anne, MD 21853
Phone: (410) 651-2200
http://www.umes.edu

MASSACHUSETTS

Bay State College
Boston, MA 02116
Phone: (617) 236-8000
http://www.baystate.edu

Fisher College
Boston, MA 02116
Phone: (617) 236-8818
http://www.fisher.edu

Framingham State College
Framingham, MA 01701
Phone: (508) 620-1220
http://www.framingham.edu

Lasell College
Newton, MA 02466
Phone: (617) 243-2000
http://www.lasell.edu

Massachusetts College of Art
Boston, MA 02115
Phone: (617) 879-7000
http://www.massart.edu

Middlesex Community College
Bedford, MA 01730
Phone: (800) 818-3434
http://www.middlesex.cc.ma.us

Newbury College
Brookline, MA 02445
Phone: (617) 730-7000
http://www.newbury.edu

University of Massachusetts–Amherst
Amherst, MA 01003
Phone: (413) 545-0111
http://www.umass.edu

University of Massachusetts–Dartmouth
North Dartmouth, MA 02747
Phone: (508) 999-8000
http://www.umassd.edu

MICHIGAN

Adrian College
Adrian, MI 49221
Phone: (800) 877-2246
http://www.adrian.edu

Baker College of Owosso
Owosso, MI 48867
Phone: (989) 729-3350
http://www.baker.edu

Central Michigan University
Mount Pleasant, MI 48859
Phone: (989) 774-4000
http://www.cmich.edu

College for Creative Studies
Detroit, MI 48202
Phone: (800) 952-2787
http://www.ccscad.edu

Delta College
University Center, MI 48710
Phone: (989) 686-9000
http://www.delta.edu

Eastern Michigan University
Ypsilanti, MI 48197
Phone: (734) 487-1849
http://www.emich.edu

Ferris State University
Big Rapids, MI 49307
Phone: (231) 591-2000
http://www.ferris.edu

Grand Rapids Community College
Grand Rapids, MI 49503
Phone: (616) 234-4722
http://www.grcc.edu

Lansing Community College
Lansing, MI 48901
Phone: (517) 483-1957
http://www.lcc.edu

Marygrove College
Detroit, MI 48221
Phone: (866) 313-1927
http://www.marygrove.edu

Michigan State University
East Lansing, MI 48824
Phone: (517) 355-1855
http://www.msu.edu

Northern Michigan University
Marquette, MI 49855
Phone: (800) 682-9797
http://www.nmu.edu

Northwood University
Midland, MI 48640
Phone: (989) 837-4200
http://www.northwood.edu/mi

Oakland Community College
Bloomfield Hills, MI 48304
Phone: (248) 341-2000
http://www.occ.cc.mi.us

Siena Heights University
Adrian, MI 49221
Phone: (517) 263-0731
http://www.sienahts.edu

University of Michigan
Ann Arbor, MI 48109
Phone: (734) 764-1817
http://www.umich.edu

Wayne State University
Detroit, MI 48202
Phone: (313) 577-2424
http://www.wayne.edu

Western Michigan University
Kalamazoo, MI 49008
Phone: (269) 387-1000
http://www.wmich.edu

MINNESOTA

Alexandria Technical College
Alexandria, MN 56308
Phone: (888) 234-1222
http://www.alextech.edu

College of St. Catherine
St. Paul, MN 55105
Phone: (800) 945-4599
http://www.stkate.edu

Concordia College
Moorhead, MN 56562
Phone: (218) 299-4000
http://www.cord.edu

Minnesota State Community and Technical College–Moorhead
Moorhead, MN 56560
Phone: (800) 426-5603
http://www.minnesota.edu

Minnesota State University–Mankato
Mankato, MN 56001
Phone: (800) 722-0544
http://www.mnsu.edu

Rasmussen College–Mankato
Mankato, MN 56001
Phone: (507) 625-6556
http://www.rasmussen.edu

Rochester Community and Technical College
Rochester, MN 55904
Phone: (507) 285-7210
http://www.roch.edu/rctc

South Central Technical College
Faribault, MN 55021
Phone: (800) 422-0391
http://www.sctc.mnscu.edu

St. Paul College
St. Paul, MN 55102
Phone: (651) 846-1600
http://www.saintpaul.edu

University of Minnesota
Minneapolis, MN 55455
Phone: (612) 625-5000
www1.umn.edu/twincities

MISSISSIPPI

Delta State University
Cleveland, MS 38733
Phone: (800) 468-6378
http://www.deltastate.edu

Hinds Community College
Raymond, MS 39154
Phone: (800) 456-3722
http://www.hinds.cc.ms.us

Holmes Community College
Goodman, MS 39079
Phone: (662) 472-2312
http://www.holmes.cc.ms.us

Mississippi College
Clinton, MS 39058
Phone: (601) 925-3000
http://www.mc.edu

Mississippi Gulf Coast Community College
Perkinston, MS 39573
Phone: (601) 928-5211
http://www.mgccc.edu

Mississippi University for Women
Columbus, MS 39701
Phone: (662) 329-4750
http://www.muw.edu

Northwest Mississippi Community College
Senatobia, MS 38668
Phone: (662) 562-3222
http://www.northwestms.edu

University of Southern Mississippi
Hattiesburg, MS 39406
Phone: (601) 266-1000
http://www.usm.edu

MISSOURI

Central Missouri State University
Warrensburg, MO 64093
Phone: (660) 543-4111
http://www.cmsu.edu

Kansas City Art Institute
Kansas City, MO 64111

Phone: (800) 522-5224
http://www.kcai.edu

Lincoln University of Missouri
Jefferson City, MO 65101
Phone: (800) 521-5052
http://www.lincolnu.edu

Lindenwood University
St. Charles, MO 63301
Phone: (636) 949-4949
http://www.lindenwood.edu

Metropolitan Community College–Penn Valley
Kansas City, MO 64111
Phone: (816) 759-4000
http://www.mcckc.edu

Missouri State University
Cape Girardeau, MO 63701
Phone: (573) 651-2000
http://www.missouristate.edu

Southwest Missouri State University
Springfield, MO 65804
Phone: (417) 836-5000
http://www.smsu.edu

Stephens College
Columbia, MO 65215
Phone: (800) 876-7207
http://www.stephens.edu

St. Louis Community College–Florissant Valley
St. Louis, MO 63135
Phone: (314) 595-4200
http://www.stlcc.cc.mo.us/fv

University of Missouri–Columbia
Columbia, MO 65211
Phone: (573) 882-2121
http://www.missouri.edu

Washington University
St. Louis, MO 63130
Phone: (314) 935-5000
http://www.wustl.edu

NEBRASKA

University of Nebraska–Lincoln
Lincoln, NE 68588
Phone: (402) 472-7211
http://www.unl.edu

University of Nebraska–Omaha
Omaha, NE 68182
Phone: (402) 554-2800
http://www.unomaha.edu

NEW HAMPSHIRE

Hesser College
Manchester, NH 03103
Phone: (603) 668-6660
http://www.hesser.edu

Southern New Hampshire University
Manchester, NH 03106
Phone: (800) 668-1249
http://www.snhu.edu

NEW JERSEY

Brookdale Community College
Lincroft, NJ 07738
Phone: (732) 224-2345
http://www.brookdale.cc.nj.us

Burlington County College
Pemberton, NJ 08068
Phone: (609) 894-4900
http://www.bcc.edu

Centenary College
Hackettstown, NJ 07840
Phone: (908) 852-1400
http://www.centenarycollege.edu

Middlesex County College
Edison, NJ 08818
Phone: (732) 548-6000
http://www.middlesex.cc.nj.us

Rowan University
Glassboro, NJ 08028
Phone: (856) 256-4000
http://www.rowan.edu

NEW MEXICO

Dona Ana Branch Community College
Las Cruces, NM 88003
Phone: (505) 527-7500
http://dabcc.nmsu.edu

New Mexico State University
Las Cruces, NM 88003
Phone: (505) 646-0111
http://www.nmsu.edu

Northern New Mexico Community College
Espanola, NM 87532
Phone: (505) 747-2100
http://www.nnm.cc.nm.us

NEW YORK

Cazenovia College
Cazenovia, NY 13035
Phone: (800) 645-3210
http://www.cazenovia.edu

Cornell University
Ithaca, NY 14853
Phone: (607) 254-4636
http://www.cornell.edu

Dutchess Community College
Poughkeepsie, NY 12601
Phone: (845) 431-8000
http://www.sunydutchess.edu

Erie Community College–City Campus
Buffalo, NY 14203
Phone: (716) 851-1155
http://www.ecc.edu

Fashion Institute of Technology
New York, NY 10001
Phone: (212) 217-7999
http://www.fitnyc.edu

Genesee Community College
Batavia, NY 14020
Phone: (585) 343-0055
http://www.genesee.edu

Herkimer County Community College
Herkimer, NY 13350
Phone: (315) 866-0300
http://www.hccc.ntcnet.com

Katharine Gibbs School
New York, NY 10018
Phone: (888) 317-6444
http://www.gibbsny.com

Kingsborough Community College
Brooklyn, NY 11235
Phone: (718) 265-5343
http://www.kbcc.cuny.edu

Laboratory Institute of Merchandising
New York, NY 10022
Phone: (800) 677-1323
http://www.limcollege.edu

Marist College
Poughkeepsie, NY 12601
Phone: (845) 575-3000
http://www.marist.edu

Marymount College
Tarrytown, NY 10591
Phone: (914) 631-3200
http://www.marymt.edu

Monroe Community College
Rochester, NY 14623
Phone: (585) 292-2000
http://www.monroecc.edu

Nassau Community College
Garden City, NY 11530
Phone: (516) 572-7501
http://www.sunynassau.edu

New York City College of Technology
Brooklyn, NY 11201
Phone: (718) 260-5500
http://www.citytech.cuny.edu

Pace University
New York, NY 10038
Phone: (800) 874-7223
http://www.pace.edu

Parsons School of Design
New York, NY 10011
Phone: (212) 229-8910
http://www.parsons.edu

Pratt Institute
Brooklyn, NY 11205
Phone: (718) 636-3600
http://www.pratt.edu

Rochester Institute of Technology
Rochester, NY 14623
Phone: (585) 475-2411
http://www.rit.edu

Sage College of Albany
Albany, NY 12208
Phone: (888) 837-9724
http://www.sage.edu/SCA

State University of New York College–Buffalo
Buffalo, NY 14222
Phone: (716) 878-4000
http://www.buffalostate.edu

State University of New York College–Oneonta
Oneonta, NY 13820
Phone: (607) 436-3500
http://www.oneonta.edu

Syracuse University
Syracuse, NY 13244
Phone: (315) 443-1870
http://www.syracuse.edu

Wood Tobé-Coburn School
New York, NY 10016
Phone: (800) 394-9663
http://www.woodtobecoburn.edu

NORTH CAROLINA

Appalachian State University
Boone, NC 28608
Phone: (828) 262-2000
http://www.appstate.edu

Art Institute of Charlotte
Charlotte, NC 28217
Phone: (800) 872-4417
http://www.artinstitutes.edu.charlotte

Bennett College
Greensboro, NC 27401
Phone: (800) 413-5323
http://www.bennett.edu

Campbell University
Buies Creek, NC 27506
Phone: (800) 334-4111
http://www.campbell.edu

Central Piedmont Community College
Charlotte, NC 28235
Phone: (704) 330-2722
http://www1.cpcc.edu

East Carolina University
Greenville, NC 27858
Phone: (252) 328-6131
http://www.ecu.edu

Institute of Textile Technology
Raleigh, NC 27695
Phone: (919) 513-7704
http://www.itt.edu

Mars Hill College
Mars Hill, NC 28754
Phone: (866) 642-4968
http://www.mhc.edu

Meredith College
Raleigh, NC 27607
Phone: (919) 760-8600
http://www.meredith.edu

North Carolina Agricultural and Technical State University
Greensboro, NC 27411
Phone: (336) 334-7500
http://www.ncat.edu

North Carolina Central University
Durham, NC 27707
Phone: (919) 530-6100
http://www.nccu.edu

North Carolina State University
Raleigh, NC 27695
Phone: (919) 515-2011
http://www.ncsu.edu

University of North Carolina–Greensboro
Greensboro, NC 27402
Phone: (336) 334-5000
http://www.uncg.edu

Western Carolina University
Cullowhee, NC 28723
Phone: (828) 227-7211
http://www.wcu.edu

NORTH DAKOTA

North Dakota State University
Fargo, ND 58105
Phone: (701) 231-8011
http://www.ndsu.edu

OHIO

Ashland University
Ashland, OH 44805
Phone: (419) 289-4142
http://www.ashland.edu

Bluffton University
Bluffton, OH 45817
Phone: (800) 488-3257
http://www.bluffton.edu

Bowling Green State University
Bowling Green, OH 43403
Phone: (419) 372-2531
http://www.bgsu.edu

Cleveland Institute of Art
Cleveland, OH 44106
Phone: (800) 223-4700
http://www.cia.edu

Columbus College of Art and Design
Columbus, OH 43215
Phone: (800) 223-4700
http://www.ccad.edu

Davis College
Toledo, OH 43623

Phone: (419) 473-2700
http://www.daviscollege.com

Kent State University
Kent, OH 44242
Phone: (330) 672-3000
http://www.kent.edu

Lourdes College
Sylvania, OH 43560
Phone: (419) 885-3211
http://www.lourdes.edu

Miami University
Oxford, OH 45056
Phone: (513) 529-1809
http://www.muohio.edu

Mount Vernon Nazarene College
Mount Vernon, OH 43050
Phone: (740) 392-6868
http://www.mvnc.edu

Ohio State University
Columbus, OH 43210
Phone: (614) 292-6446
http://www.osu.edu

Ohio University
Athens, OH 45701
Phone: (740) 593-1000
http://www.ohio.edu

Owens Community College
Toledo, OH 43699
Phone: (800) 466-9367
http://www.owens.edu

Sinclair Community College
Dayton, OH 45402
Phone: (800) 315-3000
http://www.sinclair.edu

University of Akron
Akron, OH 44325
Phone: (330) 972-7111
http://www.uakron.edu

University of Cincinnati
Cincinnati, OH 45221
Phone: (513) 556-6000
http://www.uc.edu

Ursuline College
Pepper Pike, OH 44124
Phone: (440) 449-4203
http://www.ursuline.edu

Virginia Marti College of Fashion and Art
Cleveland, OH 44107
Phone: (216) 221-8584
http://www.virginiamarticollege.com

Youngstown State University
Youngstown, OH 44555
Phone: (877) 468-6978
http://www.ysu.edu

OKLAHOMA

Langston University
Langston, OK 73050
Phone: (405) 466-2231
http://www.lunet.edu

Northeastern Oklahoma Agricultural & Mechanical College
Miami, OK 74354
Phone: (888) 464-6636
http://www.neoam.cc.ok.us

Northeastern State University
Tahlequah, OK 74464
Phone: (918) 456-5511
http://www.nsuok.edu

Oklahoma State University
Stillwater, OK 74078
Phone: (405) 744-5000
http://www.okstate.edu

Tulsa Community College
Tulsa, OK 74135
Phone: (918) 595-7000
http://www.tulsa.cc.ok.us

University of Central Oklahoma
Edmond, OK 73034
Phone: (405) 974-2000
http://www.ucok.edu

OREGON

Art Institute of Portland
Portland, OR 97201
Phone: (800) 616-2473
http://www.artinstitutes.edu/portland

George Fox University
Newberg, OR 97132
Phone: (503) 538-8383
http://www.georgefox.edu

Oregon State University
Corvallis, OR 97331
Phone: (541) 737-1000
http://www.orst.edu

University of Oregon
Eugene, OR 97403
Phone: (541) 346-1000
http://www.uoregon.edu

PENNSYLVANIA

Albright College
Reading, PA 19612
Phone: (800) 252-1856
http://www.albright.edu

Bradley Academy for the Visual Arts
York, PA 17402
Phone: (800) 864-7725
http://www.artinstitutes.edu/york

California University of Pennsylvania
California, PA 15419
Phone: (724) 938-4000
http://www.cup.edu

Cheyney University of Pennsylvania
Cheyney, PA 19319
Phone: (800) 243-9639
http://www.cheyney.edu

Community College of Allegheny County
Pittsburgh, PA 15233
Phone: (412) 237-4600
http://www.ccac.edu

Community College of Philadelphia
Philadelphia, PA 19130
Phone: (215) 751-8010
http://www.ccp.cc.pa.us

Drexel University
Philadelphia, PA 19104
Phone: (215) 895-2000
http://www.drexel.edu

Edinboro University of Pennsylvania
Edinboro, PA 16444
Phone: (814) 732-2000
http://www.edinboro.edu

Immaculata College
Immaculata, PA 19345
Phone: (610) 647-4400
http://www.immaculata.edu

Indiana University of Pennsylvania
Indiana, PA 15705
Phone: (724) 357-2100
http://www.iup.edu

Marywood University
Scranton, PA 18509
Phone: (570) 348-6211
http://www.marywood.edu

Mercyhurst College
Erie, PA 16546
Phone: (814) 824-2000
http://www.mercyhurst.edu

Moore College of Art and Design
Philadelphia, PA 19103
Phone: (215) 965-4000
http://www.moore.edu

Philadelphia University
Philadelphia, PA 19144
Phone: (215) 951-2700
http://www.philau.edu

Temple University
Philadelphia, PA 19122
Phone: (215) 204-7000
http://www.temple.edu

Westmoreland County Community College
Youngwood, PA 15697
Phone: (724) 925-4000
http://www.wccc-pa.edu

RHODE ISLAND

Community College of Rhode Island
Warwick, RI 02886
Phone: (401) 825-1000
http://www.ccri.edu

Johnson & Wales University
Providence, RI 02903
Phone: (401) 598-1000
http://www.jwu.edu

Rhode Island School of Design
Providence, RI 02903
Phone: (401) 454-6300
http://www.risd.edu

University of Rhode Island
Kingstown, RI 02881
Phone: (401) 874-1000
http://www.uri.edu

SOUTH CAROLINA

Clemson University
Clemson, SC 29634
Phone: (864) 656-3311
http://www.clemson.edu

Florence-Darlington Technical College
Florence, SC 29501
Phone: (800) 228-5745
http://www.fdtc.edu

Greenville Technical College
Greenville, SC 29606
Phone: (864) 250-8111
http://www.greenvilletech.com

Midlands Technical College
Columbia, SC 29202
Phone: (803) 738-8324
http://www.mid.tec.sc.us

South Carolina State University
Orangeburg, SC 29117
Phone: (803) 536-7000
http://www.scsu.edu

Tri-County Technical College
Pendleton, SC 29670
Phone: (864) 646-8361
http://www.tctc.edu

SOUTH DAKOTA

South Dakota State University
Brookings, SD 57007
Phone: (800) 952-3541
http://www.sdstate.edu

TENNESSEE

Carson-Newman College
Jefferson City, TN 37760
Phone: (865) 471-2000
http://www.cn.edu

Freed-Hardeman University
Henderson, TN 38340
Phone: (800) 348-3481
http://www.fhu.edu

Hiwassee College
Madisonville, TN 37354
Phone: (800) 356-2187
http://www.hiwassee.edu

Lambuth University
Jackson, TN 38301
Phone: (800) 526-2884
http://www.lambuth.edu

Lipscomb University
Nashville, TN 37204
Phone: (615) 269-1000
http://www.lipscomb.edu

Memphis College of Art
Memphis, TN 38104
Phone: (901) 272-5100
http://www.mca.edu

Middle Tennessee State University
Murfreesboro, TN 37132
Phone: (615) 898-2300
http://www.mtsu.edu

O'More College of Design
Franklin, TN 37064
Phone: (615) 794-4254
http://www.omorecollege.edu

Southwest Tennessee Community College
Memphis, TN 38101
Phone: (877) 717-7822
http://www.southwest.tn.edu

Tennessee State University
Nashville, TN 37209
Phone: (615) 963-5000
http://www.tnstate.edu

University of Tennessee–Knoxville
Knoxville, TN 37996
Phone: (865) 974-1000
http://www.utk.edu

TEXAS

Abilene Christian University
Abilene, TX 79699
Phone: (915) 674-2000
http://www.acu.edu

Alvin Community College
Alvin, TX 77511
Phone: (281) 756-3500
http://www.alvincollege.edu

Austin Community College
Austin, TX 78752
Phone: (512) 223-7000
http://www.austincc.edu

Baylor University
Waco, TX 76798
Phone: (800) 229-5678
http://www.baylor.edu

Brookhaven College
Dallas, TX 75244
Phone: (972) 860-4700
http://www.brookhavencollege.edu

Cedar Valley College
Lancaster, TX 75134

Phone: (972) 860-8201
http://www.cedarvalleycollege.edu

Collin County Community College District
McKinney, TX 75071
Phone: (972) 548-6710
http://www.ccccd.edu

El Centro College
Dallas, TX 75202
Phone: (214) 860-2037
http://www.ecc.dcccd.edu

El Paso Community College
El Paso, TX 79998
Phone: (915) 831-3722
http://www.epcc.edu

Houston Community College System
Houston, TX 77004
Phone: (713) 718-2000
http://www.hccs.cc.tx.us

Lamar University
Beaumont, TX 77710
Phone: (409) 880-7011
http://www.lamar.edu

Laredo Community College
Laredo, TX 78040
Phone: (956) 721-5117
http://www.laredo.cc.tx.us

Midland College
Midland, TX 79705
Phone: (432) 685-4500
http://www.midland.edu

Northwood University
Cedar Hill, TX 75104
Phone: (972) 291-1541
http://www.northwood.edu/tx

Palo Alto College
San Antonio, TX 78224
Phone: (210) 921-5000
http://www.accd.edu/pac

Prairie View A&M University
Prairie View, TX 77446
Phone: (936) 857-3311
http://www.pvamu.edu

Sam Houston State University
Huntsville, TX 77341
Phone: (936) 294-1111
http://www.shsu.edu

South Plains College
Levelland, TX 79336
Phone: (806) 894-9611
http://www.southplainscollege.edu

Stephen F. Austin State University
Nacogdoches, TX 75962
Phone: (936) 468-2011
http://www.sfasu.edu

St. Philip's College
San Antonio, TX 78203
Phone: (210) 531-3200
http://www.accd.edu/spc/spcmain/spc.htm

Tarrant County College District
Fort Worth, TX 76102
Phone: (817) 515-8223
http://www.tccd.edu

Texarkana College
Texarkana, TX 75501
Phone: (903) 838-4541
http://www.tc.cc.tx.us

Texas A&M University–Kingsville
Kingsville, TX 78363
Phone: (361) 593-2111
http://www.tamuk.edu

Texas Christian University
Fort Worth, TX 76109
Phone: (817) 257-7000
http://www.tcu.edu

Texas Southern University
Houston, TX 77004
Phone: (713) 313-7011
http://www.tsu.edu

Texas State University
San Marcos, TX 78666
Phone: (512) 245-2111
http://www.txstate.edu

Texas Tech University
Lubbock, TX 79409
Phone: (806) 742-2011
http://www.ttu.edu

Texas Woman's University
Denton, TX 76201
Phone: (940) 898-2000
http://www.twu.edu

University of North Texas
Denton, TX 76203
Phone: (940) 565-2000
http://www.unt.edu

University of Texas–Austin
Austin, TX 78712
Phone: (512) 475-7348
http://www.utexas.edu

University of the Incarnate Word
San Antonio, TX 78209
Phone: (800) 749-9673
http://www.uiw.edu

Wade College
Dallas, TX 75207
Phone: (214) 637-3530
http://www.wadecollege.edu

UTAH

Brigham Young University
Provo, UT 84602
Phone: (801) 378-4636
http://www.byu.edu

Dixie State College
St. George, UT 84770
Phone: (435) 652-7500
http://www.dixie.edu

Salt Lake Community College
Salt Lake City, UT 84130
Phone: (801) 957-4111
http://www.slcc.edu

Snow College
Ephraim, UT 84627
Phone: (435) 283-7000
http://www.snow.edu

Southern Utah University
Cedar City, UT 84720
Phone: (435) 586-7700
http://www.suu.edu

Utah State University
Logan, UT 84322
Phone: (435) 797-1000
http://www.usu.edu

Weber State University
Ogden, UT 84408
Phone: (801) 626-6000
http://www.weber.edu

VERMONT

Champlain College
Burlington, VT 05401
Phone: (802) 860-2700
http://www.champlain.edu

VIRGINIA

Bridgewater College
Bridgewater, VA 22812
Phone: (540) 828-8000
http://www.bridgewater.edu

J. Sargent Reynolds Community College
Richmond, VA 23285
Phone: (804) 371-3000
http://www.jsr.cc.va.us

Lord Fairfax Community College
Middletown, VA 22645
Phone: (800) 906-5322
http://www.lf.cc.va.us

Marymount University
Arlington, VA 22207
Phone: (703) 522-5600
http://www.marymount.edu

New River Community College
Dublin, VA 24084
Phone: (540) 674-3600
http://www.nr.cc.va.us

Old Dominion University
Norfolk, VA 23529
Phone: (757) 683-3000
http://www.odu.edu

Virginia Commonwealth University
Richmond, VA 23284
Phone: (804) 828-0100
http://www.vcu.edu

Virginia Polytechnic Institute and State University
Blacksburg, VA 24061
Phone: (540) 231-6000
http://www.vt.edu

WASHINGTON

Art Institute of Seattle
Seattle, WA 98121
Phone: (206) 448-0900
http://www.ais.artinstitutes.edu

Central Washington University
Ellensburg, WA 98926
Phone: (509) 963-1111
http://www.cwu.edu

Clark College
Vancouver, WA 98663
Phone: (360) 992-2000
http://www.clark.edu

Edmonds Community College
Lynnwood, WA 98036
Phone: (425) 640-1459
http://www.edcc.edu

Highline Community College
Des Moines, WA 98198
Phone: (206) 878-3710
http://www.highline.edu

Olympic College
Bremerton, WA 98337
Phone: (800) 259-6718
http://www.olympic.edu

Pierce College
Puyallup, WA 98374
Phone: (253) 840-8400
http://www.pierce.ctc.edu

Renton Technical College
Renton, WA 98056
Phone: (425) 235-2352
http://www.renton-tc.ctc.edu

Seattle Central Community College
Seattle, WA 98122
Phone: (206) 587-3800
http://www.seattlecentral.org

Seattle Pacific University
Seattle, WA 98119
Phone: (206) 281-2000
http://www.spu.edu

Shoreline Community College
Shoreline, WA 98133
Phone: (206) 546-4101
http://www.shoreline.edu

University of Washington
Seattle, WA 98195
Phone: (206) 543-2100
http://www.washington.edu

Washington State University
Pullman, WA 99164
Phone: (888) 468-6978
http://www.wsu.edu

Western Washington University
Bellingham, WA 98225
Phone: (360) 650-3000
http://www.wwu.edu

WEST VIRGINIA

Davis and Elkins College
Elkins, WV 26241
Phone: (304) 637-1900
http://www.davisandelkins.edu

Fairmont State College
Fairmont, WV 26554
Phone: (800) 641-5678
http://www.fscwv.edu

Marshall University
Huntington, WV 25755
Phone: (800) 642-3463
http://www.marshall.edu

Shepherd College
Shepherdstown, WV 25443
Phone: (304) 876-5000
http://www.shepherd.edu

West Liberty State College
West Liberty, WV 26074
Phone: (866) 937-8542
http://www.wlsc.edu

West Virginia State University
Institute, WV 25112
Phone: (800) 987-2112
http://www.wvstateu.edu

WISCONSIN

Fox Valley Technical College
Appleton, WI 54912
Phone: (800) 735-3882
http://www.fvtc.edu

Madison Area Technical College
Madison, WI 53704
Phone: (800) 322-6282
http://www.matcmadison.edu/matc

Milwaukee Area Technical College
Milwaukee, WI 53233
Phone: (414) 297-6282
http://www.matc.edu

Mount Mary College
Milwaukee, WI 53222
Phone: (414) 258-4810
http://www.mtmary.edu

Northeast Wisconsin Technical College
Green Bay, WI 54307
Phone: (800) 422-6982
http://www.nwtc.edu

University of Wisconsin–Madison
Madison, WI 53706
Phone: (608) 262-1234
http://www.wisc.edu

University of Wisconsin–Stevens Point
Stevens Point, WI 54481
Phone: (715) 346-0123
http://www.uwsp.edu

University of Wisconsin–Stout
Menomonie, WI 54751
Phone: (715) 232-1122
http://www.uwstout.edu

Waukesha County Technical College
Pewaukee, WI 53072
Phone: (262) 691-5566
http://www.wctc.edu

Western Wisconsin Technical College
La Crosse, WI 54601
Phone: (800) 322-9982
http://www.wwtc.edu

Wisconsin Indianhead Technical College
Shell Lake, WI 54871
Phone: (800) 243-9482
http://www.witc.edu

WYOMING

University of Wyoming
Laramie, WY 82071
Phone: (307) 766-1121
http://www.uwyo.edu

APPENDIX II
PROFESSIONAL, INDUSTRY, AND TRADE ASSOCIATIONS AND UNIONS

The following organizations offer opportunities for networking, job training, and union benefits. They may also be excellent sources of information about your field of interest and employment opportunities.

Advertising Photographers of America
P.O. Box 250
White Plains, NY 10605
Phone: (800) 272-6264
http://www.apanational.org

American Advertising Federation
1101 Vermont Avenue NW, Suite 500
Washington, DC 20005
Phone: (202) 898-0089
http://www.aaf.org

American Apparel and Footwear Association
1601 North Kent Street, Suite 1200
Arlington, VA 22209
Phone: (800) 520-2262
http://www.apparelandfootwear.org

American Association of Advertising Agencies
405 Lexington Avenue, 18th Floor
New York, NY 10174
Phone: (212) 682-2500
http://www.aaaa.org

American Association of Cost Engineers International
209 Prairie Avenue, Suite 100
Morgantown, WV 26501
Phone: (800) 858-2678
http://www.aacei.org

American Association of Textile Chemists and Colorists
P.O. Box 12215
Research Triangle Park, NC 27709
Phone: (919) 549-8141
http://www.aatcc.org

American Association of University Professors
1012 Fourteenth Street NW, Suite 500
Washington, DC 20005
Phone: (202) 737-5900
http://www.aaup.org

American Chemical Society
1155 16th Street NW
Washington, DC 20036
Phone: (800) 227-5558
http://www.acs.org

American Fiber Manufacturers Association
1530 Wilson Boulevard, Suite 690
Arlington, VA 22209
Phone: (703) 875-0432
http://www.fibersource.com

American Institute of Certified Public Accountants
1211 Avenue of the Americas
New York, NY 10036
Phone: (888) 777-7077
http://www.aicpa.org

American Institute of Chemical Engineers
3 Park Avenue
New York, NY 10016
Phone: (800) 242-4363
http://www.aiche.org

American Institute of Graphic Arts
164 Fifth Avenue
New York, NY 10012
Phone: (212) 807-1990
http://www.aiga.org

American Management Association
1601 Broadway
New York, NY 10019
Phone: (212) 586-8100
http://www.amanet.org

American Marketing Association
311 South Wacker Drive, Suite 5800
Chicago, IL 60606
Phone: (800) 262-1150
http://www.marketingpower.com

American Purchasing Society
North Island Center, Suite 203
8 East Galena Boulevard
Aurora, IL 60506
Phone: (630) 859-0250
http://www.american-purchasing.com

American Society for Quality
600 North Plankinton Avenue
Milwaukee, WI 53203
Phone: (800) 248-1946
http://www.asq.org

American Society for Training and Development
1640 King Street, Box 1443
Alexandria, VA 22313
Phone: (703) 683-8100
http://www.astd.org

American Society of Magazine Editors
810 Seventh Avenue, 24th Floor
New York, NY 10019
Phone: (212) 872-3700
http://www.magazine.org/editorial

American Society of Media Photographers
150 North Second Street
Philadelphia, PA 19106
Phone: (215) 451-2767
http://www.asmp.org

American Society of Transportation and Logistics
1700 North Moore Street, Suite 1900
Arlington, VA 22209
Phone: (703) 524-5011
http://www.astl.org

American Textile Machinery Association
201 Park Washington Court
Falls Church, VA 22046
Phone: (703) 538-1789
http://www.atmanet.org

American Textile Manufacturers Institute
1130 Connecticut Avenue NW, Suite 1200
Washington, DC 20036
Phone: (202) 862-0500
http://www.atmi.org

Art Directors Club
106 West 29th Street
New York, NY 10001
Phone: (212) 643-1440
http://www.adcglobal.org

Association of Information Technology Professionals
401 North Michigan Avenue, Suite 2400
Chicago, IL 60611
Phone: (800) 224-9371
http://www.aitp.org

Association for Computing Machinery
1515 Broadway
New York, NY 10036
Phone: (800) 342-6626
http://www.acm.org

Association for Financial Professionals
4520 East West Highway, Suite 750
Bethesda, MD 20814
Phone: (301) 907-2862
http://www.afponline.org

Association of Image Consultants International
431 East Locust Street, Suite 300
Des Moines, IA 50309
Phone: (515) 282-5500
http://www.aici.org

Association of Stylists and Coordinators
18 East 18th Street, SE
New York, NY 10003
http://www.stylistsasc.com/

Clothing Manufacturers Association of the U.S.A.
730 Broadway
New York, NY 10003
Phone: (212) 529-0823

Color Association of the United States
315 West 39th Street, Studio 507
New York, NY 10018
Phone: (212) 947-7774
http://www.colorassociation.com

Costume Designers Guild
4730 Woodman Avenue, Suite 430
Sherman Oaks, CA 91423
Phone: (818) 905-1557
http://www.costumedesignersguild.com

Costume Society of America
55 Edgewater Drive
P.O. Box 73
Earleville, MD 21919
Phone: (800) 272-9447
http://www.costumesocietyamerica.com

Cotton Council International
1521 New Hampshire Avenue NW
Washington, DC 20036
Phone: (202) 745-7805
http://www.cottonusa.org

Council of Fashion Designers of America
1412 Broadway, Suite 2006
New York, NY 10018
Phone: (212) 302-1821
http://www.cfda.com

Council of Supply Chain Management Professionals
2805 Butterfield Road, Suite 200
Oak Brook, IL 60523
Phone: (630) 574-0985
http://www.cscmp.org

Custom Tailors and Designers Association of America
19 Mantua Road
Mt. Royal, NJ 08061
Phone: (856) 423-1621
http://www.ctda.com

The Fashion Association
475 Park Avenue South, Ninth Floor
New York, NY 10016
Phone: (212) 683-5665
http://www.thefashion.org

Fashion Group International, Inc.
8 West 40th Street, Seventh Floor
New York, NY 10018
Phone: (212) 302-5511
http://www.fgi.org

Financial Executives International
200 Campus Drive
Florham Park, NJ 07932
Phone: (973) 765-1000
http://www.fei.org

Financial Management Association International
College of Business Administration
University of South Florida
Tampa, FL 33620
Phone: (813) 974-2084
http://www.fma.org

Garment Industry Development Corporation
275 Seventh Avenue, 15th Floor
New York, NY 10001
Phone: (212) 366-6160
http://www.gidc.org

Gemological Institute of America
The Robert Mouawad Campus
5345 Armada Drive
Carlsbad, CA 92008
Phone: (800) 421-7250
http://www.gia.edu

Graphic Artists Guild
90 John Street, Suite 403
New York, NY 10038
Phone: (212) 791-3400
http://www.gag.org

The Hosiery Association
3623 Latrobe Drive, Suite 130
Charlotte, NC 28211
Phone: (704) 365-0913
http://www.hosieryassociation.com

Institute of Electrical and Electronics Engineers
1828 L Street NW, Suite 1202
Washington, DC 20036
Phone: (202) 785-0017
http://www.ieee.org

Institute of Industrial Engineers
3577 Parkway Lane, Suite 200
Norcross, GA 30092
Phone: (800) 494-0460
http://www.iienet.org

Institute of Internal Auditors
247 Maitland Avenue
Altamonte Springs, FL 32701
Phone: (407) 937-1100
http://www.theiaa.org

Institute of Management Accountants
10 Paragon Drive
Montvale, NJ 07645

Phone: (800) 638-4427
http://www.imanet.org

Institute of Management Consultants
2025 M Street NW, Suite 800
Washington, DC 20036
Phone: (202) 367-1134
http://www.imcusa.org

Institute of Store Planners
25 North Broadway
Tarrytown, NY 10591
Phone: (914) 332-0040
http://www.ispo.org

Institute of Supply Management
P.O. Box 22160
Tempe, AZ 85285
Phone: (480) 752-6276
http://www.ism.ws

International Association of Business Communicators
1 Hallidie Plaza, Suite 600
San Francisco, CA 94102
Phone: (415) 544-4700
http://www.iabc.com

International Association of Clothing Designers and Executives
835 NW 36th Terrace
Oklahoma City, OK 73118
Phone: (405) 602-8037
http://www.iacde.com

International Colour Authority
33 Bedford Place
London WC1B 5JU
England
Phone: 011 44 2076 372211
http://www.internationalcolourauthority.com

International Textile and Apparel Association
P.O. Box 1360
Monument, CO 80132
Phone: (719) 488-3716
http://www.itaaonline.org

International Textile Manufacturers Federation
Am Schanzengraben 29
CH-8002 Zürich, Switzerland
Phone: 011 41 44 283 63 80
http://www.itmf.org

Jewelers of America
52 Vanderbilt Avenue, 19th Floor
New York, NY 10017
Phone: (800) 223-0673
http://www.jewelers.org

Manufacturers' Agents National Association
1 Spectrum Pointe, Suite 150
Lake Forest, CA 92630
Phone: (877) 626-2776
http://manaonline.org

Manufacturing Jewelers and Suppliers of America
45 Royal Little Drive
Providence, RI 02904
Phone: (800) 444-6572
http://www.mjsainc.com

Marketing Research Association
110 National Drive, Second Floor
Glastonbury, CT 06033
Phone: (860) 682-1000
http://www.mra-net.org

National Association of Fashion and Accessory Designers
6309 Cranston Lane
Fredricksburg, VA 22407
Phone: (540) 891-0633
http://www.nafad.com

National Association of Schools of Art and Design
11250 Roger Bacon Drive, Suite 21
Reston, VA 20190
Phone: (703) 437-0700
http://nasad.arts-accredit.org

National Association of Visual Merchandisers
15304 Rainbow One, Suite 201
Austin, TX 78734
Phone: (512) 266-0224
http://www.visualmerch.com

National Cotton Council
P.O. Box 820285
Memphis, TN 38182
Phone: (901) 274-9030
http://www.cotton.org

National Fashion Accessories Association
350 Fifth Avenue, Suite 2030
New York, NY 10118
Phone: (212) 947-3424
http://www.accessoryweb.com

National Retail Federation
325 Seventh Street NW, Suite 1100
Washington, DC 20004
Phone: (800) 673-4692
http://www.nrf.com

Professional Photographers of America
229 Peachtree Street NE, Suite 2200
Atlanta, GA 30303
Phone: (404) 522-8600
http://www.ppa.com

Public Relations Society of America
33 Maiden Lane, 11th Floor
New York, NY 10038
Phone: (212) 460-1490
http://www.prsa.org

Retail Industry Leaders Association
1700 North Moore Street, Suite 2250
Arlington, VA 22209
Phone: (703) 841-2300
http://www.retail-leaders.org

Retail, Wholesale, and Department Store Union
30 East 29th Street
New York, NY 10016
Phone: (212) 684-5300
http://www.rwdsu.info

Sales and Marketing Executives–International
P.O. Box 1390
Sumas, WA 98295
Phone: (312) 893-0751
http://www.smei.org

Shoe Service Institute of America
18 School Street
North Brookfield, MA 01535
Phone: (508) 867-7732
http://www.ssia.info

Society for Human Resource Management
1800 Duke Street
Alexandria, VA 22314
Phone: (703) 548-3440
http://www.shrm.org

Society of Cost Estimating and Analysis
101 South Whiting Street, Suite 201
Alexandria, VA 22304
Phone: (703) 751-8069
http://www.scea.online.org

Society of Illustrators
128 East 63rd Street
New York, NY 10021

Phone: (212) 838-2560
http://www.societyillustrators.org

Society of Professional Journalists
Eugene S. Pulliam National Journalism Center
3909 North Meridian Street
Indianapolis, IN 46208
Phone: (317) 927-8000
http://www.spj.org

Surface Design Association
P.O. Box 360
Sebastopol, CA 95473
Phone: (707) 829-3110
http://www.surfacedesign.org

Textile Society of America
P.O. Box 70
Earleville, MD 21919
Phone: (410) 275-2329
http://textilesociety.org

TRI/Princeton (formerly the Textile Research Institute)
601 Prospect Avenue, P.O. Box 625
Princeton, NJ 08542
Phone: (609) 924-3150
http://www.triprinceton.org

United Scenic Artists
29 West 38th Street
New York, NY 10018
Phone: (212) 581-0300
http://www.usa829.org

United States Association of Importers of Textiles and Apparel
13 East 16th Street
New York, NY 10003
Phone: (212) 463-0089
http://www.usaita.com

United States Small Business Administration
409 Third Street SW
Washington, DC 20416
Phone: (800) 827-5722
http://www.sba.gov

UNITE HERE
275 Seventh Avenue
New York, NY 10001
Phone: (212) 265-7000
http://www.unitehere.org

WorldatWork (formerly American Compensation Association)
14040 North Northsight Boulevard
Scottsdale, AZ 85260
Phone: (480) 951-9191
http://www.worldatwork.org

APPENDIX III FASHION AND APPAREL PERIODICALS AND WEB SITES

The following are among many consumer and trade publications and Web sites devoted to fashion/apparel and textiles.

CONSUMER PUBLICATIONS

Allure
The Condé Nast Publications
4 Times Square
New York, NY 10036
Phone: (212) 286-2860
http://www.allure.com

BRIDES
The Condé Nast Publications
4 Times Square
New York, NY 10036
Phone: (212) 286-2860
http://www.brides.com

Cosmopolitan
224 West 57th Street
New York, NY 10019
Phone: (888) 333-4948
http://www.cosmopolitan.com

Details
The Condé Nast Publications
4 Times Square
New York, NY 10036
Phone: (212) 286-2860
http://www.details.com

Elle
Lagardare Active North America
1633 Broadway, 40th Floor
New York, NY 10019
Phone: (212) 767-5800
http://www.elle.com

Esquire
250 West 55th Street
New York, NY 10019
Phone: (212) 649-4020
http://www.esquire.com

ESSENCE
135 West 50th Street, Fourth Floor
New York, NY 10020
Phone: (800) 274-9398
http://www.essence.com

Fashion Update
79 Pine Street, Suite 129
New York, NY 10005
Phone: (888) 447-2846
http://www.fashionupdate.com

Glamour
The Condé Nast Publications
4 Times Square
New York, NY 10036
Phone: (212) 286-2860
http://www.glamour.com

GQ
The Condé Nast Publications
4 Times Square
New York, NY 10036
Phone: (212) 286-2860
http://www.gq.com

Harper's BAZAAR
1700 Broadway
New York, NY 10019
Phone: (212) 903-5000
http://www.harpersbazaar.com

JANE
Fairchild Publications
750 Third Avenue
New York, NY 10017
Phone: (212) 630-4000
http://www.janemag.com

Marie Claire
1790 Broadway
New York, NY 10019
Phone: (800) 777-3287
http://www.marieclaire.com

Modern Bride
4 Times Square, 17th Floor
New York, NY 10036
Phone: (212) 286-3700
http://www.modernbride.com

O, The Oprah Magazine
1700 Broadway
New York, NY 10019
Phone: (888) 541-4438
http://www.oprah.com

People
Time & Life Building
Rockfeller Center
New York, NY 10020
Phone: (800) 541-9000
http://www.people.com

PETITE
3207 West Fifth Avenue
Spokane, WA 99224
Phone: (877) 472-4002
http://www.petitemagazine.com

Seventeen
1440 Broadway, 13th Floor
New York, NY 10018
Phone: (917) 934-6500
http://www.seventeen.com

Vanity Fair
The Condé Nast Publications
4 Times Square
New York, NY 10036
Phone: (212) 286-2860
http://www.vanityfair.com

Vogue
The Condé Nast Publications
4 Times Square
New York, NY 10036
Phone: (212) 286-2860
http://www.style.com/vogue

W
The Condé Nast Publications
4 Times Square
New York, NY 10036

Phone: (212) 286-2860
http://www.style.com/w

TRADE PUBLICATIONS

AAFA Newsbreaker
American Apparel and Footwear Association
1601 North Kent Street, Suite 1200
Arlington, VA 22209
Phone: (800) 520-2262
http://www.apparelandfootwear.org

AATCC Review
American Association of Textile Chemists and Colorists
P.O. Box 12215
Research Triangle Park, NC 27709
Phone: (919) 549-8141
http://www.aatcc.org

ACCESSORIES
185 Madison Avenue, Fifth Floor
New York, NY 10016
Phone: (212) 686-4412
http://www.accessoriesmagazine.com

Advertising Age
711 Third Avenue
New York, NY 10017
Phone: (212) 210-0100
http://www.adage.com

ADWEEK
770 Broadway, Seventh Floor
New York, NY 10003
Phone: (646) 654-5117
http://www.adweek.com

Apparel
4 Middlebury Boulevard
Randolph, NJ 07869
Phone: (978) 671-0449
http://www.apparelmag.com

The Apparel News
CaliforniaMart
110 East Ninth Street, Suite A-777
Los Angeles, CA 90079
Phone: (213) 627-3737
http://www.apparelnews.net

Apparel News South
CaliforniaMart
110 East Ninth Street, Suite A-777
Los Angeles, CA 90079
Phone: (213) 627-3737
http://www.apparelnews.net

The Apparel Strategist
P.O. Box 406
Fleetwood, PA 19522
Phone: (610) 944-5995
http://www.apparelstrategist.com

Body Fashion/Intimate Apparel
Advanstar Communications
7500 Old Oak Boulevard
Cleveland, OH 44130
Phone: (440) 243-8100
http://www.advanstar.com

Bridal Apparel News
CaliforniaMart
110 East Ninth Street, Suite A-777
Los Angeles, CA 90079
Phone: (213) 627-3737
http://www.apparelnews.net

California Apparel News
CaliforniaMart
110 East Ninth Street, Suite A-777
Los Angeles, CA 90079
Phone: (213) 627-3737
http://www.apparelnews.net

Canadian Apparel Magazine
24 O'Connor Street, Suite 504
Ottawa, Ontario K1P 5M9 Canada
Phone: (613) 231-3220
http://cam.apparel.ca/eng/index.cfm

Chain Store Age
Lebhar-Friedman, Inc.
425 Park Avenue
New York, NY 10022
Phone: (800) 766-6999
http://www.chainstoreage.com

Chicago Apparel News
CaliforniaMart
110 East Ninth Street, Suite A-777
Los Angeles, CA 90079
Phone: (213) 627-3737
http://www.apparelnews.net

Clothing and Textiles Research Journal
International Textile and Apparel Association
P.O. Box 1360
Monument, CO 80132
Phone: (719) 488-3716
http://www.itaaonline.org

Collezioni Trends
463 Seventh Avenue, Third Floor
New York, NY 10018
Phone: (212) 302-5137
http://www.mpnews.com

Custom Tailor
Custom Tailors & Designers Association of America
19 Mantua Road
Mt. Royal, NJ 08061
Phone: (856) 423-1621
http://www.ctda.com

Dallas Apparel News
CaliforniaMart
110 East Ninth Street, Suite A-777
Los Angeles, CA 90079
Phone: (213) 627-3737
http://www.apparelnews.net

***DNR* (Daily News Record)**
Fairchild Publications
750 Third Avenue, 10th Floor
New York, NY 10017
Phone: (800) 360-1700
http://www.dnrnews.com

DRESS: The Journal of the Costume Society of America
The Costume Society of America
P.O. Box 73
Earleville, MD 21919
Phone: (800) 272-9447
http://www.costumesocietyamerica.com

DSN Retailing Today
Lebhar-Friedman, Inc.
425 Park Avenue
New York, NY 10022
Phone: (212) 756-5000
http://www.dsnretailingtoday.com

Earnshaw's Review
8 West 38th Street, Suite 201
New York, NY 10018
Phone: (646) 278-1550
http://www.earnshaws.com

fashion WATCH
642 King Street West, Suite 200
Toronto, Ontario M5V 1M7 Canada
Phone: (416) 504-8044
http://www.fashionwatch.com

1st HOLD Magazine
Set the Pace Publishing Group
4237 Los Nietos Drive
Los Angeles, CA 90027
Phone: (323) 913-0500
http://www.makeuphairandstyling.com

Footwear News
Fairchild Publications
750 Third Avenue, 10th Floor
New York, NY 10017
Phone: (212) 630-4000
http://www.footwearnews.com

Hosiery News
The Hosiery Association
3623 Latrobe Drive, Suite 130
Charlotte, NC 28211
Phone: (704) 365-0913
http://www.legsource.com/tha/hos_news.htm

IMPRESSIONS
Bill Communications
770 Broadway
New York, NY 10003
Phone: (646) 654-4500
http://www.billcom.com

International Fiber Journal
7421 Carmel Executive Park Drive, Suite 105
Charlotte, NC 28226
Phone: (704) 544-1969
http://www.ifj.com

International Textile INTERIOR
463 Seventh Avenue, Third Floor
New York, NY 10018
Phone: (212) 302-5137
http://www.mpnews.com

Jewelers' Circular Keystone Magazine
360 Park Avenue South
New York, NY 10010
Phone: (800) 305-7759
http://www.jckgroup.com

KiDS CREATIONS
KiDS Creations
6900 Decarie, Suite 3110
Montreal, Quebec H3X 2T8 Canada
Phone: (514) 731-7774
http://www.cama-apparel.org

Made to Measure
830 Moseley Road
Highland Park, IL 60035
Phone: (847) 780-2900
http://www.madetomeasuremag.com

***MAN* (Men's Apparel News)**
CaliforniaMart
110 East Ninth Street, Suite A-777
Los Angeles, CA 90079
Phone: (213) 627-3737
http://www.apparelnews.net

Market Week Magazine
CaliforniaMart
110 East Ninth Street, Suite A-777
Los Angeles, CA 90079
Phone: (213) 627-3737
http://www.apparelnews.net

Marketing News
American Marketing Association
311 South Wacker Drive, Suite 5800
Chicago, IL 60606
Phone: (800) 262-1150
http://www.marketingpower.com

Modern Jeweler
3 Huntington Quadrangle, Suite 301N
Melville, NY 11747
Phone: (631) 845-2700
http://www.modernjeweler.com

MP News
Margit Publications
463 Seventh Avenue, Third Floor
New York, NY 10018
Phone: (212) 302-5137
http://www.mpnews.com

***MR* (Menswear Retailing)**
Business Journals, Inc.
185 Madison Avenue, Fifth Floor
New York, NY 10016
Phone: (212) 686-4412
http://www.mr-mag.com

National Jeweler
770 Broadway
New York, NY 10003
Phone: (646) 654-7220
http://www.national-jeweler.com

New York Apparel News
CaliforniaMart
110 East Ninth Street, Suite A-777
Los Angeles, CA 90079
Phone: (213) 627-3737
http://www.apparelnews.net

The Public Relations Strategist
Public Relations Society of America
33 Maiden Lane, 11th Floor
New York, NY 10038
Phone: (212) 460-1490
http://www.prsa.org

Retail Ad World
Visual Reference Publications
302 Fifth Avenue, 11th Floor
New York, NY 10001
Phone: (212) 279-7000
http://www.visualreference.com

Retail Merchandiser
90 Broad Street, Suite 402
New York, NY 10004
Phone: (646) 708-7300
http://www.retail-merchandiser.com

Shoe Retailing Today
National Shoe Retailers Association
7150 Columbia Gateway Drive, Suite G
Columbia, MD 21046
Phone: (410) 381-8282
http://www.nsra.org

***SMM* (Sales and Marketing Management)**
Bill Communications
770 Broadway
New York, NY 10003
Phone: (646) 654-4500
http://www.salesandmarketing.com

STORES Magazine
National Retail Federation
325 Seventh Street NW, Suite 1100
Washington, DC 20004
Phone: (202) 783-7971
http://www.nrf.com

Style
555 Richmond Street West, Suite 701
Toronto, Ontario M5V 3B1 Canada
Phone: (416) 203-6737
http://www.style.ca

The Swim Journal
609 East Oregon Avenue, Suite 100
Phoenix, AZ 85012
Phone: (602) 265-7778
http://www.theswimjournal.com

Textile HiLights
American Textile Manufacturers Institute
1130 Connecticut Avenue NW, Suite 1200
Washington, DC 20036
Phone: (202) 862-0500
http://www.atmi.org

Textile World
2100 Powers Ferry Road, Suite 300
Atlanta, GA 30339
Phone: (770) 955-5656
http://www.textileindustries.com

Textile Report
Margit Publications
463 Seventh Avenue, Third Floor
New York, NY 10018
Phone: (212) 302-5137
http://www.mpnews.com

Textile Technology Digest
Institute of Textile Technology
2401 Research Drive, Box 8310
Raleigh, NC 27695

Phone: (919) 513-7704
http://www.itt.edu

Tobe Report
Tobe Associates, Inc.
501 Fifth Avenue
New York, NY 10110
Phone: (212) 867-8677
http://www.tobereport.com

VIEW
Margit Publications
463 Seventh Avenue, Third Floor
New York, NY 10018
Phone: (212) 302-5137
http://www.mpnews.com

***VM + SD* (Visual Merchandising and Store Design)**
ST Media Group International
407 Gilbert Avenue
Cincinnati, OH 45202
Phone: (513) 421-2050
http://www.stmediagroup.com

Waterwear
CaliforniaMart
110 East Ninth Street, Suite A-777
Los Angeles, CA 90079
Phone: (213) 627-3737
http://www.apparelnews.net

Wearables Business
4800 Street Road
Trevose, PA 19053
Phone: (800) 546-1350
http://www.wearablesbusiness.com

Women's Wear Daily
750 Third Avenue
New York, NY 10017
Phone: (800) 289-0273
http://www.wwd.com

WEB SITES

About.com "Fashion" Community
http://www.fashion.about.com

The Alexander Report
http://www.thealexanderreport.com

ApparelSearch.com
http://www.apparelsearch.com

eFashion
http://www.efashion.com

fashionavenue.com
http://www.fashionavenue.com

Fashion Career Center
http://www.fashioncareercenter.com

Fashion Careers
http://www.fashioncareers.com

The Fashion Center New York City
http://www.fashioncenter.com

Fashion Icon
http://www.fashion-icon.com

Fashion Lines
http://www.fashionlines.com

Fashionmall.com
http://www.fashionmall.com

Fashmod.com
http://www.fashmod.com

Fashion Shopper
http://www.fashionshopper.com

The Fashion Web Site
http://www.fashion-411.com

Fashion Windows
http://www.fashionwindows.com

Fashion Wire Daily
http://www.fashionwiredaily.com

Focus on Style
http://www.focusonstyle.com

Hint
http://www.hintmag.com

InStyle
http://www.instyle.com

Jobs in Fashion
http://www.jobsinfashion.com

lookonline.com
http://www.lookonline.com

Lucire, The Global Fashion Magazine
http://www.lucire.com

Metrofashion
http://www.metrofashion.com

Ontone
http://www.ontone.com

Runway
runway.polo.com

7thonline
http://www.7thonline.com

Style.com
http://www.style.com

techexchange
http://www.techexchange.com

Textilecareers.com
http://www.textilecareers.com

Textile Source
http://www.textilesource.com

Textile Web
http://www.textileweb.com

Textile World
http://www.textileworld.com

Worth Global Style Network
http://www.wgsn.com

BIBLIOGRAPHY

Abbott, Langer & Associates. "Top Human Resources Income Exceeds $500,000." Available online at http://www.abbott-langer.com.

American Association of University Professors. "The Devaluing of Higher Education: The Annual Report on the Economic Status of the Profession, 2005–2006." AAUP Web site. Available online at http://www.aaup.org/surveys/06z/zrep.htm.

American Institute of Graphic Arts. "AIGA/Aquent Survey of Design Salaries 2006." Available online at http://www.designersalaries.com.

Anable, Anne. "Just Another Day in Fashion Public Relations?" Available online at http://www.lookonline.com.

Association for Financial Professionals. "AFP's 2005 Compensation Report." Available online at http://www.afponline.org/mbr/reg/pdf/2005CompSurvey_Members_Cover.pdf.

"Average Starting Salaries for Administrative Support Staff-2006." International Association of Administrative Professionals Web site. Available online at http://www.iaap-hq.org/ResearchTrends/Salaries_2006.htm.

Becker, Lee B., Tudor Vlad, Maria Tucker, and Renee Pelton. "2005 Annual Survey of Journalism & Mass Communication Graduates." James M. Cox Jr. Center for International Mass Communication Training and Research, Grady College of Journalism & Mass Communication, University of Georgia. Available online at http://www.grady.uga.edu/annualsurveys/grd05/GraduateReport.pdf. Posted August 4, 2006.

Beckett, Kathleen, Gerit Quealy, Peggy J. Schmidt, and Susan Gordon. *Fashion: Careers without College.* Lawrenceville, N.J.: Peterson's, 1999.

Berman, Jeff. "Salaries Come Back to Earth: Logistics Salaries Headed Downhill in 2005, Nearly Canceling Out 2004's Impressive Gains." *Logistics Management* online. Available at http://www.logisticsmgmt.com. Posted March 1, 2006.

Bev, Jennie S. "Fashion Event Organizer." StyleCareer.com. Available online at http://www.stylecareer.com.

———. "Fashion Illustrator." StyleCareer.com. Available online at http://www.stylecareer.com.

Brannon, Evelyn L. *Fashion Forecasting: Research, Analysis, and Presentation.* New York: Fairchild Publications, 2000.

Brooks, Joanne. "All Eyes on the Runway: Using Fashion Shows for Fund-Raising." Nishna.net. Available online at http://www.nishna.net.

Campbell, Kim. "That Size 8 Dress May Soon Be a 12." *Christian Science Monitor* online. Available online at http://www.csmonitor.com/2004/0304/p12s01-lign.html. Posted March 4, 2004.

Chancellor, Alexander. "Ice Queen Reigns over U.S. Fashion." *The Age.* Available online at http://www.theage.com.au. Posted July 24, 2000.

Collett, Stacy. "Salary Survey: Are Skimpy Raises the New Normal?" *COMPUTERWORLD* online. Available online at http://www.computerworld.com/special_report/000/001/000/special_report_0000 01001_primary_article.jsp. Posted October 25, 2005.

Colombo, Allan B. "Annual Retail Security Survey Shows Shoplifting on Increase." e-CommKiosk.com. Available online at http://tpromo.com/secmis-priv2/?p=1192.

Council of Supply Chain Management Professionals. "Careers in Logistics." CSCMP.org. Available online at http://www.cscmp.org/Downloads/Career/careerstudy.pdf.

Cromie, William J. "Solving a Real Cut-up of a Problem." *The Harvard University Gazette* online. Available online at http://www.news.harvard.edu/gazette/1996/05.16/SolvingaRealCut.html. Posted May 16, 1996.

Davis, Dick. "Career Information: Costume Designer." Bridges.com. Available online at http://www.bridges.com. Posted July 30, 2000.

Davis Burns, Leslie, and Nancy O. Bryant. *The Business of Fashion: Designing, Manufacturing, and Marketing.* New York: Fairchild Publications, 1997.

"A Day in the Life: Fashion Buyer (Fabric)." Vault Web site. Available online at http://www.vault.com/nr/main_article_detail.jsp?article_id=16710896&cat_id=0&ht_type=1. Posted February 10, 2003.

DesMarteau, Kathleen. "Making Clothes Fit: No Simple Challenge." *Apparel* online. Available online at http://www.apparelmag.com/articles/june/june05_4.shtml. Posted June 1, 2005.

Diamond, Jay, and Ellen Diamond. *Contemporary Visual Merchandising.* Upper Saddle River, N.J.: Prentice Hall, 1999.

———. *Fashion Advertising and Promotion.* New York: Fairchild Publications, 1996.

———. *The World of Fashion.* New York: Fairchild Publications, 1997.

Diamond, Jay, and Gerald Pintel. *Retail Buying.* Upper Saddle River, N.J.: Prentice Hall, 2001.

Dolber, Roslyn. *Opportunities in Fashion Careers.* Lincolnwood, Ill.: VGM Career Horizons/NTC Publishing Group, 1993.

Donnellan, John. *Merchandise Buying and Management.* New York: Fairchild Publications, 1996.

Dumas, Joseph. "A Mannequin Model: Shay Taylor Is a Perfect Fit." *Black Enterprise,* February 2005.

Everett, Judith C., and Kristen K. Swanson. *Guide to Producing a Fashion Show.* New York: Fairchild Publications, 1993.

Ezersky, Lauren. "Lunch with Lauren: Amy Spindler." *PAPERMAG.* April 23, 2001.

"Fashion Design: Could You Be a . . . Fashion Designer?" FashionClub.com. Available online at http://www.fashionclub.com/career-studio/dreamscape/articles/20041001/career-dreamscape-03.shtm.

The Fashiondex. *The Apparel Industry Sourcebook.* New York: Fairchild Publications, 2000.

———. *The Apparel Production Sourcebook.* New York: Fairchild Publications, 2000.

———. *The Directory of Brand Name Apparel Manufacturers.* New York: Fairchild Publications, 2000.

Fashion.net. "How to Become a Fashion Editor." Available online at http://www.fashion.net/howto/fashioneditor.

———. "How to Become a Fashion Photographer." Available online at http://www.fashion.net/howto/photography.

Ferguson Publishing Editors. *Careers in Focus: Fashion.* Chicago: Ferguson Publishing Company, 2001.

Fincher Winters, Peggy, and Arthur Allen Winters. *What Works in Fashion Advertising.* New York: Fairchild Publications, 1996.

Franck, Elisabeth. "Fashion Forecasting: From Denim to Fur: Fashion Forecasters See It Before You." *Fashion Windows.* Available online at http://www.fashionwindows.com. Posted March 6, 2000.

Freund, Alex. "Day in the Life: Fashion Photographer." PowerStudents.com. Available online at http://www.powerstudents.com.

Fung, Allison. "Cool Job: Fashion Editor." AWZ.com. Available online at http://www.awz.com.

"Getting Hired in Fashion Design." Vault.com. Available online at http://www.vault.com/articles/Getting-Hired-in-Fashion-Design-16677878.html.

Giacobello, John. *Careers in the Fashion Industry.* New York: Rosen Publishing Group, 1999.

———. *Choosing a Career in the Fashion Industry.* New York: Rosen Publishing Group, 2000.

Granger, Michele. *A Guide to Analyzing Your Fashion Industry Internship.* New York: Fairchild Publications, 1996.

Hansell, Saul. "High Fashion Goes on Sale on the Web." *New York Times* online. Available online at http://www.nytimes.com. Posted September 18, 2000.

Hoffman, W. Randy. "A Cut Above: An Introduction to Fashion Schools." ArtSchools.com. Available online at http://www.artschools.com/articles/fashion/intro.html. Posted September 13, 2004.

Hollinger, Richard C. "2004 National Retail Security Survey Final Report." University of Florida, Department of Criminology, Law, and Society. Available online at http://www.crim.ufl.edu/research/srp/srp.htm.

Jarnow, Jeannette, and Kitty G. Dickerson. *Inside the Fashion Business.* Upper Saddle River, N.J.: Simon & Schuster, 1997.

"Job Description for Personnel Recruiters." CareerPlanner.com. Available online at http://www.careerplanner.com/Job-Descriptions/Personnel-Recruiters.cfm.

Johnson, Maurice J., and Evelyn C. Moore. *Apparel Product Development.* Upper Saddle River, N.J.: Prentice Hall, 2000.

———. *So You Want to Work in the Fashion Business? A Practical Look at Apparel Product Development and Global Manufacturing.* Upper Saddle River, N.J.: Simon & Schuster, 1998.

Juilland, Marie-Jeanne. "Fashion Designer: What It's Like." Women.com. Available online at http://www.women.com.

Kadolph, Sara J., and Anna L. Langford. *Textiles.* Upper Saddle River, N.J.: Prentice Hall, 2002.

Kinsman, Matt. "*FOLIO*'s 2005 Editorial Management Salary Survey." *FOLIO* online. Available online at http://www.foliomag.com/viewMedia.asp?prmMID=5004. Posted August 1, 2005.

Kreger, Don. "Business, Fashion Sense Keep Buyer Clothed in Aura of Success." *Milwaukee Journal Sentinel* online. Available online at http://www.jsonline.com. Posted September 19, 2000.

Kunz, Grace I. *Merchandising: Theory, Principles, and Practice.* New York: Fairchild Publications, 1998.

Mauro, Lucia. *Careers for Fashion Plates & Other Trendsetters.* Lincolnwood, Ill.: VGM Career Horizons/NTC Publishing Group, 1996.

———. *Fashion* (VGM's Career Portraits). Lincolnwood, Ill.: VGM Career Horizons/NTC Publishing Group, 1995.

McCarthy Folse, Nancy, and Marilyn Henrion. *Careers in the Fashion Industry: Where the Jobs Are & How to Get Them.* New York: Harper & Row, 1981.

McLachlan, Michelle. "It's a Designers' Market." *DISPLAY & DESIGN Ideas* online. Available online at http://www.ddimagazine.com. Posted February 11, 2001.

Mills, Kenneth, Judith Paul, and Kay Moormann. *Applied Visual Merchandising.* Upper Saddle River, N.J.: Prentice Hall, 1995.

Mink Rath, Patricia, Jacqueline Peterson, Phyllis Greensley, and Penny Gill. *Introduction to Fashion Merchandising.* Albany, N.Y.: Delmar Publishers, 1994.

Molotsky, Iris. "Day in the Life: Fashion Stylist." Available online at http://www.powerstudents.com.

Mui, Nelson. "The Fashion Front Line: How Publicists Divvy up the Front Row." *Fashion Wire Daily.* Available online at http://www.fashionwiredaily.com. Posted February 1, 2001.

National Association of Colleges and Employers. *Salary Survey: Spring 2006.* Bethlehem, Pa.: National Association of Colleges and Employers, 2006.

Nellis, Cynthia. "All about Fit: Why Don't Clothes Ever Fit?" About.com. Available online at http://fashion.about.com/cs/tipsadvice/a/allaboutfit.htm.

———. "Day in the Life . . . of a Fashion Consultant." About.com.

O'Reilly, Eileen. "Job Q&A: Fashion Publicist." Monster.com. Available online at http://midcareer.monster.com/qanda/jtds_1215.

———. "Job Q&A: Photographer." Monster.com. Available online at http://midcareer.monster.com/qanda/fashion photographer.

Paris, Wendy. "Job Q&A: Buyer." Monster.com. Available online at http://midcareer.monster.com/qanda/ruben04051999.

Pegler, Martin M. *Visual Merchandising & Display.* New York: Fairchild Publications, 1998.

Pemberton-Sikes, Diana. "Become a Fashion Event Planner." FashionJobReview.com. Available online at http://www.fashionjobreview.com/Fashion_Event_Planner.html.

Perna, Rita. *Fashion Forecasting.* New York: Fairchild Publications, 1987.

Pflugh, Jordan. "Careers in Content." Vault.com. Available online at http://www.vault.com/nr/newsmain.jsp?nr_page=3&ch_id=409&article_id=1263550&cat_id=1831. Posted December 18, 2000.

Pizzuoto, Joseph J., with Arthur Price, Allen C. Cohen, and Ingrid Johnson. *Fabric Science.* New York: Fairchild Publications, 1999.

Ray, Kay. "Employment Trends: The Latest Patterns in the Textile Industry." Bridges.com. Available online at http://www.bridges.com. Posted November 7, 2000.

———. "Opportunities: Fashion Marketers Are in Style." Bridges.com. Available online at http://www.bridges.com. Posted February 14, 2001.

Rudolph, Barbara. "Skirting the Issues." *Time* online. Available online at http://www.time.com. Posted June 5, 1995.

Sahadi, Jeanne. "More Surprising 6-Figure Jobs." CNN/*Money* online. Available online at http://money.cnn.com/ 2003/12/09/pf/more_sixfigjobs. Posted January 9, 2004.

Salary.com. Available online at http://www.salary.com.

Samuel, Wendy, Renee Palmer, Beth Phillips, Pat Steele, Barbara McDonald, Phyllis Tama, and Joan Watkins. *Fashion Careers: The Complete Job Search Workbook.* New York: Pocket Productions, 1999.

Savage, Cassandra, and Bridges.com staff. "Career Information: Fashion Editor." Bridges.com. Available online at http://www.bridges.com. Posted April 23, 2001.

Sen, Protiti. "Silhouettes and Contours of Fashion Technology." *Financial Express.* Available online at http://www.financialexpress.com/archive.html. Posted February 9, 1998.

Shurtleff, Eric. "Still Wanted: Truly Competent Technical Designers." *Apparel,* February 2003.

Smith Bohlinger, Maryanne. *Merchandise Buying.* New York: Fairchild Publications, 2001.

Sones, Melissa. *Getting into Fashion: A Career Guide.* New York: Ballantine Books, 1984.

Stephens Frings, Gini. *Fashion: From Concept to Consumer.* 8th ed. Upper Saddle River, N.J.: Prentice Hall, 2004.

Stone, Elaine. *The Dynamics of Fashion.* New York: Fairchild Publications, 1999.

Swanson, Kristen K., and Judith C. Everett. *Promotion in the Merchandising Environment.* New York: Fairchild Publications, 2000.

Tain, Linda. *Portfolio Presentation for Fashion Designers.* New York: Fairchild Publications, 1998.

Tate, Sharon Lee, and Mona Shafer Edwards. *Inside Fashion Design.* Upper Saddle River, N.J.: Prentice Hall, 1999.

Thompson, Betsy. "New Survey Reveals Most Women Shop by Size but Don't Know Their Measurements." *Business Wire,* July 31, 2006.

Tiffany, Laura. "How to Start an Event Planning Service." *Entrepreneur,* February 22, 2001.

Tomlinson, Sarah. "Job Q&A: Wardrobe Consultant." Monster.com.

Tran, Khanh T. L. "The Life of the Perfect Fit." *Women's Wear Daily,* May 25, 2006.

Uscher, Jen. "A Q&A for Fashion Designers." Experience.com. Available online at http://www.experience.com. Posted September 8, 2000.

U.S. Census Bureau, Service Sector Statistics. "Unadjusted and Adjusted Estimates of Monthly Retail and Food Services Sales by Kind of Business: 2005." U.S. Census Bureau Web site. Available online at http://www.census.gov/mrts/www/data/html/nsal05.html.

U.S. Department of Labor, Bureau of Labor Statistics. *Career Guide to Industries, 2006–2007 Edition* online. Available online at http://www.bls.gov/oco/cg/home.htm.

———. *Occupational Outlook Handbook, 2006–2007 Edition* online. Available online at http://www.bls.gov/oco.

Vidovich, Lauren. "Administrative Professionals Are Staple That Holds Office Together, According to National Study by Swingline." Swingline.com. Available online at http://www.acco.com/swingline/docs/SwinglineOfficeOutlook SurveyResultsRelease.pdf. Posted April 24, 2006.

Wallace-Albert, Stacy. "How Do I Do It? The Fashion Editor." The Fashion Editor.com. Available online at http://www.thefashioneditor.com/become-a-fashion-editor.html.

Williams, Roshumba, and Anne Marie O'Connor. *The Complete Idiot's Guide to Being a Model.* Indianapolis, Ind.: Macmillan USA, 1999.

Wolfe, Mary G. *Fashion!* Tinley Park, Ill.: Goodheart-Willcox Company, 1998.

———. *The World of Fashion Merchandising.* Tinley Park, Ill.: Goodheart-Willcox Company, 1998.

Wood Gearheart, Susan, and Shirley Hamilton. *Opportunities in Modeling Careers.* Lincolnwood, Ill.: VGM Career Horizons/NTC Publishing, 1999.

Zissu, Alexandra. "Fashionistas Get Fed Up." *The Industry Standard Magazine* online. Posted May 15, 2000.

INDEX

Boldface page numbers denote main entries.

WITHDRAWN